The

OXFORD
Children's
THESAURUS

Chief Editor
Robert Allen

OXFORD
UNIVERSITY PRESS

OXFORD
UNIVERSITY PRESS
Great Clarendon Street, Oxford OX2 6DP

Oxford University Press is a department of the University of Oxford.
It furthers the University's objective of excellence in research, scholarship,
and education by publishing worldwide in
Oxford New York

Athens Auckland Bangkok Bogotá Buenos Aires Kolkata
Cape Town Chennai Dar es Salaam Delhi Florence Hong Kong Istanbul
Karachi Kuala Lumpur Madrid Melbourne Mexico City Mumbai
Nairobi Paris São Paulo Shanghai Singapore Taipei Tokyo Toronto Warsaw

with associated companies in Berlin Ibadan

Oxford is a registered trade mark of Oxford University Press
in the UK and in certain other countries

British Library Cataloguing in Publication Data available

Trade edition ISBN 0–19–910603-7
Educational edition 0-19-910604-5

3 5 7 9 10 8 6 4 2

Typeset by Pentacor plc, High Wycombe
Printed in Italy by G. Canale & C. S.p.A.

Preface

In this edition of the *Oxford Children's Thesaurus* we present an entirely new text which has been written in conjunction with a new edition of its companion book, the *Oxford Children's Dictionary*. It is meant for children aged 8 and upwards, and the emphasis is very much on language production. This is the process in which children look up words that they already know in order to find other words, often more interesting or more precise in a particular context, that they either do not know or cannot call to mind.

The synonyms are organized so that those considered the closest in meaning and the most useful as alternatives to the headword appear first. Every meaning of the headword is illustrated by an example of its use, and all the synonyms offered are substitutable in the examples. The examples have been devised with a close eye on children's literature written for this age group; they are not taken directly from specific sources but reflect the type of construction and immediate context found there, so as to achieve a naturalness that is not possible from intuition alone.

For noun synonyms, countability (*age* or *an age*; *conflict* or *a conflict*) is indicated by the inclusion or omission of the indefinite article *a* or *an*; in other cases the definite article *the* is included where this is a typical feature of the use of a particular synonym (in the case of the noun *extent*, for example, as in 'we need to find out the extent of the damage'). For verb synonyms, the infinitive marker *to* is given. When a headword and synonym differ in collocation (i.e. in the words used to link them with surrounding words), this is indicated after the synonym; for example you would say that someone is 'sick' *of* something, but 'fed up' or 'bored' *with* it. This is important in showing that a correspondence in meaning between one word and another does not necessarily entail a correspondence in grammatical pattern.

As in the *Children's Dictionary*, when a word falls outside the normal vocabulary range of this age group but needs to be included, it is marked as 'not an everyday word' when it is more formal or technical than normal, and 'informal' when it is more colloquial than normal.

As well as the alternative words, lists of 'word families', or sets of words used in a particular topic, are given for a number of items, including animals, birds, clothes, colours, dogs, elements, members of a family, types of houses, names of shapes, plants, religions, names of trees, etc. These word families are organized in a classified way when appropriate, the names of trees, for example, being divided into sections for conifers, deciduous, and evergreens. The purpose of these lists is to provide the terminology of a topic, and is built on linguistic rather than encyclopedic principles.

I should like to thank Jessica Feinstein for much helpful comment and advice, from which the text has benefited enormously.

Robert Allen

Text Features

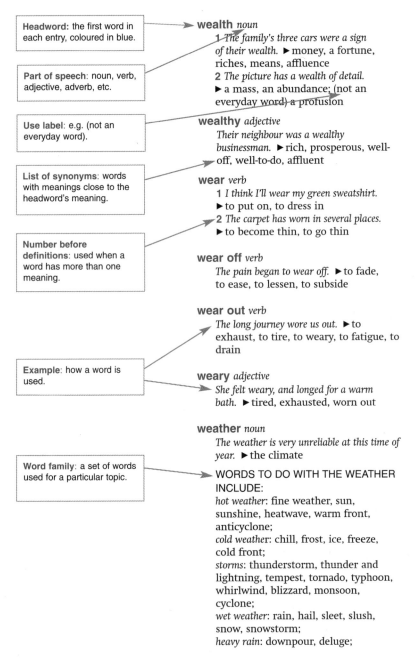

Headword: the first word in each entry, coloured in blue.

Part of speech: noun, verb, adjective, adverb, etc.

Use label: e.g. (not an everyday word).

List of synonyms: words with meanings close to the headword's meaning.

Number before definitions: used when a word has more than one meaning.

Example: how a word is used.

Word family: a set of words used for a particular topic.

wealth *noun*
1 *The family's three cars were a sign of their wealth.* ► money, a fortune, riches, means, affluence
2 *The picture has a wealth of detail.* ► a mass, an abundance; (not an everyday word) a profusion

wealthy *adjective*
Their neighbour was a wealthy businessman. ► rich, prosperous, well-off, well-to-do, affluent

wear *verb*
1 *I think I'll wear my green sweatshirt.* ► to put on, to dress in
2 *The carpet has worn in several places.* ► to become thin, to go thin

wear off *verb*
The pain began to wear off. ► to fade, to ease, to lessen, to subside

wear out *verb*
The long journey wore us out. ► to exhaust, to tire, to weary, to fatigue, to drain

weary *adjective*
She felt weary, and longed for a warm bath. ► tired, exhausted, worn out

weather *noun*
The weather is very unreliable at this time of year. ► the climate

WORDS TO DO WITH THE WEATHER INCLUDE:
hot weather: fine weather, sun, sunshine, heatwave, warm front, anticyclone;
cold weather: chill, frost, ice, freeze, cold front;
storms: thunderstorm, thunder and lightning, tempest, tornado, typhoon, whirlwind, blizzard, monsoon, cyclone;
wet weather: rain, hail, sleet, slush, snow, snowstorm;
heavy rain: downpour, deluge;

A a

abandon *verb*
1 *We will have to abandon the search after dark.* ▶ to give up, to cancel, to discontinue
2 *The villagers had abandoned their homes after the earthquake.* ▶ to evacuate, to leave, to quit, to forsake
3 *The children had been abandoned in the war.* ▶ to desert, to forsake, to leave stranded

ability *noun*
Melissa has inherited her artistic ability from her father. ▶ a talent, a skill, an aptitude, a capability, a gift, a flair, a capacity, know-how

able *adjective*
Some of the more able pupils do extra reading. ▶ skilful, skilled, capable, accomplished, competent, gifted, proficient, talented

abnormal *adjective*
It's abnormal to have frost in the summer. ▶ unusual, exceptional, odd, peculiar, strange, funny

abolish *verb*
Some people would like to abolish television licences. ▶ to get rid of, to do away with, to end, to eliminate

about *adverb*
It costs about £100. ▶ approximately, roughly, almost, nearly

abroad *adverb*
The Potters are going abroad this year. ▶ overseas

abrupt *adjective*
1 *His uncle often had abrupt changes of mood.* ▶ sudden, unexpected, rapid
2 *Her manner with the younger children was rather abrupt.* ▶ blunt, sharp, gruff, curt, rude, unfriendly, short

absent *adjective*
Jane's mother had been absent from work for three days. ▶ away, off, missing

absolute *adjective*
The holiday was absolute bliss. ▶ utter, complete, total, sheer

absorbed *adjective*
An old woman was absorbed in some needlework. ▶ engrossed, preoccupied

absurd *adjective*
It was absurd to blame the cat for the mess in the kitchen. ▶ silly, ridiculous, laughable, ludicrous, crazy, mad, preposterous, nonsensical

abundant *adjective*
(not an everyday word) *The village had an abundant water supply from an old well.* ▶ plentiful, ample, generous; (more formal) copious

abuse *verb*
1 *The RSPCA reported an increase in the number of people abusing animals.* ▶ to maltreat, to hurt
2 *The losing side began to abuse the referee.* ▶ to insult, to swear at, to curse, to be rude to

accelerate *verb*
▶ to go faster, to speed up

accent *noun*
She spoke good English but with a slight French accent. ▶ a pronunciation, an intonation

accept *verb*
1 *Police officers are not allowed to accept gifts.* ▶ to take, to receive
2 *I accept that I may have been wrong.* ▶ to admit, to acknowledge, to agree, to believe, to think

acceptable *adjective*
We found the holiday house more than acceptable. ▶ satisfactory, all right, adequate, pleasing, suitable, passable, tolerable

access *noun*
A narrow lane was the only access to the village. ▶ an approach, an entry

accident *noun*
1 *There had been another accident further down the road.* ▶ a crash, a disaster, a misfortune, a mishap
2 *They only found out by accident.* ▶ chance, coincidence

accidental *adjective*
The police said his death was accidental. ▶ unintentional, unplanned

accommodation *noun*
The council were looking for suitable accommodation for the refugees. ▶ housing, lodgings, a house, shelter, quarters, board

accompany *verb*
Shall I accompany you to the station? ▶ to go with, to come with, to escort

accomplish *verb*
The next task was accomplished very quickly. ▶ to achieve, to perform, to fulfil, to carry out, to complete, to do, to finish

accomplished *adjective*
In his spare time, Frank is an accomplished chef. ▶ gifted, expert, skilful, skilled, talented, able

account *noun*
We wrote a detailed account of our museum trip. ▶ a description, a record, a report, a narrative, a story

accumulate *verb*
A large pile of junk had accumulated in one corner. We seem to accumulate more newspapers than we can read. ▶ to collect, to heap up, to pile up, to store up

accurate *adjective*
This is an accurate description of what happened. ▶ correct, exact, precise, right, true

accuse *verb*
The money had gone and Sarah was accused of taking it. ▶ to blame (for), to charge (with), to condemn (for)
NOTE: You **accuse** someone *of* something but **blame** someone *for* something and **charge** someone *with* something

accustomed *adjective*
We went home by our accustomed route. ▶ normal, usual, customary, habitual, conventional, ordinary, regular

ache *noun*
John felt an ache spreading through his left leg. ▶ pain, pang, soreness, twinge, discomfort

ache *verb*
His leg was aching quite badly now. ▶ to hurt, to be sore, to be painful

achieve *verb*
We achieved a lot in a short time. ▶ to accomplish, to do, to complete, to finish, to fulfil, to manage

achievement *noun*
It's a great achievement to get into the county team. ▶ a feat, an accomplishment, a success, an attainment

acid *adjective*
Lemons have an acid taste. ▶ sharp, sour, tangy, tart

acknowledge *verb*
I acknowledge that you may be right. ▶ to admit, to agree, to accept, to grant

acquire *verb*
(not an everyday word) *His father is hoping to acquire a new car.* ▶ to get, to buy, to receive; (informal) to come by, to get hold of; (more formal) to purchase, to procure, to obtain

acquit *verb*
The jury acquitted him on all charges. ▶ to clear, to free, to let off; (more formal) to exonerate, to discharge

act *noun*
1 *Rushing off like that had been a foolish act.* ▶ an action, a deed, an exploit
2 *We saw a juggling act at the circus.* ▶ a turn, a performance, a routine, a show

act *verb*
1 *The children all acted sensibly.* ▶ to behave, to carry on
2 *Helen was asked to act in the school pantomime.* ▶ to perform, to appear, to take part, to play a part
3 *The medicine takes a while to act.* ▶ to work, to take effect, to have an effect

action *noun*
1 *Their prompt action prevented an accident.* ▶ an act, a deed, a move, an exploit, a feat
2 *James's father had died in action in France.* ▶ battle, fighting, combat

active *adjective*
1 *Ned had an aunt with three active young children.* ▶ lively, energetic, vigorous
2 *We lead active lives these days.* ▶ busy

activity *noun*
1 *The town is full of activity near Christmas.* ▶ liveliness, bustle, action, excitement, life
2 *Their parents tried to find time for family activities.* ▶ an interest, a pursuit, an occupation, a pastime, a hobby, a project

actual *adjective*
The story is based on actual events. ▶ real, true, genuine, authentic

actually *adverb*
It was actually rather cold outside. ▶ really, in fact, as a matter of fact

acute *adjective*
She felt an acute pain in her arm. ▶ sharp, intense, severe, sudden, keen, strong

adapt *verb*
1 *You can adapt the radio so that it works in a car.* ▶ to alter, to adjust, to convert, to modify, to transform
2 *The children quickly adapted to life in the country.* ▶ to adjust, to get used (to); (more formal) to acclimatize
NOTE: If you choose **acclimatize**, you usually say *The children quickly became acclimatized to life in the country.*

add *verb*
1 *The bill adds up to £50 altogether.* ▶ to total, to amount to, to come to
2 *Why don't we add up what we've got so far?* ▶ to count, to calculate, to reckon, to work out

additional *adjective*
The sign had additional rules about parking at weekends. ▶ more, extra, further; (more formal) supplementary

adequate *adjective*
New mothers need adequate time to rest. ▶ enough, sufficient

adjacent *preposition*
There is a river adjacent to the golf course. ▶ beside, next to, alongside, adjoining

adjust *verb*
When Susie got home someone had already adjusted the saddle on her bike. ▶ to alter, to modify, to correct, to put right, to change
NOTE: If you use **change**, be careful that it doesn't seem to mean 'replace (with a new one)' rather than 'adjust'

admirable *adjective*
The actors gave an admirable performance. ▶ excellent, fine, wonderful, marvellous; (more formal) praiseworthy, creditable

admire *verb*
1 *I stood back to admire Alex's handiwork.* ▶ to praise, to approve, to approve of, to marvel at, to wonder at
2 *This is a good spot to admire the view over the valley.* ▶ to enjoy, to appreciate
NOTE: In the first meaning you can **approve** something or (more usually) **approve of** it. **Marvel at** and **wonder at** are much stronger words in this meaning

admit *verb*
1 *The film was a 15 and the boys wondered if they'd be admitted.* ▶ to let in, to allow in
2 *Frances admitted she had been playing by the river.* ▶ to agree, to accept, to acknowledge, to confess, to own up

adopt *verb*
Schools need to adopt new methods of teaching languages. ▶ use, take on; (more formal) employ

adore *verb*
He adored his daughter and couldn't resist giving her a hug. ▶ to love, to idolize, to dote on, to revere, to worship

adorn *verb*
The room was adorned with flowers. ▶ to decorate

advance
He saw Greg advancing towards him. ▶ to move forward; (more formal) to proceed; (the following verbs take an object) to approach, to come near
NOTE: If you use **approach** or **come near**, you do not need a word like *to* or *towards*

advanced *adjective*
Freda is doing an advanced course in computing. ▶ more difficult, higher

advantage *noun*
Being tall can be an advantage. ▶ a benefit, an asset, a help

adventure *noun*
The hero returns home after his latest adventure. ▶ an exploit, a deed, a feat, an escapade, an excitement

advertise *verb*
We advertised our concert in the local shops. ▶ to publicize, to promote, to announce, to make known; (informal) to plug

advice *noun*
Henry needed some advice about what to do next. ▶ help, guidance, suggestions, tips

advisable *adjective*
It's advisable to wear safety goggles when doing experiments. ▶ sensible, wise, prudent, desirable

advise *verb*
1 *They will advise us when to go in.* ▶ to inform, to tell, to notify
2 *What does the doctor advise?* ▶ to recommend, to suggest

affair *noun*
1 *I have to do it but how I do it is my affair.* ▶ a concern, a business
2 *The rest of the game was a rather dull affair.* ▶ an occasion, an event

affect *verb*
The weather may affect tomorrow's plans. ► to influence, to alter, to change, to modify, to have an effect on

affection *noun*
She thought of the children with affection. ► fondness, devotion, friendliness, love, warmth

afflict *verb*
Harry was afflicted by all sorts of problems. ► to trouble, to distress, to burden, to plague, to torment

afford *verb*
Although a bus soon came, he couldn't afford the fare home. ► to pay, to manage, to spare

afraid *adjective*
By now it was dark and the little gang became afraid. ► frightened, scared, alarmed, anxious, fearful, apprehensive, terrified

age *noun*
In history the class was doing the Victorian age. ► a period, a time, an era

age *verb*
Frank was worried that people would think he had aged. ► to grow old, to grow older

aged *adjective*
He still lived at home with his aged mother. ► old, elderly, ancient

aggravate *verb*
1 *All the arguing and shouting only aggravated matters.* ► to make worse, to worsen, to intensify
2 (*informal*) *We tried to keep quiet so as not to aggravate anyone.* ► to irritate, to annoy, to bother, to exasperate

aggressive *adjective*
1 *Her father stomped out in an aggressive mood.* ► hostile, quarrelsome, unfriendly, attacking, belligerent, militant, pugnacious, warlike
2 *The champion played aggressive tennis and kept his title.* ► strong, forceful, vigorous

agile *adjective*
Gazelles are agile creatures. ► nimble, graceful, sure-footed

agitated *adjective*
As the traffic got worse the driver became more and more agitated. ► anxious, nervous, flustered, worried, restless, ruffled

agony *noun*
One of the victim's arms was bent back and caused him agony. ► great pain, suffering, hurt, torment, torture

agree *verb*
1 *The boy agreed to come along and help.* ► to be willing, to consent, to promise, to undertake
2 *George had to agree that his mother was right.* ► to admit, to acknowledge, to accept
3 *Spicy food doesn't agree with her.* ► to suit, to be good for

agreement *noun*
After long discussions the union leaders reached an agreement. ► a settlement, a deal, an understanding, a bargain

ahead *adverb*
The other runners were a long way ahead by now. ► in front, forwards, onwards

aid *verb*
Their efforts in the garden were aided by a spell of good weather. ► to help, to support; (*more formal*) to facilitate

aid *noun*
Aid came in the form of food parcels.
▶ help, support, cooperation

aim *verb*
1 *She turned and saw a man aiming a gun at her.* ▶ to point
2 *The driver said he aimed to reach Dover by eight o'clock.* ▶ to plan, to intend

aim *noun*
The manager said his aim was not to draw but to win. ▶ an intention, an ambition, a goal, an object, an objective, a plan, a purpose

alarm *verb*
They approached the man slowly, anxious not to alarm him. ▶ to startle, to frighten, to scare, to surprise, to terrify, to panic; (informal) to put the wind up

alarm *noun*
The woman turned round in alarm and saw a dog chasing after her. ▶ fright, fear, panic, surprise, anxiety, disquiet, consternation, distress, dismay

alert *adjective*
She was tired but had to stay alert while she drove us home. ▶ sharp, bright, wary, observant, vigilant, watchful, attentive, quick, keen

alien *adjective*
Simon painted a weird alien landscape.
▶ strange, foreign, remote, unfamiliar

alike *adjective*
The three youngest brothers all looked alike. ▶ identical, similar, the same

alive *adjective*
Police said the woman was still alive when she was thrown in the river.
▶ living, surviving, breathing

allow *verb*
1 *Their father would not allow them to stay out after dark.* ▶ to permit, to let, to authorize
2 *They only allowed £5 for bus fares and it wasn't enough.* ▶ to grant, to provide, to set aside, to allocate, to earmark
NOTE: In the first meaning, if you use **let** you do not use *to* after it.

all right *adjective*
1 *She said she was perfectly all right.*
▶ well, fine, fit, healthy; (informal) OK
2 *Is everything all right?*
▶ satisfactory, acceptable, adequate, passable, tolerable; (informal) OK

almost *adverb*
Alicia jumped forward and almost banged her head on the glass. ▶ nearly, practically

alone *adjective*
1 *Don't you mind staying here alone?*
▶ by yourself, on your own, unaccompanied
2 *She felt lost and alone after they had gone.* ▶ lonely, abandoned, deserted, isolated, forlorn, forsaken, desolate

alter *verb*
He altered his expression when he heard the news. ▶ to change, to adjust, to modify, to transform

altogether *adverb*
The excuse was not altogether convincing. ▶ completely, entirely, absolutely, quite, totally, utterly, wholly

always *adverb*
1 *It always seems to be raining.*
▶ continuously, all the time, unceasingly
2 *The family always go for a long walk on Sundays.* ▶ regularly, invariably
NOTE: In the first meaning, you would put

the alternative words at the end of the sentence, for example *It seems to be raining all the time.*

amaze *verb*
We were amazed that our phone bill was so low. ▶ to astonish, to astound, to surprise, to stagger
NOTE: Other words such as **shock** and **bewilder** usually mean that someone is upset as well as surprised

amazing *adjective*
My brother was ill for weeks but made an amazing recovery. ▶ astonishing, astounding, staggering, surprising, extraordinary, incredible, remarkable

ambition *noun*
Polly's ambition was to become a doctor like her mother. ▶ a goal, an aim, an intention, an objective, a wish

ambush *verb*
Three men ambushed a couple of trucks one evening. ▶ to attack, to pounce on, to jump out on, to swoop on, to intercept

amend *verb*
We have amended the rules so that girls can play too. ▶ to change, to alter, to adjust, to modify

amiable *adjective*
Jenny's aunt had been noticeably amiable during her Christmas visit. ▶ friendly, kind, agreeable, nice, pleasant

amount *noun*
We were alarmed at the amount of blood running down Jennifer's face. ▶ the quantity, the volume

ample *adjective*
There was food in the fridge and an ample supply of coal and logs in the shed outside. ▶ plentiful, abundant, generous, copious

amuse *verb*
The story amused the children and made them chuckle. ▶ to entertain, to delight, to cheer up, to divert

amusing *adjective*
I was lucky to have such a lively and amusing friend. ▶ funny, witty, humorous

ancestor *noun*
He could trace his ancestors back to the reign of James I. ▶ a forebear, a forefather

ancient *adjective*
The walls of the cave were covered with ancient carvings. ▶ old, early, prehistoric, primitive

anger *noun*
Emily found it hard to hide her anger. ▶ fury, rage, temper; (not an everyday word) wrath

anger *verb*
Their silly behaviour angered everyone. ▶ to annoy, to enrage, to infuriate, to irritate, to exasperate, to incense

angry *adjective*
The king became angry and went about shouting. ▶ cross, furious, enraged, infuriated, irritated, incensed, bad-tempered, irate, livid; (not an everyday word) wrathful

anguish *noun*
The man screwed up his face in anguish and let out a long moan. ▶ distress, agony, suffering, torment, misery, pain, torture

animal *noun*
The zoo has animals of all kinds. ▶ a creature, a living thing, (large animal) a beast
KINDS OF ANIMAL ARE:
vertebrates (animals with skeletons): mammals (warm-blooded, have body hair, young feed on milk, e.g. humans,

elephants, rats, whales), birds (warm-blooded, have feathers, lay eggs, e.g. sparrows, larks, ostriches), reptiles (cold-blooded, have scaly skin, most lay eggs, e.g. snakes, crocodiles), amphibians (have damp skin, young have gills, adults have lungs, e.g. frogs, newts), fish (cold-blooded, have scaly skin, have gills, most lay eggs, e.g. plaice, sharks, catfish);
invertebrates (animals with no skeleton): arthropods (have bodies in sections, have legs, e.g. spiders, crabs), starfish (five arms in a circle), molluscs (soft body usually with a shell, feet that can cling, e.g. snails, octopuses), worms (flatworms, roundworms, segmented worms), jellyfish (body with an opening surrounded by tentacles), sponges (body like a bag)

announce *verb*
The results will be announced over loudspeakers. ▶ to declare, to give out, to proclaim, to publish, to report, to broadcast

announcement *noun*
There will be an announcement about sports day after lunch. ▶ a notice, a bulletin, a statement, a message, a communication, a declaration, a proclamation

annoy *verb*
1 *The traffic queues were beginning to annoy us.* ▶ to irritate, to bother, to make someone cross, to aggravate, to displease, to exasperate, to anger, to upset, to trouble
2 *There was a young child annoying its mother in the shop.* ▶ to pester, to harass, to vex, to disturb, to bother

answer *noun*
1 *She told me to think about it and give her an answer tomorrow.* ▶ a reply, a response, a reaction

2 *It's a problem and I don't know the answer.* ▶ a solution, an explanation, a remedy

anticipate *verb*
The police were anticipating trouble at the football match. ▶ to expect, to foresee, to forecast, to predict

anxious *adjective*
1 *Before every holiday, Dad is anxious about flying.* ▶ nervous, worried, apprehensive, concerned, uneasy, fearful, jittery
2 *Her mother was anxious to get to work and couldn't wait any longer.* ▶ eager, keen

apart *adverb*
The friends were living apart now. ▶ separately, on your own

apologize *verb*
I wanted to apologize for my rudeness the other day. ▶ to say sorry, to beg pardon, to express regret

appal *verb*
The violence appalled everyone. ▶ to disgust, to horrify, to shock, to outrage, to dismay, to alarm

apparent *adjective*
It soon became apparent that they had taken the wrong road. ▶ clear, obvious, plain, evident, unmistakable

appeal *verb*
1 *The hospital is appealing for money to build a new kidney unit.* ▶ to ask, to request
NOTE: If you use **request**, you leave out the word *for*
2 *The idea of going to bed early didn't appeal to us much.* ▶ to attract, to interest, to tempt

appear *verb*
1 *A ship appeared on the horizon.* ▶ to become visible, to be seen, to come

into view, to emerge
2 *They appeared very anxious.* ▶ to look, to seem

appearance *noun*
On her way out, Daisy checked her appearance in the mirror. ▶ a look, looks, an expression

appetite *noun*
All this exercise had given him an appetite for dinner. ▶ a desire, a longing, a hunger, a craving, a relish

applaud *verb*
1 *The spectators applauded a brilliant goal.* ▶ to cheer, to clap, to acclaim
2 *You have to applaud his efforts.* ▶ to praise, to commend, to admire, to approve of

apply *verb*
1 *We need to apply another coat of paint.* ▶ to put on, to spread
2 *These rules apply to you too.* ▶ to concern, to be relevant to

appoint *verb*
We will appoint a new captain for Saturday's game. ▶ to select, to choose, to name, to nominate

appreciate *verb*
It is good to perform for people who appreciate good singing. ▶ to like, to enjoy, to admire, to approve of, to prize, to respect, to value

approach *noun*
The approach to the house had trees on each side. ▶ an entrance, a drive, an access, an entry, a way in

approach *verb*
The lion approached its prey stealthily. ▶ to come near, to draw near, to move towards

appropriate *adjective*
Red is not an appropriate colour to wear at a funeral. ▶ suitable, fitting, apt, proper, right; (not an everyday word) seemly

approve *verb*
The committee approved the plan at its last meeting. ▶ to authorize, to accept, to pass, to allow

approve of *verb*
I don't think she approves of the idea. ▶ to like, to support, to admire, to applaud, to commend, to think much of, to value

approximately *adverb*
The two houses are approximately the same size. ▶ roughly, nearly, about, around

apt *adjective*
1 *The younger children are apt to wander off.* ▶ liable, likely, inclined, prone
2 *Let's find some apt pieces of music for the party.* ▶ suitable, appropriate, fitting; (not an everyday word) apposite

area *noun*
1 *Jan's family has just moved to a smarter area.* ▶ a district, a region, a locality, a neighbourhood, a part, a vicinity
2 *The plane was flying over an area of desert.* ▶ an expanse, a stretch; (not an everyday word) a tract

argue *verb*
1 *His parents were arguing about money again.* ▶ to quarrel, to disagree, to fight, to wrangle, to bicker; (usually used about children) to squabble
2 *She argued that flying is safer than going by train.* ▶ to reason, to maintain, to insist, to contend

argument *noun*
1 *We had an argument about what to watch on TV.* ► a disagreement, a dispute, a quarrel, a controversy, a debate
2 *The bloody knife was the biggest argument against him.* ► evidence, grounds, justification, proof, reason

arid *adjective*
The film was set in an arid desert landscape. ► barren, dry, lifeless, parched

arise *verb*
Some confusion has arisen over what exactly happened. ► to occur, to emerge, to come up, to come to light, to appear, to result, to ensue; (informal) to crop up

arouse *verb*
1 *We were aroused by the sound of thunder.* ► to awaken, to rouse, to wake up
2 *Their comments aroused a lot of interest.* ► to excite, to incite, to inspire, to provoke, to stimulate, to stir

arrange *verb*
1 *He was arranging his books on the shelf.* ► to sort, to order, to put in order, to classify, to group
2 *At the start of the holiday we arranged a river trip.* ► to plan, to organize, to fix, to devise, to set up

arrest *verb*
The police arrested several pickpockets at the racecourse. ► to seize, to detain, to hold, to take prisoner, to catch; (informal) to nab

arrive *verb*
1 *She didn't want to arrive at the party with her face in a mess.* ► to come to, to reach
2 *When will the train arrive?* ► to come, to appear, to turn up

arrogant *adjective*
The new queen's daughters were very arrogant. ► haughty, proud, conceited, boastful, bumptious, lordly, disdainful, self-important, snobbish, vain; (informal) cocky, stuck-up

artful *adjective*
Nigel had an artful way of dealing with people. ► crafty, clever, cunning, knowing, astute, sly, shrewd, wily

article *noun*
The bag was full of old articles put aside for the jumble sale. ► an item, an object, a thing

artificial *adjective*
The necklace contained artificial jewels. ► man-made, false, unnatural, bogus, faked, synthetic, unreal; (informal) phoney

artistic *adjective*
The flower arrangement was colourful and artistic. ► creative, imaginative, attractive, tasteful, beautiful

ascend *verb*
We ascended the hill. ► to climb, to go up, to mount, to scale

ashamed *adjective*
Tom crawled back under the bedclothes, ashamed of his behaviour. ► sorry (for), distressed (by), embarrassed (by), upset (about), mortified (by)
NOTE: **Ashamed** is followed by *of*, but the other words are followed by *about, by,* or *for*

ask *verb*
1 *I'll ask what time the bus goes.* ► to enquire, to find out
2 *Did you ask her about it?* ► to query, to interrogate; (informal) to quiz
NOTE: If you use **interrogate** it means 'to ask a lot of hard questions'
3 *Did you ask them to our party?* ► to invite

ask for *verb*
Children were asking for money in the street. ▶ to beg (for), to demand, to request

asleep *adjective*
The tortoise stayed asleep all winter.
▶ sleeping; (not an everyday word) dormant

aspect *noun*
The book deals with every aspect of keeping birds. ▶ a part, a feature, an element, a detail, a side, a facet

assault *verb*
The youths assaulted him as he was walking his dog. ▶ to attack, to beat, to beat up, to set on, to molest, to mug, to hit

assemble *verb*
1 *The children assembled on the village green.* ▶ to gather, to come together, to crowd together, to collect, to group, to meet; (more formal) to convene, to congregate
2 *We assembled our belongings ready to leave.* ▶ to gather, to get together, to bring together, to collect, to pile up
3 *You have to assemble the shelves with nails or screws.* ▶ to make, to build, to fit together, to put together; (more formal) to construct, to erect

assert *verb*
The writer asserts that art is a reflection of real life. ▶ to state, to claim, to contend, to declare, to argue, to insist, to maintain, to proclaim, to stress, to emphasize

assess *verb*
Jack bravely went on to the roof to assess the damage to his TV aerial. ▶ to estimate, to calculate, to work out, to evaluate, to determine, to gauge, to reckon

assign *verb*
A different teacher is assigned to each subject. ▶ to appoint, to allocate, to choose (for), to designate (for), to select (for)
NOTE: **Assign** is followed by *to*, but some of the other words are followed by *for*

assist *verb*
During the holidays Steve and Lynn usually assisted their father in the shop.
▶ to help, to aid, to lend a hand, to support
NOTE: If you use **help** or **lend a hand** you can say *usually helped in the shop* or *usually lent a hand in the shop,* but if you use **aid** or **support** you have to say *usually aided their father in the shop* or *usually supported their father in the shop*

assistant *noun*
The manager wanted to find an assistant to help at busy times.
▶ a helper, an associate, a deputy, a right-hand man, a right-hand woman, a partner

assorted *adjective*
The racks outside the shop contained shoes of assorted sizes. ▶ various, different, diverse, miscellaneous, mixed

assortment *noun*
The chair was covered with an assortment of cushions. ▶ a collection, a selection, a mixture, a variety

assume *verb*
I assume you will be coming tomorrow.
▶ to suppose, to presume, to imagine, to believe, to guess, to expect, to gather

assure *verb*
He assured us we had a good chance of seeing a badger. ▶ to promise, to guarantee, to give your word to, to tell

astonish *verb*
The anger in his voice astonished her.
▶ to amaze, to astound, to surprise, to stagger, to shock, to dumbfound, to flabbergast
NOTE: See the note at **amaze**

astound *verb*
Fiona's recovery from her illness has astounded her doctors. ▶ to astonish, to amaze, to surprise, to stagger, to dumbfound, to flabbergast
NOTE: See the note at **amaze**

atrocious *adjective*
The gang had committed atrocious crimes. ▶ wicked, terrible, dreadful, brutal, savage

attach *verb*
Sign the form and attach it to your entry for the competition. ▶ to fasten, to fix, to join, to tie, to connect, to link, to secure

attack *verb*
The old people were attacked in their homes in broad daylight. ▶ to assault, to beat, to beat up, to set on, to molest, to mug, to hit

attain *verb*
Three clarinet pupils attained Grade 3 last term. ▶ to obtain, to gain, to achieve, to reach, to secure, to win, to get

attempt *verb*
Three athletes were attempting to break the record. ▶ to try, to endeavour, to strive, to make an effort, to exert yourself

attend to *verb*
1 *Please attend to what I am saying.*
▶ to concentrate on, to pay attention to, to think about
2 *Their neighbour asked them to attend to the cat and parrot while they were away.* ▶ to look after, to take care of

attentive *adjective*
Most of the audience was attentive but some people were chatting or fidgeting.
▶ alert, paying attention, observant, watchful, vigilant, awake

attitude *noun*
1 *John was amused by his father's attitude to cooking the dinner.*
▶ a reaction, an approach, a point of view (on), a position (on)
2 *What's your attitude towards smoking?* ▶ an opinion (about, on), a feeling (about), an opinion (about, on), a standpoint (on), a view (about, on)
NOTE: **Attitude** is followed by *to* or *towards*, but the other words are followed by *about* or *on*

attract *verb*
Bags of nuts are hung in the branches to attract birds. ▶ to lure, to entice, to fascinate, to tempt, to interest

attractive *adjective*
1 *I looked back and saw an attractive young woman behind us.* ▶ pretty, good-looking, pleasing, charming, fetching, appealing, captivating, handsome, beautiful
2 *It may seem an attractive idea but in fact it's quite dangerous.* ▶ appealing, tempting, interesting, agreeable, pleasant

available *adjective*
The theme music is now available on a CD. ▶ obtainable, ready

average *adjective*
On an average day the store will get about two thousand customers.
▶ typical, usual, normal, ordinary

avid *adjective*
Susan is an avid reader but her sister is not so keen. ▶ keen, eager, enthusiastic, fervent

avoid *verb*
His aunt and uncle used country roads to avoid the traffic. ▶ to escape, to get out of, to evade

aware *adjective*
I was soon aware of something running through the grass. ▶ conscious, sensitive (to)

awe *noun*
The mountains filled him with awe.
▶ wonder, admiration, respect, reverence, fear, amazement

awful *adjective*
1 *Sharon had an awful pain in her stomach.* ▶ bad, severe, unpleasant, horrible, nasty
2 *Everyone agrees that war is awful.*
▶ terrible, dreadful, appalling, hateful, abominable, shocking, fearful

awkward *adjective*
1 *The doors were narrow and awkward to get through.* ▶ inconvenient, difficult, troublesome, unwieldy
2 *John felt awkward in a bow tie.*
▶ embarrassed, uncomfortable, clumsy, gawky, ungainly

B b

baby *noun*
Maria's sister was still a baby. ▶ an infant, a child, a toddler

babyish *adjective*
He behaved in a babyish way.
▶ childish, immature, infantile

back *noun*
Jack walked towards the back of the house. ▶ the rear, the end, the far end

back *verb*
Would you be willing to back our scheme? ▶ to support, to sponsor, to promote, to endorse, to subsidize, to aid, to assist, to help

back away *verb*
He shook his head and began to back away. ▶ to move back, to withdraw, to retreat

backer *noun*
We are looking for a backer for the youth club scheme. ▶ a sponsor, a supporter, a patron, a promoter

backing *noun*
I knew that I had my parents' backing.
▶ support, approval, endorsement, encouragement, assistance, help, sponsorship

bad *adjective*
1 *a bad person a bad thing to do*
▶ wicked, evil, wrong, sinful, vile, immoral, beastly, cruel, detestable, shameful, reprehensible, deplorable, villainous, rotten
2 *a bad child* ▶ naughty, disobedient, mischievous
3 *a bad mistake* ▶ serious, severe, shocking, terrible, dreadful, frightful, ghastly, unfortunate, appalling, awful, horrible
4 *a bad performance a bad piece of work* ▶ poor, inadequate, imperfect, inferior, weak, abysmal, atrocious, appalling, awful, dreadful, defective; (informal) lousy
5 *a bad apple* ▶ rotten, decayed, decomposing, putrid, tainted; (informal) off
6 *a bad smell* ▶ nasty, unpleasant, revolting, vile, odious, repellent, repulsive, nauseating
7 *Smoking is a bad habit.* ▶ harmful, dangerous, damaging, unhealthy
8 *I feel bad today.* ▶ ill, unwell, sick; (informal) poorly, under the weather; (more formal) indisposed
NOTE: **Bad** has many meanings depending on the words you use it with. There are other words you can use as well, but these are the most important

bad-tempered *adjective*
Long queues made my father bad-tempered. ▶ cross, angry, grumpy, irritable, irascible, morose, sullen, gruff, testy, moody, short-tempered

baffle *verb*
The crime has baffled the police for months. ▶ to perplex, to mystify, to fox, to puzzle, to frustrate, to bewilder, to confuse, to confound, to stump

bag *noun*
I'll take your bag out to the car. ▶ a case, a handbag, a basket, a carrier bag, a suitcase, a briefcase

bald *adjective*
A bald man came into the shop. ▶ bald-headed, hairless

ball *noun*
1 *He screwed the paper up into a tight ball.* ▶ a globe, a sphere
2 *The ball was being held in a grand house in the country.* ▶ a dance, a party, a disco, a social

ballot *noun*
The boys decided to hold a ballot to choose their leader. ▶ a vote, a poll, an election

ban *verb*
Large lorries have been banned from the town centre. ▶ to bar, to prohibit, to forbid, to make illegal, to outlaw, to banish

band *noun*
1 *The flag was white with a band of blue.* ▶ a strip, a stripe, a line, a ribbon
2 *The boy was kidnapped by a band of pirates.* ▶ a gang, a group, a company, a troop, a horde, a crew
3 *The band began to play a dance tune.* ▶ a group, an orchestra, an ensemble

bandit *noun*
The merchants knew how to protect themselves against pirates and bandits. ▶ a robber, a brigand, a thief, a highwayman, a buccaneer

bang *noun*
1 *He's had a terrific bang on the back of his head.* ▶ a blow, a knock, a hit
2 *There was a loud bang and a dreadful shriek.* ▶ a noise, a crash, a blast, a thud, a thump, a boom, an explosion, a report
NOTE: **crash**, **blast**, **explosion**, and **report** are all sharp sounds whereas **thud**, **thump**, and **boom** are all dull heavy sounds

bang *verb*
His mother got cross and banged the table. ▶ to hit, to thump, to knock, to strike, to hammer, to rap, to pound, to beat

banish *verb*
He was banished from the court for offending the Queen. ▶ to expel, to exile, to eject, to send away, to deport
NOTE: Note that to **deport** means to banish someone from the country they live in

bank *noun*
We had our picnic on a grassy bank by the river. ▶ a slope, a shore, an embankment, a mound, a knoll

bank *verb*
The little plane banked to the left. ▶ to tilt, to lean, to slant, to list, to incline, to pitch

banner *noun*
Each knight carried a banner. ▶ a flag, a standard, an ensign, colours, a streamer

banquet *noun*
More than a thousand people came to the king's banquet. ▶ a feast, a meal, a dinner; (informal) a spread

bar *noun*
The door was locked with a metal bar.
▶ a rod, a stick, a beam, a girder

bar *verb*
1 *All three of them were barred from the library for the rest of the term.* ▶ to ban, to exclude, to prohibit, to keep out, to banish
2 *A locked door barred her from going into the room.* ▶ to block, to obstruct, to impede, to check, to prevent, to stop

barbaric *adjective*
Alexandra had nightmares about wild barbaric people. ▶ savage, cruel, brutal, violent, fierce, atrocious

bare *adjective*
1 *The water was lapping round their bare legs.* ▶ naked, nude, unclothed, uncovered, undressed
2 *They walked up the bare hillside.*
▶ bleak, barren, desolate, windswept
3 *They were surprised to find the house bare and everyone gone.* ▶ empty, vacant, unfurnished, stripped

barely *adverb*
I reached home with barely enough time to eat. ▶ hardly, scarcely

bargain *noun*
I'd like to make a bargain with you.
▶ a deal, an agreement, an arrangement, a pact

bargain *verb*
They bargained for hours about the price. ▶ to haggle, to barter, to argue, to discuss terms, to negotiate

barrel *noun*
The barrel contained beer and not wine as they had thought. ▶ a cask, a tub, a keg

barren *adjective*
It was a landscape of jagged mountain peaks and barren slopes. ▶ bare, lifeless, arid, sterile

barrier *noun*
There was a barrier across the road.
▶ an obstruction, a barricade, a fence, a hurdle, an obstacle

base *noun*
1 *The statue stood on a large concrete base.* ▶ a stand, a support, a foundation, a rest
2 *The company has its base in Birmingham.* ▶ a depot, a headquarters

base *verb*
The story is based on actual events.
▶ to found

bashful *adjective*
The youngest children looked nervous and bashful. ▶ shy, timid, self-conscious, coy, diffident, reticent, reserved, sheepish, timorous

basic *adjective*
The course gave them a good basic training. ▶ essential, elementary, fundamental, primary, principal

basin *noun*
She poured water into a basin.
▶ a bowl, a dish, a tub, a pan, a sink

basis *noun*
These players will be the basis of a new team. ▶ a starting-point, a base, a foundation

batch *noun*
I put another batch of mince pies into the oven. ▶ a collection, a bunch, a consignment, a group, a set

batter *verb*
The prince went up to the door and battered boldly on it. ▶ to knock, to bang, to hammer, to pound, to thump; (with an object) to hit, to strike
NOTE: If you use hit you have to say *hit it* and not *hit on it*.

battle *noun*
A battle took place just outside the town.
▶ a fight, fighting, a conflict, a struggle, a clash, hostilities, an encounter

bawl *verb*
The sergeant turned his head to bawl to the men behind him. ▶ to yell, to roar, to shout, to bellow, to call, to cry, to scream, to shriek

bay *noun*
We watched the fishing boats in the bay.
▶ an inlet, a cove, an estuary, a gulf, a fiord
NOTE: You can use **fiord** when you are talking about Norway

be *verb*
1 *The mountains will be there for ever.*
▶ to remain, to exist, to stand, to stay, to continue, to endure
2 *The school concert will be in November.* ▶ to take place, to happen, to occur

beach *noun*
Some children and a dog were playing on the beach. ▶ the shore, the sand, the sands, the coast
NOTE: You can also use **seaside** but that means the place where the beach is rather than the beach itself.

beam *noun*
1 *Three beams hold up the ceiling.*
▶ a joist, a girder, a bar, a rafter
2 *A beam of light shone into the room.*
▶ a ray, a shaft, a gleam

bear *verb*
1 *His body looked too weak to bear the weight of his head.* ▶ to support, to carry, to hold up, to prop up
2 *She is too old to bear children.* ▶ to give birth to, to produce
3 *The old man couldn't bear the thought of going back alone.* ▶ to stand, to endure, to abide, to cope with, to put up with, to tolerate

bearings *plural noun*
Once she got her bearings she could head for home. ▶ a position, a direction, a course, a way

beast *noun*
Tom drew a picture of a jungle, full of wild beasts. ▶ a creature, an animal

beat *verb*
1 *They came across a man beating a dog.* ▶ to flog, to thrash, to hit, to chastise, to cane, to whip, to birch, to strike; (informal) to clout, to wallop, to whack, to knock about, to thump
2 *You have to beat the eggs to make omelettes.* ▶ to whisk, to whip, to blend, to mix, to stir
3 *The other team beat them 6-0.* ▶ to defeat, to overcome, to crush, to trounce; (informal) to lick, to thrash
4 *My heart beat faster with the excitement.* ▶ to throb, to thump, to pound

beat *noun*
1 *They like music with a strong beat.*
▶ a rhythm, a pulse, a throb
2 *I listened to the beat of the baby's heart.* ▶ a pulse, a throb, a beating, a flutter

beautiful *adjective*
1 *A beautiful woman stood by the door.*
▶ lovely, gorgeous, attractive, good-looking, pretty, radiant, stunning, glamorous, fair, graceful, elegant, handsome, delightful, charming
2 *Sunday was another beautiful day.*
▶ fine, lovely, sunny, fair, gorgeous, brilliant
3 *The scenery from the top of the hill was beautiful.* ▶ lovely, glorious, spectacular, splendid, superb, magnificent

become *verb*
1 *As Toby became tired the job became a lot harder.* ▶ to grow, to begin to be

2 *Isn't it strange that tiny babies can become big hairy men?* ▶ to grow into, to develop into, to turn into

bed *noun*
1 *She lay on the bed and fell asleep.*
▶ a divan, a bunk, a couch, a bedstead, a berth, a four-poster, a hammock
2 *The little garden has a flower bed at one end.* ▶ a plot, a patch, a border, a strip
3 *Fish were swimming along the bed of the river.* ▶ the bottom

bedraggled *adjective*
They came in from the rain looking wet and bedraggled. ▶ dishevelled, dirty, untidy, muddy, scruffy

before *adverb*
1 *You should have told me before.*
▶ earlier, sooner
2 *Have you been to Paris before?*
▶ previously, in the past, already

beg *verb*
He begged the old woman to let him go into the house. ▶ to entreat, to implore, to plead (with); (less strong) to ask, to request

begin *verb*
1 *Trouble began when the boys returned.*
▶ to start, to arise, to happen, to occur; (not an everyday word) to commence
2 *His father had begun a newsagent's business in the town.* ▶ to start, to establish, to set up, to found, to create, to undertake, to initiate, to open

beginner *noun*
I've been playing hockey for years but Joanna here's a beginner. ▶ a learner, a novice, a newcomer

beginning *noun*
They were studying the beginning of life on earth. ▶ an origin, a start, a birth, a creation; (not an everyday word) a commencement

behave *verb*
1 *Don't behave like a fool.* ▶ to act, to conduct yourself
2 *George sometimes found it difficult to behave.* ▶ to be good, to act well

behaviour *noun*
Their behaviour had been excellent.
▶ conduct, manners, attitude

belief *noun*
Do you have any religious beliefs?
▶ faith, a principle, a conviction, an opinion, a view, an attitude

believe *verb*
1 *I believe what they say, don't you?*
▶ to accept, to trust, to rely on, to have confidence in, to have faith in
2 *I believe the party's next week.* ▶ to think, to reckon, to suppose, to assume, to consider

belong *verb*
1 *The pencil belongs to me.* ▶ to be owned by
2 *The butter belongs in the fridge.*
▶ to go

belongings *noun*
Megan had few belongings left by the time she arrived in London.
▶ possessions, things, property

bend *verb*
1 *The shelves started to bend under the weight of so many books.* ▶ to buckle, to warp, to curve, to distort, to twist
2 *Molly had to bend to see under the car.* ▶ to crouch, to bow, to kneel, to stoop, to duck

bend *noun*
They came to a bend in the road.
▶ a curve, an angle, a corner, a twist, a turn

benefit *noun*
Having so many shops is one of the benefits of living in the city. ▶ an advantage, an asset, a blessing

bent *adjective*
A bent nail was sticking out of the fence.
► crooked, twisted, angled, curved,
distorted, warped

besides *adverb*
*I don't mind coming for a swim. Besides,
it will do me good.* ► anyway, also,
moreover; (more formal)
furthermore; (less formal) what's
more

best *adjective*
1 *Her mother was the best person to ask.*
► right, correct, most suitable, most
appropriate, most likely
2 *The visitors wanted to know where
the best restaurant was. Kate is the best
tennis player we know.* ► finest,
foremost, leading

betray *verb*
*Connor tried not to betray his true
feelings.* ► to reveal, to expose, to
disclose

better *adjective*
1 *Her Mum has got a better job.*
► superior, nicer, preferable, more
rewarding
2 *We need some better weather.*
► finer, nicer, more suitable
3 *I hope you are better now.* ► well,
recovered, healthier, cured, healed,
improved; (informal) on the mend

bewilder *verb*
*The strange look on his face bewildered
her.* ► to perplex, to mystify, to puzzle,
to baffle, to confuse, to confound, to
fox

biased *adjective*
*The commentators were extremely
biased.* ► one-sided, prejudiced,
unfair, partial

bid *verb*
*George wanted the watch but he wasn't
sure how much to bid for it.* ► to offer,
to propose

big *adjective*
1 *Polly's family lived in a big house in
the country.* ► large, enormous, huge,
great, grand, immense, colossal,
gigantic, massive, sizeable, substantial,
extensive, vast, mighty, tremendous
2 *It was amazing how big Tom had
grown.* ► tall, large, huge
3 *The big moment had come.* ► great,
important, significant

bill *noun*
*Some post lay on the floor: two cards
and what looked like a bill.* ► invoice,
account

bind
*A piece of old ribbon was used to bind
the package together.* ► to tie, to
secure, to fasten, to join

bird *noun*
KINDS OF BIRD ARE:
wild birds: sparrow, thrush, blackbird,
robin, starling, tit, bluetit, finch,
chaffinch, greenfinch, swallow, wren,
martin, jay, swift, lark, skylark, crow,
rook, raven, magpie, pigeon, dove,
jackdaw, linnet, nightingale,
woodpecker
water birds: duck, swan, goose, heron,
flamingo, stork, pelican, kingfisher,
mallard, moorhen, coot, plover,
peewit, dipper, crane
sea birds: seagull, gull, guillemot, tern,
albatross, gannet, cormorant, auk,
penguin, puffin
cage birds: canary, budgerigar
((informal) budgie), lovebird, parrot,
parakeet, cockatoo, cockatiel, myna
bird, macaw, toucan, bird of paradise,
kookaburra
birds of prey: eagle, hawk, owl, falcon,
kestrel, buzzard, vulture, condor

running birds: emu, ostrich, kiwi
fowl: chicken, turkey, hen
game birds: pheasant, grouse, quail

bit *noun*
1 *There's a bit of food on the floor.*
▶ a piece, a chunk, a lump, a scrap,
a crumb, a slice, a dollop, a morsel,
a particle, a speck
2 *Can I have a bit of the newspaper?*
▶ a part, a piece, a section, a share

bite *verb*
*The hamster bit a hole through the
carpet.* ▶ to chew, to gnaw, to nibble,
to chomp

bitter *adjective*
1 *The drink had a bitter taste.* ▶ sour,
sharp, acrid, unpleasant
2 *People who suffer bad injuries can
become quite bitter.* ▶ resentful, angry,
envious, embittered, jealous, sour
3 *The weather turned cold with bitter
winds.* ▶ cold, biting, freezing,
piercing, raw, icy, wintry; (informal)
perishing

black *adjective*
1 *It was a black night out on the moors.*
▶ dark, starless, moonless, inky, pitch-
black, pitch-dark
2 *Rachel has black hair.* ▶ dark, coal-
black, raven, jet-black

blame *verb*
Who can blame her for being angry?
▶ to criticize, to reproach, to chide, to
condemn, to denounce, to rebuke, to
reprimand, to scold

blame *noun*
It was Karl who took the blame. ▶ the
responsibility

blank *adjective*
1 *John started to write on a blank piece
of paper.* ▶ clean, unused, unmarked,
empty

2 *Mark looked blank and shook his
head.* ▶ vacant, expressionless,
absent-minded

blare *verb*
*Car horns were blaring in the evening
traffic.* ▶ to blast, to sound

blast *noun*
1 *An icy blast of air hit him full in the
face.* ▶ gust, burst, rush, draught
2 *A blast like that would destroy the
whole building.* ▶ an explosion

blaze *verb*
The fire started to blaze brightly. ▶ to
burn, to flame, to flare

bleak *adjective*
1 *The countryside looked cold and
bleak.* ▶ desolate, barren, dreary,
dismal, grim, cheerless, wintry, bare,
raw, exposed, windswept
2 *The future is looking bleak.*
▶ gloomy, grim, hopeless

blend *verb*
The colours blend well. ▶ to mix, to
combine, to mingle, to match, to go
together

blind *adjective*
1 *A blind man with a dog came round
the corner.* ▶ sightless
2 *His mother is blind to all his faults.*
▶ unaware (of), ignorant (of)

blink *verb*
Lights were blinking in the distance.
▶ to twinkle, to flicker, to wink, to
glitter

bliss *noun*
She had a look of utter bliss.
▶ happiness, joy, delight, ecstasy,
rapture, pleasure

blob *noun*
*A blob of ice cream had fallen on the
floor.* ▶ a lump, a drop, a spot

block *noun*
A block of stone lay across the path.
▶ a slab, a chunk, a lump, a hunk

block *verb*
1 *A mass of wet leaves had blocked the drains.* ▶ to bung up, to stop up, to clog; (more formal) to obstruct
2 *A massive pillar blocked our view of the altar.* ▶ to obstruct, to hinder, to hamper, to impede

bloodshed *noun*
The city surrendered to avoid further bloodshed. ▶ killing, slaughter, carnage, butchery

bloodthirsty *adjective*
The people in the tribe are no longer seen as bloodthirsty killers. ▶ cruel, barbaric, vicious, brutal, murderous, savage, ferocious, ruthless

bloom *verb*
The roses had bloomed early this year.
▶ to flower, to open

blot *verb*
The sheet was blotted with dried blood.
▶ to stain, to mark, to smudge, to spot

blot out *verb*
A factory building blotted out the view.
▶ to hide, to conceal, to obscure, to obliterate, to mask

blow *noun*
1 *As he walked in, the burglar gave him a sharp blow on the head.* ▶ a knock, a thump, a smack, a bang, a bump, a hit
2 *The news came to her as quite a blow.*
▶ a shock, a surprise, a jolt, a bombshell

blow up *verb*
1 *It was time to blow up the balloons.*
▶ to inflate, to fill, to pump up
2 *The bomb blew up in the early hours of the morning.* ▶ to go off, to explode, to detonate

bluff *verb*
We think they must be bluffing us. ▶ to hoodwink, to fool, to hoax, to deceive, to trick; (informal) to kid, to take in

blunder *noun*
They lost the game through a series of blunders. ▶ a mistake, an error, a slip; (more informal) a clanger, a howler, a slip-up

blunt *adjective*
Their request was met with a blunt refusal. ▶ abrupt, curt, frank, direct, outspoken, plain, rude

blurred *adjective*
When Kim came round at last everything looked blurred. ▶ hazy, fuzzy, confused, misty, unclear, indistinct, dim, faint

blush *verb*
When she saw Arthur she blushed and giggled. ▶ to flush, to go red, to turn red, to redden, to colour

boast *verb*
Soon they'll be boasting about their smart new kitchen. ▶ to brag, to crow, to show off, to gloat; (informal) to swank

boastful *adjective*
The group preferred Penny to her smug boastful sister. ▶ conceited, arrogant, haughty, vain, proud; (informal) cocky, stuck-up

bog *noun*
Police think he may have got lost and fallen into a bog. ▶ a marsh, a swamp, a quagmire

bogus *adjective*
The man showed us his ID card but it turned out to be bogus. ▶ false, faked, feigned, spurious, sham, pretended; (informal) phoney

boil *verb*
The water began to boil. ▶ to bubble,
to simmer

boisterous *adjective*
*The old grandmother sat at one end of
the table, and the boisterous children at
the other.* ▶ noisy, lively, rowdy,
unruly, frisky, disorderly, wild

bold *adjective*
*He wanted to look bold but felt a little
frightened.* ▶ daring, brave,
adventurous, courageous, heroic,
intrepid, fearless, valiant, enterprising

bolt *verb*
1 *Don't forget to bolt the door at night.*
▶ to lock, to fasten, to secure
2 *When he returned the animals had all
bolted.* ▶ to run away, to escape, to
flee, to dash away, to stampede
3 *Charlie was in a hurry but didn't
want to bolt his food.* ▶ to gobble, to
gulp, to guzzle, to wolf

bond *noun*
*There is a strong bond between a parent
and a child.* ▶ a tie, an attachment, a
relationship, a connection, a link

bonus *noun*
*His father earns a good income and
sometimes gets a bonus.* ▶ an extra, a
supplement, an addition

boom *noun*
*They could hear the boom of guns in the
distance.* ▶ an explosion, a bang, a
blast, a crash, a thunder

boost *noun*
*All the attention she was getting boosted
Jill's self-confidence.* ▶ to increase,
to raise, to bolster, to enhance, to help,
to encourage, to improve, to promote,
to foster

border *noun*
1 *We showed our passports at the
border.* ▶ frontier, boundary
2 *The picture had a white border.* ▶ an
edge, an edging, a verge, a margin

boring *adjective*
The speech was long and boring.
▶ tedious, dull, dreary, dry,
monotonous, uninteresting, tiresome,
humdrum

boss *noun*
*June went to work early to talk to her
new boss.* ▶ a chief, a head, a director,
a supervisor, a manager, a proprietor,
a controller, a superintendent, a
foreman, an employer, a governor,
a leader, a master

bossy *adjective*
*Her voice sounded more bossy than
usual.* ▶ bullying, domineering,
dictatorial, overbearing, masterful,
tyrannical

bother *noun*
1 *It was all a lot of bother about
nothing.* ▶ fuss, trouble, commotion,
disorder, disturbance
2 *It was a real bother keeping the
drinks cold during the summer.*
▶ a nuisance, an inconvenience, an
annoyance, a trouble, a worry

bother *verb*
1 *The noise outside was beginning to
bother them.* ▶ to disturb, to annoy, to
irritate, to upset, to worry, to harass, to
vex, to trouble, to exasperate
2 *Try not to bother your father while
he's working.* ▶ to disturb, to pester, to
trouble, to worry, to annoy

bottom *noun*
1 *The others were waiting at the bottom
of the hill.* ▶ the foot, the base
2 *He fell back and landed on his
bottom.* ▶ your seat, your rear;

(informal) your behind, your backside; (more formal) your buttocks, your posterior, your rump
3 *The wreck still lies on the bottom of the sea.* ▶ the floor, the bed, the depths

bough *noun*
A large bird had settled in one of the higher boughs. ▶ a branch, a limb

bounce *verb*
The ball bounced over his head and into the net. ▶ to rebound, to bound, to ricochet

bound *adjective*
1 *The train is bound to come soon.* ▶ certain, sure, very likely
2 *His mother felt bound to say he was wrong.* ▶ compelled, obliged, forced, constrained
3 *The cattle were put on a truck bound for Colombo.* ▶ heading, going (to)

bound *verb*
The labrador bounded up in the back seat. ▶ to jump, to leap, to spring

boundary *noun*
A stone wall marked the boundary of the Empire in the north. ▶ a frontier, a limit, a border, an edge, bounds, a margin, an extremity, a perimeter

bouquet *noun*
The bride carried a bouquet of flowers. ▶ a spray, a bunch, a posy, an arrangement

bout *noun*
1 *He was knocked out in the last bout.* ▶ a fight, a match, a contest
2 *He never had any illnesses apart from the odd bout of flu.* ▶ a spell, an attack, a fit

bowl *verb*
He bowled three good balls in a row. ▶ to throw, to pitch, to hurl, to fling

box *noun*
Someone had put all the old clothes in a box in the corner. ▶ a chest, a case, a carton, a crate

boy *noun*
Harry was a good boy. ▶ a lad, a kid, a youngster

brag
They didn't like to brag, but the party had been quite a success. ▶ to boast, to crow, to show off, to gloat; (informal) to swank

brain *noun*
They were good in school and had brains. ▶ intelligence, intellect, sense; (informal) grey matter

brainy *adjective*
The family was full of brainy brothers and weird grannies. ▶ intelligent, clever, bright, academic, intellectual

branch *noun*
1 *The branches of the tree were creaking in the wind.* ▶ a bough, an arm, a limb, a shoot
2 *The bank is opening a new branch.* ▶ a department, an office, a section

branch *verb*
The road branches into two just past the phone box. ▶ to divide, to split, to fork

brand *noun*
There are plenty of other brands you could try. ▶ a make, a sort, a kind, a line, a label

brandish *verb*
He marched into the room brandishing his diary. ▶ to wave, to flourish, to shake, to wield

brave *adjective*
After a while I became brave enough to ask a question. ▶ courageous, bold,

daring, plucky, adventurous, fearless, gallant, heroic, valiant, intrepid, spirited

bravery *noun*
She received an award for bravery.
▶ courage, heroism, gallantry, daring, determination, fortitude, valour, prowess, spirit, pluck; (*informal*) guts, grit

brawl *noun*
When a brawl broke out the landlord decided to call the police. ▶ a fight, a quarrel, a scuffle, a tussle, a clash, a scrap, a confrontation, a struggle, a squabble

brazen *adjective*
Their story turned out to be a brazen lie.
▶ shameless, brash, cheeky, insolent, impertinent, impudent

break *verb*
1 *Jim admitted he'd broken another plate.* ▶ to smash, to shatter, to crack, to destroy
2 *I've broken the CD player.* ▶ to damage, to wreck, to ruin
3 *Stella broke her arm in a hockey game.* ▶ to fracture, to shatter
4 *We may have broken the law.* ▶ to disobey, to disregard; (*more formal*) to violate, to infringe

break *noun*
1 *There was a break in the pipe.*
▶ a hole, a gap, a breach, a chink, a crack, a split, a cut, a gash, a leak, an opening, a rift, a slit, a tear
2 *We asked for a short break between rehearsals.* ▶ a pause, a rest, an interval, a lull, a respite, an interlude, a lapse; (*informal*) a breather

breathe *verb*
1 *Breathe in through your nose.* ▶ to inhale
2 *Breathe out through your mouth.*

▶ to exhale
NOTE: These are both more formal and technical words than **breathe**

breed *verb*
Some wild birds do not breed well in captivity. ▶ to reproduce, to have young, to produce young, to increase, to multiply

breed *noun*
This is the only breed of cat to have such small ears. ▶ a type, a kind, a species, a variety

breezy *adjective*
The day started cold and breezy and later it rained. ▶ windy, blowy, blustery, fresh

brief *adjective*
1 *She gave Jack a brief glance and went back to her work.* ▶ quick, short, momentary, fleeting, passing, temporary
2 *They gave a brief account of what had happened.* ▶ short, concise, abridged, compact, condensed, terse

brigand *noun*
The story was about a gang of brigands in the mountains. ▶ a robber, a bandit, a thief, a highwayman, a buccaneer

bright *adjective*
1 *Her hair looked red in the bright light from the kitchen.* ▶ shining, brilliant, blazing, intense, dazzling, clear, gleaming, glowing, radiant, luminous, sparkling
2 *The bright young faces belonged to girls of the local Brownie pack.* ▶ lively, cheerful, jolly, joyful, happy, animated
3 *Sarah was a bright child and she enjoyed going to school.* ▶ clever, intelligent, brainy, accomplished, brilliant, quick; (*informal*) smart

brighten *verb*
The good news brightened our day. ▶ to cheer up, to light up, to lighten

brilliant *adjective*
1 *His face was glistening in the sports hall's brilliant lights.* ▶ shining, bright, blazing, intense, dazzling, clear, gleaming, glowing, radiant, luminous, sparkling
2 *Her father had been a brilliant scientist.* ▶ clever, gifted, intelligent, brainy, outstanding, talented, accomplished
3 *They gave a brilliant performance.* ▶ outstanding, superb, excellent, masterly, marvellous, wonderful; (informal) fabulous, fantastic

brim *noun*
The glass was too full, with water spilling over the brim. ▶ the top, the rim, the edge, the brink

bring *verb*
1 *Shall I bring the picnic things?* ▶ to fetch, to take, to carry
2 *Selina wanted to bring her friend as well.* ▶ to invite
3 *She gave me a charm which was supposed to bring good luck.* ▶ to cause, to attract, to lead to, to result in, to create, to generate, to give rise to, to provoke

bring about *verb*
The new manager wanted to bring about some changes. ▶ to introduce, to effect, to create.

bring up *verb*
She had been brought up on a farm and understood country ways. ▶ to raise, to educate, to rear

brink *noun*
They found themselves standing at the brink of a deep pit. ▶ the edge, the rim

brisk *adjective*
He gets his exercise riding his bicycle or taking a brisk walk. ▶ quick, lively, energetic, fast, rapid, speedy, sprightly

brittle *adjective*
Cheap wallpaper tends to become brittle and crack. ▶ fragile, crisp, crumbly, frail, delicate

broad *adjective*
1 *She looked out of the window, and saw the broad plain thousands of feet below.* ▶ wide, large, great, extensive, vast, expansive, spacious, sweeping
2 *He gave a broad outline of what had happened.* ▶ general, rough, vague, imprecise

brutal *adjective*
In those days soldiers could be brutal. ▶ cruel, barbaric, vicious, bloodthirsty, murderous, savage, ferocious, ruthless

bubble *verb*
The water began to bubble furiously. ▶ to boil, to fizz, to foam, to seethe, to froth

bubbly *adjective*
Peter decided that his drink was not bubbly enough. ▶ fizzy, sparkling, foaming, frothy; (more formal) effervescent

buckle *noun*
The belt had a heavy brass buckle. ▶ a clasp, a catch, a fastening, a fastener, a clip

buckle *verb*
The beam began to buckle under the weight. ▶ to bend, to twist, to curve, to collapse, to crumple, to distort

budge *verb*
She refused to budge until she'd sorted out the problem. ▶ to move, to shift

buffet *noun*
He made his way to the buffet and bought two drinks. ▶ a café, a cafeteria, a snack bar, a bar

build *verb*
1 They want to knock the old house down and build a new one. ▶ to construct, to erect, to put up, to assemble, to make, to put together
2 The excitement was building up inside him. ▶ to develop, to increase, to strengthen, to enlarge, to intensify, to escalate

bulge *noun*
He noticed a bulge in the wallpaper above the light switch. ▶ a bump, a lump, a swelling

bulge *verb*
His eyes bulged as if they were coming out of his head. ▶ to stick out, to protrude, to swell, to pop

bulk *noun*
The statue's bulk was more obvious in the daylight. ▶ size, magnitude, largeness, volume

bully *verb*
Sometimes the bigger girls bullied us little ones. ▶ to intimidate, to torment, to frighten, to persecute, to terrorize, to threaten

bump *noun*
1 It took a few bumps on the head for him to get used to the low ceilings. ▶ a bulge, a lump, a swelling
2 The car hit the wall with a bump. ▶ a thud, a thump, a bang, a crash

bump *verb*
Andrew fell off the bed and bumped his head. ▶ to hit, to knock, to bang, to strike, to thump, to wallop

bumpy *adjective*
We had a bumpy ride across town in an old car. ▶ rough, jerky, uneven, bouncy, shaky

bunch *noun*
1 There was a bunch of flowers at the spot where the accident happened. ▶ a bouquet, a posy, a spray, a bundle
2 He picked up a bunch of bananas and threw them at her. ▶ a clump, a bundle, a cluster
3 He went out to play football with a bunch of friends. ▶ a group, a gang, a band, a crowd, a gathering

bundle *noun*
Les handed the bundle of papers to the girl. ▶ a batch, a bunch, a clump, a sheaf, a package, a parcel, a packet, a pile

burden *noun*
1 The donkey was carrying a heavy burden up the hill. ▶ a load, a weight
2 They felt as if a burden had been taken from them. ▶ a worry, a care, a trouble, a problem, a millstone

burly *adjective*
In the back of the car, a girl was squashed between two burly men. ▶ brawny, hefty, beefy, husky, stocky, muscular, strong, tough, big, large

burn *verb*
1 The fire was burning steadily. ▶ to blaze, to flare, to flame, to glow, to flicker, to smoulder
NOTE: You use **flicker** when something is burning gently with small flames, and **smoulder** when it is burning without any flames
2 Wayne lit a bonfire to burn the garden rubbish. ▶ to set fire to, to set alight, to kindle; (more formal) to incinerate

burrow *verb*
The rabbits had burrowed holes in the garden. ▶ to dig, to excavate, to tunnel, to hollow out

burst *verb*
The pillow burst and left feathers all over the room. ▶ to break, to split, to give way, to tear, to explode

bury *verb*
The dog kept burying bones in the garden. ▶ to hide, to cover, to conceal

business *noun*
1 *The company does good business abroad.* ▶ trade, trading, commerce, dealings, buying and selling
2 *What kind of business do you want to go into?* ▶ a career, an occupation, a job, work, employment
3 *His uncle ran a small engineering business in Birmingham.* ▶ a company, a firm, an establishment, an organization, a concern, an enterprise, a corporation
4 *My uncle left the room, saying he had some urgent business to deal with.*
▶ affairs, matters, duties
5 *It was none of Carolyn's business, but she still wanted to know more.*
▶ concern, affair

busy *adjective*
1 *The next day everyone was busy cleaning up the house.* ▶ occupied, active, engaged, employed, involved
2 *After a busy day she was too tired to go exploring.* ▶ active, full, hectic, energetic, strenuous, exciting
3 *The ambulance raced through the busy streets.* ▶ bustling, crowded, lively

butt *verb*
The next moment the goat had butted her. ▶ to bump, to ram, to jab, to knock, to strike, to hit

butt in *verb*
If you've got something to say, do butt in. ▶ to interrupt

buy *verb*
You can buy it much cheaper at the supermarket. ▶ to get, to obtain; (more formal) to acquire, to purchase; to procure

C c

cabin *noun*
You can hire a cabin by the lake during the summer. ▶ a hut, a shelter, a chalet, a shack, a shed

cable *noun*
1 *The boat was held to the jetty by a cable.* ▶ a cord, a rope, a line, a chain, a hawser
2 *An electric cable stretched across the corner of the room.* ▶ a lead, a wire, a flex

cadge *verb*
We missed the last bus and had to cadge a lift. ▶ to scrounge, to beg

café *noun*
If you find a café, bring me back a cheese sandwich. ▶ a snack bar, a coffee shop, a coffee bar, a tea room, a cafeteria, a canteen, a bar, a buffet

caked *adjective*
Our shoes were caked with mud.
▶ covered, coated, plastered, encrusted

calamity *noun*
They regarded their holiday as rather a calamity. ▶ a disaster, a catastrophe, a misfortune, a tragedy

calculate *verb*
It was difficult to calculate the size of the room. ▶ to work out, to estimate, to add up, to assess, to compute, to reckon, to figure out

call *verb*
1 *William could hear someone calling to him.* ▶ to cry out, to shout, to yell
2 *The head called three people to his office.* ▶ to summon, to order, to invite
3 *I said I'd call again later.* ▶ to ring, to phone, to telephone
4 *Harriet's mother called the next day.* ▶ to visit; (informal) to drop in, to drop by
5 *I'd better call you early tomorrow.* ▶ to wake, to wake up, to rouse, to awaken
6 *Why did you call your cat Albert?* ▶ to name

call off *verb*
Tomorrow's game has been called off. ▶ to put off, to cancel, to postpone, to abandon, to scrap
NOTE: You use **cancel** if you mean calling off for good, and **postpone** if you mean calling off until a later date. You often use **abandon** to refer to things that have been started but cannot be completed.

calling *noun*
The priest was more fun than most men of his calling. ▶ an occupation, a profession, a job, a career, a line of work

callous *adjective*
Callous thieves dumped a baby from the car they had stolen. ▶ cruel, brutal, heartless, pitiless, uncaring, ruthless, cold-blooded, hard-hearted, insensitive

calm *adjective*
1 *a calm sea* ▶ still, smooth, placid, flat, motionless
2 *a calm mood* ▶ peaceful, quiet, sedate, serene, tranquil, untroubled
3 *Please keep calm.* ▶ cool, collected, level-headed, relaxed, quiet, patient

calm *verb*
He took her by the arm and tried to calm her. ▶ to quieten, to soothe, to pacify, to comfort, to settle

cancel *verb*
When his father was ill they had to cancel their holiday. ▶ to call off, to abandon, to give up, to scrap, to postpone, to put off

capable *adjective*
They called in a team of highly capable engineers. ▶ competent, accomplished, able, efficient, proficient, skilful, skilled, talented, clever

capacity *noun*
1 *Measure the capacity of the container.* ▶ the size, the volume
2 *They have a great capacity for hard work.* ▶ an ability, a capability, an aptitude, a talent

caper *verb*
Lambs capered about in the fields. ▶ to frolic, to gambol, to dance, to frisk, to romp, to jump, to leap, to skip, to prance

capsize *verb*
A group of students had drowned when their sightseeing boat capsized. ▶ to overturn, to keel over, to turn over, to tip over, to turn turtle

captive *noun*
PC Brown put handcuffs on the captive and then fastened him to a convenient railing. ▶ a prisoner, a convict

capture *verb*
Most of the escaped prisoners were later captured. ▶ to catch, to seize, to arrest; (more formal) to apprehend, to take into custody

care *verb*
1 *She cares very much about her children.* ▶ to mind, to bother, to concern yourself, to trouble, to worry
2 *Rob's sister has a job caring for old people.* ▶ to look after, to take care of, to mind, to attend to, to tend, to watch over, to nurse, to provide for

care *noun*
1 *They did the work with great care.* ▶ attention, carefulness, thoroughness, diligence, concentration, exactness
2 *She tripped along without a care in the world.* ▶ a trouble, a worry, an anxiety, a concern
3 *In the end they left the child in the care of a nanny.* ▶ the charge, the keeping, the protection, the safe-keeping, the custody

career *noun*
Kate wants a career in journalism. ▶ a job, an occupation, a profession, employment

carefree *adjective*
1 *We want our journey to be smooth and carefree.* ▶ easy, untroubled, straightforward, pleasant, comfortable
2 *The children were smiling and carefree.* ▶ happy, cheerful, cheery, untroubled, light-hearted

careful *adjective*
1 *Be careful on the wet floors.* ▶ wary, watchful, alert, attentive, vigilant, cautious, observant
2 *In his report Tom's work was said to be careful and steady.* ▶ thorough, methodical, conscientious, meticulous, neat, painstaking, accurate, precise

careless *adjective*
1 *His brother had been careless and left the door open.* ▶ thoughtless, absent-minded, negligent, rash, inattentive, remiss, inconsiderate, irresponsible,

reckless, uncaring, scatter-brained
2 *His work seems more careless than usual.* ▶ slovenly, slapdash, shoddy, sloppy, disorganized, messy, untidy

caress *verb*
She gently caressed the baby's cheek with her fingers. ▶ to stroke, to fondle, to kiss, to pat, to pet

carry *verb*
1 *I wanted to carry my own suitcase.* ▶ to take, to bring, to lift, to move, to hold, to fetch
2 *Electric trains carry visitors from the station to the pier.* ▶ to take, to transport, to ferry, to ship; (more formal) to convey
3 *The foundations may not be strong enough to carry the weight.* ▶ to support, to bear, to hold up

carry on *verb*
We wondered if the rain would carry on all afternoon. ▶ to continue, to go on, to keep on, to last, to persevere

carry out *verb*
They hoped to carry out the work in their spare time. ▶ to do, to perform, to complete, to finish, to achieve; (more formal) to accomplish, to execute

case *noun*
1 *Their valuables were all packed up in cases.* ▶ a container, a box, a crate, a chest, a trunk, a carton
2 *It was a clear case of dishonesty.* ▶ an instance, an example, an illustration, an occurrence

cast *verb*
1 *They invented a game of casting stones into the lake.* ▶ to throw, to toss, to fling, to sling, to lob, to pitch, to hurl, to heave; (informal) to chuck
NOTE: You normally use **hurl** and **heave** when you are talking about heavy things that

are difficult to throw
2 *The statue is cast in pure gold.* ▶ to mould, to form, to shape

casual *adjective*
1 *It was just a casual remark.*
▶ chance, random, offhand, careless, unintentional, unplanned, accidental, unexpected, spontaneous
2 *They were all wearing casual clothes.*
▶ informal, comfortable, everyday, easygoing
3 *There was a casual atmosphere in the room.* ▶ relaxed, informal, easygoing, pleasant; (informal) laid-back

catastrophe *noun*
Two accidents in the same day seemed like a catastrophe. ▶ a disaster, a calamity, a misfortune, a tragedy

catch *verb*
1 *Edward's arm shot out to catch the ball.* ▶ to grab, to seize, to grasp, to clutch, to snatch, to grip
2 *The fish they caught was lying on the table.* ▶ to hook, to net, to get
3 *The suspect was caught getting on a train in Newcastle.* ▶ to arrest, to capture, to corner, to stop; (informal) to nab
4 *If we stay in this damp house any longer we'll catch pneumonia.* ▶ to get, to come down with, to be infected by; (more formal) to contract

catch *noun*
The car was so cheap there had to be a catch. ▶ a snag, a drawback, a disadvantage, a hitch

category *noun*
A prize is awarded in each age category.
▶ a group, a set, a class

cater for *verb*
The library caters for a wide range of readers. ▶ to provide for, to serve

cause *noun*
1 *The cause of the problem seemed to be faulty wiring.* ▶ a reason (for), an origin, a root, a basis, a source, a beginning
2 *They are collecting money for a good cause.* ▶ a purpose, an objective, a project

cause *verb*
Heavy rain has been causing floods near the river. ▶ to result in, to bring about, to give rise to, to lead to, to produce

caution *noun*
1 *There are good reasons for caution when young children are around.*
▶ care, attentiveness, vigilance, watchfulness, wariness, alertness, prudence
2 *As it was their first offence they were all let off with a caution.* ▶ a warning, a reprimand

cautious *adjective*
Ali took a cautious step towards the edge of the pool. ▶ careful, discreet, wary, deliberate, prudent

cease
(not an everyday word) *We were told to cease work immediately.* ▶ to stop, to finish, to break off, to discontinue, to end; (formal) to terminate

celebrate *verb*
The villagers celebrated the end of the war by singing and dancing. ▶ to mark, to honour

censure *noun*
Their actions deserve the strongest censure. ▶ criticism, disapproval, condemnation

centre *noun*
The pictures were in the centre of the book. ▶ the middle, the midpoint, the inside, the heart

certain *adjective*
1 *A rise in prices now seems certain.*
▶ sure, unavoidable, inescapable,
inevitable
2 *We are certain that we saw a boat in
the harbour yesterday.* ▶ sure, positive,
definite, assured, confident

chain *noun*
*The chain of helpers were swinging
buckets of water from hand to hand.*
▶ a row, a line, a cordon, a string, a
column, a series

chance *noun*
1 *The two boys met by chance on the
beach.* ▶ accident, coincidence, luck
2 *There's a slight chance of snow.*
▶ a possibility, a risk
3 *On Thursday there will be a chance to
see the eclipse.* ▶ an opportunity, a
possibility (of)
NOTE: If you use **possibility** you have to say
'... a possibility of seeing the eclipse'.

change *verb*
1 *Just as we got used to the new phone
numbers they decided to change them
again.* ▶ to alter, to modify, to adjust,
to adapt, to reorganize, to amend, to
convert, to vary
2 *Do you want to change places?* ▶ to
swop, to switch, to exchange

change *noun*
*There has been little change in her
condition since the operation.*
▶ difference, alteration, variation,
progress

changeable *adjective*
*The weather is changeable at this time
of year.* ▶ variable, unreliable,
inconsistent, unpredictable, unsettled,
erratic, unstable

chaos *noun*
A burst water pipe was causing chaos.
▶ confusion, turmoil, disorder,
upheaval, anarchy, pandemonium,
bedlam

chaotic *adjective*
*The intruders left the house in a chaotic
state.* ▶ confused, messy, muddled,
disorderly, disorganized, jumbled,
topsy-turvy

character *noun*
1 *Julie thought the old man was an odd
character.* ▶ a person, an individual;
(informal) a chap, a bloke
NOTE: You only use **chap** and **bloke** about a
man
2 *Chinese tea has a special character of
its own.* ▶ a quality, a flavour, a nature
3 *He is a gentleman of good character.*
▶ reputation
4 *It was not in Angie's character to start
an argument.* ▶ nature, personality,
disposition, manner, temperament

charge *noun*
1 *There's a charge for using the
photocopier.* ▶ a fee, a cost, a
payment, a price
2 *The Black Prince led a cavalry charge.*
▶ an attack, an assault, an advance

charge *verb*
1 *The cavalry charged the enemy.* ▶ to
attack, to assault, to storm
2 *The police decided not to charge him
with the crime.* ▶ to accuse (of), to
prosecute (for)
NOTE: You **charge** someone *with* something
but **accuse** someone *of* something and
prosecute someone *for* something

charity *noun*
*She showed great charity towards the
poor people in her neighbourhood.*
▶ generosity, kindness, humanity,
compassion

charm *verb*
The young woman was charmed by their singing. ► to delight, to enchant, to entrance, to attract, to bewitch, to captivate, to fascinate, to spellbind

charming *adjective*
His mother always told him he had been a charming baby. ► lovely, delightful, appealing, attractive, captivating, enchanting

chase *verb*
The young dog was chasing rabbits in a field. ► to pursue, to run after, to hunt, to track, to trail, to follow

cheap *adjective*
1 *They tried to find a cheap meal in town.* ► inexpensive, economical, reasonable
2 *She was wearing cheap jewellery and smelly make-up.* ► inferior, poor, poor-quality, shoddy, tawdry, worthless; (informal) tacky

cheat *verb*
The man in the paper shop tried to cheat us. ► to trick, to deceive, to defraud, to swindle, to dupe, to fool, to hoax; (informal) to rip off, to take in

check *verb*
1 *She realized she'd forgotten to check her lottery numbers.* ► to look at, to confirm, to examine, to compare, to test; (informal) to check out
2 *I'd better check that the door is locked.* ► to make sure, to ensure, to establish; (more formal) to ascertain
3 *Doctors have managed to check the spread of the disease.* ► to curb, to reduce, to control, to halt, to restrain, to slow

check *noun*
Ron went into the house to give the bedrooms a quick check. ► an inspection, an examination

cheeky *adjective*
Sarah often got into trouble for being cheeky. ► rude, impolite, disrespectful, impertinent, insolent, impudent, saucy

cheer *verb*
The audience clapped and cheered in delight. ► to applaud, to shout, to yell

cheer up *verb*
The thought of a meal in town cheered them up a little. ► to comfort, to console, to hearten, to raise your spirits, to elate, to gladden; (informal) to perk up

cheerful *adjective*
In the end he relaxed and gave a cheerful smile. ► happy, jolly, lively, bright, sunny, friendly, cheery, jovial, joyful, light-hearted, merry, animated

cherish *verb*
Their happy memories were something to cherish. ► to treasure, to value, to prize, to hold dear, to cling to

chief *adjective*
1 *The chief reason for going was that Maisie would be there.* ► main, principal, major, dominant, basic, essential, fundamental, most important, key, prime, primary
2 *Surinder's been promoted from cook to chief cook.* ► head, top, senior, principal, leading

chief *noun*
1 *The village chief had been killed.* ► the head, the leader, the chieftain
2 *After Christmas they would all meet the new chief of the firm.* ► the boss, the head, the manager, the director, the proprietor

chiefly *adverb*
Polly chiefly remembered her aunt for the special puddings she used to make

her. ▶ mainly, mostly, principally, especially, predominantly, primarily, particularly

child *noun*
I lived abroad for several years as a child. ▶ a boy, a girl, a baby, an infant, a minor, a youngster; (informal) a kid, a nipper

childish *adjective*
The letter had lots of childish jokes in it. ▶ immature, silly, babyish, infantile, juvenile

chilly *adjective*
It was a chilly April day with grey skies. ▶ cold, cool, crisp, fresh, frosty, wintry; (informal) nippy

chink *noun*
Jane noticed a light through a chink in the curtains. ▶ a slit, an opening, a crack, a gap

chip *noun*
Linda's glass had a small chip in it. ▶ a crack, a nick, a splinter, a flaw

choice *noun*
1 *We had no choice but to agree.* ▶ an option, an alternative
2 *The Lake District is a good choice for an outdoor holiday.* ▶ a selection, an idea

choke *verb*
1 *A huge cloud of dust threatened to choke them.* ▶ to suffocate, to smother, to stifle, to strangle, to throttle
2 *Her collar was so tight it seemed to be choking her.* ▶ to throttle, to strangle, to suffocate

choose *verb*
1 *Each team had to choose its own leader.* ▶ to pick, to appoint, to decide on, to select, to elect, to name, to nominate, to settle on

2 *Mary came, but her sister chose to stay at home.* ▶ to decide, to opt, to elect, to prefer

chop *verb*
Dave could see his father in the back yard, chopping wood. ▶ to cut, to cut up, to hack, to hew

chubby *adjective*
He peeped in the pushchair and saw a chubby baby. ▶ plump, podgy, dumpy, fat

chuck *verb*
(informal) *Some boys were chucking stones into the river.* ▶ to throw, to toss, to sling, to fling, to hurl, to lob, to cast

chunk *noun*
Their drinks had large chunks of ice in them. ▶ a lump, a hunk, a piece, a block, a portion, a slab, a cube

civil *adjective*
They were angry, but they managed to keep pleasant and civil. ▶ polite, courteous, considerate, respectful, well-mannered

claim *verb*
1 *You are allowed to claim the money for your train fares.* ▶ to request, to ask for, to demand
2 *They claimed they had been at home all evening.* ▶ to maintain, to insist, to assert, to state, to declare, to say, to pretend

clamp *verb*
A pair of earphones were clamped to her head. ▶ to fix, to attach, to secure, to fasten, to stick

clap *verb*
The audience clapped loudly. ▶ to applaud, to cheer

clarify *verb*

Can you please clarify what you want us to do? ▶ to make clear, to explain, to define

clash *noun*

There have been several clashes between rival gangs. ▶ a fight, a conflict, a struggle, a confrontation, a battle, a collision, a contest

clash *verb*

Supporters clashed with police outside the ground. ▶ to fight, to come to blows, to quarrel

clasp *verb*

Ruth clasped her sister's hand as they crossed the busy road. ▶ to grip, to grasp, to clutch, to grab, to seize, to hold, to squeeze, to cling to

clasp *noun*

Her hair fell in waves from a gold clasp. ▶ a fastening, a fastener, a brooch, a slide, a clip, a buckle

class *noun*

1 *The programme showed different classes of paintings.* ▶ a category, a kind, a sort, a type, a group, a set
2 *Here are several different classes of plants.* ▶ a species, a division, a kind, a type, a category, a sort

classify *verb*

The animals are classified according to breed. ▶ to arrange, to group, to class, to sort, to organize, to order, to rank

clean *adjective*

1 *We'll have to spend ages getting the floor clean.* ▶ washed, scrubbed, spotless
2 *The air in the mountains is beautifully clean.* ▶ fresh, pure, clear
3 *She held the tip of her pen above the clean page.* ▶ blank, unused, clear, unmarked, untouched

clean *verb*

1 *He had to clean the floor at least twice a day.* ▶ to wash, to sweep out, to brush, to hoover, to vacuum, to mop, to rinse, to tidy
2 *Have you cleaned your hands?* ▶ to wash, to scrub, to soap, to cleanse

clear *adjective*

1 *One window had clear glass so you could see into the room.* ▶ transparent, see-through, clean, colourless, pure
2 *He gave a clear explanation of the problem.* ▶ lucid, plain, simple, coherent, understandable, comprehensible, intelligible
3 *They had a clear choice.* ▶ obvious, plain, straightforward, definite
4 *It was clear who was going to win.* ▶ obvious, plain, apparent, evident
5 *He finished the letter in his usual clear writing.* ▶ legible, simple, neat, plain, tidy
6 *Jenny's voice was clear and bright.* ▶ audible, distinct
7 *The window gave a clear view across the valley.* ▶ open, uninterrupted, unimpeded
8 *Next day the sky was clear.* ▶ cloudless, sunny, bright
9 *Keep a space clear to sit down on.* ▶ free, empty, uncluttered, open

clear *verb*

1 *After the storm, the sky began to clear.* ▶ to brighten, to lighten, to become clear
2 *They cleared a space on the floor to sit on.* ▶ to leave, to make, to empty
3 *The horse cleared the first three fences but fell at the fourth.* ▶ to jump, to jump over, to leap over, to bound over, to spring over

clear up *verb*

1 *I'll have to clear up my room.* ▶ to tidy, to tidy up, to clean, to clean up
2 *The man's confession cleared up the*

mystery. ► to solve, to explain
3 *The weather cleared up in the
afternoon.* ► to brighten, to improve

clever *adjective*
1 *James had found a clever way of
making extra money.* ► shrewd, smart,
astute, ingenious, cunning, bright
2 *You're a clever girl, you know that?*
► smart, intelligent, bright, capable,
able, gifted, sharp, talented,
accomplished; (informal) brainy

climax *noun*
*The climax of the day was to be a
fireworks party in the evening.* ► a high
point, a highlight, a peak; (not an
everyday word) an acme

climb *verb*
*He had to climb a ladder to reach the
window.* ► to go up, to scale; (more
formal) to ascend

cling *verb*
1 *Ivy was clinging to the walls.* ► to
adhere, to stick
2 *'Can I stay?' she said, clinging to Jim's
hand.* ► to clasp, to clutch, to grasp, to
hold on to
NOTE: You do not use *to* with the first three
words: *'Can I stay?' she said, clasping Jim's
hand.*

clip *verb*
It's my job to clip the hedge. ► to cut, to
trim, to snip, to prune, to crop, to
shear

clog *verb*
Wet leaves had clogged the drains. ► to
block, to bung up, to stop up, to
obstruct

close *verb*
1 *Beth went out of the room and closed
the door behind her.* ► to shut, to lock,
to fasten, to bolt, to secure
NOTE: The best alternative word is **shut**. All
the others are about locking, and this is

sometimes what **close** means
2 *The road has been closed for building
works.* ► to block, to close off, to bar,
to barricade
3 *The chairman closed the meeting at
eight o'clock.* ► to end, to conclude, to
bring to a close, to finish, to stop;
(informal) to wind up

close *adjective*
1 *They have moved to a new house close
to the supermarket.* ► near, adjacent
(to), adjoining, close by
NOTE: **Adjoining** means 'touching another
building'
2 *The boys had been close friends for
several years.* ► fond, firm, dear,
affectionate, intimate
3 *It was getting close in their small
room.* ► stuffy, muggy, humid, airless,
oppressive, stifling
4 *The car squeezed into the garage but
it was a close fit.* ► tight
5 *The girls came in to take a close look
at my new poster.* ► careful, thorough,
detailed, intent

clothes *plural noun*
DIFFERENT TYPES OF CLOTHES ARE:
outdoor clothes: anorak, cagoule, cape,
cloak, coat, duffel coat, gloves,
mackintosh, mittens, overcoat, parka,
poncho, raincoat, scarf, shawl, wind-
cheater, yashmak
indoor clothes: blazer, blouse,
cardigan, dress, frock, gown, jacket,
jeans, jersey, jumper, kilt, pinafore,
pullover, sari, shirt, shoes, shorts,
singlet, skirt, slacks, smock, socks,
stockings, suit, sweater, sweatshirt, tie,
trousers, T-shirt, tunic, waistcoat
underclothes: boxer shorts, bra, briefs,
corset, knickers, panties, pants,
petticoat, slip, tights, underpants, vest,
Y-fronts
work clothes: apron, cassock,
dungarees, oilskins, overalls, pinafore,
smock

clothes worn for sport and recreation:
bikini, football jersey, jodhpurs,
leotard, shorts, tracksuit, wetsuit
clothes worn at bedtime: dressing
gown, nightdress, pyjamas, slippers

clothing *noun*
*The boys will need warm clothing for
their camp.* ▶ clothes, dress, gear;
(more formal) garments, attire,
apparel

cloudy *adjective*
1 *After a fine morning the sky became
cloudy.* ▶ overcast, dull, grey, gloomy
2 *The glass contained a cloudy liquid.*
▶ murky, milky, misty, opaque,
steamy, unclear

clout *verb*
(informal) *She clouted him on the back
of his head.* ▶ to hit, to strike, to
smack, to whack, to wallop, to thump,
to knock, to punch, to swipe

club *noun*
1 *Someone had hit him with a club.*
▶ a stick, a cudgel, a baton, a
truncheon
2 *His parents were members of a local
club.* ▶ a society, an association, a
group, a union, a league, an
organization

clue *noun*
*The police needed a clue about who the
woman was.* ▶ a hint, an indication, a
sign, a lead, a piece of evidence, a
suggestion, an inkling

clump *noun*
*At the back of the house there were
small clumps of bushes.* ▶ a cluster, a
group, a collection, a bunch

clumsy *adjective*
He was a big clumsy boy of thirteen.
▶ awkward, ungainly, careless,
blundering, fumbling, gawky,
accident-prone

cluster *noun*
1 *There were clusters of jackets and
raincoats hanging from the pegs.* ▶ a
bunch, a clump, a collection
2 *A cluster of people still stood at the
bus stop.* ▶ a group, a crowd, a
collection, a gathering

clutch *verb*
*He started to run again, still clutching
his sister's hand.* ▶ to grip, to grasp, to
clasp, to hold, to squeeze, to cling to

clutter *noun*
Sarah gazed at the clutter on the table.
▶ a mess, a muddle, a jumble, a
confusion, a disarray

coarse *adjective*
1 *The curtains were made of a heavy
coarse material.* ▶ rough, thick, hard,
scratchy, hairy, harsh
2 *You have a very coarse sense of
humour.* ▶ crude, rude, indecent,
uncouth, vulgar, foul, lewd

coax *verb*
*The children were now hungry and it
was easy to coax them back into the
house.* ▶ to tempt, to persuade, to
entice, to induce

cocky *adjective*
(informal) *Kevin gets cocky when he's
nervous.* ▶ cheeky, insolent, rude,
arrogant, conceited, brash, boastful,
bumptious

coil *verb*
The rope was coiled round a post. ▶ to
loop, to wind, to twist, to entwine, to
curl

coincide *verb*
*The rain coincided with the guests'
arrival.* ▶ to clash

cold *adjective*
1 *It had been a cold day and the ground
was frozen.* ▶ chilly, freezing, bitter,
biting, wintry, raw, perishing, cool,

frosty, icy; (informal) nippy
2 *Donna's parents were always a bit cold towards her husband.*
▶ unfriendly, unkind, unfeeling, distant, aloof, indifferent, uncaring (about), unconcerned (about)
NOTE: If you use **uncaring** or **unconcerned** you would usually say *about* rather than *towards*

cold-blooded *adjective*
The papers called the killer a cold-blooded brute. ▶ cruel, savage, ruthless, callous, barbaric, inhuman, heartless, merciless, pitiless

collapse *verb*
1 *Cathy felt unsteady and collapsed on the floor.* ▶ to faint, to fall down
2 *Thousands of buildings collapsed in the earthquake.* ▶ to fall down, to fall in, to tumble down, to subside, to cave in, to crumple

collect *verb*
1 *We collected the dead leaves into a large heap.* ▶ to gather, to pile up, to sweep, to accumulate, to assemble, to bring together, to cluster
2 *A crowd was collecting outside the hospital.* ▶ to gather, to assemble, to come together, to converge
3 *Mum had to collect Vicky from the station.* ▶ to fetch, to bring, to get, to pick up

collection *noun*
Jim's uncle had a valuable collection of paintings. ▶ a set, an assortment, a group, a batch, a hoard

collide *verb*
The car collided with a lorry. ▶ to hit, to strike, to crash into, to run into, to smash into, to bump into, to knock

collision
There was a collision at the end of the road. ▶ accident, bump, crash, impact, knock, smash

colossal *adjective*
There was a colossal statue of the general in the town square. ▶ huge, enormous, giant, gigantic, immense, mighty, massive, big

colour *noun*
The walls were painted a soft pink colour. ▶ a hue, a shade, a tint, a tone, a tinge
THE RANGE OF COLOURS INCLUDES:
red: crimson, scarlet, vermilion, cherry, maroon, ruby, rosy, claret, burgundy, pink, orange
brown: bronze, chestnut, mahogany, auburn, copper, chocolate, beige, tan, khaki, fawn
yellow: lemon, amber, ochre, saffron, gold, cream
green: emerald, jade
blue: turquoise, aquamarine, azure, cobalt, indigo, navy, sky blue, lavender, violet, purple, mauve
grey: silver, pearl, ashen
black: charcoal, ebony, jet
white: chalky, milky, ivory

colourful *adjective*
1 *Colourful pictures give your baby something to focus on.* ▶ bright, brilliant, gaudy, showy, flashy, striking, rich, vivid
2 *The film was a colourful story of life on board a pirate ship.* ▶ exciting, lively, vivid, animated, graphic

combine *verb*
1 *To get the job done quickly they combined their efforts.* ▶ to pool, to unite, to merge, to add together, to put together, to join, to amalgamate
2 *Try to combine work with pleasure.* ▶ to mix, to mingle, to blend; (more formal) to integrate

come *verb*
1 *Some visitors came last night.* ▶ to arrive, to appear; (informal) to turn up, to show up

2 *She was much happier since she had come to London.* ▶ to arrive at, to arrive in, to reach, to get to, to move to
NOTE: You use **move to** about someone who has come to a place to live
3 *New Year comes a week after Christmas.* ▶ to occur, to fall, to happen, to take place

comfort *noun*
1 *Most people want good food and comfort.* ▶ ease, well-being, contentment, affluence, luxury, relaxation
2 *It's a comfort to know they will help us.* ▶ a consolation, a relief; (not an everyday word) a solace

comfort *verb*
He was upset, so we tried to comfort him. ▶ to calm, to console, to cheer up, to reassure, to soothe, to sympathize with

comfortable *adjective*
He pushed himself back in his comfortable armchair. ▶ cosy, snug, restful, relaxing, luxurious, soft

comic, comical *adjectives*
1 *The story she told sounded comic.* ▶ funny, amusing, humorous, witty
2 *Jake looked comical in his shorts and sandals.* ▶ funny, absurd, laughable, ludicrous, ridiculous, silly
NOTE: **Comic** and **comical** often mean much the same, but **comic** is more often used about things that are meant to be funny whereas **comical** is used about things that are funny although they are not meant to be

command *noun*
1 *Wait till I give the command.* ▶ an order, an instruction, the word
2 *By the end of their stay the students had a good command of English.*
▶ a knowledge, a mastery, an ability (in), a skill (in)

command *verb*
1 *He'd commanded the twins not to quarrel that day.* ▶ to order, to tell, to instruct, to require
2 *A colonel usually commands a regiment.* ▶ to be in charge of, to control, to lead, to direct, to head, to manage

commence *verb*
We will send your hotel details a week before you are due to commence your holiday. ▶ to begin, to start, to embark on

comment *noun*
No one had any comment to make.
▶ a remark, an observation, an opinion, a statement, a view, a criticism

comment *verb*
He commented that the heating had stopped working. ▶ to remark, to mention, to observe, to note, to point out, to state, to say

commit *verb*
The day after he was released from prison he committed another robbery.
▶ to carry out, to perform, to do; (more formal) to execute, to perpetrate

common *adjective*
1 *They had a common interest in cooking.* ▶ joint, mutual, shared
2 *Shorter holidays are now a common practice.* ▶ normal, usual, ordinary, familiar, commonplace, regular, customary, everyday, conventional, frequent, habitual, typical, widespread

commonplace *adjective*
Foreign travel is a commonplace event.
▶ normal, usual, ordinary, familiar, common, everyday

commotion *noun*
He didn't look back at the commotion behind him. ▶ the noise, the din, the

disorder, the disturbance, the confusion, the racket, the rumpus, the pandemonium, the upheaval, the turmoil, the bedlam, the hubbub, the row

compact *adjective*
The kitchen is well equipped and compact. ► small, neat

company *noun*
1 *They enjoyed the food and the good company.* ► friendship, society, companionship, fellowship
2 *Maggie had a cousin who worked for an insurance company.* ► a firm, a business, an organization, a concern

compare *verb*
1 *Compare your answer with someone else's.* ► to check (against), to contrast with
2 *Our track cannot compare with an Olympic stadium.* ► to equal, to match, to compete with; (informal) to come up to

compartment *noun*
The toolbox had rows of tiny compartments. ► a division, a section, a part

compassion *noun*
Stephen had a great deal of warmth and compassion for others. ► feeling, sympathy, tenderness, concern, pity

compel *verb*
Shortage of money compelled them to find work. ► to force, to oblige, to drive, to make
NOTE: If you use **make** you do not need the word *to* after *them*

compete *verb*
Henry is competing in three events. ► to take part, to enter (for), to participate

competent *adjective*
The hotel is run by a highly competent staff. ► capable, able, effective, efficient, proficient, accomplished, qualified, skilful, skilled, experienced, expert

competition *noun*
His brothers had entered for a darts competition. ► a tournament, a championship, a contest, an event, a match, a game

compile *verb*
She compiled a collection of children's poems. ► to edit, to assemble, to put together, to compose

complacent *adjective*
We are doing a good job but we must not be complacent. ► self-satisfied, smug, contented, pleased with yourself, self-righteous

complain *verb*
People like it here and don't complain much. ► to grumble, to protest, to find fault, to grouse, to moan, to object; (informal) to whinge

complaint *noun*
1 *The children had no complaints about the refreshments.* ► a criticism, a grievance, an objection, a protest
2 *I've got a serious stomach complaint.* ► a disorder, an ailment, an infection, a sickness

complete *adjective*
1 *By evening the jigsaw puzzle was complete.* ► finished, entire, intact, whole
2 *We heard the news in complete silence.* ► total, utter, absolute

complete *verb*
The builders say they will complete the work next week. ► to finish, to get done, to conclude, to end, to accomplish, to achieve

complex *adjective*
Each movement of the body uses a complex system of muscles.
▶ complicated, elaborate, intricate, involved, sophisticated

complicated *adjective*
They chose a complicated route in case anyone was following them. ▶ complex, intricate, elaborate, difficult, involved

compose *verb*
She began to compose a poem in her head. ▶ to make up, to think up, to write, to create, to devise, to produce

composed of *adjective*
There appeared a hideous monster composed of a leathery body and a horny head. ▶ made of, made up of, consisting of

comprehend *verb*
He was beginning to comprehend just how clever his friend had been. ▶ to understand, to appreciate, to perceive, to grasp, to realize, to see, to follow; (informal) to take in

compress *verb*
The man was compressing the snow into hard blocks. ▶ to squeeze, to crush, to press, to squash

comprise *verb*
The exhibition comprises forty paintings. ▶ to consist of, to contain, to include, to be made up of

compulsory *adjective*
Wearing cycle helmets should be compulsory. ▶ obligatory, required, necessary

conceal *verb*
It was hard to conceal his anger. ▶ to hide, to cover up, to disguise

conceited *adjective*
Without wishing to sound conceited, I think we offer the best service.

▶ arrogant, immodest, boastful, bumptious, proud, self-satisfied, self-important; (informal) cocky

conceive *verb*
Jake was always conceiving wild and fantastic ideas. ▶ to think up, to invent, to create, to imagine, to plan

concentrate *verb*
Jennifer tried to concentrate on her letter, despite the noise outside. ▶ to think about, to put your mind to, to attend to

concept *noun*
Paying tax on what you earn seems a simple concept. ▶ an idea, a notion, a principle, a thought

concern *verb*
1 *The decision did not concern him one way or the other.* ▶ to affect, to interest, to involve, to be important to, to matter to
2 *It concerned Mary that the family was so late back.* ▶ to worry, to bother, to trouble, to upset, to distress

concern *noun*
1 *I think that is my concern.*
▶ a business, an affair, a matter
2 *My uncle has a job with a banking concern.* ▶ a firm, a company, an organization
3 *We expressed our concern about the cost of long-distance phone calls.*
▶ a worry, an anxiety, a fear

concerning *preposition*
They wrote to us concerning our rubbish collection. ▶ about, regarding, relating to, involving, respecting

concise *adjective*
The story is written in a clear concise style. ▶ brief, terse, succinct

conclude *verb*
1 *John concluded his speech with another joke.* ▶ to end, to close, to

finish, to complete, to round off, to stop
2 *The inquiry concluded that the crash was caused by a bomb.* ▶ to decide, to infer, to deduce, to judge

conclusion *noun*
1 *At the conclusion of the meeting everyone went home.* ▶ an end, a close, a finish
2 *Have you reached any conclusion about the accident?* ▶ a decision, a judgement, a verdict, an opinion

condemn *verb*
We condemn violence completely. ▶ to denounce, to disapprove of, to criticize, to reject

condense *verb*
The story is condensed into a short space of time. ▶ to compress, to shorten, to squeeze, to abridge

condition *noun*
For sale: mountain bike in good working condition. ▶ order, state, shape

conduct *verb*
1 *An official conducted us to our seats.* ▶ to guide, to escort, to lead, to show
2 *The council conducted a survey of rubbish collection in the area.* ▶ to organize, to carry out, to direct

conduct *noun*
He had come out of prison early for good conduct. ▶ behaviour

confess *verb*
Gina confessed that she had eaten the cake. ▶ to admit, to acknowledge, to own up

confidence *noun*
1 *You have to have confidence to sing in front of an audience.* ▶ self-assurance, courage, nerve, self-confidence
2 *I was pleased that my parents had confidence in me.* ▶ faith, belief, trust

confident *adjective*
They were confident that things would work out. ▶ optimistic, positive, certain, sure, hopeful

confine *verb*
1 *The animals were confined in a small space.* ▶ to enclose, to coop up, to shut in, to cramp
2 *Fortunately the pain was confined to his right side.* ▶ to restrict, to limit

confirm *verb*
The news confirmed what they had always feared. ▶ to prove, to verify, to demonstrate, to establish, to show

conflict *noun*
1 *The area was a scene of constant conflict.* ▶ hostility, war, warfare, antagonism, confrontation
2 *Thousands were killed in the conflict.* ▶ a battle, a fight, fighting, an action, a clash, a combat, an encounter, a struggle

conflict *verb*
Your version of what happened conflicts with hers. ▶ to disagree, to clash, to differ (from), to contradict
NOTE: If you use **contradict**, you would say *Your version of what happened contradicts hers.*

conform *verb*
We have to conform to the rules. ▶ to obey, to follow, to comply (with), to abide (by), to keep (to)

confront *verb*
1 *There were too many problems to confront all at once.* ▶ to tackle, to face, to face up to
2 *He went back to confront Jane there and then.* ▶ to challenge, to stand up to, to defy

confuse *verb*
1 *They asked him difficult questions just to confuse him.* ▶ to baffle, to bewilder,

to muddle, to fox, to fluster, to perplex, to mystify, to puzzle, to frustrate, to confound
2 *Perhaps Kenny was confusing the two sisters.* ▶ to mix up, to muddle up, to jumble

confusion *noun*
The prisoners managed to escape in all the confusion. ▶ disorder, chaos, muddle, turmoil, uproar, rumpus, upheaval, disturbance, commotion, tumult, hubbub, bedlam, pandemonium, shambles

congested *adjective*
It was a hard drive through the congested streets. ▶ crowded, overcrowded, packed, blocked, jammed

congratulate *verb*
We thanked the boy and congratulated him on his English. ▶ to compliment, to applaud (for), to commend (for), to praise (for)

connect *verb*
The plumber arrived to connect the pipes. ▶ to join, to attach, to fasten, to fix, to link

connection *noun*
There may be a connection between the two crimes. ▶ a link, a relationship, an association

conquer *verb*
The English kings had been trying to conquer and rule France. ▶ to defeat, to overcome, to overpower, to beat, to crush, to subdue, to suppress, to capture, to seize, to occupy, to overthrow, to defeat; (not an everyday word) to vanquish

conscientious *adjective*
Your dad was a loyal and a conscientious worker. ▶ diligent, hard-working, careful, dutiful, scrupulous, meticulous, thorough

conscious *adjective*
1 *Ruth lifted her head and we knew she was conscious again.* ▶ awake, alert
2 *I was conscious of a knocking on the wall.* ▶ aware

consent *verb*
In the end Rose consented to our request. ▶ to agree to, to approve of, to allow, to permit, to authorize

consent *noun*
Debbie needed her parents' consent to go on the trip. ▶ permission, agreement, approval

consequence *noun*
Getting burnt was a consequence of staying in the sun for too long.
▶ a result, an effect, an outcome

consider *verb*
1 *After considering the matter they announced their decision.* ▶ to think about, to contemplate, to ponder, to meditate on, to reflect on, to study
2 *We consider that the criticism was fair.* ▶ to believe, to reckon, to judge

considerable *adjective*
There is a considerable difference between the two versions of the story.
▶ big, large, significant, substantial, important, noticeable, sizeable

considerate *adjective*
That morning he had seemed more gentle and considerate towards her.
▶ kind, thoughtful, generous, friendly, helpful, obliging, polite

consist of *verb*
The mixture consists of flour, water, and an egg. ▶ to comprise, to include, to

be composed of, to be made up of, to contain; (not an everyday word) to incorporate

consistent *adjective*
The two explanations are not consistent.
▶ compatible, in agreement

console *verb*
She was very upset and it was not easy to console her. ▶ to comfort, to soothe, to calm, to sympathize with, to support

conspicuous *adjective*
The bird has a conspicuous black patch on its head. ▶ noticeable, remarkable, striking, notable, prominent, pronounced, obvious, unmistakable, marked

constant *adjective*
1 *There was a constant hum of traffic in the background.* ▶ continuous, endless, ceaseless, incessant, permanent, persistent, non-stop, unending, uninterrupted
2 *The speaker was interrupted by constant chatter.* ▶ continual, incessant, persistent, repeated, relentless

construct *verb*
An iron bridge was constructed to span the river. ▶ to build, to erect, to assemble, to make, to put up, to set up

consult *verb*
1 *I consulted the doctor about my cough.*
▶ to ask, to discuss with, to talk to
2 *Judy consulted the atlas to see where Portugal was.* ▶ to look at, to refer to

consume
1 *We consumed an enormous amount of food.* ▶ to devour, to digest, to eat, to gobble up, to swallow
2 *If we buy a video, it'll consume all our savings.* ▶ to exhaust, to use up

contact *verb*
It was a pity he didn't contact us immediately. ▶ to communicate with, to get in touch with, to notify, to correspond with, to phone, to ring, to write to, to speak to, to talk to

contain *verb*
The box contained a complete Superman outfit. ▶ to hold, to have inside, to include

contemplate *verb*
1 *We sat contemplating the view.* ▶ to gaze at, to look at, to observe, to regard
2 *After a cup of strong coffee she contemplated the day ahead.* ▶ to consider, to reflect on, to think about, to ponder

contempt *noun*
She felt contempt for people who worried about money. ▶ disgust, loathing, disapproval, scorn

contend *verb*
He contended that he had been right.
▶ to maintain, to claim, to argue, to assert, to declare

content *adjective*
She had been content to stay in the house all day cleaning up. ▶ happy, willing, satisfied

contest *noun*
The winner in this month's singing contest is Barbara. ▶ a competition, a tournament, a match, a championship

contest *verb*
It was such a bad decision we had to contest it. ▶ to challenge, to oppose, to resist, to argue against

continual *adjective*
She needs continual encouragement.
▶ constant, repeated, incessant, ceaseless, eternal, perpetual, frequent
NOTE: See the note at **continuous**

continue *verb*
The noise outside continued all afternoon. ▶ to carry on, to go on, to keep on, to last, to persist, to endure, to linger, to remain

continuous *adjective*
They could hear the continuous hum of the traffic. ▶ constant, non-stop, incessant, ceaseless, eternal, perpetual
NOTE: **Continuous** means 'going on all the time' (without a break) and **continual** means 'happening many times with breaks in between'

contract *noun*
The building contract is for twenty new houses. ▶ an agreement, a deal

contract *verb*
Substances contract when they get colder. ▶ to shrink, to reduce, to diminish, to get smaller, to decrease

contradict *verb*
Graham didn't like to contradict her, but she was clearly wrong. ▶ to oppose, to speak against

contradictory *adjective*
The two statements seem to be contradictory. ▶ opposite, conflicting, incompatible, inconsistent

contrary *adjective*
1 *What actually happened was contrary to what had been expected.* ▶ opposite, counter, the reverse (of)
2 *John's mother always described his aunt as contrary.* ▶ obstinate, awkward, stubborn, difficult, uncooperative, wilful, perverse

contrast *noun*
There was quite a contrast between the grey skies of home and the sunny landscape of their new surroundings. ▶ a difference, an opposition, a distinction

contribute *verb*
Everyone had to contribute one item of food. ▶ to give, to donate, to provide, to supply, to subscribe

control *verb*
1 *A computer controls the whole production process.* ▶ to direct, to manage, to handle, to regulate, to govern, to guide, to monitor, to deal with, to cope with, to look after
2 *He found it hard to control his anger.* ▶ to restrain, to check, to curb, to hold back

control *noun*
We have no control over what happens next. ▶ power, authority, command, direction, jurisdiction

controversy *noun*
The controversy over the safety of mobile phones continues. ▶ a disagreement, a dispute, an argument, a debate, a quarrel, an issue

convenient *adjective*
Nick sank down on a convenient chair. ▶ useful, handy, accessible, available, suitable

conventional *adjective*
'Good morning' is a conventional greeting. ▶ customary, standard, normal, regular, proper, ordinary, traditional, common, commonplace, everyday

converge on *verb*
Thousands of people converged on Trafalgar Square for the demonstration. ▶ to come together (at), to meet (at), to approach, to merge (at)
NOTE: **Approach** takes an object:
Thousands of people approached Trafalgar Square.

convert *verb*
They have converted the old house into flats. ▶ to adapt, to change, to turn, to alter, to modify, to transform

convey *verb*
1 *The car was waiting to convey them back to Hampstead.* ▶ to take, to carry, to drive, to bear, to transport, to deliver, to transfer
2 *She squeezed Edward's hand to convey her feelings.* ▶ to show, to communicate, to indicate

convince *verb*
They put on a good act and almost convinced us. ▶ to persuade, to win over, to satisfy

cool *adjective*
1 *The weather turned cool.* ▶ cold, chilly
2 *We need to keep cool and not panic.* ▶ calm, sensible, level-headed, composed, unruffled, unflustered
3 *Jake tried to be friendly but Lisa's response was cool.* ▶ aloof, distant, unfriendly, indifferent, half-hearted, reserved, unenthusiastic, cold, lukewarm

cooperate with *verb*
The villagers were reluctant to cooperate with the police. ▶ to help, to assist, to aid, to collaborate with, to support, to work together with

cooperative *adjective*
If people are cooperative we can get a lot done today. ▶ helpful, accommodating, constructive, willing

cope *verb*
She was eighty now and no longer able to cope on her own. ▶ to manage, to survive; (informal) to get by

cope with *verb*
The explorers had to cope with storms, fast-flowing rivers, and poisonous snakes. ▶ to deal with, to handle, to contend with, to grapple with, to endure, to bear

copy *noun*
The pictures on the walls were only copies. ▶ a replica, a reproduction, an imitation, a forgery, a fake
NOTE: You use **forgery** and **fake** to mean something that is meant to deceive or fool people

copy *verb*
1 *See if you can copy this noise.* ▶ to mimic, to reproduce, to imitate, to repeat, to echo
2 *I told Francis not to copy my work.* ▶ to reproduce, to duplicate, to plagiarize, to steal, to crib

core *noun*
The earth's core is intensely hot. ▶ a centre, a nucleus, a middle, a heart, an inside

corner *noun*
We went round a sharp corner and arrived home. ▶ a bend, a turn, a turning

correct *adjective*
Please check that the address is correct. ▶ right, accurate, exact, precise, true

correct *verb*
Before Joe sent the letter he wanted to correct a few spelling mistakes. ▶ to put right, to rectify, to remedy, to amend

correspond *verb*
1 *I've been corresponding with a French penfriend.* ▶ to communicate, to write (to), to exchange letters
2 *Your story corresponds to what I heard.* ▶ to agree (with), to tally (with), to coincide (with), to match

corrupt *adjective*
We suspect that some of the officials may be corrupt. ▶ dishonest, crooked, bribable, criminal, immoral, untrustworthy, wicked

44

cost *noun*
They wondered what the cost of a holiday in Italy would be. ▶ price, amount, charge (for), expense

costly *adjective*
Frank bought his mother a costly perfume. ▶ expensive, valuable, high-priced, dear, precious, priceless; (informal) pricey

costume *noun*
The puppets wore red costumes and nightcaps with bells on the end. ▶ an outfit, a uniform, a suit, a set of clothes

cosy *adjective*
The dog preferred his cosy old basket in the corner of the kitchen.
▶ comfortable, snug, warm, restful, relaxing, secure, soft

count *verb*
Frances began counting the number of steps up to the cathedral. ▶ to add up, to calculate, to work out, to figure out, to total, to compute

count on *verb*
You can count on us to help. ▶ to depend on, to rely on, to bank on, to trust

countless *adjective*
He made countless pots of tea for all the visitors. ▶ endless, many, innumerable, many, numberless

country *noun*
1 *The visitors came from many countries.* ▶ a nation, a land, a state
2 *They went for a drive in the country.*
▶ countryside

couple *verb*
At Crewe a second engine was coupled to the back of the train. ▶ to join, to attach, to link, to fix, to fasten

courage *noun*
It takes courage to fight back when someone attacks you. ▶ daring, bravery, valour, audacity, nerve, spirit, heroism; (informal) pluck, guts, grit

courageous *adjective*
We had all been too frightened to be courageous. ▶ brave, bold, daring, fearless, heroic, valiant, plucky, determined, intrepid

course *noun*
The river follows a winding course.
▶ a path, a route, a direction, a way

courteous *adjective*
Their children are courteous and thoughtful. ▶ civil, polite, considerate, well-mannered, respectful

courtesy *noun*
His unfailing courtesy made Henry popular with the older aunts.
▶ politeness, civility, good manners

cover *verb*
1 *A thick mist covered the countryside.*
▶ to envelop, to shroud, to cloak, to lay over, to obscure, to conceal
2 *The French course covers most of what you'll need on holiday.* ▶ to include, to deal with, to incorporate

cover *noun*
1 *The ground has a thin cover of snow.*
▶ a covering, a coating, a layer, a blanket
2 *The soldiers found cover in an old house.* ▶ protection, refuge, shelter

cowardly *adjective*
She refused to be cowardly and stared back at him. ▶ timid, faint-hearted, weak, fearful, spineless, unheroic; (informal) lily-livered

cower *verb*
The animal cowered helplessly against a mound of rubbish. ▶ to cringe, to crouch, to shrink, to flinch, to grovel

coy *adjective*
He looked away, trying not to seem too coy. ► shy, timid, bashful, modest, self-conscious, sheepish

crack *noun*
The plate has a crack in it. ► a break, a chip, a chink, a split, a fracture

crack *verb*
The plate has cracked. ► to chip, to break, to fracture

crafty *adjective*
The boys thought up a crafty way of making some money. ► cunning, clever, artful, deceitful, devious, sly, foxy, wily

cram *verb*
1 *People crammed every street along the procession route.* ► to pack, to fill, to crowd, to throng, to jam
2 *Perhaps I can cram in a few more things.* ► to squeeze, to pack, to stuff, to press, to force, to jam

cramped *adjective*
Living conditions in those days were very cramped. ► crowded, overcrowded, confined, tight, uncomfortable, enclosed, restricted

crash *verb*
I nearly crashed into the back of the car in front. ► to collide (with), to hit, to bump, to smash, to knock

crash *noun*
There has been a crash on the motorway. ► a collision, an accident, a smash, a pile-up

crawl *verb*
She crawled across to the wall by the front door. ► to edge, to creep, to worm your way

craze *noun*
There's a new yo-yo craze. ► an enthusiasm, a fashion, a fad, a trend, a mania

crazy *adjective*
1 *I think you'd be crazy to own up now.* ► mad, insane, out of your mind, daft, silly; (informal) barmy, potty
2 *The inventor had come up with another crazy idea.* ► absurd, daft, ludicrous, idiotic, ridiculous, preposterous, strange, peculiar, odd, weird, silly, stupid, zany

crease *verb*
Melanie folded the sheets carefully so as not to crease them. ► to crumple, to wrinkle, to crush, to crinkle

create *verb*
Cycling is a form of transport that doesn't create any pollution. ► to make, to generate, to produce, to cause, to bring about, to result in, to lead to

creative *adjective*
If you have creative ideas, write in and tell us about them. ► imaginative, inventive, ingenious, artistic, original

credible *adjective*
They weren't able to give any credible explanation for their torn clothes. ► believable, convincing, plausible, likely, reasonable

credit *noun*
You have to give them credit for trying. ► praise, approval

creep *verb*
1 *After a while Carla crept back to bed and went to sleep.* ► to slink, to crawl, to slip, to sneak
2 *A snake was creeping across the floor.* ► to crawl, to slither, to wriggle, to edge

crest *noun*
A large car with a crest on the front was parked outside. ► an emblem, a badge, a sign, a seal, a symbol

crevice *noun*
Tiny plants were growing in crevices in the rock. ▶ a crack, a cranny, a cleft, a chink, a slit, an opening, a gap

crime *noun*
The judge told him he was guilty of a serious crime. ▶ a wrong, a wrongdoing, a misdeed, an offence, an evil

criminal *noun*
She was accused of being a criminal. ▶ a crook, an offender, a convict, a wrongdoer, an outlaw; (more formal) a malefactor

cringe *verb*
She cringed back in her chair and frowned. ▶ to cower, to shrink, to crouch

crippled *adjective*
The accident had left him crippled. ▶ disabled, handicapped, maimed, lame

crisp *adjective*
1 *Do you like your toast crisp or soft?* ▶ brittle, crunchy, crackly, hard
2 *He served a crisp salad to go with the fish.* ▶ fresh, firm

criticism *noun*
We may face criticism if we don't do better. ▶ disapproval, censure

criticize *verb*
They criticized Tim for not being adventurous enough. ▶ to reproach, to find fault with, to blame, to judge, to rebuke

crooked *adjective*
1 *The old woman had a crooked finger.* ▶ bent, twisted, deformed, misshapen
2 *There was a crooked path leading through the wood.* ▶ winding, twisting, curving, zigzag, meandering
3 *Mum said my poster was crooked.* ▶ slanting, askew, not straight, at an angle, lopsided, tilted, uneven
4 *He ran a crooked operation selling forged passports.* ▶ dishonest, illegal, fraudulent, criminal, corrupt

crop *verb*
1 *The goat had lowered its head and was cropping the grass.* ▶ to eat, to nibble, to graze on
2 *A problem has cropped up.* ▶ to arise, to occur, to come up, to appear, to happen, to emerge

crop *noun*
We had a good crop of fruit this year. ▶ a harvest, a yield

cross *adjective*
It made her cross to think of good food being wasted. ▶ angry, annoyed, irritated, bad-tempered, grumpy, indignant, vexed

cross *verb*
A bit further on the road crossed a river. ▶ to go across, to pass over, to go over, to span

cross out *verb*
Someone had crossed out Tim's name. ▶ to erase, to cancel, to delete, to blot out, to strike out, to put a line through; (not an everyday word) to obliterate

crouch *verb*
She could see Julie crouching under the table. ▶ to bend, to bend down, to stoop, to squat, to cower

crowd *noun*
A crowd of people had gathered outside the house. ▶ a mob, a group, a throng, a horde, a mass, a gathering

crowd *verb*
People crowded round the area where the band was playing. ▶ to gather, to flock, to assemble, to congregate, to throng

crowded *adjective*
They were fed up with the crowded car parks and the traffic jams. ► congested, packed, jammed, busy, full

crude *adjective*
1 *Huge amounts of crude oil had spilled into the sea.* ► natural, unrefined, unprocessed, raw
2 *It was a crude way of finding the answer, but it worked.* ► rough, simple, clumsy, primitive
3 *James always had a crude sense of humour.* ► coarse, rude, indecent, dirty, smutty, vulgar

cruel *adjective*
He had been a cruel man all his life, and had done cruel things. ► brutal, barbaric, callous, vicious, savage, bloodthirsty, murderous, merciless, ferocious, ruthless

crumb *noun*
Some birds were pecking at a few crumbs on the grass. ► a speck, a bit, a particle, a fragment, a scrap

crumble *verb*
They took care climbing over the wall as it was already beginning to crumble. ► to fall apart, to disintegrate, to collapse, to dissolve, to break up

crumple *verb*
He crumpled the chocolate wrapper slowly in his hand. ► to crush, to screw up, to wrinkle, to crease

crunch *verb*
The dog was crunching a bone under the table. ► to chew, to crush, to grind, to munch

crush *verb*
1 *Now crush the nuts into a fine powder.* ► to grind, to pound, to crunch, to crumble, to mash, to squash, to break, to squeeze
2 *The rebellion was crushed in a matter*

of days. ► to defeat, to overcome, to overthrow, to subdue, to put down, to quash, to quell, to suppress

cry *verb*
1 *He was tired and angry and about to cry.* ► to sob, to weep, to shed tears, to blubber
2 *I heard someone cry 'Help!'* ► to call, to shout, to yell, to shriek, to scream, to screech

cuddle *verb*
Some people love to cuddle babies. ► to hug, to fondle, to caress, to embrace, to hold

culprit *noun*
Looking at the mess, they decided that the culprit might have been a dog. ► an offender, a wrongdoer

cunning *adjective*
They had been cunning enough to leave before the trouble started. ► clever, astute, crafty, wily, sly, shrewd, foxy, knowing

curb *verb*
He tried hard to curb his anger. ► to control, to check, to restrain, to suppress, to repress, to hold back

curdle *verb*
The milk has curdled. ► to clot, to turn sour

cure *verb*
1 *Sean wears glasses to cure his squint.* ► to correct, to put right, to remedy
2 *She went to see if the doctor could cure her arthritis.* ► to heal, to make better, to relieve, to ease

curious *adjective*
1 *We became very curious about what they were doing in the next garden.* ► interested (in), inquisitive, nosy, puzzled

2 *The next day a curious thing happened.* ► strange, unusual, peculiar, odd, queer, abnormal

curl *verb*
I wanted to make the ends of the ribbon curl. ► to bend, to twist, to coil, to wind, to spiral, to loop

curse *noun*
He was like a madman, shrieking curses at the children. ► an oath, a swear word, an exclamation; (not an everyday word) a profanity

curt *adjective*
He waved them away with a curt flick of his hand. ► abrupt, rude, blunt

curve *verb*
The road curved round to the left. ► to bend, to curl, to twist, to wind

custom *noun*
There is a local custom of naming children after their grandparents. ► a practice, a habit, a tradition, a convention, an institution

customer *noun*
A customer came into the shop. ► a buyer, a shopper, a client

cut *noun*
Imran had a nasty cut on his leg. ► a wound, a gash, a graze
NOTE: A **gash** is a deep cut, and a **graze** is a light cut without much bleeding

cut *verb*
1 *Kirsty is going to cut some meat for the sandwiches.* ► to slice, to carve, to chop, to chop up
2 *John cut his finger on a piece of broken glass.* ► to gash, to wound, to nick
3 *The supermarkets are cutting prices on lots of things.* ► to reduce, to lower, to decrease; (informal) to slash

cut off *verb*
1 *Tom cut off a branch from the tree.* ► to remove, to sever
2 *They forgot to pay their phone bill and got cut off.* ► to disconnect

D d

dainty *adjective*
She wiped her eyes with a dainty lace handkerchief. ► delicate, fine, exquisite, pretty

damage *verb*
1 *The jolt she got in the crash damaged her spinal cord.* ► to injure, to hurt, to harm
2 *The house was badly damaged in the fire.* ► to harm, to spoil, to wreck, to ruin

damage *noun*
Damage to wildlife was much less than they feared. ► harm, injury, destruction, loss, suffering, devastation, havoc

damp *adjective*
He put his bare feet down on the cool damp sand. ► moist, wet, clammy
NOTE: You use **clammy** to mean that something is damp and rather sticky and unpleasant

dance *verb*
Soon they were dancing about and having fun. ► to leap, to skip, to prance, to caper, to jig, to hop, to twirl

danger *noun*
1 *He could see there was a danger of seeming rude.* ► a risk, a chance, a possibility
2 *Animals with good eyesight can detect danger from far off.* ► harm, a threat, trouble, peril

dangerous *adjective*
1 *There is a dangerous crossing near the supermarket.* ► unsafe, hazardous, precarious
2 *It is dangerous to cycle without lights.* ► unsafe, risky, chancy, hazardous, perilous
3 *The motorway was closed when a lorry spilled its load of dangerous chemicals.* ► harmful, deadly, poisonous, destructive

dangle *verb*
Della sat by the side of the pool with her legs dangling in the water. ► to hang, to swing, to sway, to be suspended

dare *verb*
Her friends seemed to be daring her to jump. ► to challenge, to defy, to urge, to urge on, to provoke

daring *adjective*
1 *The stunts became more daring.* ► bold, adventurous, audacious, reckless, foolhardy
2 *Some of the more daring boys tried to climb the wall.* ► bold, brave, adventurous, fearless, intrepid, audacious, reckless, foolhardy

dark *adjective*
It was dark outside when he went out to go home. ► black, pitch-black, dim, gloomy, starless

dash *verb*
Anne hastily dashed back to the kitchen. ► to rush, to run, to bolt, to fly, to speed

dawdle *verb*
Ruth dawdled in the wood, reluctant to return. ► to linger, to dally, to hang about, to loiter

dazed *adjective*
He hit his head on the fridge door and felt dazed. ► stunned, bewildered, confused

dazzle *verb*
The bright lights dazzled them. ► to blind, to daze, to bedazzle

dead *adjective*
1 *He often thought about his dead father.* ► deceased, late
2 *Will you forget me when I'm dead?* ► gone, departed, passed away
3 *The place is dead at weekends.* ► dull, lifeless, boring, uninteresting

deaden *verb*
Thick panels were used to deaden the noise between rooms. ► to muffle, to soften, to reduce, to stifle, to suppress, to quieten

deadly *adjective*
The kitchen was soon full of deadly fumes. ► poisonous, lethal, fatal

deafening *adjective*
There was a deafening roar from the engines. ► loud, overwhelming, overpowering, penetrating

deal *noun*
Next day they completed the deal and Tom handed over the money. ► an agreement, a bargain, a contract, a pact, a negotiation, an arrangement

deal with *verb*
1 *We have a few problems to deal with.* ► to attend to, to see to, to cope with, to handle, to tackle, to sort out, to manage, to overcome
2 *There are a lot of good books that deal with this subject.* ► to cover, to explain, to include, to be concerned with

dear *adjective*
1 *Annabel said good morning to her dear friend Maria.* ► beloved, adored, darling
2 *Food is quite dear in some countries.* ► expensive, costly, high-priced; (informal) pricey

debate *verb*
We had been debating whether to phone them or go and see them. ▶ to discuss, to argue, to dispute

debate *noun*
The debate on modern art is likely to continue. ▶ a discussion, an argument, a dispute, a controversy

debris *noun*
They spent the day lifting debris from the river bed. ▶ remains, wreckage, fragments, ruins

decay *verb*
The wet leaves started to decay. ▶ to rot, to decompose

deceitful *adjective*
George soon realized that I was being deceitful and couldn't be trusted.
▶ dishonest, false, untruthful, untrustworthy, unreliable, insincere

deceive *verb*
She deceived us about who she really was. ▶ to mislead, to fool, to cheat, to trick, to dupe, to take in; (informal) to con

decent *adjective*
1 *Jim's jokes aren't always decent.*
▶ polite, suitable, proper, respectable
2 *We'd like to buy a decent car.* ▶ good, adequate, satisfactory, nice, pleasant

deceptive *adjective*
It was bitterly cold and the bright sunshine was deceptive. ▶ misleading, unreliable

decide *verb*
1 *I couldn't decide which pudding to have.* ▶ to choose, to settle (on), to make up your mind, to resolve
2 *The jury decided they were not guilty.*
▶ to rule, to conclude, to come to a conclusion, to judge, to determine

decisive *adjective*
The decisive battle of the war was fought here. ▶ crucial, conclusive, significant

declare *verb*
He declared that he would not enter the race. ▶ to state, to proclaim, to announce, to assert, to maintain ,

decline *verb*
1 *We had to decline the offer of help.*
▶ to refuse, to reject, to turn down, to say no to
2 *His enthusiasm continued to decline.*
▶ to diminish, to decrease, to weaken, to flag, to fail, to lessen, to sink

decorate *verb*
We decorated the tree and stood it in the window. ▶ to adorn, to embellish, to beautify

decrease *verb*
If we criticize them, their confidence may well decrease. ▶ to diminish, to decline, to weaken, to flag, to fail, to lessen, to sink

decrepit *adjective*
Tom's uncle lived in a decrepit old house by the canal. ▶ dilapidated, ramshackle, ruined, run-down, rickety, derelict

dedicate *verb*
She dedicated her life to helping the poor. ▶ to devote, to give, to commit

deduce *verb*
We deduced that Thomas and Marilyn were Jennifer's children. ▶ to conclude, to work out, to gather, to infer, to reason

deduct *verb*
She deducted £5 from their money to pay for the broken window. ▶ to subtract, to take away; (informal) to knock off

deed *noun*
She sank back in her seat, pleased with a daring deed well done. ▶ an act, an exploit, an action, a feat, an achievement

deep *adjective*
1 *She woke up with a deep feeling of contentment.* ▶ strong, intense, profound, genuine
2 *The house was painted a deep green.* ▶ dark, strong, rich, vivid
3 *He spoke with a deep voice.* ▶ low, bass, low-pitched, booming

defeat *verb*
Napoleon was defeated at Waterloo. ▶ to beat, to overcome, to conquer, to crush, to overthrow, to overpower, to rout

defect *noun*
The glass had a small defect in one side. ▶ a fault, a weakness, a blemish, a flaw, an imperfection, a failing

defective *adjective*
The equipment they were using proved to be defective. ▶ faulty, imperfect, flawed, deficient

defence *noun*
1 *They had no defence for their actions.* ▶ an excuse, an explanation, a justification
2 *The town has surviving medieval defences.* ▶ fortifications, ramparts

defend *verb*
1 *A small force was left to defend what was left of the town.* ▶ to protect, to guard, to fortify, to safeguard
2 *When her son was accused, she did her best to defend him.* ▶ to support, to speak up for, to stand up for

defer *verb*
The court case has been deferred for two months. ▶ to adjourn, to postpone, to put off, to delay

defiant *adjective*
She marched out of the room with a defiant glare. ▶ disobedient, obstinate, rebellious, insolent

deficient *adjective*
The doctor told Katy her diet was deficient in vitamins. ▶ lacking, scarce, short (of), defective

definite *adjective*
1 *Are you holiday plans definite now?* ▶ settled, fixed, decided, certain, assured, sure
2 *The weather showed a definite improvement the next day.* ▶ distinct, clear, marked, noticeable, unmistakable, plain, obvious, pronounced

defy *verb*
1 *Nancy defied her doctor's advice and went swimming as usual.* ▶ to disobey, to ignore, to go against, to resist
2 *I defy you to walk out of here.* ▶ to dare, to challenge

dejected *adjective*
He went away dejected and spent the rest of the day feeling gloomy. ▶ sad, depressed, downcast, disheartened, dispirited, discouraged, despondent, unhappy; (informal) down, low

delay *verb*
1 *Bad weather and heavy traffic delayed us, I'm afraid.* ▶ to hold up, to detain, to hinder, to slow down
2 *They'll have to delay the start of their journey.* ▶ to postpone, to defer, to put off

deliberate *adjective*
1 *Did you spot my deliberate mistake?* ▶ intentional, calculated, conscious, planned, premeditated
2 *She has a deliberate way of talking.* ▶ careful, methodical, thoughtful, unhurried, painstaking

deliberately *adverb*
They deliberately avoided coming to the house. ▶ intentionally, purposely, consciously, on purpose

delicate *adjective*
1 *Although it is a delicate fabric it is also very strong.* ▶ fine, soft, exquisite, dainty, silky
2 *Laura was a delicate child.* ▶ weak, frail, unhealthy, feeble, sickly
3 *The spices have a delicate flavour.* ▶ gentle, subtle, mild

delicious *adjective*
I chose a delicious pasta dish at the restaurant. ▶ appetizing, tasty, enjoyable, luscious; (informal) yummy

delight *noun*
When she came into the room she heard squeals of laughter and delight.
▶ enjoyment, joy, pleasure, happiness, bliss, ecstasy

delight *verb*
Mary and Kevin managed to earn £10, which delighted them. ▶ to please, to thrill, to gladden, to cheer, to excite

deliver *verb*
The firm promises to deliver parcels the next day. ▶ to bring, to distribute, to convey, to supply, to take round

delude *verb*
We mustn't delude ourselves about the work we have to do. ▶ to fool, to deceive, to mislead, to trick, to hoodwink

demand *verb*
He demanded to see the person in charge. ▶ to insist (on), to ask, to request, to beg, to require
NOTE: If you use **insist** you say 'insist on seeing'. **Ask** and **request** are much milder words, and **beg** shows strong feeling

demolish *verb*
There used to be a cricket pavilion over there, but they demolished it. ▶ to knock down, to pull down, to bulldoze, to destroy, to dismantle

demonstrate *verb*
1 *Shall I demonstrate how I did it?* ▶ to show, to explain, to describe, to illustrate
2 *The incident demonstrated their incompetence.* ▶ to prove, to establish

demonstration *noun*
1 *There will be a cookery demonstration next week.* ▶ a presentation, a display, a show, an exhibition, an explanation
2 *A political demonstration was going on in the town square.* ▶ a rally, a protest, a march; (informal) a demo

denounce *verb*
He feared he would be denounced as a traitor. ▶ to condemn, to accuse, to blame, to expose

dense *adjective*
1 *The fog was becoming even more dense.* ▶ thick, heavy, impenetrable
2 *The building blocks are made of a dense material.* ▶ thick, solid, compact

deny *verb*
At first they denied all knowledge of the incident. ▶ to dispute, to reject, to disclaim

depart *verb*
Paul would have to depart early in the morning. ▶ to leave, to start, to set off, to set out; (informal) to get going

depend on *verb*
The old man next door depends on me to do his shopping. ▶ to rely on, to need, to count on; (informal) to bank on

dependable *adjective*
Molly is hard-working and dependable.
▶ trustworthy, reliable, loyal, faithful, honest

depict *verb*
The cave paintings depicted animals that looked like bulls. ▶ to show, to portray, to represent, to illustrate, to picture

deplorable *adjective*
In the last century miners worked in deplorable conditions. ▶ dreadful, disgraceful, shameful

deplore *verb*
We supported the demonstration but deplored the violence. ▶ to condemn, to regret, to disapprove of, to abhor

depress *verb*
The mess in the kitchen depressed me. ▶ to dishearten, to upset, to sadden, to discourage

depressed *adjective*
They drove home, exhausted and depressed, at the end of the day. ▶ dejected, fed up, despondent, downhearted, unhappy

derelict *adjective*
The land had several derelict cottages on it. ▶ dilapidated, ruined, ramshackle, run-down, neglected, abandoned, deserted, rickety, decrepit

derive *verb*
They derived a lot of pleasure from travelling. ▶ to get, to gain, to obtain, to acquire, to receive

descend *verb*
1 *Mark reached the staircase and descended into the living room.* ▶ to go down, to move down, to come down, to climb down
2 *The plane began to descend.* ▶ to go down, to drop, to fall, to plummet

describe *verb*
Emma tried to describe what she had seen. ▶ to recount, to explain, to relate, to depict, to tell, to express, to outline

description *noun*
You will need to write a detailed description of what happened. ▶ an account, a report, an explanation, an outline, a version

desert *verb*
The story was about a woman who deserted her husband and stole his fortune. ▶ to leave, to abandon, to forsake, to walk out on

deserve *verb*
We all deserve a day off after our hard work. ▶ to be entitled to, to merit, to earn

design *verb*
When Michael wrote a book, his wife designed the cover. ▶ to draw, to plan, to sketch, to devise

desire *verb*
All she desired was a few moments' peace. ▶ to want, to wish for, to long for, to crave, to yearn for

desire *noun*
1 *He stole because of his desire for money.* ▶ an ambition, an appetite, a craving, a hunger, an itch, a longing, a love, a lust, a passion, a thirst, an urge, a wish
2 *Next morning Kim had a strong desire to go on sleeping.* ▶ a wish, an urge, a longing, a craving
NOTE: You usually use **craving** when you are talking about something to eat: *She had a strong craving for some chocolate.*

desolate *adjective*
(not an everyday word) *He was desolate after his dog died.* ▶ lonely, unhappy, miserable, wretched, dejected, fed up, despondent

despair *noun*
The heroine gives a cry of despair and
hurls herself into the sea.
▶ hopelessness, depression,
desperation

desperate *adjective*
1 We were in desperate trouble.
▶ serious, grave, dire, urgent
2 Alice made a desperate grab at a
branch as she fell from the tree. ▶ wild,
frantic, determined

despise *verb*
She despised him for the nasty way he
spoke to people. ▶ to detest, to dislike,
to look down on, to be contemptuous
of, to scorn

destiny *noun*
He thought that marriage was an
important part of his destiny. ▶ fate,
fortune

destroy *verb*
The house was totally destroyed by fire.
▶ to demolish, to ruin, to wreck

detach *verb*
Detach the voucher and hand it in with
your order. ▶ to remove, to separate,
to cut off, to cut out

detain *verb*
1 They promised not to detain us for too
long. ▶ to delay, to keep, to hold up
2 After the fire the police detained two
teenagers. ▶ to arrest, to hold, to
confine

detect *verb*
He thought he detected a note of regret
in her voice. ▶ to discover, to notice, to
discern, to observe

deter *verb*
The warning did not deter them from
trying. ▶ to prevent, to discourage, to
put off, to hinder, to stop, to dissuade

deteriorate *verb*
In the afternoon the weather began to
deteriorate. ▶ to worsen, to get worse

determined *adjective*
You can succeed if you are determined
enough. ▶ firm, resolute, resolved,
single-minded, strong-willed,
persevering, purposeful, unwavering

detest *verb*
He detested working at night. ▶ to
hate, to dislike, to loathe

develop *verb*
1 The chick starts to develop inside the
egg. ▶ to grow, to mature
2 Try to develop some of the minor
characters in your story. ▶ to expand,
to elaborate, to fill out, to expand, to
work on
3 The money will go towards helping
the region to develop. ▶ to advance, to
prosper, to progress, to grow, to
flourish, to expand
4 Doctors have developed a new way of
treating the disease. ▶ to invent, to
think up, to work out, to devise, to
discover; (informal) to come up with

device *noun*
This handy little device will fit in any
pocket. ▶ a gadget, a tool, an
implement, a utensil, an instrument, a
contraption, a contrivance

devious *adjective*
1 The coach took a devious route to
avoid the traffic jams. ▶ roundabout,
indirect
2 It's good to know that not everyone is
as devious as he is. ▶ cunning,
scheming, deceitful, dishonest,
underhand, sly, wily; (informal)
sneaky

devise *verb*
It is a good idea to devise a way of checking your results. ▶ to invent, to think up, to design, to contrive, to prepare, to plan

devoted *adjective*
During his illness the old man was looked after by his devoted wife Harriet.
▶ loyal, loving, dedicated, faithful

devour *verb*
Her brother was devouring hunks of bread covered with peanut butter. ▶ to gobble, to gobble up, to eat up, to consume, to gulp, to gulp down

devout *adjective*
The merchants were devout Muslims and needed to pray during the day.
▶ sincere, devoted, committed, dedicated, religious, pious

diagram *noun*
Make a good diagram of how you want your garden to look. ▶ a plan, an outline, a sketch, a chart

die *verb*
1 *Edward's grandfather had died a few years before.* ▶ to pass away, to perish
NOTE: There are no ordinary alternatives for this meaning of **die**. **Pass away** is a kind of euphemism (a way of saying something unpleasant in a more pleasant way) and **perish** is normally used about dying in wars or accidents
2 *Water your sunflower or it will die.*
▶ to wilt, to wither, to shrivel

die out *verb*
The tiger is beginning to die out. ▶ to disappear, to decline, to decrease, to become extinct

differ *verb*
1 *We differed about what to do next.*
▶ to disagree, to argue, to quarrel
2 *The two photographs differed in several ways.* ▶ to be different, to contrast, to vary

different *adjective*
1 *All the dresses are available in different colours.* ▶ various, varied, several, assorted, miscellaneous
2 *The sails on the boat all have different names.* ▶ special, distinct, particular, specific, individual, separate
3 *When we fed the information into the computer again, the answer was different.* ▶ changed, conflicting, contradictory
4 *Can you think of something different to do?* ▶ new, unusual, original

difficult *adjective*
1 *We have some difficult decisions to make.* ▶ hard, complicated, complex, demanding, tricky
2 *The next stage of the climb was more difficult.* ▶ arduous, tough, demanding, strenuous
3 *Harry can be a difficult person.*
▶ awkward, tiresome, trying, troublesome, obstinate

difficulty *noun*
1 *When the weather changed the travellers faced severe difficulty.*
▶ hardship, trouble, problems, adversity
2 *We have a lot of difficulties to overcome.* ▶ a problem, a complication, an obstacle, a snag

dig *verb*
The first thing I do on the beach is to dig a hole to hide in. ▶ to excavate, to burrow, to hollow out, to scoop out, to tunnel

dignified *adjective*
The doctor had a dignified manner but no sense of humour. ▶ noble, grand, calm, solemn, serious, proper

dilemma *noun*
Their dilemma was whether to stay and be attacked or to run and be called cowards. ▶ a quandary, a difficulty, a predicament, a plight; (informal) a fix

diligent *adjective*
Clive is a diligent worker. ▶ careful, conscientious, earnest, hardworking, persevering, scrupulous, thorough

dim *adjective*
They caught sight of a dim shape in the distance. ▶ faint, hazy, indistinct, blurred, dark, obscure, shadowy, misty, murky, unclear

diminish *verb*
The army's supplies diminished rapidly over the next few days. ▶ to lessen, to reduce, to shrink, to dwindle, to decrease, to decline

din *noun*
Cleo called out, straining to be heard above the din. ▶ a noise, a racket, a row, a commotion, an uproar, a rumpus, a hubbub

dingy *adjective*
A cat was sitting on an old chair in the dingy back room. ▶ gloomy, dull, drab, dismal, dreary, dim, dirty
NOTE: It is interesting how many of these words begin with the letter 'D'

dip *verb*
Sarah dipped her head in the water once more and reached for her towel. ▶ to immerse, to lower, to plunge, to submerge

dip *noun*
1 *After the bend there was a dip in the road.* ▶ a hollow, a depression, a slope
2 *I'm going for a dip in the sea.*
▶ a swim, a plunge

dire *adjective*
The refugees are in dire need of food and shelter. ▶ serious, urgent, desperate, extreme, terrible

direct *adjective*
1 *From here it is a direct route back to the airport.* ▶ straight
2 *He tried to give her a direct answer.*
▶ plain, frank, honest, candid, blunt, straight, straightforward

direct *verb*
1 *We asked the guard if he could direct us to the exit.* ▶ to guide, to show the way
2 *The official directed them to go in.*
▶ to instruct, to tell, to order, to command
3 *The chief decided to direct operations himself.* ▶ to manage, to control, to supervise, to run, to be in charge of, to mastermind, to regulate

dirt *noun*
Jenny had fallen over in the dirt.
▶ dust, muck, filth, grime

dirty *adjective*
1 *Kim saw that Mike's clothes were dirty.* ▶ filthy, dusty, grubby, messy, grimy, soiled; (informal) mucky
2 *They spent the morning swopping dirty jokes.* ▶ rude, crude, vulgar, offensive, coarse, indecent, smutty

disadvantage *noun*
The only disadvantage was having to stay indoors on a lovely day.
▶ a drawback, a snag, an inconvenience

disagree *verb*
People disagree about which road to take. ▶ to differ, to argue, to quarrel

disagreeable *adjective*
He could be very disagreeable at times.
▶ unpleasant, unfriendly, rude, difficult, nasty, offensive

disagreement *noun*
The family had had a disagreement that morning. ▶ an argument, a quarrel, a squabble, a dispute; (not an everyday word) an altercation

disappear *verb*
1 *Elaine disappeared and was never seen again.* ▶ to vanish, to go away, to be lost to view
2 *By lunch-time the fog had disappeared.* ▶ to vanish, to dissolve, to fade away, to evaporate, to clear, to melt away

disappointed *adjective*
Did you feel disappointed when you weren't chosen? ▶ dejected, dissatisfied, downcast, down-hearted, let down, discouraged

disapprove of *verb*
I disapprove of people smoking on buses. ▶ to dislike, to deplore, to condemn, to frown on, to censure, to rebuke, to criticize

disaster *noun*
There was nearly a disaster on the motorway. ▶ a calamity, a catastrophe

discard *verb*
They had discarded a lot of old clothes in a corner of the room. ▶ to get rid of, to dispose of, to abandon, to throw away, to throw out, to dispense with, to jettison, to dump, to scrap

discontented *adjective*
How can we cheer up this discontented crowd? ▶ dissatisfied, unhappy, upset, disappointed, displeased

discourage *verb*
Jack hoped that his criticisms would not discourage them too much. ▶ to deter, to put off, to dishearten, to dismay, to demoralize

discover *verb*
The police discovered a lorry full of explosives. ▶ to find, to uncover, to come across, to locate, to stumble upon, to unearth, to reveal

discreet *adjective*
We need to be discreet about what we tell them. ▶ careful, prudent, cautious, wary, guarded, tactful, diplomatic

discriminate *verb*
1 *We had to discriminate between the different shapes and give them names.* ▶ to tell the difference, to distinguish, to differentiate, to tell apart
NOTE: If you use **tell apart**, you leave out between: *We had to tell the different shapes apart and give them names.* If you use **distinguish** or **differentiate**, you can use between or leave it out: *We had to distinguish between the different shapes and give them names* or *We had to distinguish the different shapes and give them names.*
2 *Some people were saying the law discriminated against foreigners.* ▶ to be biased, to be prejudiced

discuss *verb*
He discussed the matter with Hazel and decided to take the next day off. ▶ to talk over, to debate, to consider

discussion *noun*
They had a quick discussion among themselves. ▶ a talk, a conversation, a chat, a debate

disease *noun*
The hospital specializes in heart diseases. ▶ an illness, a sickness, a complaint, an ailment; (more formal) an affliction, a disorder, an infirmity, a malady; (informal) a bug

disgrace *noun*
It's no disgrace to be poor. ▶ shame, dishonour, stigma, humiliation

disgraceful *adjective*
The dogs were found to be living in disgraceful conditions. ▶ shameful, appalling, dreadful, shocking, terrible, intolerable

disgust *noun*
It was difficult to hide our feeling of disgust. ▶ revulsion, distaste, repugnance, aversion, contempt, loathing

disgust *verb*
The story of the abandoned children disgusted them. ▶ to sicken, to revolt, to appal, to horrify, to nauseate

disgusting *adjective*
The room was in a disgusting mess. ▶ revolting, shocking, dreadful, appalling

dishonest *adjective*
The newspaper claimed that the mayor had been dishonest. ▶ untruthful, cheating, lying, untrustworthy, dishonourable, deceitful, corrupt, unscrupulous

disintegrate *verb*
The old building was beginning to disintegrate. ▶ to fall apart, to break up, to decay, to crumble, to deteriorate, to rot

disinterested *adjective*
His opinion was not entirely disinterested. ▶ impartial, objective, unbiassed, neutral, detached, impartial
NOTE: **Disinterested** does not mean the same as **uninterested**, which means 'not interested' or 'bored'

dislike *verb*
The survey showed that most children dislike cabbage. ▶ to hate, to loathe, to detest, to despise

dislike *noun*
Her dislike for her cousins was getting stronger. ▶ hatred, disgust, aversion, contempt, loathing, revulsion

dismal *adjective*
They had spent a dismal winter and were looking forward to spring. ▶ gloomy, miserable, dreary, bleak, dull, dingy, cheerless

dismay *noun*
She looked at the ruined meal in dismay. ▶ consternation, horror, alarm, dread, anxiety, disappointment, trepidation

dismay *verb*
I was dismayed to hear that the plan had been scrapped. ▶ to appal, to alarm, to distress, to disappoint, to disgust, to shock, to horrify

dismiss *verb*
1 *Later that day, Terry was dismissed without any explanation.* ▶ to sack, to fire, to lay off
2 *She tried to dismiss the idea as unrealistic.* ▶ to reject, to ignore, to disregard, to discard, to set aside

disobedient *adjective*
The king accused his ministers of being disobedient. ▶ rebellious, insubordinate, defiant, mutinous

disorder *noun*
1 *Mona's bedroom was in disorder.* ▶ a mess, a muddle, a shambles, confusion
2 *Police were ready to deal with any disorder after the match.* ▶ a disturbance, a commotion, rioting, fighting, unrest, chaos

display *noun*
The day ended with a grand firework display. ▶ a show, an exhibition, a presentation

display *verb*
They displayed great skill during the performance. ▶ to show, to exhibit, to present, to reveal

displease *verb*
Jim tried hard not to displease anyone that day. ▶ to annoy, to upset, to irritate, to trouble, to vex, to offend

dispose of *verb*
We've got quite lot of junk to dispose of. ▶ to get rid of, to dump, to discard, to throw away

dispute *noun*
They asked their uncle to settle their dispute. ▶ a quarrel, a disagreement, an argument

disregard *verb*
Sarah tried to attract his attention, but he disregarded her. ▶ to ignore, to take no notice of, to pay no attention to, to overlook, to neglect

disrupt *verb*
The bad weather has disrupted all our plans. ▶ to disturb, to upset, to interrupt, to interfere with

dissatisfied *adjective*
He felt dissatisfied with what he had done. ▶ disappointed, discontented, unhappy, displeased, frustrated

dissolve *verb*
The acids dissolve in water. ▶ to melt, to disperse

dissuade *verb*
They tried to dissuade their friend from going. ▶ to discourage, to deter, to warn (against)

distant *adjective*
1 *She wanted to visit distant countries.*
▶ remote, faraway, far-off, far-flung
2 *His manner was noticeably distant.*
▶ unfriendly, cool, reserved, unenthusiastic, unwelcoming

distinct *adjective*
1 *There was a distinct tapping noise coming from the shed.* ▶ definite, clear, unmistakable, obvious
2 *The work falls into three distinct kinds.* ▶ separate, individual, different

distinctive *adjective*
The letter had been written in a distinctive green ink. ▶ special, particular, characteristic, distinct, unique

distinguish *verb*
We can distinguish three main stages in the process. ▶ to identify, to discern, to make out, to perceive, to recognize

distinguished *adjective*
On Sunday they had a distinguished visitor. ▶ famous, eminent, celebrated, important, well-known

distress *noun*
She lowered her head in distress.
▶ suffering, torment, anguish, misery, agony, sorrow, heartache

distress *verb*
It distressed us that we could do nothing to help. ▶ to trouble, to upset, to dismay, to worry, to grieve, to pain, to sadden, to disturb

distribute *verb*
Students were distributing leaflets about the drama festival. ▶ to hand out, to give out, to circulate

district *noun*
Most people in the district use buses to get to work. ▶ a region, an area, a locality, a neighbourhood; (more formal) a vicinity

distrust *verb*
After what had happened the day before, Shaun distrusted everyone. ▶ to mistrust, to suspect, to be suspicious of, to be wary of, to doubt

disturb *verb*
1 *She had instructed everyone not to disturb her that evening.* ▶ to bother, to interrupt, to pester, to trouble
2 *A fox had disturbed the chickens in the night.* ▶ to scare, to frighten, to terrify, to agitate

disturbing *noun*
The news of the crash was very disturbing. ▶ alarming, upsetting, troubling, distressing, frightening

dither *verb*
He had to stop dithering and make a choice. ▶ to hesitate, to waver, to fuss

dive *verb*
Cathy walked to the edge of the river and dived into the water. ▶ to jump, to leap, to plunge

diverse *adjective*
The nature reserve has badgers, foxes, and diverse kinds of bird life. ▶ various, varied, different, assorted, miscellaneous, mixed

divide *verb*
1 *The road divides at the phone box.* ▶ to fork, to branch, to split
2 *How shall we divide the money?* ▶ to share out, to split, to separate; (more formal) to allocate, to distribute, to allot

division *noun*
1 *The room had divisions for people to work in.* ▶ a compartment, a section, a part, a segment
2 *Harry was now working for a different division of the business.* ▶ a department, a branch, a part, a sector

dizzy *adjective*
The dizzy feeling in his head got much worse. ▶ giddy, confused, faint, unsteady, light-headed, wobbly

do *verb*
1 *He had a few jobs to do.* ▶ to carry out, to perform, to undertake, to attend to, to deal with
2 *I did the work in two hours.* ▶ to accomplish, to complete, to finish, to achieve
3 *There's one question I can't do.* ▶ to answer, to work out, to solve
4 *Georgia said she had done as he asked.* ▶ to act, to behave
5 *There's not much food but perhaps an omelette will do.* ▶ to be enough, to serve; (more formal) to suffice
NOTE: **Do** has many meanings depending on the words you use with it. The other words given here are only some of the ones you can use

docile *adjective*
The dog that had caused so much havoc was now looking remarkably docile. ▶ gentle, quiet, tame, meek, obedient

dodge *verb*
Sara ducked her head to dodge some low branches. ▶ to avoid, to fend off, to duck

dog *noun*
▶ a bitch (= a female dog), a hound (= a large strong dog), a mongrel (= a dog of mixed breeds), a puppy (= a young dog)
SOME BREEDS OF DOG ARE:
small pet dogs: chihuahua, corgi, dachshund, King Charles spaniel, Pekinese, poodle, pug, Scottish terrier, Sealyham, Welsh terrier, Yorkshire terrier;
dogs used in hunting and sport: basset hound, beagle, bloodhound, bull terrier, cocker spaniel, foxhound, fox terrier, greyhound, Jack Russell, pointer, retriever, springer spaniel, terrier, whippet;
working dogs: Alsatian, husky, sheepdog;
large strong dogs: Afghan hound,

Alsatian, borzoi, boxer, bulldog, bull
terrier, chow, collie, Dalmatian,
Dobermann pinscher, German
shepherd (= Alsatian), golden
retriever, Great Dane, Labrador,
mastiff, Rottweiler, setter, St Bernard,
wolf hound

dogged *adjective*
*Her dogged efforts had led to enough
money being raised.* ► determined,
persistent, resolute, unwavering

dominant *adjective*
*The business has bought some more
shops and is now in a dominant
position.* ► leading, commanding,
powerful, prominent, superior,
influential, supreme

dominate *verb*
*Her desire to make money had come to
dominate her life.* ► to control, to rule,
to govern, to influence

donate *verb*
Please donate some money to our fund.
► to give, to contribute

donation *noun*
*The library has received a donation of
books from a local business.* ► a gift, a
present, a contribution, an offering

doom *noun*
*All day I felt a sense of approaching
doom.* ► fate, ruin, catastrophe,
downfall, death

doubt *noun*
I still had some doubts about going.
► uncertainty, reservations, hesitation,
misgivings

doubt *verb*
*Frank was beginning to doubt her
honesty.* ► to question, to distrust, to
mistrust, to suspect

doubtful *adjective*
*The woman sounded doubtful, but let us
in anyway.* ► uncertain, undecided,
unsure, dubious, hesitant

downcast *adjective*
*Neil did his best to cheer her up but she
remained downcast all the way home.*
► sad, dejected, depressed, dispirited,
down-hearted, unhappy

drab *adjective*
*Ellie took them into a drab little room at
the back of the house.* ► dull, dreary,
dowdy, dingy, cheerless, dismal,
gloomy

draft *noun*
*Tom sat down to write a draft of his
speech.* ► an outline, a plan, a sketch,
a rough version

drag *verb*
*Then we had to drag the car out of the
ditch.* ► to pull, to haul, to draw, to
tow, to tug

drain *verb*
The long walk drained our energy. ► to
exhaust, to sap, to consume, to use up

dramatic *adjective*
*Ben told us about his dramatic escape
from the avalanche.* ► exciting,
sensational, thrilling, spectacular,
tense, startling

drastic *adjective*
*The family now faced a drastic reduction
in its income.* ► severe, extreme,
sharp, radical

draw *verb*
1 *Sam was drawing a house on the back
of an envelope.* ► to sketch, to depict,
to design
2 *She drew a handkerchief from her
pocket.* ► to pull, to take out
3 *The circus will draw large crowds.*
► to attract, to bring in, to lure,

to entice

4 *The two sides drew after extra time.*
► to tie, to be level, to be equal

drawback *noun*
It was a lovely house, but the small garden was a drawback.
► a disadvantage, a handicap, a hindrance, an inconvenience

dread *noun*
They all shared the same dread of being out of work. ► fear, horror, terror, anxiety (about)

dreadful *adjective*
1 *The hotel was comfortable but the food was dreadful.* ► bad, unpleasant, nasty, awful, terrible, appalling, ghastly
2 *Everyone agrees that war is dreadful.*
► terrible, awful, appalling, hateful, abominable, shocking

dreary *adjective*
Tuesday was another dreary grey day.
► gloomy, miserable, dismal, bleak, dull, cheerless

dress *noun*
1 *Emma had changed into a black dress.*
► a frock; (more formal) a gown
2 *Don't forget to wear casual dress.*
► clothes, clothing; (more formal) attire, costume

drift *verb*
The little boat was drifting in the breeze.
► to float, to be carried along

drill *verb*
After a while they realized they must be drilling through concrete. ► to bore, to penetrate, to pierce
NOTE: If you use **penetrate** or **pierce** you do not need to use the word *through*. You can drill a hole or bore a hole.

drink *verb*
Jerry sat down and drank his tea. ► to sip, to gulp, to guzzle, to slurp, to swig; (not an everyday word) to quaff

NOTE: To **sip** is to drink gently. To **gulp** is to drink hard and fast. To **slurp** and **guzzle** are to drink greedily. **Quaff** is a word you usually find in stories about the past. If you are talking about a cat or a dog you can also use **to lap**.

drip *verb*
Water was dripping from the ceiling.
► to trickle, to drop, to dribble, to splash, to ooze
NOTE: To **trickle** is to drip slowly and in small amounts. You use **ooze** when you are talking about thicker liquids such as oil

drive *verb*
1 *The gales were driving ships on to the rocks.* ► to force, to hurl, to push, to propel
2 *Hunger was driving the villagers to steal and loot.* ► to make, to compel, to force, to press
NOTE: If you use **make** you do not use the word *to*: *Hunger was making the villagers steal and loot.*
3 *John is learning to drive a car.* ► to operate, to control
4 *Please drive carefully.* ► to go, to travel

drive *noun*
1 *After lunch they all went for a drive.*
► an outing, an excursion, a trip, a jaunt; (informal) a spin
2 *The job needed a lot of drive, and Sally sometimes found it exhausting.*
► energy, determination, enthusiasm, initiative, enterprise, ambition

droop *verb*
The flowers began to droop in the heat.
► to wilt, to sag, to flop, to hang down

drop *verb*
1 *Leaves were dropping from the trees.*
► to fall, to tumble; (more formal) to descend
2 *Some trees drop their leaves in autumn.* ► to shed, to discard
3 *House prices have dropped this year.*

▶ to fall, to lower, to go down, to come down, to tumble, to plunge

4 *Three players were dropped after failing a fitness test.* ▶ to exclude, to remove, to leave out, to omit

5 *In the end they dropped the idea for lack of support.* ▶ to give up, to reject, to discard, to abandon, to scrap

drop *noun*
We expect a drop in the number of students next year. ▶ a fall, a decrease, a reduction

drown
1 *The floods drowned everything for miles around.* ▶ to engulf, to flood, to immerse, to inundate, to overwhelm, to sink, to submerge, to swamp

2 *The music drowned our voices.* ▶ to overpower, to overwhelm, to muffle, to drown out

drowsy *adjective*
She went on feeling drowsy long after she had woken up. ▶ sleepy, dozy

dry *adjective*
1 *The eastern part of the country is dry and hot in the summer.* ▶ arid, parched, dehydrated

2 *I thought the cake was rather dry.* ▶ stale, hard

3 *Liz went to a rather dry talk on German poetry.* ▶ dull, boring, tedious, uninteresting, dreary

dubious *adjective*
Sarah felt dubious about the whole idea. ▶ doubtful, uncertain, disbelieving, sceptical, unconvinced

duck *verb*
They ducked under the low branches. ▶ to crouch, to stoop, to bend, to bend down

due *adjective*
1 *The money is due at the end of the month.* ▶ payable, owed, outstanding, owing

2 *After due thought they decided to turn the offer down.* ▶ suitable, appropriate, proper, enough

3 *Find out when the next train is due.* ▶ expected, scheduled

dull *adjective*
1 *It was a dull day.* ▶ cloudy, overcast, grey, sunless

2 *The room was painted in dull colours.* ▶ drab, sombre, gloomy, dingy, dowdy, subdued

3 *What a dull programme.* ▶ boring, tedious, dry, uninteresting

4 *Then there was a dull thud upstairs.* ▶ muffled, indistinct

dumb *adjective*
1 *She was dumb for several minutes.* ▶ silent, mute, speechless

2 *We made some pretty dumb mistakes.* ▶ stupid, silly, foolish

dumbfounded *adjective*
He shook his head and looked completely dumbfounded. ▶ astonished, nonplussed, amazed, astounded, stunned

dump *noun*
1 *Take these things to the rubbish dump.* ▶ a tip, a heap

2 *The building used to be an ammunition dump.* ▶ a store, a depot, a cache, a hoard

dump *verb*
1 *Someone had dumped an old car by the side of the road.* ▶ to leave, to discard, to dispose of, to get rid of

2 *Sheila rushed in and dumped her bags on the floor.* ▶ to drop, to put, to throw down

duplicate *noun*
I've lost my licence but I can get a duplicate. ▶ a copy, a replica

durable *adjective*
The coat had deep pockets and a durable lining. ▶ strong, lasting, sturdy, hard-wearing, tough

dusk *noun*
They wanted to set out before dusk.
▶ sunset, nightfall, twilight, evening, dark

duty *noun*
She didn't much like the idea but felt she had a duty to support her friends.
▶ a responsibility, an obligation

dwell *verb*
An elderly couple dwelt in the cottage by the lake. (not an everyday word)
▶ to live in, to inhabit, to occupy, to reside in

dwelling *noun*
The mountainside was dotted with various small dwellings. ▶ a building, a home, a house, a residence; (more formal) an abode

dwindle *verb*
By the end of the day their energy had dwindled. ▶ to lessen, to decline, to ebb, to diminish, to decrease, to reduce, to subside

dynamic *adjective*
The business has just appointed a dynamic new director. ▶ energetic, forceful, active, vigorous

E e

eager *adjective*
1 *Jake was very eager to see what his father had brought home.* ▶ keen, enthusiastic, anxious, avid, impatient, intent (on)
2 *Sue was an eager football fan.*
▶ keen, avid, enthusiastic, fervent, zealous

early *adjective*
1 *I'm doing a project on early civilizations.* ▶ primitive, ancient, prehistoric
2 *Please send an early reply to our letter.* ▶ quick, prompt, speedy

early *adverb*
At this rate we may well arrive early.
▶ ahead of time, in advance, in good time, too soon; (more formal) prematurely

earn *verb*
1 *How much do your parents earn?*
▶ to receive, to get, to gain, to make, to take home
2 *They all thought Michael had earned a day off.* ▶ to deserve, to merit

earnest *adjective*
1 *Martin was sticking in stamps with an earnest expression on his face.*
▶ serious, solemn, grave, thoughtful, determined, intense
2 *The girls made an earnest promise that they would help.* ▶ solemn, sincere, heartfelt, fervent, wholehearted

earnings *plural noun*
Frank pays a quarter of his earnings into a savings fund. ▶ income, pay, wages, salary

earth *noun*
1 *You can see the earth clearly from satellite photographs.* ▶ the globe, the world
2 *Some dogs were sniffing about in the earth.* ▶ the soil, the ground

ease *noun*
For the next two weeks the family would be having a life of ease, or so they thought. ▶ leisure, comfort, contentment, relaxation, luxury, rest

ease *verb*
1 *The doctor gave him a prescription to ease the pain.* ▶ to relieve, to reduce, to lessen, to soothe, to calm
2 *The pain was beginning to ease.* ▶ to reduce, to lessen, to diminish; (more formal) to abate

easy *adjective*
1 *We had to give the answers to three easy questions.* ▶ simple, straightforward, elementary, undemanding
2 *Our dog has an easy life.* ▶ leisurely, comfortable, carefree, untroubled, peaceful, relaxed, relaxing, restful

eat *verb*
1 *A man was standing by the door eating an apple.* ▶ to feed on, to gobble, to munch, to chew, to gnaw, to nibble, to chomp on; (more formal) to consume, to devour
2 *Are you ready to eat?* ▶ to have a meal, to dine
3 *The sea air has eaten the woodwork away.* ▶ to rot, to corrode, to erode

eatable *adjective*
The potatoes were burnt and hardly eatable. ▶ edible
NOTE: You use **eatable** about food that is fit to be eaten, and **edible** about anything you can eat without it harming you. The two words do not mean quite the same.

ebb *verb*
Towards the end of the day her strength began to ebb. ▶ to fade, to decline, to lessen, to subside, to flag, to sink, to weaken, to diminish

eccentric
He was born into a rich family with lots of eccentric aunts. ▶ odd, strange, mad, weird, peculiar, unconventional; (informal) dotty, batty, nutty, cranky, zany

echo *verb*
1 *His words were still echoing in my head days later.* ▶ to resound, to reverberate
2 *What Frances said echoed the opinion of most people.* ▶ to repeat, to represent, to reflect, to imitate

economical *adjective*
1 *I'm trying to be economical while I'm saving.* ▶ careful, sparing, frugal, thrifty
2 *It may be more economical to use a cheaper form of fuel.* ▶ cheap, cost-effective, efficient, inexpensive, reasonable

ecstasy *noun*
My idea of ecstasy is sun, sea, and plenty of good food. ▶ bliss, rapture, joy, delight, happiness, pleasure

edge *noun*
1 *He walked to the edge of the grass and turned round.* ▶ a border, a boundary
2 *There was an old car by the edge of the road.* ▶ a side, a verge
3 *The edge of the cup had a smear of lipstick.* ▶ a rim, a brim, a lip

edge *verb*
She edged back to her seat. ▶ to creep, to slink, to sidle, to steal

edgy *adjective*
Jo seemed edgy and was beginning to fidget. ▶ nervous, irritable, jittery, on edge, jumpy, tense, touchy; (informal) uptight

edible *adjective*
Some mushrooms are edible but toadstools aren't. ▶ eatable
NOTE: See the note at **eatable**

educate *verb*
We need to educate young people to drink responsibly. ▶ to train, to teach, to instruct, to bring up, to coach

eerie *adjective*
The house was dark and inside there was an eerie silence. ▶ weird, creepy, frightening, ghostly, scary, spooky

effect *noun*
1 *Their efforts with buckets of water had little effect.* ▶ a consequence, an impact, an influence, a result, an outcome
2 *The lights had a colourful effect.* ▶ an impression

effective *adjective*
Local newspapers provide a cheap and effective form of advertising.
▶ successful, efficient, productive, useful, serviceable

efficient *adjective*
She was an efficient woman who enjoyed organizing things.
▶ proficient, capable, competent, well-organized, effective, productive

effort *noun*
1 *They had put a lot of effort into the concert.* ▶ work, energy, trouble, exertion, toil
2 *Dad made an effort to give up smoking.* ▶ an attempt, a try, an endeavour

eject *verb*
1 *Click on the screen to eject the disk.*
▶ to remove, to push out, to force out
2 *Police had to eject the troublemakers.*
▶ to expel, to throw out, to banish, to get rid of; (informal) to kick out

elaborate *adjective*
The game has an elaborate set of rules.
▶ complicated, complex, intricate, involved, detailed

elated *adjective*
The next day Charles was feeling elated by his success. ▶ delighted, joyful, overjoyed, ecstatic

elderly *adjective*
Two elderly men were talking by the pond. ▶ aged, old

elect *verb*
The committee elects a new chairman each year. ▶ to choose, to vote for, to select, to appoint

elegant *adjective*
A large elegant house stood at the end of the drive. ▶ handsome, graceful, beautiful, noble, dignified, refined, stately

element *noun*
1 *There are three main elements in the problem.* ▶ a factor, a component, a part (of), a feature (of)
2 A chemical element is a substance that cannot be broken down into simpler substances. Most elements are metals, but some are liquids or gases.
Metal elements include: calcium, copper, gold, iron, lead, silver, sodium, tin.
Gases include: chlorine, fluorine, helium, hydrogen, nitrogen, oxygen.
Liquid elements include: mercury.
Solid elements include: iodine, sulphur.

elementary *adjective*
The course covers elementary computer skills. ▶ basic, fundamental, simple, easy, uncomplicated

eligible *adjective*
He did so much work he became eligible for a bonus. ▶ qualified, authorized, suitable

eliminate *verb*
1 *The authorities are looking for ways to eliminate cheating.* ▶ to get rid of, to remove, to eradicate, to stamp out, to put an end to
2 *The local team was eliminated in the first round.* ▶ to knock out

elude *verb*
So far a large number of offenders have managed to elude justice. ▶ to escape, to avoid, to evade, to dodge

embark on *verb*
Stella embarked on a new career in her thirties. ▶ to undertake, to begin, to start; (more formal) to commence

embarrassed *adjective*
Sharon felt embarrassed at not knowing the answer. ▶ awkward, uncomfortable, ashamed, humiliated, disconcerted, flustered

emblem *noun*
America's national emblem is the bald eagle. ▶ a symbol, a badge, a crest, a seal, a sign

embrace *verb*
The old man looked at his son and embraced him. ▶ to grasp, to hold, to clasp, to hug

emerge *verb*
The door opened and a funny-looking dog emerged. ▶ to appear, to come out, to evolve, to issue, to materialize, to show, to surface

emergency *noun*
She came to offer a helping hand in an emergency. ▶ a crisis, a danger, a predicament

eminent *adjective*
The exhibition had been the idea of an eminent scientist. ▶ famous, respected, distinguished, important, prominent, notable, renowned, celebrated, well-known

emit *verb*
A row of chimneys emitted foul dark fumes. ▶ to give out, to give off, to pour out, to discharge, to belch, to secrete

emotion *noun*
He stood for a while without showing any sign of emotion. ▶ feeling, passion

emotional *adjective*
The Prime Minister gave an amusing and emotional speech. ▶ moving, touching, passionate, stirring, intense

emphasize *verb*
We emphasized the importance of having a good library. ▶ to stress, to underline, to highlight, to insist on

employ *verb*
1 He had to employ a builder to put up the shed. ▶ to engage, to take on, to hire
2 The organization employs the latest technology. ▶ to use, to apply, to utilize

empty *adjective*
1 They walked into an empty room.
▶ bare, unfurnished
2 The house seemed to be empty.
▶ unoccupied, uninhabited, vacant, deserted

empty *verb*
Jack decided he would empty the bottle on to the floor. ▶ to pour out, to drain

enable *verb*
1 The extra money enabled them to have a holiday. ▶ to allow, to help, to make it possible for
2 A visa will enable you to visit the country for a longer period. ▶ to authorize, to entitle, to permit, to allow

enchant *verb*
The young woman enchanted us with her singing. ▶ to delight, to charm, to entrance, to attract, to bewitch, to captivate, to fascinate, to spellbind

enclose *verb*
1 The larger animals were enclosed in a separate compound. ▶ to confine, to

fence in, to restrict, to shut in
2 *Jane enclosed a few stamps with her letter.* ▶ to include, to put in

enclosure *noun*
1 *The cemetery lay within a high walled enclosure.* ▶ a compound, an area
2 *The lion and tiger enclosures are further on.* ▶ a cage, a compound, an area

encounter *verb*
We suddenly encountered a tailback of traffic on the motorway. ▶ to meet, to come across, to come upon, to run into, to experience

encourage *verb*
1 *The losing side needed someone to encourage them.* ▶ to support, to cheer on, to rally, to hearten, to spur on, to reassure; (informal) to egg on
2 *Having plenty of attractions encourages tourists to spend more money.* ▶ to prompt, to urge, to invite, to influence, to spur on

end *noun*
1 *Did you stay to watch the end of the film?* ▶ the ending, the close, the conclusion, the finish
2 *The outbreak of war marked an end of many people's hopes.* ▶ a collapse, a ruin, a downfall, a death; (more formal) an extinction
3 *Join the end of the queue.* ▶ the back, the tail, the rear
4 *Soon they reached the end of the path.* ▶ a limit
5 *Mohammed bit the end of his pencil.* ▶ a tip, a point, a top

end *verb*
1 *My subscription ends at the end of the month.* ▶ to expire, to lapse, to stop, to finish, to cease, to close
2 *Frank and Jill ended their friendship after many years.* ▶ to finish, to break off; (more formal) to cease, to

discontinue, to conclude, to terminate
3 *The author ended his story with a mystery.* ▶ to conclude, to finish, to round off
4 *The outbreak of war ended all our hopes.* ▶ to destroy, to extinguish

endeavour *verb*
He endeavoured to rescue the trapped bird. ▶ to try, to try hard, to attempt, to make an effort, to strive

endless *adjective*
1 *Their grandchildren gave them endless delight.* ▶ constant, ceaseless, continual, everlasting, unending
2 *The endless noise is very annoying.* ▶ constant, ceaseless, continual, interminable, incessant, persistent
NOTE: You use **interminable**, **incessant**, and **persistent** when you are talking about something unpleasant or unwelcome

endure *verb*
1 *The prisoners had to endure months of torture.* ▶ to undergo, to bear, to stand, to withstand, to suffer, to put up with, to submit to, to cope with
2 *The feelings of fear endured for years.* ▶ to continue, to last, to remain, to persist, to survive, to carry on

enemy *noun*
They knew who their enemies were. ▶ an opponent, an adversary, an antagonist, a foe, a rival
NOTE: You normally find the word **foe** in stories and poems. A **rival** is someone who wants to do the same thing as you and wants to stop you doing it.

energetic *adjective*
By the next day she was well again, and her usual bouncing energetic self. ▶ active, lively, vigorous, dynamic, spirited, brisk

energy *noun*
The puppies have loads of energy and a good sense of fun. ▶ vigour, zest, drive, life, stamina, vitality; (informal) pep, go

enforce *verb*
The law is the law and must be enforced. ▶ to apply, to impose, to administer, to carry out

engage *verb*
The boss is going to engage a new secretary. ▶ to employ, to take on, to hire

engaged *adjective*
Jeremy was engaged in some weird exercise. ▶ involved, occupied, employed, engrossed, absorbed, busy (with)

engrossed *adjective*
An old woman was engrossed in some needlework. ▶ absorbed, preoccupied, busy (with)

enjoy *verb*
People enjoy beautiful walks along the river. ▶ to like, to love, to be fond of, to appreciate, to be pleased by, to delight in

enjoyable *adjective*
They wanted an enjoyable evening in town. ▶ pleasant, agreeable, entertaining, pleasurable, amusing, delightful

enlarge *verb*
1 *Enlarge the picture before you print it out.* ▶ to magnify, to make larger, to expand; (informal) to blow up
2 *Philip wants to enlarge his CD collection.* ▶ to increase, to extend, to expand, to build up, to add to, to develop, to widen, to broaden, to augment

enlist *verb*
Sam went off to enlist in the army. ▶ to enrol, to sign up, to join up, to register, to volunteer (for)

enormous *adjective*
1 *Jenny came home with an enormous pile of work to do.* ▶ huge, immense, massive, vast
2 *An enormous statue stood at the entrance.* ▶ colossal, gigantic, huge, massive, immense

enough *adjective*
Do we have enough time? ▶ sufficient, adequate

enquire *verb*
May I enquire what you are doing? ▶ to ask, to question

enraged *adjective*
As she tried to weave her way back, she became enraged by the traffic. ▶ angered, incensed, infuriated, exasperated

enrol *verb*
We are going to enrol for a first-aid course. ▶ to enlist, to register, to join up, to sign on

ensure *verb*
We need to ensure that the doors are locked. ▶ to make sure, to make certain, to confirm

enter *verb*
1 *You enter the house through a large door at the side.* ▶ to go into, to come into
2 *It's still not too late to enter the competition.* ▶ to go in for, to take part in; (more formal) to participate in

entertain *verb*
The band will entertain guests with dance music. ▶ to amuse, to delight, to please, to divert

enthusiasm *noun*
They were cautious at first, but in the end they had a lot of enthusiasm for the idea. ▶ eagerness, keenness, fervour, commitment (to)

enthusiast *noun*
The store was full of DIY enthusiasts looking for bargains. ▶ a devotee, an addict, a fan, a fanatic, a supporter; (informal) a buff

enthusiastic *adjective*
Jim's mother was an enthusiastic gardener. ▶ keen, fervent, avid, eager, passionate, energetic

entire *adjective*
She had spent her entire life trying to support her family. ▶ whole, complete

entitle *verb*
A special pass entitles you to admission to five museums. ▶ to authorize, to allow, to enable, to permit, to qualify

entrance *noun*
The entrance to the house is round the side. ▶ an access, an entry, a way in, a door

entrance *verb*
Maggie stood unable to move, entranced by the beauty of the scene. ▶ to delight, to charm, to enchant, to bewitch, to captivate, to fascinate, to spellbind, to attract

entreat *verb*
His wife entreated him to drive more carefully. ▶ to beg, to implore, to plead (with), to appeal to, to ask

entry *noun*
1 *The police needed to gain entry to the house.* ▶ access, admission, entrance
2 *The entry is round the side.* ▶ an entrance, a way in, a door, a gate, an opening, a turnstile

envelop *verb*
The mountain was enveloped in mist. ▶ to surround, to wrap, to cover, to hide, to enclose

envious *adjective*
The thing that made her a little envious of Kim was her weekly visit to the riding club. ▶ jealous, grudging, resentful

environment *noun*
1 *They enjoyed the country but preferred to live in a city environment.* ▶ surroundings, neighbourhood
2 *The school provides a good environment for learning.* ▶ an atmosphere, a setting, a background, a situation, conditions

envy *verb*
James envied his brother's reputation as an actor. ▶ to begrudge, to be jealous of, to resent

episode *noun*
1 *The story is told in seven episodes, each covering a day.* ▶ an instalment, a part
2 *She went back to sleep hoping she could forget the whole episode.* ▶ an affair, an incident, an occurrence, an experience, an event, a happening

equal *adjective*
The two boys are of equal height. ▶ the same, identical, matching, equivalent

equip *verb*
It took several years to build the boat, equip it, and send it to sea. ▶ to prepare, to supply, to fit out, to kit out

equipment *noun*
The equipment needs to be strong and reliable. ▶ gear, kit, apparatus, tackle, supplies, hardware, paraphernalia

erase *verb*
Some of the tapes had been erased by mistake. ▶ to wipe out, to rub out, to obliterate, to delete, to cancel

erect *verb*
They needed to erect a building capable of holding 60 cars. ▶ to build, to construct, to put up, to raise

erect *adjective*
Doreen was standing with her head erect, full of confidence. ▶ upright, straight, stiff, vertical

erode *verb*
Powerful waves have eroded the cliffs. ▶ to wear away, to eat away

errand *noun*
If you come back tomorrow I may have an errand for you. ▶ a job, a task, a mission, a chore

erratic *adjective*
Up to then her career had been erratic, and she hoped for a new start. ▶ unreliable, variable, changeable, irregular, inconsistent

error *noun*
They noticed that the letter had a lot of errors in it. ▶ a mistake, a slip, a fault, an inaccuracy, a blunder, a lapse; (informal) a howler

erupt *verb*
The next day they are all killed when lava suddenly erupts from the volcano. ▶ to pour out, to burst out, to gush, to belch, to issue, to overflow, to be discharged

escape *verb*
1 *Very few people managed to escape from the Tower.* ▶ to get away, to break out, to flee
2 *He ran into the road and narrowly escaped injury.* ▶ to avoid, to elude

escape *noun*
The escape wasn't discovered until next morning. ▶ a breakout, a getaway

escort *verb*
The waiter escorted us to the door. ▶ to accompany, to conduct, to see, to guide

especially *adverb*
The river gets very dirty, especially in the summer. ▶ chiefly, principally, particularly, above all

essential *adjective*
It was essential to find them before dark. ▶ necessary, vital, crucial, imperative, important

establish *verb*
1 *The business was first established in the 1890s.* ▶ to found, to create, to set up, to start, to initiate
2 *He established that he had not been there at the time.* ▶ to confirm, to show, to prove, to demonstrate, to verify

estate *noun*
1 *There is a housing estate at the edge of the town.* ▶ a development, an area
2 *The family estate was worth millions.* ▶ wealth, property, a fortune, an inheritance

estimate *verb*
The builders estimated that the work would take two months. ▶ to work out, to calculate, to reckon, to judge, to assess

eternal *adjective*
1 *They have been good to us and deserve our eternal gratitude.* ▶ everlasting, endless, unending, never-ending, enduring, infinite
2 *A day out would make a change from the eternal rounds of housework.* ▶ constant, continual, ceaseless, incessant, interminable, repeated, relentless, perpetual

evacuate *verb*
1 *The day before, people were evacuated from the factory after a bomb scare.*
▶ to move out, to clear, to remove
2 *They decided to evacuate the city during the invasion.* ▶ to abandon, to leave, to flee

evade *verb*
By trying to evade him that morning she had just increased his suspicions. ▶ to avoid, to dodge, to escape from, to elude

even *adjective*
1 *The ground was more even beyond the ridge.* ▶ level, flat, smooth
2 *He has a very even temper.* ▶ calm, cool, placid
3 *The scores were even.* ▶ equal, level, balanced, the same

event *noun*
I wrote an account of the day's events in my diary. ▶ a happening, an incident, an occurrence, an affair, an experience

everlasting *adjective*
The gift would be an everlasting reminder of their evening together.
▶ eternal, endless, unending, never-ending, enduring, infinite

everyday *adjective*
1 *Everyday life has changed a lot in the last fifty years.* ▶ ordinary, daily
2 *Everyone stared when he turned up at the funeral in his everyday clothes.*
▶ normal, usual, ordinary, regular

evict *verb*
The army had ruthlessly evicted the families from their homes. ▶ to expel, to eject, to remove, to turn out, to throw out

evident *adjective*
The problems faced by hospitals in London are becoming more evident by the day. ▶ apparent, obvious, noticeable, clear, plain, unmistakable

evil *adjective*
1 *There are myths about evil gods as well as kind ones.* ▶ wicked, bad, vile, base, devilish, malevolent, treacherous
2 *They read stories about the king's evil deeds.* ▶ wicked, foul, atrocious, bad, vile, wrong, sinful

exact *adjective*
They needed to work out the exact size of the room. ▶ precise, correct, accurate, right, true

examine *verb*
1 *The vet began to examine the calf.*
▶ to check, to inspect, to investigate, to probe
2 *We need to examine all the facts.*
▶ to analyse, to look into, to assess, to explore, to investigate, to weigh up, to appraise

example *noun*
The play we are reading is a good example of a tragedy. ▶ an illustration, an instance, a case

exasperate *verb*
The traffic queues were beginning to exasperate us. ▶ to annoy, to irritate, to anger, to bother, to aggravate

exceed *verb*
We managed to exceed out target. ▶ to beat, to do better than, to go beyond, to surpass, to pass

excellent *adjective*
The old car was in excellent condition.
▶ very good, outstanding, first-class, superb, fine, great, remarkable, marvellous, wonderful, admirable,

magnificent, exceptional, notable,
distinguished; (informal) fabulous,
fantastic, terrific, tremendous

except *preposition*
Everyone came except Kerry. ▶ besides,
apart from, excluding

exceptional *adjective*
He was a man of exceptional generosity.
▶ remarkable, outstanding,
extraordinary, rare, unusual,
uncommon

excessive *adjective*
*After a while the noise became excessive,
and work was impossible.* ▶ extreme,
too much, unreasonable, unbearable

exchange *verb*
*Terry exchanged his old gold clubs for a
new set.* ▶ to change, to swap, to
trade, to trade in

excite *verb*
*He said he liked climbing and it excited
him.* ▶ to thrill, to stir, to stimulate, to
arouse

excited *adjective*
*I was so excited about everything, I only
slept for a couple of hours.* ▶ thrilled,
elated, stimulated, aroused, eager,
enthusiastic, frantic; (informal) wild

exciting *adjective*
*They hoped she would come up with
something more exciting than a picnic
on the downs.* ▶ interesting, thrilling,
stimulating, gripping, rousing,
exhilarating, eventful, dramatic

exclude *verb*
*After the incident they were excluded
from the club for a month.* ▶ to bar, to
ban, to prohibit, to shut out, to keep
out

excuse *verb*
*Sarah found it hard to excuse her
brothers for what they had done.* ▶ to
forgive, to pardon

execute *verb*
1 *She executed a perfect somersault.*
▶ to perform, to accomplish, to carry
out, to complete, to do
2 *In some countries murderers are still
executed.* ▶ to put to death

exercise *noun*
*Fresh air, exercise, and a sensible diet
are all equally important.* ▶ physical
activity, running, training

exertion *noun*
*She fell into a chair, dizzy from the
exertion.* ▶ effort, strain, work, labour,
toil

exhaust *verb*
1 *They had exhausted all their money,
even the fare home.* ▶ to use up, to
spend, to get through
2 *Her day out had exhausted her.* ▶ to
wear out, to tire, to weary, to weaken,
to drain

exhausted *adjective*
She lay there, too exhausted to move.
▶ worn out, tired out, weary, drained,
fatigued

exhausting *adjective*
The long journey had been exhausting.
▶ tiring, gruelling, arduous, hard,
laborious, strenuous

exhibition *noun*
*We went to see an exhibition of Dutch
paintings.* ▶ a display, a presentation,
a show

exile *verb*
Napoleon was exiled to Elba. ▶ to
banish, to deport, to expel, to send
away

exist *verb*
They existed on biscuits and water. ▶ to survive, to live, to keep going, to endure

exit *noun*
The building only has one exit. ▶ a way out, a door

expand *verb*
The company wants to expand its business in Europe. ▶ to increase, to build up, to enlarge, to broaden, to extend, to spread

expect *verb*
1 *Are you expecting visitors?* ▶ to wait for, to await, to look for
2 *I expect it will rain.* ▶ to think, to imagine, to suppose, to believe

expedition *noun*
They are going on a shopping expedition. ▶ an excursion, a trip, a journey, an outing

expel *verb*
The authorities had expelled them from the country. ▶ to deport, to banish, to eject, to evict; (informal) to throw out

expensive *adjective*
Most good modern furniture is expensive. ▶ costly, dear; (informal) pricey

experience *noun*
Walking round the old house had been a strange experience. ▶ an event, an occurrence, a happening, an affair

experienced *adjective*
She is an experienced lawyer, and very good at her job. ▶ expert, qualified, accomplished, competent, proficient

expert *adjective*
Sally is an expert photographer. ▶ skilful, skilled, experienced, talented, qualified, proficient, knowledgeable

expire *verb*
The licence expires at the end of March. ▶ to run out, to lapse, to finish

explain *verb*
Mary tried to explain what had happened. ▶ to describe, to show, to make clear, to clarify

explode *verb*
Later, a bomb exploded at the embassy in London. ▶ to blow up, to burst, to detonate, to go off

exploit *noun*
She spoke of his exploits with great admiration. ▶ a deed, an act, a feat, an adventure

exploit *verb*
Many people thought he was exploiting her good nature. ▶ to take advantage of, to make use of

explore *verb*
The project will give us the chance to explore the subject from different angles. ▶ to analyse, to investigate, to examine, to inquire into, to probe, to look into, to research

explosion *noun*
There was a loud explosion followed by sounds of people running. ▶ a bang, a blast

expose *verb*
1 *She lowered the newspaper, exposing her startled face.* ▶ to reveal, to uncover, to show
2 *They threatened to expose the truth if he didn't pay up.* ▶ to divulge, to reveal, to disclose, to uncover, to betray

express *verb*
It is hard to express your true feelings. ▶ to describe, to communicate, to explain, to make known, to speak, to utter

expression noun
1 *His expression changed when Dora came into the room.* ► a face, a look, an appearance, a countenance
2 *I was trying to find the right expression to say how I felt.* ► a phrase, a term, a word, wording

exquisite adjective
She handed me the fruit in an exquisite glass dish. ► beautiful, delicate, dainty, elegant, lovely

extend verb
1 *The street lighting extends for three miles along the main road.* ► to continue, to reach, to go on
2 *We extended our holiday for another week.* ► to increase, to lengthen, to continue, to prolong, to stretch

extent noun
We need to find out the extent of the damage. ► the amount, the size, the scope, the degree, the level, the range

exterior noun
The exterior of the house needs repainting. ► the outside

external adjective
The external walls were covered in graffiti. ► outer, outside, exterior

extinguish verb
Some local men helped to extinguish the fire. ► to put out, to quench, to snuff out

extra adjective
Ann took an extra dose of her medicine that evening. ► additional, further, added

extract verb
She extracted her spare set of keys from the jar by the fireplace. ► to take out, to pull out, to remove, to draw out, to fish out

extract noun
The poem was long, so we just read an extract. ► an excerpt, a clip, a passage, a quotation

extraordinary adjective
We hardly believed his extraordinary story. ► unusual, strange, remarkable, astonishing, astounding, staggering, surprising, amazing, incredible, exceptional

extreme adjective
1 *She lives in the extreme north of the country.* ► far
2 *He is suffering from extreme cold.* ► intense, severe, acute, great, excessive

F f

fable noun
I like the fable about the fox and the crow. ► a legend, a story, a myth, a fantasy

fabric noun
The room had a big bed covered in pink fabric. ► cloth, material

fabulous adjective
1 (everyday meaning) *There was a fabulous view from the top window.* ► wonderful, great, terrific, amazing, lovely
2 *The picture showed winged dragons and other fabulous monsters.* ► legendary, mythical, imaginary, fictional
SOME FABULOUS CREATURES ARE:
animals: dragon, unicorn;
huge people: giant, monster, ogre;
little people: dwarf, elf, gnome, goblin, imp, troll;
ordinary-sized people: vampire, wizard;
women: fairy, mermaid, nymph, witch

face *noun*
1 *The children had happy faces.* ▶ an expression, a countenance, features; (not an everyday word) a visage
2 *A French team is planning to climb the north face of the Eiger next year. A cube has six faces.* ▶ a side, a surface

face *verb*
1 *The harbour faces south.* ▶ to look towards
2 *The expedition faced many dangers in the jungle.* ▶ to encounter, to meet, to confront

fact *noun*
1 *The hardest thing about history is remembering all the facts. We need to look at all the facts.* ▶ a circumstance, a detail, a piece of information
2 *It is a fact that most dogs are good swimmers.* ▶ a truth, a reality, a certainty

factory *noun*
The workers at the factory went on strike. ▶ a works, a workshop, a plant, a mill, a foundry

fade *verb*
1 *The curtains were beginning to fade in the sunlight.* ▶ to grow pale, to discolour, to bleach, to whiten
2 *The light was slowly fading.* ▶ to dim, to fail, to vanish, to weaken, to disappear, to dwindle, to decline, to diminish, to wane, to melt away

fail *verb*
1 *All our plans have failed.* ▶ to be unsuccessful, to go wrong, to fall through, to miscarry, to misfire
2 *The lights in the house suddenly failed. The old man's health was failing.* ▶ to grow weak, to fade, to weaken, to decline, to wane
3 *He failed to warn me of the danger.* ▶ to neglect, to omit

failing *noun*
He doesn't have many failings but one of them is his bad temper. ▶ a fault, a weakness, a defect, an imperfection, a shortcoming, a vice

failure *noun*
Fear of failure stops people doing interesting things. ▶ a lack of success; (stronger words) a disaster, a fiasco

faint *adjective*
1 *There was a faint outline of a tower in the distance.* ▶ indistinct, weak, faded, hazy, misty, pale, blurred, dim, shadowy, unclear
2 *When I called out I could hear faint answering hellos.* ▶ soft, gentle, quiet, low, muffled
3 *As Mary climbed up the stairs she began to feel faint.* ▶ giddy, dizzy, light-headed, wobbly, weak, unsteady

faint *verb*
My uncle felt giddy and said he was going to faint. ▶ to pass out, to black out, to lose consciousness, to collapse

fair *adjective*
1 *Sophie is fair but her sister is dark. The sisters both had fair hair.* ▶ blond (man or boy), blonde (woman or girl), light-skinned, fair-haired, pale
NOTE: Some of these words describe people and others describe hair and skin, so be careful which you use. You use **blond** about a man or boy, and you use **blonde** about a woman or girl.
2 (old-fashioned) *The story was about a fair princess.* ▶ beautiful, pretty, lovely
3 *The club wanted to be fair to its supporters. It was a fair decision to award a penalty.* ▶ just, proper, right, impartial, even-handed, unbiased, honest
4 *He got a fair number of cards on his birthday. His report said his work had only been fair.* ▶ reasonable, middling,

moderate, ordinary, indifferent,
mediocre, satisfactory, all right,
goodish
NOTE: **Fair** can mean something quite good
or something not very good, depending on
how you use it, so you need to choose other
words carefully.
5 *The day turned out fair after all.*
▶ fine, dry, bright, cloudless, clear,
sunny, pleasant

fair *noun*
1 *Last year I won a tiny little goldfish at
the fair.* ▶ a fun-fair, a carnival
2 *She makes jewellery and sells it at the
Christmas fair.* ▶ a market, a sale, a
bazaar, an exhibition, a fête

fairly *adverb*
I have brown hair, which is fairly curly.
▶ rather; (informal word) pretty; (not
everyday words) somewhat,
moderately
NOTE: The usual words are **fairly** and **rather**.
You normally only use **pretty** in
conversation, because it is more informal

faith *noun*
1 *A team manager must have faith in
the players.* ▶ confidence, trust, belief
2 *They belong to the Muslim faith.*
▶ a religion, a conviction, a creed

faithful *adjective*
*The group's most faithful fans had been
waiting for hours.* ▶ devoted, loyal,
reliable, dependable, true, constant,
trustworthy

fake *noun*
*The painting turned out to be a clever
fake.* ▶ a forgery, a counterfeit, a
sham, a hoax, a fraud
NOTE: A **fake**, like all the other words given
here, means something that is made to look
real so as to fool or deceive people. Words for
a thing that is made to look like something
else but is not meant to fool people are **copy**,
duplicate, **imitation**, **replica**, and
reproduction.

fake *adjective*
*Some fake furs look just as good as the
real ones.* ▶ imitation, artificial, false,
bogus; (slang) phoney

fake *verb*
*Some people had faked a letter to the
local newspaper.* ▶ to forge, to copy, to
counterfeit

fall *verb*
1 *The ball rolled off the roof and fell on
to the grass.* ▶ to drop, to plunge, to
tumble
2 *Prices of computers have fallen again
this year.* ▶ to come down, to become
less, to decrease, to decline, to
diminish, to lessen
3 *Be careful or you'll fall.* ▶ to trip, to
fall over, to fall down, to stumble, to
slip, to go head over heels

false *adjective*
1 *He gave the police a false name.*
▶ made-up, incorrect, unreal,
fabricated, wrong, inaccurate,
misleading, mistaken, deceptive
2 *He proved false when I really needed
him.* ▶ unfaithful, disloyal, deceitful,
dishonest, treacherous, lying
3 *The old man had to wear false teeth.*
▶ artificial, imitation, unreal, man-
made, synthetic; (slang) phoney
4 *The local newsagent had discovered a
false £5 in the till.* ▶ fake, bogus,
counterfeit

falsehood *noun*
She was telling a deliberate falsehood.
▶ a lie, an untruth

fame *noun*
*The Brontë sisters did not all live long
enough to enjoy their fame.* ▶ renown,
glory, distinction, reputation, esteem,
honour, prestige, importance

familiar *adjective*
1 *Their old car was a familiar sight.*
▶ well-known, common, everyday,

ordinary, normal, regular, usual
2 *She was very familiar with me
although we hadn't met before.*
▶ friendly, close, intimate
3 *Are you familiar with this story?*
▶ acquainted with, knowledgeable
about

family *noun*
Some of my family live in America.
▶ relatives, relations, kin, kinsmen, a
clan
NOTE: **Kin** and **kinsmen** are words you
normally find in stories and literature
MEMBERS OF A FAMILY ARE:
same generation: brother, sister, twin,
stepbrother, stepsister, cousin, fiancé
(= the man a woman is going to
marry), fiancée (= the woman a man
is going to marry), spouse (= a
husband or wife), husband, wife,
widow (= a woman whose husband
has died), widower (= a man whose
wife has died);
older generation: parent, father,
mother, step-parent, stepfather,
stepmother, guardian, godparent,
godfather, godmother, uncle, aunt,
grandfather, grandmother;
younger generation: child, son,
daughter, stepchild, stepson,
stepdaughter, ward (= a child looked
after by a guardian), godchild, godson,
goddaughter, grandchild, grandson,
granddaughter, nephew, niece

famous *adjective*
Her sister is a famous film star. ▶ well-
known, celebrated, prominent,
notable, noted, renowned,
distinguished, important, outstanding,
eminent, great, legendary

fan *noun*
His cousins were all football fans.
▶ a supporter, an enthusiast, a
follower, an addict, a fanatic

fanatic *noun*
*She is a bit of a fitness fanatic these
days.* ▶ an addict, an enthusiast, a fan

fanciful *adjective*
1 *Some of the stories may sound
fanciful, but they are all true.*
▶ fantastic, make-believe, imaginary,
romantic, pretended, unreal
2 *Maria is a fanciful girl with an
ambition to be a writer.* ▶ imaginative,
inventive

fancy *adjective*
They were all wearing fancy hats.
▶ decorated, elaborate, ornamental

fancy *verb*
1 *Fancy having another baby at his age!*
▶ to imagine, to think of
2 *James didn't fancy working in an
office.* ▶ to like, to like the idea of, to
want to, to hanker after, to long for, to
prefer, to wish for; (not an everyday
word) to desire

fantastic *adjective*
1 *He was tying the balloons into the
most fantastic shapes. The story they
told was quite fantastic.* ▶ strange,
amazing, extraordinary, fabulous,
remarkable, odd, weird, unbelievable,
unreal
2 (everyday meaning) *To win a
fantastic prize you just have to answer a
simple question.* ▶ wonderful,
fabulous, great, marvellous,
sensational

fantasy *noun*
*The idea of going to the North Pole was
just a fantasy.* ▶ make-believe, a
dream, a day-dream, an illusion

far *adjective*
They wanted to travel to far places.
▶ distant, remote, far-away

far-fetched *adjective*
It may sound far-fetched, but what I'm going to tell you really happened.
▶ incredible, improbable, unlikely, unbelievable, implausible, dubious, unconvincing

farm *noun*
SOME WORDS TO DO WITH A FARM:
buildings and parts of a farm:
farmhouse, farmyard, field, barn, shed, cow-shed, milking-shed, outhouse, granary, pigsty, haystack, rick, silo (for storing grain), stable, sty;
machines and tools: tractor, trailer, combine harvester, mower, plough, harrow, pitchfork, planter, scythe;
animals: livestock (= all the animals on a farm), cattle (plural), cow, bull, bullock, heifer (= a cow that has not yet borne a calf), horse, sheep (singular and plural), ewe (= female sheep), lamb, hen, chicken, chick (= young chicken), duck, goose, turkey;
crops: cereal, corn (= any type of cereal, including wheat and oats), wheat, maize, oats, rye, barley

fascinate *verb*
The attic with its great collection of junk really fascinated him. ▶ to enchant, to delight, to enthral, to entrance, to engross, to interest, to attract, to bewitch, to captivate, to entice, to spellbind, to charm

fascinating *adjective*
Helicopter trips around the city are fascinating and great fun.
▶ enthralling, enchanting, engrossing, interesting, delightful

fashion *noun*
1 *The fashion this year is for bright colours.* ▶ a trend, a vogue, a craze, a style, a taste
2 *I wonder why they were behaving in such an odd fashion.* ▶ a manner, a way, a style

fashionable *adjective*
It isn't fashionable any more to wear such huge earrings. ▶ stylish, tasteful, modern, smart, sophisticated, up-to-date; (informal) trendy, in

fast *adjective*
1 *He's a fast runner.* ▶ quick, rapid, swift, speedy, brisk, hasty, smart; (everyday word) nippy
NOTE: You can describe people or things (for example, a car or train) as **fast** when they move quickly. You would say that someone is **quick** at doing something when they get it done in a short time. You normally use **rapid** to describe something that happens in a short time: *There was a rapid change in the weather.* You can use **hasty** to describe someone who does something a bit too fast, or something that someone does in a hurry. **Swift** is a word you usually find in poems and stories.
2 *We'd better get a T-shirt with fast colours.* ▶ fixed, permanent, indelible

fast *adverb*
A small white boat was tied fast to the jetty. ▶ firmly, securely

fast *verb*
The monks had to fast for three days.
▶ to go without food, not to eat, to starve

fasten *verb*
1 *There was a sign on the gate asking people to fasten it.* ▶ to close, to secure, to clamp, to chain, to lock
2 *I'll fasten the rope to the hook on the wall.* ▶ to fix, to tie, to tie up, to attach, to bind, to tether

fat *adjective*
1 *The police officer was little and fat with a booming voice.* ▶ plump, stout, tubby, chubby, podgy, overweight, dumpy, flabby, gross, heavy, portly, stocky
NOTE: When you are talking about people, **plump**, **tubby**, and **chubby** are fairly kind

words, but **dumpy**, **flabby**, and **gross** are unkind or even rude. You normally use **portly** and **stocky** to describe older people. **Overweight** means too heavy as well as too big.
2 *Oliver Twist is quite a fat book.*
▶ thick, big; (not an everyday word) substantial

fatal *adjective*
1 *She had a heart attack but it wasn't fatal.* ▶ terminal, final, incurable
2 *He died after taking a fatal overdose.* ▶ lethal, deadly

fate *noun*
Fate saved England from defeat when rain stopped play. ▶ fortune, destiny, chance, luck, providence, lot

fatigue *noun*
He closed his eyes and was overcome with fatigue. ▶ tiredness, weariness, weakness, exhaustion

fault *noun*
1 *It was difficult to work out whose fault it had been.* ▶ responsibility
2 *Philip had few faults, but a bad temper was one of them.* ▶ a defect, a weakness, a failing, an imperfection, a shortcoming
3 *Their work contained a lot of faults.* ▶ a mistake, an error, an inaccuracy, a slip, a blemish

faulty *adjective*
If the goods are faulty, you are entitled to your money back. ▶ defective, imperfect, damaged, flawed, out of order

favour *noun*
Julie said she had a favour to do for someone. ▶ a service, a good deed, a kindness, a courtesy

favour *verb*
A lot of people now favour American wines. ▶ to like, to prefer, to approve of, to choose, to opt for, to go for; (informal) to fancy

favourite *adjective*
The old man was sitting in his favourite chair. ▶ best-loved, chosen, preferred

fear *noun*
She screamed and jumped back in fear. ▶ fright, alarm, apprehension, terror, horror, panic
NOTE: **Terror** and **horror** are much stronger words than **fear**

fear *verb*
You don't need to fear anyone here. ▶ to be afraid of, to be frightened of, to be scared of

fearful *adjective*
1 *The frog is fearful of the scorpion's sting.* ▶ afraid, frightened, scared, terrified, apprehensive (about), anxious (about)
NOTE: **Terrified** is a stronger word than the others
2 *There was a fearful din coming from the classroom.* ▶ awful, dreadful, terrible, frightful, horrid, unpleasant

fearless *adjective*
She was completely fearless about the dangers. ▶ unafraid, brave, bold, daring, courageous, intrepid

feasible *adjective*
The escape plan seemed feasible, and they decided to go ahead. ▶ possible, realistic, workable, practicable, viable

feast *noun*
After the wedding there was a grand feast in the castle. ▶ a banquet, a dinner

feat *noun*
Martha recited the whole poem off by heart, and after this feat people took more notice of her. ▶ an achievement, a deed, an act, a performance, an exploit

feature *noun*
The old wooden ceiling is one of the interesting features of the church. ▶ an aspect, a point, a detail, a characteristic

feeble *adjective*
1 *The old man looked pale and feeble.* ▶ poorly, sickly, weak, delicate, frail
2 *He gave a feeble chuckle.* ▶ weak, faint, slight

feed *verb*
She had a family to feed, and would need more money. ▶ to nourish, to support, to provide for

feel *verb*
1 *She reached out her hand and felt his forehead.* ▶ to touch, to stroke, to caress
2 *I feel the cold much more these days.* ▶ to notice, to sense, to suffer from, to experience

feeling *noun*
1 *He was upset, but tried not to think too much about his own feelings.* ▶ an emotion, a sentiment
2 *My feeling is that everyone is afraid to say anything.* ▶ a belief, an impression, an opinion, a thought

fence *noun*
Two women were talking on the other side of the fence. ▶ a barrier, a railing, a hedge, a wall

fence in *verb*
Some of the animals need to be fenced in. ▶ to confine, to enclose, to hedge in, to pen in

ferocious *adjective*
The dog growled and looked even more ferocious. ▶ fierce, wild, savage, vicious, violent, brutal, cruel, bloodthirsty

fertile *adjective*
The river valleys are surrounded by good fertile land. ▶ productive, fruitful, flourishing, lush

fervent *adjective*
He is a fervent supporter of animal rights. ▶ keen, enthusiastic, eager, avid, passionate, zealous

festival *noun*
Most major cities have some kind of festival every year. ▶ a carnival, a gala, a fête, a celebration

festive *adjective*
I love the festive atmosphere at New Year. ▶ joyful, joyous, merry, jolly, happy, cheerful, gay

fetch *verb*
1 *Jo threw a stick for the dog to fetch.* ▶ to retrieve, to bring back, to get
2 *Dad's gone to fetch his cousin from the station.* ▶ to collect, to get, to pick up, to bring

fetching *adjective*
a fetching dress ▶ appealing, attractive, charming, lovely, pretty

fête *noun*
The village fête is on Saturday. ▶ a carnival, a fair, a gala, a festival, a jamboree

fickle *adjective*
It was fickle of him to let you down like that. ▶ unreliable, disloyal, unfaithful

fiddle *verb*
A man sat in the corner fiddling with a radio. ▶ to play, to fidget, to twiddle; (informal) to mess about

NOTE: If you use **twiddle** you do not use
with: *A man sat in the corner twiddling a
radio.*

fidget *verb*
*He looked very nervous and was
beginning to fidget.* ▶ to be restless, to
wriggle, to squirm, to twitch

field *noun*
*There is a path back home across the
fields.* ▶ a meadow, an enclosure, a
paddock, a pasture

fierce *adjective*
1 *The new enemy was even more fierce.
Fierce fighting continued through the
day.* ▶ ferocious, wild, savage, vicious,
violent, brutal, cruel, bloodthirsty
2 *They felt the fierce heat from the
bonfire.* ▶ strong, intense, blazing,
burning

fiery *adjective*
1 *Her hair was the colour of a fiery
sunset.* ▶ burning, flaming, blazing,
red, red-hot
2 *Tom was a big strong lad with a fiery
temper.* ▶ violent, strong, hot, angry,
furious, raging, livid

fight *noun*
1 *The king's army was losing the fight.*
▶ a battle, an action; (more formal)
an engagement, a contest, an
encounter
2 *There was a fight going on in the
street outside.* ▶ a scrap, a scuffle, a
brawl, a disturbance, a fracas

fight *verb*
Some men were fighting in the street.
▶ to brawl, to quarrel, to wrangle, to
exchange blows

figure *noun*
1 *Someone had written a row of figures
across the page.* ▶ a number, a
numeral, a digit, an integer

2 *Rose has a slim figure and can wear
what she likes.* ▶ a form, a shape, a
build, an outline

figure *verb*
I'm trying to figure how much we owe.
▶ to calculate, to add up, to work out,
to reckon

fill *verb*
*By the time he had finished shopping he
had filled three trolleys.* ▶ to load, to
pack, to cram, to stuff, to use up

film *noun*
*The table was covered with a film of
grease.* ▶ a layer, a coating, a
covering, a sheet, a skin

filter *verb*
*A grill at the bottom of the machine
filters out bits of fluff.* ▶ to sieve, to
strain

filth *noun*
Filth littered the path. ▶ dirt, grime,
mess, sludge; (informal) muck

filthy *adjective*
*When they took the bandage off it was
blood-stained and filthy.* ▶ dirty,
messy, soiled, stained, foul; (informal)
mucky, grubby

final *adjective*
Tonight is the show's final night. ▶ last,
closing, concluding

finally *adverb*
*Finally, they put him on a train to
London.* ▶ eventually, in the end,
ultimately

find *verb*
1 *The children found crabs in the rocks.*
▶ to discover, to come across, to dig
up, to locate, to uncover, to unearth
2 *We'll have to call in an electrician to
find the cause of the fault.* ▶ to detect,
to discover, to trace, to locate, to
diagnose, to identify

3 *She found that the job was quite pleasant.* ▶ to discover, to realize, to learn, to become aware

fine *adjective*
1 *It turned out to be a fine day for sailing.* ▶ bright, sunny, clear, fair, cloudless, pleasant
2 *A fine thread hung from the ceiling.* ▶ slender, slim, thin, narrow
3 *The curtains were made of a fine material.* ▶ delicate, dainty, exquisite
4 *Sylvia gave a fine performance.* ▶ excellent, good, enjoyable, admirable, first-class

finish *verb*
1 *Sam had some work to finish.* ▶ to complete, to conclude, to get done, to accomplish, to round off
2 *We've finished all the coffee.* ▶ to use up, to consume, to exhaust; (informal) to polish off
3 *The concert finishes at nine o'clock.* ▶ to end, to conclude, to come to an end; (more formal) to cease

finish *noun*
The race had an exciting finish. ▶ a conclusion, an end, a close, a completion

fire *noun*
A fire had broken out across the street. ▶ a blaze; (more formal) a conflagration

fire *verb*
1 *Suddenly, someone fired a gun.* ▶ to let off, to shoot; (more formal) to discharge, to explode
2 *Jack's boss decided to fire him.* ▶ to dismiss; (informal) to sack

firm *adjective*
1 *She was glad to get off the boat and be on firm land.* ▶ hard, solid, stable, secure
2 *We have to reach a firm decision.*

▶ definite, agreed, settled, fixed
3 *Jackie was a firm friend.* ▶ loyal, faithful, constant, dependable, devoted
4 *Steve had a firm grip on my shoulder.* ▶ strong, tight, hard, unshakeable

firm *noun*
She had joined the firm as a trainee. ▶ a company, a business

first *adjective*
1 *Her brother was the first to speak.* ▶ earliest, soonest
2 *The first flying machines had wings that flapped.* ▶ earliest, original, initial, primitive
3 *The first thing you need is patience.* ▶ chief, principal, main, basic, fundamental

first *adverb*
First we must finish our work. ▶ to begin with, first of all, before anything else

first-class *adjective*
This was a first-class opportunity to try out her French. ▶ excellent, exceptional, first-rate, outstanding, superb, fine, great, remarkable, marvellous, wonderful

fit *adjective*
1 *The old house was no longer in a fit state to live in.* ▶ suitable, appropriate, fitting, proper, right
2 *She looked remarkably fit for 62.* ▶ healthy, strong, well, robust, sturdy, in good shape

fit *verb*
A carpenter arrived to fit the new door. ▶ to install, to fix, to assemble, to build

fit *noun*
Mary was in the kitchen trying to control her coughing fit. ▶ an attack, a bout, a convulsion, a spasm

fitting *adjective*
It was hardly a fitting occasion for making jokes. ▶ suitable, appropriate, proper, right, apt, timely

fix *verb*
1 *Jake was fixing shelves to the bathroom wall.* ▶ to fit, to fasten, to secure, to attach, to screw
2 *A date was fixed for the trial at the end of January.* ▶ to arrange, to agree, to settle, to decide, to establish, to determine
3 *We need to find someone to fix the broken window.* ▶ to mend, to repair, to put right

fix *noun*
(informal) *Harry was in a bit of a fix over some money he owed.*
▶ a difficulty, a jam, a predicament

fizz *verb*
The lemonade fizzed furiously and overflowed. ▶ to bubble, to fizzle, to foam, to froth; (more formal) to effervesce

fizzy *adjective*
They seemed to live on a diet of fizzy drinks and hamburgers. ▶ sparkling, bubbly, foaming; (more formal) effervescent, carbonated

flabby *adjective*
Vanessa looked at her flabby arms in the mirror. ▶ fat, sagging, limp, feeble

flag *noun*
The street was decorated with flags in time for the carnival. ▶ a banner (large and square with a message on it), a streamer (long and narrow), a pennant (tapering to a point), an ensign (especially on a ship)

flag *verb*
By the end of the walk the younger children were flagging. ▶ to weaken, to tire, to droop, to flop, to wilt, to weary

flap *verb*
Flags were flapping in the wind. ▶ to flutter, to wave

flash *verb*
Lights flashed in the distance. ▶ to blaze, to shine, to gleam, to glimmer, to sparkle, to burn, to flare

flat *adjective*
Jenny looked round for a flat surface to do her work on. ▶ even, level, smooth, horizontal

flatten *verb*
He flattened the crumpled page on the table. ▶ to press, to smooth

flavour *noun*
The local food has a spicy flavour.
▶ a taste, a tang

flaw *noun*
The one flaw in his character was his temper. ▶ a fault, a defect, a weakness, a blemish, a failing, an imperfection

flee *verb*
She had fled screaming from the house.
▶ to run away, to escape, to rush, to fly, to dash

flexible *adjective*
The shower had a flexible tube with a large spray at the end. ▶ bendable, supple, pliable, elastic, springy; (informal) bendy

flicker *verb*
Lights flickered in the distance. ▶ to blink, to glimmer, to twinkle, to sparkle, to glint

flimsy *adjective*
Roger put his cup on the flimsy table.
▶ rickety, fragile, shaky, wobbly, weak, frail

flinch *verb*
I put a hand out to the dog but it flinched again. ▶ to recoil, to draw back, to cringe, to quail, to wince, to shrink back

fling *verb*
Some boys were flinging stones into the water. ▶ to throw, to toss, to sling, to lob, to pitch, to hurl, to heave, to cast; (informal) to chuck
NOTE: You normally use **heave** when you are talking about heavy things that are difficult to throw

float *verb*
Toy boats were floating on the pond. ▶ to sail, to drift

flog *verb*
Sailors were once flogged for some offences. ▶ to beat, to whip, to thrash, to lash, to cane

flood *noun*
The river was rising and there was danger of a flood. ▶ a deluge, a torrent; (formal) an inundation

flood *verb*
Water was flooding the houses on lower ground. ▶ to engulf, to swamp, to inundate, to submerge, to immerse, to overflow

flop *verb*
1 *She poured herself more coffee and flopped into a chair.* ▶ to fall, to drop, to collapse, to slump
2 *The plant had long leaves that were flopping in the heat.* ▶ to dangle, to droop, to wilt, to sag

flounder *verb*
They were floundering chest-deep in quicksand. ▶ to struggle, to wallow

flourish *verb*
1 *Several rare plants flourish in the valleys.* ▶ to prosper, to blossom, to thrive, to bloom, to grow

2 *John flourished a large hat in his left hand.* ▶ to brandish, to wield, to wave, to shake, to twirl

flow *verb*
A river flowed through the town. ▶ to run, to stream, to glide, to swirl, to rush

fluffy *adjective*
She went back into the bedroom wrapped in a big fluffy towel. ▶ woolly, fleecy, downy, soft, feathery

flush *verb*
He put out his hand, feeling awkward and flushing slightly. ▶ to blush, to colour, to redden, to go red

flustered *adjective*
He felt so flustered he got his shoelaces in a complete tangle. ▶ confused, nervous, embarrassed

flutter *verb*
1 *The letter slipped from her hand and fluttered to the floor.* ▶ to quiver, to flicker, to flap, to float
2 *The bird fluttered its wings gently.* ▶ to wave, to flap, to beat

fly *verb*
1 *The day was glorious and birds were flying overhead.* ▶ to flutter, to glide, to soar, to rise, to swoop, to wing, to flit
NOTE: All these words mean special ways of flying. **Rise** and **soar** mean to fly high, and **swoop** means to fly rapidly downwards. **Wing** is a verb you use in poetry
2 *A flag was flying from the roof.* ▶ to wave, to flap, to flutter

foam *noun*
Inside the washing machine was a thick mass of foam. ▶ lather, bubbles, suds, froth

fog *noun*
There's often a thick fog out on the moors. ▶ a mist, a haze

foil *verb*
An observant police officer foiled the bombers. ▶ to stop, to frustrate, to defeat, to prevent, to thwart, to obstruct, to check

fold *verb*
She folded the newspaper and put it back in her case. ▶ to crease, to double over

fold *noun*
She took a few folds of the dress in her hands. ▶ a pleat

follow *verb*
1 *Dora followed him out of the house and up the road.* ▶ to go after, to run after, to shadow, to stalk, to track
2 *There's a police car following them.* ▶ to pursue, to chase
3 *The king needed an heir to follow him on the throne.* ▶ to succeed, to come after
4 *She followed the instructions carefully.* ▶ to observe, to obey, to comply with, to heed, to keep to
5 *I'm afraid I didn't follow what you said.* ▶ to understand, to comprehend, to grasp
6 *Which team do you follow?* ▶ to support, to be interested in

fond *adjective*
Looking through their photographs brought back fond memories. ▶ loving, tender, affectionate

fondle *verb*
She sat in a dream, idly fondling her long flowing hair. ▶ to stroke, to caress, to pat, to pet

food *noun*
1 *The traveller's cart needed repairing and he needed food and shelter.* ▶ nourishment, sustenance, provisions, refreshment
2 *There is not enough food for the sheep and cattle.* ▶ fodder, feed, forage

fool *noun*
He felt a fool for saying something so silly. ▶ an idiot, an ass, a half-wit, a moron, an imbecile; (informal) a twerp, a twit, a nitwit, a booby, a dope
NOTE: Many of these words are offensive if you use them about someone else

fool *verb*
Your plastic scorpion wouldn't fool anyone. ▶ to trick, to deceive, to mislead, to take in, to bluff, to hoodwink; (informal) to kid

foolish *adjective*
It would be foolish to give in now. ▶ stupid, silly, unwise, crazy

forbid *verb*
They have forbidden smoking in the shopping centre. ▶ to prohibit, to ban, to bar

force *noun*
It took a lot of force to get the door open. ▶ strength, power, energy, might, vigour

force *verb*
The bad weather forced them to return home. ▶ to compel, to make, to drive, to oblige
NOTE: If you use **make** you do not need the word *to* after *them*

forecast *verb*
The company is forecasting higher profits next year. ▶ to predict, to prophesy, to foresee, to foretell

forecast *noun*
The forecast proved to be wrong. ▶ a prediction, a prophecy, an outlook

foreign *adjective*
Angus felt as if he had strayed into a foreign country. ▶ distant, overseas, strange, unfamiliar, alien

foresee *verb*
Nobody could foresee what might happen next. ► to predict, to forecast, to foretell, to prophesy

forge *verb*
They later discovered that the cheque had been forged. ► to fake, to falsify, to counterfeit

forgery *noun*
The paintings turned out to be forgeries. ► a fake, an imitation; (informal) a phoney
NOTE: A **forgery**, like all the other words given here, means something that is made to look real so as to fool or deceive people. Words for a thing that is made to look like something else but is not meant to fool people are **copy**, **duplicate**, **imitation**, **replica**, and **reproduction**.

forget *verb*
1 *Last year their aunt forgot every one of their birthdays.* ► to neglect, to overlook, to disregard, to ignore
2 *When he got to the airport he realized he'd forgotten his passport.* ► to leave behind, to overlook

forgetful *adjective*
As he grew older he became more careless and forgetful. ► absent-minded, vague

forgive *verb*
He found it hard to forgive them for walking out on him. ► to excuse, to pardon, to let off

forlorn *adjective*
Some refugees sat wrapped in blankets, looking forlorn. ► unhappy, sad, miserable, dejected, pitiful, wretched, abandoned, neglected

form *noun*
1 *They could see a dim human form coming towards them.* ► a shape, an outline, a figure
2 *There are many forms of life to study.* ► a type, a kind, a sort, a variety

form *verb*
1 *The clay is smoothed by hand to form the side of the pot.* ► to make, to create, to fashion, to shape, to mould
2 *The buildings on the other side of the road form part of the factory.* ► to make up, to constitute, to compose
3 *Icicles formed on the window sill.* ► to develop, to grow, to appear, to take shape

formal *adjective*
1 *Although she'd started as a trainee she'd received no formal training.* ► regular, official, proper, standard
2 *The conference ended with a formal dinner.* ► ceremonial, official, smart; (informal) posh

forsake *verb*
She did not want to forsake her friends. ► to desert, to abandon, to leave

fortunate *adjective*
He reminded himself that he was fortunate to have any kind of job. ► lucky

fortune *noun*
1 *By a piece of good fortune she met an old friend in the town.* ► luck, chance, fate
2 *He had to spend his fortune on repairing the house.* ► wealth, money

forward *adjective*
She wondered if she had been a bit forward in answering back. ► bold, brazen, impudent, cheeky

foul *adjective*
1 *There was a foul mess on the floor.* ► dirty, filthy, disgusting
2 *The fruit smells foul but tastes good.* ► nasty, disgusting, vile, rotten, revolting, unpleasant

3 *The weather had been foul for several days.* ▶ nasty, rainy, stormy
4 *A foul crime had been committed in that street years before.* ▶ wicked, evil, atrocious, vile

found *verb*
The college had been founded in the eighteenth century. ▶ to create, to establish, to set up

fragile *adjective*
He sipped his tea from a cup of pale fragile china. ▶ delicate, brittle, frail, thin, breakable

fragment *noun*
Fragments of glass were spread across the road. ▶ a bit, a piece, a remnant, a particle, a scrap, a sliver, a shard

frail *adjective*
The woman was old and frail, and lived alone. ▶ weak, infirm, feeble, delicate

frame *noun*
The shed is built round a strong steel frame. ▶ a framework, a shell, a skeleton, a structure, a body

frank *adjective*
He made a frank appeal for help. ▶ direct, open, plain, candid, honest, sincere, straightforward

frantic *adjective*
She started to make frantic gestures to attract our attention. ▶ hectic, excited, wild, desperate, frenzied, furious

fraud *noun*
Later they admitted that the offer had been a fraud. ▶ a sham, a trick, a cheat, a fake, a hoax, a pretence

fraudulent *adjective*
They are accused of fraudulent business dealings. ▶ dishonest, crooked, cheating, underhand, deceitful

free *adjective*
1 *You get a free book with every £20 you spend.* ▶ complimentary
2 *They were now free to leave.*
▶ allowed, permitted, enabled, able, at liberty
3 *After eight years in captivity they were free again.* ▶ at liberty, liberated, released
4 *There isn't a phone box free.*
▶ available, unoccupied

free *verb*
1 *The judge freed him.* ▶ to acquit, to discharge, to let off, to let go, to pardon, to spare
2 *They would have to pay a ransom to free the prisoners in the castle.* ▶ to liberate, to release, to save, to rescue, to set free

freedom *noun*
They demand the freedom to live where they like. ▶ independence, liberty

freeze *verb*
The pond froze last night. ▶ to ice, to ice up, to ice over

frequent *adjective*
1 *The telephone calls became more frequent in the evenings.* ▶ numerous, persistent, recurrent, constant, continual
2 *Jack was a frequent visitor all the following week.* ▶ regular, habitual, constant, familiar

fresh *adjective*
1 *After a while we thought up some fresh suggestions.* ▶ new, original, different
2 *I'll put fresh sheets on the bed.*
▶ clean, washed, unused
3 *Mae felt fresher after her rest.*
▶ refreshed, invigorated, revived
4 *The air in the hills is fresh.* ▶ clean, clear, pure

fret *verb*
Lauren was fretting about how much the new tyres would cost. ▶ to worry, to fuss, to brood, to agonize, to be upset

friend *noun*
Julie and Alice were good friends.
▶ a companion, an acquaintance; (informal) a pal, a chum, a mate
NOTE: An **acquaintance** is someone you know slightly.

friendly *adjective*
1 *He enjoyed being with such a friendly and amusing girl.* ▶ kind, affectionate, agreeable, good-natured, tender, amiable, genial, likeable, loving, helpful, sociable
2 *The local shops offer good service and a friendly welcome.* ▶ warm, cordial, hospitable

friendship *noun*
Their friendship goes back many years.
▶ affection, attachment, fondness, intimacy

fright *noun*
1 *I jumped up in fright and almost tripped over the cat.* ▶ alarm, fear, dread, terror, panic, horror
2 *They got their second fright of the day when the car refused to start.* ▶ a scare, a shock, a surprise

frighten *verb*
The angry man had frightened the children. ▶ to scare, to alarm, to startle, to terrify

frightened *adjective*
Donald felt nervous and a little frightened. ▶ scared, afraid, alarmed, fearful, apprehensive, terrified
NOTE: You do not use **afraid** before a noun. You say *a frightened rabbit* or *a scared rabbit*, but not *an afraid rabbit*.

frightening *adjective*
The house was a frightening place even with all the lights on. ▶ alarming, terrifying; (informal) scary, spooky, creepy

frightful *adjective*
There has been a frightful accident.
▶ terrible, awful, appalling, dreadful, horrible, fearful, ghastly, shocking, horrific

fringe *noun*
1 *The curtain had a long fringe that trailed across the floor.* ▶ a frill, a border, an edging
2 *There is a picnic area at the fringe of the wood.* ▶ an edge

frisky *adjective*
The dancers made quick frisky movements. ▶ playful, lively, sprightly, spirited

fritter *verb*
He had an uncle who frittered all his money on gambling. ▶ to squander, to waste, to misuse

frivolous *adjective*
The man in the shop was making frivolous remarks about his family.
▶ trivial, flippant, unimportant, silly, foolish

frock *noun*
Sarah was wearing her best summer frock. ▶ a dress, a gown
NOTE: A **gown** is usually a more formal kind of dress worn for special occasions

front *noun*
In the end we reached the front of the queue. ▶ the head, the beginning, the start

frontier *noun*
We showed our passports at the frontier.
▶ a border

frosty *adjective*
It was not easy getting up at 5 o'clock on a frosty morning. ▶ freezing, icy, bitter, wintry, cold

froth *noun*
Froth was beginning to ooze out of the washing machine. ▶ lather, suds, bubbles, foam

frown *verb*
She frowned again as another thought came into her head. ▶ to scowl, to glower

fruitful *adjective*
1 *It was disappointing that the day had not been more fruitful.* ▶ successful, profitable, useful
2 *He'd worked hard to have a fruitful garden.* ▶ fertile, flourishing, lush, productive

fruitless *adjective*
The search had been fruitless and was called off when it grew dark.
▶ unsuccessful, pointless, futile, useless

frustrate *verb*
We were planning an outing, but the weather frustrated us. ▶ to thwart, to prevent, to stop, to foil, to hinder

fugitive *noun*
Eventually they caught the fugitive.
▶ an escapee, a runaway, a deserter, a refugee
NOTE: A **deserter** is a soldier who runs away from the army. A **refugee** is someone who has to leave their country and has nowhere to go.

fulfil *verb*
1 *They have fulfilled all they had to do.*
▶ to achieve, to accomplish, to complete, to carry out, to perform
2 *The new shopping centre fulfils many important needs.* ▶ to satisfy, to meet, to answer

full *adjective*
1 *When the weather is bad, the museums tend to be full.* ▶ filled, crowded, packed, congested, crammed, bursting
2 *They gave us a full account of what happened.* ▶ complete, thorough, detailed, comprehensive, exhaustive
3 *The other car was now driving at full speed towards them.* ▶ maximum, high, highest

fun *noun*
I could do with some fun.
▶ amusement, enjoyment, entertainment, recreation

function *noun*
1 *One function of language is to help people communicate.* ▶ a purpose, a use, a role, a job, an aim
2 *There is a function at the hotel this weekend.* ▶ a reception, a gathering, a party, an occasion; (informal) a do

function *verb*
1 *The chair also functions as a small table.* ▶ to serve, to act
2 *There's a number to ring if your computer isn't functioning properly.*
▶ to work, to operate

fund *noun*
1 *They decided to start a holiday fund.*
▶ a collection, a reserve; (informal) a kitty
2 *Shortage of funds is always a problem.*
▶ money, resources, capital, savings

fundamental *adjective*
The new managers made some fundamental changes. ▶ basic, important, elementary, essential

funny *adjective*
1 *They looked funny standing there in their pyjamas.* ▶ comic, comical, amusing, ridiculous, ludicrous
2 *Jim was fond of telling funny stories.*
▶ humorous, amusing, witty

3 *I thought I heard a funny noise outside the window.* ▶ strange, odd, curious, peculiar, queer, unusual

furious *adjective*
The woman was furious when she missed the bus. ▶ angry, infuriated, enraged, irate, livid, cross, fuming, incensed

furnish *verb*
The workshop had been furnished with all the necessary tools. ▶ to equip, to provide, to supply, to fit

further *adjective*
They agreed that the idea needed further thought. ▶ extra, more, additional, fresh

furtive *adjective*
They kept to the back of the crowd in a furtive way. ▶ secretive, stealthy, shifty, sneaky, sly, deceitful

fury *noun*
His face went white with fury. ▶ rage, anger; (not an everyday word) wrath

fuss *noun*
There was a lot of fuss at the time but the incident was soon forgotten.
▶ bother, excitement, commotion, trouble, turmoil

fussy *adjective*
Isabel was especially fussy about keeping the bathroom tidy. ▶ finicky, particular, fastidious; (informal) choosy, picky
NOTE: You use **choosy** and **picky** especially when you are talking about food

futile *adjective*
It was futile to pretend that they had not been there. ▶ useless, pointless, fruitless, ineffective

fuzzy *adjective*
1 *The baby already had a mass of fuzzy hair.* ▶ fluffy, woolly, downy
2 *Some of the pictures looked fuzzy.*
▶ unclear, blurred, hazy, indistinct

G g

gadget *noun*
The kitchen drawer was full of gadgets for opening cans and bottles. ▶ a device, a contraption, a tool, a utensil, a contrivance

gain *verb*
1 *We may gain an advantage by arriving early.* ▶ to win, to get, to achieve, to secure, to acquire, to earn, to obtain
2 *Trevor raised his head to gain a better view from the window.* ▶ to get, to achieve

gala *noun*
A swimming gala is held in July.
▶ a competition, a tournament, a meeting

gale *noun*
We were worried that the tree would fall down in the gale. ▶ a storm, a squall, a hurricane
NOTE: A **squall** is a strong wind that does not last long. A **hurricane** is much stronger than a gale.

gallant *adjective*
1 *They wrote a story about beautiful maidens and gallant knights.* ▶ brave, courageous, chivalrous, heroic, fearless
2 *A gallant gentleman at the next table came and helped us.* ▶ courteous, polite, helpful, chivalrous, valiant

game *noun*
1 *They spent the evening thinking up new games.* ▶ a pastime, an

amusement, an entertainment
2 *That was a silly game to play on us.*
▶ a trick, a joke
3 *If you like draughts let's have a game tomorrow.* ▶ a contest, a match, a competition

gang *noun*
A lively gang of youths stood on one corner. ▶ a group, a band, a bunch, a company, a crowd, a horde

gangster *noun*
The gangsters tied up the family and took everything they could find.
▶ a crook, a criminal, a robber, a gunman

gap *noun*
1 *By peeping through gaps in the trees she could just see what they were doing.*
▶ an opening, a hole, a chink, a space, a break
2 *There was a gap of about a month between the doctor's visits.* ▶ an interval, a pause

gape *verb*
Molly gaped at the diamond in wonder.
▶ to gaze, to stare; (informal) to goggle

garbage *noun*
Jack needed help carrying the garbage out because of his bad back. ▶ refuse, rubbish, trash, junk, litter, waste

garbled *adjective*
He gave us a garbled account of what the film had been about. ▶ confused, incoherent, jumbled

garments *plural noun*
The shop has a wide range of knitted garments. ▶ clothes, clothing, attire, dress
NOTE: **Clothing**, **attire**, and **dress** are all singular nouns. If you want an alternative for **garment** you have to use **piece of clothing**

gash *noun*
Tim slipped on the tiles and got a nasty gash in the top of his head. ▶ a cut, a wound, a slash

gasp *verb*
She gasped and stepped back, her face pale. ▶ to gulp, to catch your breath, to choke, to pant

gate *noun*
He walked out of the gate and back along the street. ▶ an entrance, a gateway, a door

gather *verb*
1 *A crowd had gathered outside the house.* ▶ to assemble, to come together, to collect, to congregate
2 *We'd better gather everyone in the hall.* ▶ to call, to summon, to assemble, to bring together, to round up
3 *Josie began to gather all her things.*
▶ to collect, to assemble, to pick up
4 *Will you go and gather some flowers?*
▶ to pick, to pluck
5 *I gather you've been on holiday.* ▶ to understand, to believe, to hear

gathering *noun*
1 *There is a small gathering of people in the garden.* ▶ a group, a crowd, a meeting, a collection, a company
2 *There will be a family gathering at Christmas.* ▶ a party, a function; (informal) a do

gaudy *adjective*
She preferred plain colours and avoided anything too gaudy. ▶ bright, showy, flashy, lurid

gauge *verb*
I tried to gauge how high the building was. ▶ to measure, to calculate, to estimate, to judge, to determine

gay *adjective*
1 *Some of the men were gay.*
▶ homosexual

2 *The party was lively and gay.*
▶ cheerful, merry, bright, light-hearted, happy

gaze at *verb*
As she passed the mirror she stopped to gaze at her reflection. ▶ to look at, to stare at, to watch, to contemplate, to regard

gem *noun*
The gold chain was covered with gems of various colours. ▶ a jewel, a precious stone

general *adjective*
1 *The general opinion is that we are right.* ▶ widespread, common, popular, universal
2 *As a general rule we leave after lunch.* ▶ normal, customary, regular, usual, everyday, habitual
3 *She pointed in the general direction of the office.* ▶ broad, rough, approximate, vague

generally *adverb*
It's generally easier to shop in the evening. ▶ usually, normally, mostly, as a rule, on the whole

generous *adjective*
1 *It was generous of them to let Michael stay.* ▶ kind, good, noble, charitable
2 *The fund has received several generous donations.* ▶ liberal, large, sizeable, lavish

genial *adjective*
He had a bright manner and a genial smile. ▶ kind, pleasant, cordial, friendly

genius *noun*
He was showing a genius for carpentry. ▶ a gift, a talent, a flair, an aptitude

gentle *adjective*
1 *She is very gentle with the young children.* ▶ kind, kindly, tender, good-tempered, mild, pleasant

2 *The place was silent except for the sound of a gentle breeze.* ▶ faint, slight, light, soft
3 *They had to cycle up a gentle slope.* ▶ gradual, easy, slight, moderate

genuine *adjective*
1 *Many people thought the painting was a fake but it turned out to be genuine.* ▶ authentic, real
2 *Gill showed a genuine interest in what we were saying.* ▶ sincere, honest, real, true, candid

germ *noun*
Some diseases are caused by germs. ▶ a bug, a microbe, a bacterium, a virus
NOTE: You normally use **bacterium** in the plural, **bacteria**

gesture *noun*
The queen silenced the crowd with a gesture. ▶ a sign, a signal, an action, a movement

get *verb*
1 *Where can we get some tea?* ▶ to find, to buy, to get hold of, to obtain
2 *Jane got a letter from her cousin.* ▶ to receive, to be sent
3 *Three people got prizes.* ▶ to win, to earn, to take, to secure
4 *I'm afraid I've got a cold.* ▶ to catch, to develop, to contract, to come down with
5 *See if you can get him to play the banjo.* ▶ to persuade
6 *Molly's mother went indoors to get the dinner.* ▶ to prepare, to cook, to make ready
7 *It wasn't easy to get what he meant.* ▶ to understand, to grasp, to follow, to comprehend
8 *We can get to York by train.* ▶ to go, to travel
9 *We'll get to York after dark.* ▶ to reach, to arrive at
10 *It began to get cold in the New Year.* ▶ to become, to grow, to turn

ghastly *adjective*
There has been a ghastly accident.
▶ terrible, awful, appalling, dreadful, horrible, frightful, fearful, shocking, horrific

ghost *noun*
Eddie claimed he saw a ghost. ▶ a spirit, a phantom, a spectre, an apparition; (*informal*) a spook

ghostly *adjective*
On the back was painted a ghostly figure with a hood. ▶ spooky, eerie, creepy, weird, scary, unearthly

giant *adjective*
One of the things they brought back from their holiday was a giant bar of chocolate. ▶ enormous, huge, colossal, gigantic, immense, massive

gibberish *adjective*
He kept up a stream of gibberish all the way home. ▶ nonsense, drivel, rubbish, balderdash; (*informal*) tripe, twaddle

giddy *adjective*
She woke up in the mornings feeling giddy. ▶ dizzy, faint, unsteady, reeling

gift *noun*
1 *The king gave the old man his horse as a gift.* ▶ a present, an offering
2 *Stella has a gift for music.* ▶ an ability, a talent, a genius, a flair

gifted *adjective*
She is a gifted musician. ▶ able, talented, accomplished, skilful, skilled, expert

gigantic *adjective*
Under the water they saw a gigantic fish. ▶ enormous, huge, colossal, giant, immense, massive

giggle *verb*
They looked away, trying hard not to giggle. ▶ to snigger, to titter

girl *noun*
She's a lovely girl. ▶ a lass, a kid, a youngster

give *verb*
1 *She gave me a small box of chocolates with a thank-you card.* ▶ to present (with), to award, to hand over
2 *I'd like to give some of the money to a charity.* ▶ to donate, to contribute
3 *He gave a loud gasp.* ▶ to utter, to let out
4 *We were afraid the branch might give under the weight.* ▶ to break, to give way, to snap, to collapse

glad *adjective*
I'm glad your husband is feeling better. ▶ pleased, happy, delighted

glamorous *adjective*
The place was swarming with film stars and glamorous models. ▶ dazzling, elegant, glittering, beautiful, lovely, gorgeous, attractive, good-looking

glance *verb*
She glanced across at the clock on the wall. ▶ to look, to peep, to glimpse

glare *verb*
They stood glaring at each other for several minutes. ▶ to stare, to scowl, to glower

gleam *verb*
The newly-washed car gleamed in the sunlight. ▶ to shine, to glimmer, to glint, to glisten, to glow, to shimmer

gleam *noun*
There was a gleam of light in one corner of the room. ▶ a glimmer, a glint, a beam, a ray, a shaft

glee *noun*
Margot danced with glee at the news. ▶ joy, delight

glide *verb*
Skaters were gliding across the ice. ► to slide, to skim, to drift

glimmer *verb*
A light glimmered in the darkness. ► to shine, to gleam, to glint, to glisten, to glow, to twinkle, to shimmer

glint *verb*
Her bright eyes glinted in the sun. ► to shine, to gleam, to twinkle, to sparkle, to glow

glisten *verb*
The car's lights glistened on the wet road. ► to shine, to gleam, to glint, to glimmer, to glow, to twinkle, to shimmer
NOTE: It is interesting how many of these words begin with the letters 'GL'

glitter *verb*
Something bright glittered in his hand. ► to gleam, to twinkle, to sparkle, to glow

gloomy *adjective*
1 *The large gloomy bedroom had no pictures and no mirror.* ► dreary, dingy, dark, dismal, sombre, cheerless
2 *The weather was even more gloomy the next day.* ► dull, dreary, cloudy, overcast, sunless
3 *He was hardly ever gloomy, but when he was it took a lot to cheer him up.* ► glum, downcast, sad, miserable, melancholy, depressed, down-hearted

glorious *adjective*
1 *It had been a glorious sunny day and he had woken up early.* ► splendid, magnificent, beautiful, brilliant, gorgeous, wonderful, lovely, marvellous
2 *The king's army has won a glorious victory.* ► brilliant, magnificent, splendid, famous, celebrated, great

gloss *noun*
The flicker of the television was reflected in the gloss of the half-open door.
► sheen, polish, shine, brightness, lustre

glossy *adjective*
The bushes had bright flowers and glossy green leaves. ► shiny, bright, gleaming, polished, lustrous

glow *verb*
The fire glowed and the lights sparkled.
► to shine, to gleam, to glimmer, to radiate

glower *verb*
She turned and glowered sulkily back at him. ► to scowl, to glare, to frown

glue *noun*
Some brushes and a squashed tube of glue had fallen on the floor.
► adhesive, gum, paste

glue *verb*
Kelly carefully glued a gold bow on the top of the parcel. ► to stick, to paste, to fix

glum *adjective*
He sat down wearily, looking glum.
► sad, depressed, dispirited, dejected, despondent, downcast, down-hearted, gloomy, melancholy, miserable, unhappy

gnaw *verb*
The dog was gnawing an old bone. ► to chew, to bite, to munch

go *noun*
James wanted to have a go at putting up wallpaper. ► a turn, a chance, an opportunity

go *verb*
1 *I'd like to go to Fiji.* ► to travel, to journey, to visit
NOTE: If you use **visit** you do not need the word *to*: *I'd like to visit Fiji.*

2 *We'll have to go soon.* ► to leave, to set off; (more formal) to depart

3 *The car started to go forward.* ► to move, to advance, to progress

4 *When they returned the car had gone.* ► to disappear, to vanish

5 *The road on the left goes to the village.* ► to lead to, to reach, to take you to

6 *My watch isn't going.* ► to work, to function, to run, to operate

7 *The time goes very quickly.* ► to pass, to elapse

8 *The fruit has gone mouldy.* ► to turn, to become, to grow

9 *The box goes on the top shelf.* ► to belong, to fit, to have a place

go away *verb*
Why don't they go away? ► to leave, to depart

go back *verb*
It's time to go back home now. ► to return

go in for *verb*
I'm going in for a competition. ► to enter, to take part in, to compete in

go off *verb*
A bomb went off during the night. ► to explode, to blow up, to detonate

go on *verb*
Let's go on talking. ► to continue, to carry on, to keep on

goal *noun*
Their goal was to finish the decorating by Christmas. ► an aim, an ambition, an objective, a target

gobble *verb*
Jim gobbled up whatever he could find and went to bed. ► to eat up, to guzzle, to devour

good *adjective*
1 *They are very good people.*
► virtuous, honourable, honest, upright, moral, praiseworthy, worthy

2 *It was good of you to come.* ► kind, considerate, helpful, caring

3 *He's a good musician.* ► able, talented, capable, accomplished, skilful, proficient

4 *We all had a good time.* ► enjoyable, nice, pleasant, agreeable, lovely, delightful, excellent, fine, pleasing, wonderful, marvellous

5 *It was good that she helped you.* ► right, correct, fitting

goods *plural noun*
The goods are delivered by road every week. ► freight, merchandise, cargo
NOTE: All these words take a singular verb:
The freight is delivered by road every week, not *The freight are delivered … .*

gorgeous *adjective*
The models were pretty and their clothes were gorgeous. ► magnificent, splendid, beautiful, glorious, lovely; (informal) stunning

govern *verb*
She became an MP because she wanted to help govern the country. ► to administer, to control, to be in charge of, to manage, to rule, to run, to direct

gown *noun*
Rose wore a dark gown with white gloves. ► a dress, a costume, a frock

grab *verb*
Robert grabbed his case and rushed out of the room. ► to grasp, to seize, to snatch, to pick up, to clutch

graceful *adjective*
The dancers were tall and graceful.
► beautiful, elegant, dignified

gracious *adjective*
She gave them a gracious smile.
► courteous, agreeable, friendly, kind, polite

grade *noun*
The pottery is sorted by hand into different grades. ▶ a class, a category, a quality, a standard

gradual *adjective*
There has been a gradual change in public opinion. ▶ steady, gentle, moderate, slow

grand *adjective*
1 A grand dinner will be held on Saturday. ▶ splendid, magnificent, lavish, big, great, important
2 The house is large and grand.
▶ stately, imposing, noble, majestic, elegant, impressive

grant *noun*
Students can get a grant towards the cost of their travel. ▶ an allowance, a subsidy, an award, a donation

grant *verb*
The queen granted all her enemies a royal pardon. ▶ to give, to allow, to bestow, to confer

grapple *verb*
In South America there are wasps that can grapple with bird-eating spiders.
▶ to fight, to struggle, to wrestle

grasp *verb*
1 The boy turned to his mother and grasped her hand. ▶ to grip, to clasp, to clutch, to grab, to seize, to hold, to squeeze, to cling to
2 After the accident he found it difficult to grasp what had happened. ▶ to understand, to comprehend, to follow, to realize

grateful *adjective*
We are very grateful for your help.
▶ thankful, appreciative, glad (of)

grave *adjective*
1 Everyone in the room was looking at Shaun, their faces grave and thoughtful.
▶ serious, solemn, grim, subdued

2 We have had some grave news.
▶ serious, important, momentous
NOTE: Grave news is normally bad news, whereas important or momentous news can also be good.

great *adjective*
1 A new coat of paint makes a great difference. ▶ big, large, enormous, huge, immense, tremendous, significant
2 The poor man seemed to be in great pain. ▶ severe, acute, extreme, intense
3 The royal wedding would be a great occasion. ▶ grand, important, splendid, magnificent, spectacular
4 Their grandfather was a great musician as well as a writer.
▶ important, major, leading, eminent, distinguished, prominent, celebrated, notable, well-known
5 We all thought it was a great game.
▶ excellent, good, wonderful, marvellous; (informal) fantastic, terrific

greedy *adjective*
We like Jim but he can be greedy when he wants something. ▶ grasping, selfish

greet *verb*
When Jenny arrived, Tom stepped forward to greet her. ▶ to welcome, to receive

grief *noun*
The old man could not hide his grief when his wife died. ▶ sorrow, sadness, distress

grievance *noun*
If you have a grievance, let us know about it. ▶ a complaint, a grumble, a protest

grieve *verb*
In the back of her mind she was grieving for her mother constantly. ▶ to mourn, to lament
NOTE: If you use **mourn** or **lament** you do

not need to use *for*. You could say: *She was mourning her mother's death* or *She was lamenting the death of her mother.*

grim *adjective*
1 *The coastguard gave a grim warning about the storms at sea.* ▶ stern, severe, gloomy, ominous
2 *Driving home in the dense fog had been a grim experience.* ▶ dreadful, terrible, grisly, awful, frightful, frightening

grimy *adjective*
The windows were cracked and grimy. ▶ dirty, filthy, grubby, dusty

grin *verb*
Paul grinned and winked. ▶ to beam, to smile

grind *verb*
1 *You need to grind the beans in a machine.* ▶ to crush, to pound, to powder
2 *The knives need grinding.* ▶ to sharpen, to polish

grip *verb*
She gripped the handle firmly and pulled. ▶ to grasp, to clasp, to clutch, to grab, to seize, to hold, to squeeze, to clench

grisly *adjective*
They came across the grisly remains of a dead sheep. ▶ gruesome, ghastly, gory, grim, horrible, horrid, nasty

groan *verb*
She woke up, groaned, and pulled the pillow over her head. ▶ to moan, to sigh, to wail

groove *noun*
The rock has tiny grooves cut in its surface. ▶ a channel, a furrow, a hollow, a cut, a rut, an indentation

grope *verb*
Jane groped for the keys at the bottom of her bag. ▶ to fumble, to fish, to feel about

gross *adjective*
1 *He looked gross and disgusting.* ▶ fat, ugly, revolting, overweight, obese, flabby
2 *Leaving the baby alone in the house was gross stupidity.* ▶ shocking, flagrant, blatant, plain, extreme

grotesque *adjective*
They saw some huge statues with grotesque faces. ▶ ugly, weird, deformed, distorted, misshapen

ground *noun*
1 *The badger disappeared down a hole in the ground.* ▶ the earth, the soil
2 *The ground is too wet to play on.* ▶ a pitch, a field

grounds *plural noun*
There are good grounds for suspecting their story. ▶ a reason, a cause, a basis, a justification, a case, an argument

group *noun*
1 *A group of people was waiting on the platform.* ▶ a crowd, a collection, a party, a gang, a throng; (informal) a bunch
2 *The choir was divided into three groups to lead the singing.* ▶ a section, a part, a division

grow *verb*
1 *Some plants grow in dark corners.* ▶ to develop, to flourish, to thrive, to prosper
2 *The business has grown a lot in the last year.* ▶ to develop, to expand, to improve, to flourish, to prosper
3 *The family grew their own potatoes at the end of the garden.* ▶ to cultivate, to produce

grown-up *adjective*
Jill had a grown-up sister who lived in America. ▶ adult, mature

growth *noun*
There has been a big growth in the population in the last few years. ▶ an increase, a development, an expansion

grubby *adjective*
The man was wearing a grubby coat with the collar turned up. ▶ dirty, filthy, shabby, grimy

gruelling *adjective*
They looked tired after their gruelling journey back from the Himalayas. ▶ arduous, strenuous, exhausting, tiring, wearying, hard, laborious

gruesome *adjective*
The stories she told were gruesome and frightening. ▶ grisly, gory, bloody, disgusting, grim, hideous, horrible, ghastly, revolting, sickening

gruff *adjective*
His voice was gruff in the darkness. ▶ hoarse, husky, rough, harsh

grumble *verb*
There was a long line of people at the bus stop, most of them grumbling about the wait. ▶ to complain, to moan, to grouse, to protest; (informal) to whinge

grumpy *adjective*
Alan is always grumpy when someone wakes him up. ▶ cross, bad-tempered, irritable, peevish, tetchy, testy, irascible

guarantee *verb*
1 He guaranteed that he would return. ▶ to promise, to pledge, to vow, to swear
2 Booking now will guarantee a ticket. ▶ to secure, to ensure

guard *verb*
Two security men guarded the entrance. ▶ to defend, to watch, to watch over, to protect

guard *noun*
An armed guard stood in the doorway. ▶ a sentry, a watchman, a security man, a security officer, a lookout

guess *verb*
She guessed the baby must be about eighteen months. ▶ to suppose, to assume, to estimate

guest *noun*
The next day more guests arrived. ▶ a caller, a visitor

guide *noun*
A guide will take us round the city tomorrow. ▶ a leader, an escort, a courier

guide *verb*
Shaun put a hand on the old lady's elbow to guide her to the door. ▶ to lead, to show, to direct, to escort, to conduct

guilty *adjective*
1 The jury decided that the man was guilty. ▶ to blame, at fault
2 Polly felt guilty about being horrid to her sister. ▶ ashamed, remorseful, regretful, conscious-stricken, contrite, sheepish

gulp *verb*
He reached across the table for the pudding and gulped it down. ▶ to bolt, to gobble, to guzzle

gush *verb*
Wet steam gushed out of the kitchen. ▶ to pour, to stream, to spurt, to squirt, to flow

guts *plural noun*
(informal) *It needed guts to take a boat out in the storm.* ▶ courage, nerve, daring, spirit, grit; (informal) pluck

guzzle *verb*
They all sat there, guzzling crisps. ▶ to gobble, to gulp down
NOTE: With drinks you can use **swill** instead of **guzzle**

H h

habit *noun*
1 *Jack has a habit of nodding when he speaks.* ▶ a way, a mannerism, a quirk
2 *It had always been our habit to go out after lunch.* ▶ a practice, a custom, a routine

hack *verb*
The boys had to hack back the brambles that had grown across the path. ▶ to chop, to slash, to cut

haggard *adjective*
She was sitting still, looking pale and haggard. ▶ tired, exhausted, worn out, drawn, drained

haggle *verb*
They spent hours haggling over a few pence. ▶ to bargain, to argue, to dispute, to negotiate

hairy *adjective*
A large hairy youth came out of the bathroom. ▶ bristly, shaggy
NOTE: If you are describing an animal you can also use **woolly**, **fleecy**, or **fuzzy**

half-hearted *adjective*
Some of the girls were half-hearted about the whole idea.
▶ unenthusiastic, cool, indifferent, lukewarm

hall *noun*
The telephone was in the hall. ▶ the lobby, the foyer, the passage; (more formal) the vestibule
NOTE: These words are mostly used about theatres or other large buildings

halt *verb*
1 *Gus halted at the front door instead of driving on to the garage.* ▶ to stop, to pull up, to draw up, to come to a standstill
2 *All work will halt at 5 o'clock sharp.* ▶ to stop, to finish, to end, to cease, to break off; (more formal) to terminate

hammer *verb*
Someone was hammering on the door. ▶ to beat, to thump, to batter, to bash, to knock

hamper *verb*
Thick foliage outside the prison walls hampered the escape. ▶ to hinder, to foil, to frustrate, to impede, to obstruct, to interfere with, to hold up, to check

hand *verb*
He handed her a blanket as she had no shawl. ▶ to pass, to give, to offer

hand in *verb*
We have some work to hand in by Monday. ▶ to give in, to deliver, to submit, to present

hand round *verb*
Some people at the meeting were handing round leaflets. ▶ to pass round, to hand out, to give out, to distribute

handicap *noun*
1 *Ruth enjoyed France but not speaking the language was a handicap.*
▶ a disadvantage, a drawback, a difficulty, an obstacle

2 *John suffers from a severe physical handicap.* ► a disability, an impediment

handle *verb*
1 *The glass was fragile and had to be handled with care.* ► to touch, to hold, to feel
2 *Unfortunately her mother was left to handle the problem by herself.* ► to deal with, to cope with, to manage, to control

handsome *adjective*
1 *Tara wanted a new boyfriend who was handsome and honest.* ► attractive, good-looking
2 *The house was handsome and stood at the top of a hill.* ► elegant, smart, good-looking, beautiful
3 *After a few years the company made a handsome profit.* ► large, big, sizeable, substantial

handy *adjective*
1 *A handy little leaflet tells you about local walks.* ► convenient, useful, helpful, practical
2 *You need to be handy with a screwdriver.* ► clever, skilful, capable, competent, proficient

hang *verb*
1 *Flags were hanging from the mast.* ► to dangle, to droop, to be suspended
2 *Dirty smoke hung low across the city.* ► to drift, to float, to hover

hang about *verb*
After a while they decided not to hang about any longer. ► to linger, to dally, to wait

hang back *verb*
The child came over reluctantly, hanging back when I took his hand. ► to hesitate, to pause, to shrink back, to recoil

hang on to *verb*
1 *Hang on to the railing.* ► to hold, to hold on to, to grasp, to grab, to grip, to clutch, to cling to
2 *They hung on to their tickets until the journey was over.* ► to keep, to hold, to hold on to, to save; (more formal) to retain

haphazard *adjective*
The stamp collection looked haphazard, but in fact it had been carefully planned. ► disorganized, random, unplanned, unsystematic, confused

happen *verb*
Something strange happened. ► to occur, to take place, to come about

happening *noun*
Meg welcomed the chance to talk over the day's happenings. ► an event, an incident, an occurrence

happiness *noun*
Everyone deserves some happiness in their life. ► joy, pleasure, cheerfulness, gladness, cheer, gaiety

happy *adjective*
1 *Sam felt happy when he heard the news.* ► cheerful, content, contented, pleased, merry, glad, joyful, overjoyed, delighted, ecstatic, elated, exultant
2 *They hoped the party would be a happy time for everyone.* ► cheerful, merry, jolly, joyous, joyful, lively
3 *It was a happy chance they were still at home when we called.* ► lucky, fortunate, favourable

harass *verb*
Leslie was being harassed about some bills he hadn't paid. ► to bother, to pester, to annoy, to trouble, to badger, to harry, to disturb, to worry

harbour *verb*
The family had harboured refugees during the war. ▶ to shelter, to give refuge to, to give asylum to, to hide, to protect

hard *adjective*
1 *The ground was hard, with frost in places.* ▶ firm, solid, rock-like, unyielding, rigid
2 *She had a hard task ahead of her after the birth of her second baby.* ▶ difficult, tough, arduous, strenuous, exhausting, gruelling, harsh, heavy, laborious
3 *It was a hard question to answer.* ▶ difficult, complicated, complex, baffling, involved, puzzling
4 *She gave the door a quick hard knock, and waited.* ▶ forceful, sharp, strong, heavy, powerful
5 *Her parents had had a hard life.* ▶ harsh, difficult, grim, unpleasant, uncomfortable, severe

hardly *adverb*
Tom could hardly wait for the morning to arrive. ▶ barely, scarcely

hardship *noun*
The expedition would face great hardship and danger. ▶ suffering, difficulty, adversity, misery, unhappiness

hardy *adjective*
There is a special route for hardy walkers. ▶ strong, tough, fit, vigorous, robust, sturdy

harm *verb*
1 *She didn't want to harm the fish by giving them the wrong food.* ▶ to hurt, to injure
2 *Bad weather might harm our chances of winning.* ▶ to damage, to spoil, to ruin

harm *noun*
They have to do the repair work without causing any harm to the old buildings. ▶ damage, injury

harmful *adjective*
Pollution was having a harmful effect on the city. ▶ damaging, injurious, dangerous, unhealthy, destructive

harmless *adjective*
The joke had been silly but fairly harmless. ▶ innocent, innocuous, inoffensive, safe

harmony *noun*
For a while they were able to live in harmony. ▶ friendship, agreement, understanding, concord

harsh *adjective*
1 *The man spoke in a loud harsh voice.* ▶ shrill, strident, grating, jarring, raucous
2 *The room was painted in harsh colours.* ▶ lurid, glaring, gaudy, bright, brilliant, dazzling
3 *Conditions in the prison are harsh.* ▶ tough, severe, hard, arduous, austere, unpleasant, difficult
4 *The cloth has a harsh texture.* ▶ bristly, coarse, hairy, rough, scratchy
5 *We thought the decision had been much too harsh.* ▶ strict, hard, severe, stern, unkind

hasty *adjective*
They all agreed that their action had been hasty. ▶ hurried, rushed, abrupt, impetuous, impulsive, rash, foolhardy

hate *verb*
She hates anyone seeing her with her hair untidy. ▶ to dislike, to loathe, to detest, to abhor
NOTE: **Detest** and **abhor** are much stronger words

hatred *noun*
You could see the hatred in their eyes.
▶ hate, loathing, enmity, hostility, dislike, contempt

haughty *adjective*
He looked away with a haughty toss of his head. ▶ proud, arrogant, conceited, scornful, lofty, lordly, disdainful, self-important

haul *verb*
Strong rope was needed to haul the car out of the water. ▶ to drag, to pull, to draw, to tow, to tug

have *verb*
1 *Judy wanted to have her own car.*
▶ to own, to possess
2 *Their new house has two bathrooms and a study.* ▶ to contain, to include
3 *What did you have for your birthday?*
▶ to get, to receive, to be given; (more formal) to acquire, to obtain
4 *Did you have a good time?* ▶ to enjoy, to experience
NOTE: **Have** has many meanings. These are only some of the other words you can use
5 *We had a terrible experience.* ▶ to suffer, to go through, to endure, to undergo

haven *noun*
She was pleased to be back in the familiar haven of her own room.
▶ a refuge, a shelter, a retreat, an asylum, safety

havoc *noun*
The gales have caused havoc along the coast. ▶ damage, destruction, devastation

hazard *noun*
The journey was full of hazards.
▶ a danger, a peril, a risk, a threat

hazardous *adjective*
Removing the old tree proved to be a hazardous operation. ▶ dangerous, risky, perilous, unsafe, chancy

hazy *adjective*
1 *They stepped out into the hazy morning sunshine.* ▶ misty, blurred, dim, faint, unclear
2 *Mohan's memory of what happened was only hazy.* ▶ faint, dim, vague, sketchy

head *noun*
1 *The head of the organization is coming on a visit.* ▶ a chief, a boss, a director
2 *The head gardener was standing by the door.* ▶ chief, principal, senior

head *verb*
He heads a research team. ▶ to lead, to be in charge of, to run, to direct, to manage

head for *verb*
The car was heading for Birmingham when the accident happened. ▶ to go to, to make for

headlong *adjective*
They ended up in a headlong rush for the exit. ▶ breakneck, reckless, impetuous, impulsive

heal *verb*
1 *The ointment heals cuts and bruises.*
▶ to cure, to make better, to treat
2 *Kitty's leg had healed already.* ▶ to get better, to mend, to recover

healthy *adjective*
He looks healthy for his age. ▶ fit, well, strong, robust, sound

heap *noun*
Someone's clothes lay in a heap in one corner. ▶ a pile, a mass, a mound

heap *verb*
Old newspapers were heaped under the table. ► to pile, to collect, to mass, to stack, to accumulate

hear *verb*
1 *I didn't hear what you said.* ► to listen to, to catch
2 *We heard that they had moved to America.* ► to learn, to find out, to discover, to be told

heart *noun*
The monument is in the heart of the city. ► the centre, the middle, the hub

heartless *adjective*
I couldn't believe that people could be so heartless. ► unkind, unfeeling, pitiless, uncaring, cruel, callous

hearty *adjective*
1 *They gave us a hearty welcome.* ► warm, enthusiastic, sincere
2 *Darren always had a hearty appetite.* ► big, healthy, robust

heat *noun*
The summer heat was becoming unbearable. ► warmth, hotness
NOTE: A long period of hot weather is called a **heatwave**

heave *verb*
Sabina heaved the basket of wet washing on to the table. ► to haul, to pull, to hoist, to tug, to drag, to raise, to lift

heavenly *adjective*
(informal) *It promised to be another heavenly day.* ► lovely, beautiful, pleasing, pleasant, delightful, blissful

heavy *adjective*
1 *Maisie staggered in with heavy bags of shopping in each arm.* ► weighty, hefty, burdensome, massive
2 *It was heavy work digging the garden.* ► hard, arduous, difficult, laborious, tough, strenuous

3 *Gradually the drizzle increased to heavy rain.* ► severe, torrential
NOTE: **Torrential** is a stronger word than **heavy**

hectic *adjective*
Shopkeepers said it was the most hectic day they had known. ► busy, active, lively, bustling, excited, frantic

heed *verb*
It is important to heed what they say. ► to listen to, to take note of, to take notice of, to note, to mark, to mind, to act on, to follow

hefty *adjective*
The man was strong and hefty. ► heavy, beefy, brawny, burly, large, tough, muscular

height *noun*
The mountain has a height of 5,000 feet. ► an altitude, an elevation

help *verb*
1 *We must help the police to catch the thief.* ► to assist, to aid, to support, to cooperate with
NOTE: With all these words you say … *in catching the thief*: *We must assist the police in catching the thief.*
2 *Kate couldn't help a slight shiver running down her back.* ► to prevent, to stop, to avoid

help *noun*
1 *The girl seemed to be in need of help.* ► assistance, aid, support
2 *It had been a help for Rachel to have her friends with her.* ► an advantage, a support

helpful *adjective*
1 *We were impressed by the friendly helpful girl in the shop.* ► considerate, obliging, willing, thoughtful, accommodating, cooperative

2 *The guidebook has helpful suggestions about which places to visit.* ▶ useful, valuable, informative, instructive

helping *noun*
There was quite a good helping of potato but only a tiny piece of meat.
▶ a portion, a serving, a share

helpless *adjective*
1 *When chicks are born they are quite helpless.* ▶ weak, defenceless, feeble, vulnerable, unprotected, dependent
2 *He just stood there helpless as the car began to roll away.* ▶ powerless, impotent, forlorn

hem in *verb*
They found themselves hemmed in by the crowds outside the gate. ▶ to enclose, to encircle, to surround, to confine, to hedge in

herd *noun*
A few cows were wandering towards the lake, and the rest of the herd looked like following.
NOTE: You use **herd** about cattle, sheep, pigs, goats, and large wild animals such as buffalo and elephants. You can use other words about other animals: a **flock** of birds or sheep, a **gaggle** of geese, a **pack** of hounds, a **pride** of lions, a **school** of dolphins or whales, a **shoal** of fish, a **swarm** of bees

heritage *noun*
Museums play an important part in looking after a country's heritage.
▶ a culture, a history, a tradition, a legacy

hero *noun*
Napoleon had always been his great hero. ▶ a champion, an idol

heroic *adjective*
The ship's crew made heroic efforts to reach land. ▶ brave, courageous, daring, gallant, noble, valiant, fearless

hesitate *verb*
He hesitated at first, then held out his hand to her. ▶ to pause, to wait, to waver, to falter, to hang back

hide *verb*
1 *He had no time to think, and hid the book hurriedly under a towel.* ▶ to conceal, to secrete
2 *Their view across the fields was hidden by a row of tall trees.* ▶ to blot out, to obscure, to mask, to screen
3 *She hid in the garden until everyone had gone.* ▶ to conceal yourself, to lie low, to keep out of sight

hideous *adjective*
The mouth of the lifeless body showed a hideous grin. ▶ ugly, repulsive, gruesome, frightful, ghastly, grisly

high *adjective*
1 *The city has many high buildings.*
▶ tall, towering, lofty
2 *The old cot had high sides.* ▶ tall, raised, elevated
3 *House prices are high at the moment.*
▶ great, dear, exorbitant
4 *His father had a high position in one of the big banks.* ▶ important, leading, powerful, prominent, top, eminent
5 *The bridge had to be closed for a while when the wind was high.* ▶ strong, intense, powerful
6 *When he pinched her she let out a high squeaky sound.* ▶ sharp, shrill, piercing

hilarious *adjective*
They thought the joke was hilarious, but we didn't get it at all. ▶ funny, amusing, hysterical
NOTE: **Funny** and **amusing** are less strong in meaning than **hilarious**; **hysterical** is about equally strong

hill *noun*
As they walked up the hill a little way, they noticed the car. ▶ a rise, a summit, a slope, an incline, a ridge, a peak

hinder *verb*
We need to help the work of farmers and not hinder it. ▶ to hamper, to impede, to obstruct, to interfere with, to hold up, to prevent, to frustrate, to check

hindrance *noun*
Having her young cousins about was more a hindrance than a help.
▶ a disadvantage, a difficulty, a handicap, an impediment, an inconvenience

hint *noun*
The programme contained a few hints on cooking vegetables. ▶ a suggestion, a tip, a clue

hint *verb*
They hinted we might be lucky today.
▶ to indicate, to suggest, to imply

historic *adjective*
A historic battle was fought near here.
▶ important, decisive, crucial, famous, notable, celebrated

historical *adjective*
Archaeologists have shown that the Trojan War was a historical event.
▶ real, real-life, actual, authentic, genuine

hit *verb*
1 *The car hit a post.* ▶ to strike, to run into, to crash into, to knock into, to bump into, to collide with
2 *I saw you hit your dog.* ▶ to strike, to smack, to slap; (informal) to clout, to bash, to whack, to wallop
3 *A hurricane hit central America.* ▶ to strike, to affect, to devastate, to overwhelm, to damage
4 *They've hit the ball into the neighbours' garden.* ▶ to strike, to knock, to kick, to send, to bat

hit *noun*
1 *He seems to have got a bad hit on the head.* ▶ a blow, a knock, a thump, a bump

2 *The show was a big hit in London, but a flop in New York.* ▶ a success, a triumph

hoard *verb*
Fearing a war, many people began to hoard food. ▶ to store away, to collect, to stock up, to buy up, to save, to gather, to pile up, to accumulate, to stockpile, to mass

hoard *noun*
A hoard of gold was found under the floorboards. ▶ a store, a secret store, a supply, a secret supply, a treasure-house, a collection

hoarse *adjective*
She had a cold and her voice was hoarse. ▶ gruff, husky, croaking, croaky, grating, harsh, rough, rasping

hoax *noun*
We had all been the victim of a hoax.
▶ a trick, a deception, a fraud, a practical joke

hoax *verb*
Someone has been hoaxing us. ▶ to trick, to fool, to cheat, to play a trick on, to take in, to deceive, to hoodwink

hobby *noun*
Reading is a hobby of mine. ▶ an interest, a pursuit, a pastime

hoist *verb*
Gordon hoisted a huge rucksack on to his back. ▶ to heave, to haul, to pull, to tug, to drag, to raise, to lift

hold *verb*
1 *He came in holding a large torch.* ▶ to grip, to grasp, to clasp, to clutch
2 *Tanya held the little boy in her arms and kissed him.* ▶ to take, to embrace, to hug
3 *Do you hold a driving licence?* ▶ to possess, to have
4 *I'm not sure my suitcase will hold all my things.* ▶ to contain, to take, to

enclose, to include
5 *The car can hold six people.* ▶ to take, to carry, to seat, to accommodate
6 *I couldn't hold her and she struggled free.* ▶ to restrain, to confine, to detain, to keep
7 *They decided to hold a meeting in the village hall.* ▶ to have, to organize, to conduct
8 *The good weather should hold until the weekend.* ▶ to last, to continue, to persist, to carry on, to stay

hold on *verb*
Hold on while I see who's at the door.
▶ to wait, to stay; (informal) to hang on

hold out *verb*
1 *She held out her hand and smiled.*
▶ to reach out, to stretch out, to offer, to extend
2 *They were not sure if their supplies would hold out.* ▶ to last, to remain

hold up *verb*
1 *Several people held up their hands.*
▶ to raise, to lift, to put up
2 *They arrived late, complaining that they had been held up by the traffic.*
▶ to delay, to obstruct, to hinder, to slow down

hold-up *noun*
1 *There was a hold-up at the bank.*
▶ a robbery
2 *Traffic was slow, but it was hard to see what was causing the hold-up.*
▶ a delay, a wait, a jam

hole *noun*
1 *Someone had dug several large holes in the ground.* ▶ a crater, a chasm, a pit, a cavity, a hollow
2 *There is a hole in the wall where it was hit by a car.* ▶ a gap, an opening, a breach, a break, a chink

NOTE: A **chink** is a small narrow hole
3 *Meg had a hole in one sock.* ▶ a tear, a slit, a split, a rip

hollow *adjective*
The beach ball was light and hollow.
▶ empty, unfilled

hollow *noun*
They nearly fell into a hollow in the ground. ▶ a hole, a depression, a dip

hollow *verb*
You can make a lantern by hollowing out a pumpkin. ▶ to scoop, to dig, to gouge

holy *adjective*
1 *Part of the old city was a holy place.*
▶ sacred, blessed, hallowed, consecrated
2 *We met a Tibetan holy man.*
▶ religious, pious, saintly

home *noun*
Jay's home was just round the corner.
▶ a house; (informal) a place; (not everyday words) an abode, a dwelling, a residence
NOTE: You use **house** to mean a building and **home** to mean the building and the people and things inside it

homely *adjective*
This is a family hotel that offers a warm welcome and a homely atmosphere.
▶ friendly, relaxed, informal, pleasant, easy-going, comfortable

honest *adjective*
1 *She was an honest girl who loved him.*
▶ good, upright, trustworthy, sincere, conscientious, honourable, virtuous, law-abiding, moral
2 *I'll try to give an honest answer.*
▶ frank, sincere, candid, direct, straightforward, truthful

honesty *noun*
They trusted people's honesty and left a box out for the money. ▶ honour, integrity, uprightness, morality, sincerity

honour *noun*
1 *They were offered the honour of taking part in the Lord Mayor's show.* ▶ the distinction, the privilege
2 *They are all people of honour.* ▶ honesty, integrity, decency, sincerity

honour *verb*
The minute's silence is to remember and honour the dead. ▶ to respect, to show respect to, to pay tribute to, to praise, to pay homage to

honourable *adjective*
Kevin did the honourable thing and owned up. ▶ decent, honest, right, worthy, virtuous, noble, respectable, admirable

hook *verb*
The caravan was hooked to a large estate car. ▶ to fasten, to fix, to couple

hooligan *noun*
A gang of hooligans were scaring people in the town. ▶ a ruffian, a lout, a thug, a delinquent

hop *verb*
After her shower Sue hopped on to the bath mat. ▶ to jump, to leap, to step, to spring, to bound

hope *noun*
There seemed little hope of getting their money back. ▶ likelihood, prospect

hope *verb*
I hope they'll be happy together. ▶ to trust, to expect, to have confidence, to have faith

hopeful *adjective*
1 *We're hopeful of success.* ▶ confident, optimistic

2 *There is some hopeful news about the hostages.* ▶ encouraging, promising, reassuring, favourable

hopeless *adjective*
1 *The situation seems hopeless.* ▶ impossible, desperate, incurable
2 *Jenny admitted she was hopeless at making conversation.* ▶ bad, incompetent, useless, poor, feeble

horde *noun*
Hordes of people arrived on the day of the funeral. ▶ a crowd, a swarm, a throng, a mob

horrible *adjective*
The glue had a horrible smell. ▶ nasty, unpleasant, bad, awful, dreadful, horrid, terrible, appalling, ghastly

horrid *adjective*
Sinbad had to carry the horrid old man on his back. ▶ nasty, unpleasant, bad, awful, dreadful, horrible, terrible, appalling, ghastly

horrific *adjective*
People suffered horrific injuries in the fire. ▶ dreadful, frightful, appalling, horrifying, shocking

horrify *verb*
We were horrified to see the men starting to fight. ▶ to shock, to terrify, to appal, to frighten, to scare

horror *noun*
He stood with his eyes wide open in horror. ▶ dread, terror, dismay, fear, shock, disgust

hospitable
The family we stayed with were very hospitable. ▶ friendly, welcoming, sociable, kind

hostile *adjective*
She stared back at him, looking hostile. ▶ aggressive, unfriendly, antagonistic

hot *adjective*
1 *After a few days the weather turned hot.* ▶ warm, boiling, baking, scorching, burning, sweltering, sizzling
NOTE: **Warm** is less strong than **hot**, but the other words are all stronger
2 *The pies can be served hot.* ▶ warm, heated
3 *Charles has a hot temper.* ▶ fierce, angry, raging, violent, passionate
4 *Do you like hot food?* ▶ spicy, peppery, pungent, sharp

hound *verb*
The family was hounded by newspaper reporters. ▶ to chase, to hunt, to pursue, to track down

house *noun*
Come to my house. ▶ a home; (informal) a place; (not everyday words) an abode, a dwelling, a residence, quarters
KINDS OF HOUSE ARE:
small houses: a cottage, a bungalow, a croft;
large houses: a mansion, a manor, a palace, a villa;
special kinds of house: a detached house (not joined to another house), a semi-detached house (joined to another on one side), a terraced house (joined to others on both sides), a chalet (in the mountains), a farmhouse, a lodge (at the gateway to a larger house), a rectory (where a rector lives), a vicarage (where a vicar lives), a villa (a large house in the country or suburbs);
poor houses: a hovel, a shack, a shanty

hover *verb*
1 *She hovered by the phone while Michael finished his call.* ▶ to linger, to wait; (informal) to hang about
2 *A great black cloud hovered over their heads.* ▶ to hang, to float, to drift

hubbub *noun*
It was hard to hear anything above the hubbub. ▶ a din, a row, a noise, a commotion, pandemonium, a rumpus, a racket, an uproar

huddle *verb*
People huddled together to keep warm. ▶ to snuggle, to cuddle, to curl up, to nestle, to crowd, to press

hue *noun*
The view across the valley was of soft green and brown hues of autumn. ▶ a colour, a tint, a shade, a tinge

hug *verb*
I could have hugged my Mum that day for saving the tortoise. ▶ to cuddle, to squeeze, to embrace, to clasp, to hold close

huge *adjective*
I turned my head and saw a huge cat. ▶ enormous, colossal, gigantic, massive, immense, great, very large

humane *adjective*
What is the most humane way of getting rid of garden pests? ▶ kind, merciful, compassionate, considerate, benevolent

humble *adjective*
One day the boat got stranded and the girl was rescued by a humble fisherman. ▶ modest, lowly, meek, simple, unassuming, unpretentious

humid *adjective*
The weather turned hot and humid. ▶ muggy, sultry, close, clammy, dank

humiliate *verb*
Her father's remarks had humiliated her deeply. ▶ to shame, to embarrass, to mortify, to disgrace, to humble, to make ashamed

humorous *adjective*
He was full of humorous stories about their holiday. ▶ amusing, funny, comic, facetious, witty

humour *noun*
1 *Her good humour suddenly vanished.* ▶ a mood, a temper, a disposition, a state of mind
2 *I like stories that have humour in them.* ▶ wit, comedy, funniness, jokes

hump *noun*
There was a low hump at the other end of the field and beyond it some trees. ▶ a lump, a mound, a hill, a bulge, a bump, a swelling

hunch *noun*
His suggestion had been no more than a hunch. ▶ a feeling, an idea, a suspicion, an inkling, an intuition

hunger *noun*
1 *The meal hardly satisfied their hunger.* ▶ an appetite, a desire, a need
2 *Ben looked filthy and weak from hunger.* ▶ lack of food, starvation, malnutrition

hungry *adjective*
She was very hungry and ate twice as much as usual. ▶ famished, ravenous, starving; (informal) peckish
NOTE: You do not use *very* with the first three words. They are all stronger words, whereas **peckish** means 'slightly hungry'

hunt *verb*
The people of the forest were forbidden to cut down trees or hunt animals. ▶ to chase, to track, to stalk, to poach

hunt for *verb*
Laura had got out of the bath and was hunting for the shampoo. ▶ to look for, to search for, to seek

hurdle *noun*
One last hurdle and they would be free to leave. ▶ an obstacle, a barrier, a difficulty, a problem

hurl *verb*
Soldiers hurled grenades into the building. ▶ to throw, to toss, to fling, to sling, to lob, to pitch, to cast; (informal) to chuck

hurry *verb*
1 *He dropped the tray and hurried back into the kitchen.* ▶ to dash, to rush, to hasten, to speed, to scurry, to hurtle
2 *You'll have to hurry if you want to finish on time.* ▶ to speed up; (informal) to buck up, to get a move on

hurt *verb*
1 *The wasp sting began to hurt.* ▶ to smart, to sting, to ache, to be painful, to be sore
2 *He'd hurt his leg in a fall.* ▶ to injure, to damage, to wound, to harm
3 *Peter's comments were unkind and hurt her.* ▶ to upset, to distress, to offend, to wound

hurtle *verb*
The car hurtled on round the corner. ▶ to speed, to career, to dash, to race, to speed; (informal) to zoom

hush *verb*
She felt David's hand on her arm, and heard his voice gently hushing her. ▶ to calm, to soothe, to quieten

husky *adjective*
He spoke in a low husky voice. ▶ gruff, hoarse, croaking, croaky, throaty, grating, harsh, rough, rasping

hustle *verb*
Dinah hustled the children out of the room. ▶ to push, to shove, to hurry, to rush

hut *noun*
There are huts by the sea to get changed in. ▶ a shack, a cabin, a shelter, a shed

hygienic *adjective*
Hotel kitchens have to be hygienic.
▶ clean, sanitary, germ-free

hysterical *adjective*
Kate had become hysterical and started screaming. ▶ frenzied, distraught, demented, frantic, delirious, beside yourself

I i

icy *adjective*
1 *They didn't like the thought of being woken up at dawn on icy mornings.*
▶ freezing, frosty, bitter, cold, wintry
2 *The roads were icy and dangerous.*
▶ frozen, freezing, slippery, glassy

idea *noun*
1 *Vicky had an idea she wanted to share with the others.* ▶ a thought, a plan, a notion, a proposal, a suggestion; (informal) a brainwave
2 *He does have some strange ideas.*
▶ a view, an opinion, a belief, a theory, a notion
3 *Give me an idea of what you want.*
▶ a clue, a hint, an inkling, an impression

ideal *adjective*
The next day would be an ideal time to work in the garden. ▶ perfect, suitable, excellent

identical *adjective*
The two cars were almost identical, but one had a dent in the side. ▶ the same, alike, indistinguishable, similar

NOTE: If you use **similar**, this can mean 'alike in some ways' rather than 'completely alike'

identify *verb*
The police have identified the person seen in the video. ▶ to recognize, to pick out, to single out, to name

idiotic *adjective*
They asked us a lot of idiotic questions.
▶ silly, stupid, ridiculous, ludicrous, absurd, foolish, crazy

idle *adjective*
1 *The machinery is often idle for several days during the summer holidays.*
▶ inactive, unused, unemployed, not working
NOTE: If you use **not working**, this can also mean 'broken down'
2 *Toby spent a lot of time wandering round feeling idle.* ▶ lazy, slothful, sluggish, slow

idol *noun*
1 *The idols were made of gold and were very valuable.* ▶ a statue, an image, a god
2 *Harry had been his idol as well as his friend.* ▶ a hero, a favourite, a star

idolize *verb*
Grandfather had been kind and the children idolized him. ▶ to love, to adore, to worship, to revere

ignite *verb*
1 *After a while they ignited another flare and watched it shoot up into the sky.* ▶ to light, to set fire to, to set alight, to kindle
NOTE: You can use **kindle** when you are talking about a fire
2 *The boiler wouldn't ignite.* ▶ to light, to fire, to burn, to catch fire, to burst into flames

ignorant *adjective*
1 *He was ignorant of the fact that his mother was right behind him.*
▶ unaware, uninformed
2 *My older cousins always make me feel ignorant.* ▶ uneducated, illiterate, stupid

ignore *verb*
1 *The driver ignored a red light and drove on.* ▶ to take no notice of, to disobey, to disregard, to overlook
2 *Ignore the first question and go on to the second.* ▶ to omit, to leave out, to miss out, to skip, to disregard
3 *I called to them but they just ignored me.* ▶ to pay no attention to, to take no notice of, to turn your back on, to snub, to disregard

ill *adjective*
1 *Vicky was feeling ill and went home.*
▶ sick, unwell, poorly; (informal) queer, under the weather
NOTE: You use these words about short less serious illnesses
2 *Uncle Jock had been ill for years.*
▶ sick, infirm, diseased, bedridden
NOTE: You use these words about serious illnesses
3 *The boys braved the storm and reached home without any ill effects.*
▶ harmful, bad, unfavourable; (more formal) detrimental

illegal *adjective*
The organization agreed to hand over any illegal weapons. ▶ forbidden, unlawful, banned, unauthorized; (more formal) prohibited

illegible *adjective*
Parts of the letter were illegible, and she rewrote them in her neat writing.
▶ unreadable, unclear, indecipherable

illness *noun*
Mr Eden's illness grew worse every day.
▶ (serious illness) a disease, a
sickness, an infection, an infirmity, a malady, an affliction, an attack; (less serious illness) an ailment, an upset, a disorder, a complaint; (informal) a bug

illogical *adjective*
He knew his fears were illogical but still he couldn't shake them off.
▶ irrational, unreasonable, unfounded, baseless

illuminate *verb*
Rows of lights illuminated the ship at night. ▶ to light up, to decorate

illusion *noun*
Holograms create the illusion of depth in a picture. ▶ the appearance, the delusion, the deception, the fantasy

illustrate *verb*
The story seemed to illustrate the differences between Kate and her sister.
▶ to demonstrate, to show, to make clear

illustration *noun*
1 *The illustrations and photographs in the book help make the instructions clearer.* ▶ a picture, a drawing, a diagram
2 *Give me an illustration of what you mean.* ▶ an example, an instance, a case

image *noun*
1 *The little girl could see an image of herself in the glass.* ▶ a likeness, a picture, a reflection, a portrait
2 *The temple contained the god's image.*
▶ a carving, a figure, a representation, a statue

imaginary *adjective*
Her story was set in an imaginary underworld kingdom. ▶ unreal, fanciful, fictitious, invented, mythical, non-existent

imaginative *adjective*
Kevin wrote an imaginative story about a journey into space. ► creative, inventive, original, ingenious, inspired

imagine *verb*
1 *He'd close his eyes and imagine a hot sun and a sandy beach.* ► to picture, to think up, to think of, to visualize, to dream up, to dream of, to conceive
2 *I imagine they are on their way.* ► to presume, to suppose, to assume, to believe, to guess, to think

imitate *verb*
He likes to tease Diana by imitating the way she nods her head when she speaks. ► to copy, to mimic, to reproduce, to impersonate, to ape

imitation *noun*
In the film they weren't able to use a real gun but they could use an imitation. ► a fake, a dummy, a copy, a replica

immature *adjective*
He seems very immature for his age. ► childish, babyish, juvenile, infantile, puerile, young

immediate *adjective*
1 *We'd like an immediate answer to our question.* ► instant, prompt, speedy, quick, swift, direct
2 *Their immediate neighbours had lived in the street for years.* ► closest, nearest, next-door, adjacent

immediately *adverb*
We decided to leave immediately. ► at once, straightaway, directly, instantly, promptly, forthwith

immense *adjective*
The cost of the expedition was immense. ► huge, enormous, colossal, gigantic, massive, great, very large

immerse *verb*
The bird immersed its whole beak in the water. ► to plunge, to dip, to lower, to submerge

immersed *adjective*
He was immersed in a magazine he'd bought. ► absorbed, preoccupied, engrossed, interested, concentrating (on)

immobile *adjective*
He sat immobile at the window. ► motionless, paralysed, fixed, immobilized, immovable, static, stationary

immoral *adjective*
He thought it was immoral to be rich when so many people were starving. ► bad, evil, wicked, wrong, sinful, depraved, vile, unprincipled

immortal *adjective*
The ancient gods were immortal, but heroes died in battle. ► undying, eternal, endless, everlasting

imp *noun*
The story was about a mischievous imp. ► a devil, a demon, an elf, a rascal, a scamp

impact *noun*
1 *The woman suffered bruising in the impact.* ► a collision, a crash, a blow, a knock, a bump, a smash
2 *The advertising campaign has had a major impact on the company's sales.* ► an effect, an impression, an influence

impair *verb*
Her vision was impaired in the fall. ► to damage, to injure, to harm, to weaken

impartial *adjective*
We need some impartial advice. ► neutral, fair, unprejudiced, unbiased, detached, objective, disinterested

impatient *adjective*
1 *He gets impatient if the journey takes too long.* ▶ restless, anxious, irritable, apprehensive, edgy
2 *We were impatient to begin.* ▶ eager, anxious

imperfect *adjective*
These vases are cheaper because they are imperfect. ▶ damaged, defective, faulty, flawed, incomplete

impersonate *verb*
Who are you trying to impersonate? ▶ to copy, to mimic, to imitate

impertinent *adjective*
She thought his remarks were impertinent. ▶ cheeky, rude, impolite, insolent, impudent, arrogant, disrespectful, discourteous

implement *noun*
The shed was full of gardening implements. ▶ a tool, a utensil, a device, a gadget, an instrument

implore *verb*
He implored the chief to let the prisoners go. ▶ to beg, to plead (with), to entreat, to ask, to request
NOTE: **Ask** and **request** are not as strong as the other words

imply *verb*
The games teacher implied that I would be in the netball team. ▶ to suggest, to hint, to indicate

impolite *adjective*
The food looked dreadful but it would be impolite not to eat it. ▶ rude, discourteous, disrespectful, insulting

important *adjective*
1 *These are the important points to remember.* ▶ major, principal, significant, essential, basic, fundamental, main, primary
2 *We have an important visitor.* ▶ prominent, distinguished, eminent, well-known, celebrated, famous

impose *verb*
A speed limit of 20 miles per hour has been imposed on the road through the village. ▶ to enforce, to inflict

imposing *adjective*
A large and imposing house stood at the end of the drive. ▶ grand, stately, magnificent, impressive, splendid, striking

impossible *adjective*
Escape from the dungeon seemed impossible. ▶ inconceivable, unthinkable, out of the question, hopeless, unimaginable, impracticable

impractical *adjective*
They described the scheme as impractical. ▶ impossible, unworkable, unrealistic

impress *verb*
The story impressed them all. ▶ to affect, to move, to influence, to make an impression on

impression *noun*
1 *I had the impression they were writers.* ▶ the idea, the feeling, the notion
2 *He thought he had made a good impression on Vicky.* ▶ an effect, an impact, a mark

impressive *adjective*
Vancouver is a modern and impressive city. ▶ grand, great, splendid, imposing, striking, magnificent

imprison *verb*
He was imprisoned for stirring up riots in the city. ▶ to put in prison, to gaol, to detain, to confine, to lock up, to shut up

improbable *adjective*
It was an improbable story, and no one believed it. ► unlikely, incredible, unbelievable, unconvincing, dubious, implausible, far-fetched

improper *adjective*
1 *Improper use of the equipment could damage it.* ► wrong, incorrect, inappropriate
2 *Their language was considered improper.* ► indecent, coarse, crude, vulgar, unseemly

improve *verb*
1 *You will have to practise more if you want to improve.* ► to get better, to recover, to advance, to develop, to move on, to progress
2 *Our work has improved.* ► to get better, to progress, to develop
3 *You can get a grant to improve your house.* ► to renovate, to repair, to restore, to modernize, to upgrade

impudent *adjective*
The dinner lady told the children not to be so impudent. ► cheeky, rude, impolite, insolent, impertinent, arrogant, disrespectful, discourteous

impulsive *adjective*
It was a generous gesture, but impulsive. ► hasty, sudden, impetuous, rash, spontaneous, unconsidered, unplanned

impure *adjective*
Avoid drinking impure water. ► contaminated, polluted, dirty, unclean, foul, filthy, infected

inaccessible *adjective*
1 *The tool is useful for getting into inaccessible corners.* ► awkward, unreachable, hidden, hard to reach
2 *The airport used to be in an inaccessible part of the island.* ► remote, isolated, cut off, unreachable

NOTE: If you use **hard to reach** (in the first meaning) and **cut off** (in the second meaning) you have to use *corners that are hard to reach* and *a part of the island that is cut off.*

inaccurate *adjective*
The information proved to be inaccurate. ► incorrect, wrong, mistaken, false, untrue

inactive *adjective*
Some animals are inactive in winter. ► idle, dormant, hibernating

inadequate *adjective*
The food supply was inadequate. ► insufficient, not enough, unsatisfactory

inanimate *adjective*
Stones are inanimate objects. ► lifeless

inappropriate *adjective*
It was a handsome gift but rather inappropriate. ► unsuitable, irrelevant, out of place

incapable *adjective*
They are incapable of understanding the problem. ► unable (to), useless (at)

incense *verb*
We were incensed by all the delays. ► to anger, to enrage, to infuriate, to madden

incentive *noun*
Leo was promised a new football as an incentive to stop biting his nails. ► an encouragement, a stimulus, a motivation

incident *noun*
In another incident, a pensioner was mugged in broad daylight. ► an event, an episode, a happening, an affair, an occurrence, an occasion

incidental *adjective*
The news report went on to give some incidental details. ► unimportant, secondary, minor, trivial

incite *verb*
A group of trouble-makers incited the crowd to violence. ▶ to provoke, to encourage, to excite, to stir up, to urge, to arouse, to rouse

inclination *noun*
Philip has an inclination to eat too much. ▶ a tendency, a disposition, a habit (of), a willingness, a readiness
NOTE: If you use **habit**, you have to use *of* and not *to*: *Philip has a habit of eating too much.*

incline *verb*
1 They were inclined to accept the invitation. ▶ be disposed to, be willing to
2 The door is inclined to creak. ▶ be liable to, tend to

incline *noun*
Stuart changed gear when he saw the sharp incline ahead. ▶ a slope, a hill, an ascent, a gradient

include *verb*
Does the price include VAT? ▶ to contain, to cover, to incorporate, to allow for, to take into account, to take account of

income *noun*
Her total weekly income was less than £80. ▶ pay, earnings, salary, wages
NOTE: If you use **earnings** or **wages** you need to say: *Her total weekly earnings were less than £80*, not *Her total weekly earnings was less than £80.*

incompetent *adjective*
They were too lazy or incompetent to do an honest job. ▶ useless, ineffective, incapable, inept; (informal) hopeless

incomplete *adjective*
The story is incomplete. ▶ unfinished, deficient

incomprehensible *adjective*
Their actions seemed incomprehensible. ▶ hard to understand, unintelligible, inexplicable, baffling, puzzling, mysterious

inconceivable *adjective*
It's inconceivable that anyone could swim the Atlantic. ▶ impossible, unimaginable, incredible, unthinkable, beyond belief

incongruous *adjective*
She felt incongruous in her black dress when everyone else was wearing jeans. ▶ odd, out of place, inappropriate, unsuitable

inconsiderate *adjective*
Motorists were criticized for being inconsiderate to pedestrians. ▶ insensitive (to), unkind (to), thoughtless (about), selfish (towards), heedless (of), uncaring (about)
NOTE: The words you use after these words are shown in round brackets

inconsistent *adjective*
1 We didn't know what to believe because their stories were inconsistent. ▶ contradictory, conflicting, incompatible
2 The referee's performance was as inconsistent as everyone else's. ▶ erratic, variable, uneven, changeable, unpredictable, unreliable

inconspicuous *adjective*
He tried to look inconspicuous as he hurried into the hotel. ▶ unnoticeable, ordinary, insignificant, unremarkable, unexceptional

inconvenient *adjective*
The men offered to return later if now was inconvenient. ▶ awkward, inappropriate, difficult, unsuitable, troublesome, bothersome

incorrect *adjective*
The first answer was incorrect.
▶ wrong, erroneous, inaccurate, mistaken, untrue

increase *verb*
1 *As the other instruments joined in, the noise increased.* ▶ to build up, to rise, to swell, to strengthen
2 *Traffic delays increased our journey by an hour.* ▶ to lengthen, to extend, to prolong
3 *The main bus company has increased its fares.* ▶ to raise, to put up
4 *House prices continue to increase.*
▶ to rise, to go up, to mount, to escalate

incredible *adjective*
It seemed incredible that anyone could be so generous. ▶ extraordinary, unbelievable, unlikely, improbable, far-fetched

incredulous *adjective*
She gave an incredulous little shake of her head. ▶ disbelieving, dubious, suspicious, sceptical, unconvinced

indecent *adjective*
They were accused of indecent behaviour.
▶ improper, offensive, crude, coarse, obscene, dirty, foul, impure

indefinite *adjective*
He was indefinite about how long he would be away. ▶ uncertain, unsure, unclear, vague, undecided

independent *adjective*
1 *We need some independent advice on business matters.* ▶ impartial, neutral, objective
2 *The country became independent in the 1960s.* ▶ free, self-governing; (more formal) autonomous

indicate *verb*
1 *Barbara indicated that her glass was empty.* ▶ to point out, to make known, to signal, to register, to show

2 *Red usually indicates danger.* ▶ to stand for, to signal, to signify, to be a sign of, to mean, to express, to symbolize

indication *noun*
The pile of newspapers and rows of milk bottles were an indication that the family was away. ▶ a sign, a clue, a hint, a signal, a warning

indifferent *adjective*
1 *He seemed indifferent to their problems.* ▶ unconcerned (about), uninterested (in), half-hearted (about)
2 *He is an indifferent cook.*
▶ mediocre, average, ordinary, unexceptional, moderate

indignant *adjective*
At first Anne felt indignant about Joe, but later she forgave him. ▶ angry, cross, annoyed, irritated, incensed, resentful, furious, infuriated

indirect *adjective*
We went home by an indirect route.
▶ roundabout, devious, rambling

indispensable *adjective*
A good library was indispensable to Becky to get her work finished.
▶ essential, necessary, vital, crucial

indistinct *adjective*
Mike's memory of the accident was very indistinct. ▶ unclear, hazy, dim, faint, blurred, confused, fuzzy, misty

individual *adjective*
She sings in a very individual style.
▶ distinctive, characteristic, special, particular, peculiar, personal
NOTE: **Peculiar** can also mean 'odd, strange', and so you can't always use it

indulgent *adjective*
Robin's uncle was sometimes too indulgent towards him. ▶ kind, lenient, easygoing, tolerant, patient, genial

industrious *adjective*
William is very bright, but Alex is more industrious. ▶ hard-working, conscientious, diligent, keen, enterprising

ineffective *adjective*
The boys' attempts to find the toad proved ineffective. ▶ unsuccessful, futile, useless

inevitable *adjective*
A few mistakes were inevitable.
▶ unavoidable, inescapable, certain

inexcusable *adjective*
Their behaviour was inexcusable.
▶ unforgivable, wrong

inexpensive *adjective*
The girls were looking for inexpensive earrings. ▶ cheap, low-price, cut-price, economical

infallible *adjective*
He had found an infallible cure for headaches. ▶ unfailing, foolproof, dependable, reliable

infect *verb*
Fumes from the factories infect the atmosphere. ▶ to pollute, to contaminate, to poison

infected *adjective*
The wound had become infected.
▶ septic, poisoned

inferior *adjective*
When they became poor, the family had to move to inferior accommodation.
▶ poor-quality, cheap, indifferent

infinite *adjective*
You need an infinite amount of patience to do this job. ▶ unlimited, endless, limitless, everlasting, unending, immeasurable, immense

infirm *adjective*
Those who are aged or infirm can only enjoy the park by car. ▶ frail, ill, sick, poorly

inflate *verb*
The cover can be inflated with air to form a cushion. ▶ to pump up, to blow up

inflexible *adjective*
The rules about smoking are fairly inflexible. ▶ firm, strict, rigid, invariable

influence *noun*
Tod's stepfather had a lot of influence on him. ▶ control (over), authority (over), power (over)

influence *verb*
He tried not to be influenced too much by what other people said. ▶ to affect, to sway, to control, to guide, to impress

influential *adjective*
Jack's mother was an influential business woman. ▶ important, powerful, leading

inform *verb*
I will inform you of the cost. ▶ to notify, to advise, to let you know, to tell
NOTE: If you use **tell** or **let you know**, you do not use of: *I will tell you the cost.*

inform on *verb*
He denied that he had ever informed on his friends. ▶ to denounce, to report, to complain about

informal *adjective*
The party was a pretty informal affair.
▶ relaxed, casual, easygoing, friendly

information *noun*
1 *The local paper contains information about the road closures.* ▶ news, details, reports, announcements, notices, advice, communications,

statements
2 *The Internet is a good source of information.* ▶ facts, data, knowledge

infrequent *adjective*
Her invitations to parties were becoming infrequent. ▶ rare, uncommon, occasional, unusual

infuriate *verb*
The noises in the street began to infuriate them. ▶ to anger, to enrage, to exasperate, to incense, to madden, to irritate, to annoy
NOTE: **Irritate** and **annoy** are less strong words

ingenious *adjective*
Everyone agreed it was an ingenious idea. ▶ clever, artful, shrewd, smart, cunning, imaginative, inventive

inhabit *verb*
People had inhabited the town for centuries. ▶ to occupy, to populate, to live in, to dwell in

inherit *verb*
He inherited a fortune from a distant uncle. ▶ to acquire, to be left, to succeed to, to receive, to come into

inheritance
He got a small inheritance from his uncle's will. ▶ bequest, estate, fortune, legacy

inhospitable *adjective*
They reached an inhospitable rocky island. ▶ desolate, unwelcoming

inhuman *adjective*
The treatment of the prisoners was inhuman. ▶ cruel, barbaric, brutal, pitiless, heartless, savage, merciless

initial *adjective*
Several students dropped out in the initial stages of the course. ▶ first, opening, earliest

initiate *verb*
The police initiated a widespread search of the area. (not an everyday word)
▶ to undertake, to embark on, to launch, to begin, to start, to commence

initiative *noun*
He used some initiative and found the answer on the Internet. ▶ imagination, enterprise, resourcefulness

injure *verb*
Several people were injured in the accident. ▶ to hurt, to harm, to damage, to wound
NOTE: You normally use **damage** when you are talking about things, and **wound** when you are talking about an injury caused by a weapon such as a gun or knife

inkling *noun*
Jim had an inkling that something strange was about to happen. ▶ an idea, an intuition, a suspicion, an impression

innocent *adjective*
1 *The Inspector realized he had arrested an innocent man.* ▶ blameless, guiltless
2 *They were just having some innocent fun.* ▶ harmless, inoffensive, playful, innocuous

innumerable *adjective*
The sky was full of innumerable stars.
▶ countless, numberless

inquire into *verb*
The officials will inquire into the causes of the crash. ▶ to investigate, to examine, to look into, to probe

inquisitive *adjective*
Vanessa has an inquisitive mind.
▶ inquiring, curious, interested, nosy, prying
NOTE: **Nosy** and **prying** are unkind words suggesting that someone is too inquisitive

insane *adjective*
Jill told him the idea was insane.
▶ crazy, mad, foolish, idiotic, stupid,
senseless; (informal) daft

insect *noun*
SOME INSECTS ARE:
crawling insects: ant, cockroach,
earwig, louse, woodworm;
flying insects: bee, bumble-bee, wasp,
hornet (a large wasp), fly, bluebottle,
horsefly, crane-fly (daddy-long-legs),
gnat, mosquito, midge, beetle,
ladybird, butterfly, moth, locust,
dragonfly, damselfly (small
dragonfly);
jumping insects: flea, grasshopper,
cricket
NOTE: Spiders and scorpions are not insects,
but are called *arachnids*

insecure *adjective*
*After the storm many buildings were
looking insecure.* ▶ unsafe, unsteady,
precarious, dangerous, perilous,
unstable, shaky

insensitive *adjective*
*Mandy apologized for making
insensitive remarks about deaf people.*
▶ thoughtless, tactless, unfeeling,
heartless, uncaring

insert *verb*
You have to insert a coin in the slot.
▶ to put in, to push in; (informal) to
stick in

inside *noun*
*The inside of the building was bright
and spacious.* ▶ the interior, the
middle, the centre, the core, the heart

insignificant *adjective*
*The effect of the changes was
insignificant.* ▶ unimportant, small,
trivial, negligible, minor,
imperceptible, inconsequential, trifling

insincere *adjective*
*She flashed him a gleaming, insincere
smile.* ▶ false, deceitful, dishonest,
disingenuous

insist *verb*
1 *He insisted that he was innocent.*
▶ to assert, to maintain, to declare,
to emphasize, to stress
2 *We insist on seeing the manager.*
▶ to demand (to)

insolent *adjective*
*There was something insolent about the
way he looked at her.* ▶ cheeky, rude,
impolite, impertinent, impudent,
arrogant, disrespectful, discourteous

insoluble *adjective*
The problem seemed to be insoluble.
▶ inexplicable, unsolvable,
unanswerable, baffling

inspect *verb*
*The library sometimes inspects books
when they are returned.* ▶ to check, to
examine, to look over, to scrutinize, to
investigate

inspire *verb*
*His early successes inspired him to
continue.* ▶ to encourage, to stimulate,
to prompt

install *verb*
We want to install central heating. ▶ to
fit, to put in, to set up

instance *noun*
*I'll give you an instance of what I
mean.* ▶ an example, an illustration, a
case

instant *adjective*
The suggestion was an instant success.
▶ immediate, instantaneous, quick,
rapid, speedy

instant *noun*
His words flashed through her mind in an instant. ▶ a moment, a second, a flash

instinct *noun*
The bandit had an animal's instinct for survival. ▶ a feeling, an inclination, an intuition

instruct *verb*
1 *Jill's mother instructs disabled people in swimming.* ▶ to teach, to train, to coach
2 *She instructed them to wait at the door.* ▶ to tell, to order, to direct, to command

instrument *noun*
This is an instrument for measuring rainfall. ▶ a device, a tool, an apparatus, a gadget, an implement

insufficient *adjective*
We have insufficient money for the rest of the week. ▶ inadequate, not enough

insult *verb*
He insulted her by saying she was a liar. ▶ to offend, to snub, to be rude to

intact *adjective*
Several windows were broken but two were still intact. ▶ unbroken, undamaged, whole, complete, untouched

integrate *verb*
The information will be integrated into one database. ▶ to combine, to merge, to join, to amalgamate, to unite

integrity *noun*
Among his qualities are courage and great integrity. ▶ honesty, sincerity, honour, principle, virtue

intelligence *noun*
They seem to manage with a lot of luck rather than intelligence. ▶ intellect, brains, cleverness, reason, sense, ability

intelligent *adjective*
All the students in Michael's group were intelligent. ▶ clever, bright, brainy, intellectual

intelligible *adjective*
The message was barely intelligible. ▶ understandable, comprehensible, clear

intend *verb*
Rosy intended to go and see her grandfather that evening. ▶ to mean, to propose, to determine, to be determined, to resolve, to plan

intense *adjective*
1 *The pain from the wound was becoming intense.* ▶ acute, sharp, extreme, strong, keen
2 *She looked at them with intense feeling in her eyes.* ▶ deep, burning, passionate, profound, earnest

intent *adjective*
They were intent on finishing the work in the garden before it grew dark. ▶ determined (to), eager (to), keen (to)
NOTE: With all these words, you use *to* and not *on*: *They were determined to finish the work.*

intention *noun*
Their intention was to raise the money by doing a sponsored walk. ▶ an aim, a plan, an objective, an ambition, a goal, a purpose, a target

intentional *adjective*
The joke seemed to be intentional and not just a silly slip. ▶ deliberate, intended, conscious, considered

intercept *verb*
Two sentries stepped forward to intercept the visitors. ► to stop, to check, to deflect, to head off

interest *verb*
What interested them most about the poem was the choice of words. ► to attract, to appeal to, to absorb, to engross, to intrigue, to fascinate

interest *noun*
1 *She showed a lot of interest.*
► enthusiasm, attention, concern
2 *His interests include chess and games.*
► a hobby, a pastime, a pursuit, an amusement

interested *adjective*
They all seemed interested in what they were doing. ► absorbed, engrossed, involved, intent (on)

interfere *verb*
1 *Jules always seemed to be interfering in the girls' plans.* ► to meddle, to pry, to snoop, to intrude
2 *I hope the weather won't interfere with our picnic.* ► to spoil, to hamper, to hinder, to upset

interlude *noun*
There will be a short interlude at the end of Act 2. ► an interval, a break, an intermission

internal *adjective*
We painted all the internal walls blue.
► inside, inner, interior

interpret *verb*
1 *We interpreted their signal as meaning we should walk towards them.* ► to understand, to explain, to make out
2 *The ancient writing was hard to interpret.* ► to decipher, to make out, to translate

interrogate *verb*
The police interrogated two of the men for several hours. ► to question, to cross-examine, to examine

interrupt *verb*
1 *Steve held up a hand to interrupt.*
► to cut in, to break in, to butt in, to intervene
2 *The meeting was interrupted by a disturbance outside.* ► to hold up, to disrupt, to cut short, to delay, to disturb

interruption *noun*
The discussion went on for three hours without an interruption. ► a break, a pause, a gap

intersect *verb*
The two roads intersect here. ► to cross, to pass across each other, to converge

intersection *noun*
There are traffic lights at the intersection. ► crossroads, junction, interchange

interval *noun*
1 *The women returned after an interval of several days.* ► a break, a space, a period
2 *During the interval, they went for some fresh air in the street outside.* ► an interlude, a break, an intermission

intervene *verb*
The police had to intervene to stop the argument becoming violent. ► to step in, to butt in, to interrupt

intimate *adjective*
1 *The two girls have been intimate since nursery school. The guest house was run with an intimate atmosphere.*
► friendly, affectionate, familiar, close, loving
2 *The reporter wanted to know all the intimate details.* ► personal, confidential, private

intimidate *verb*
When Jock couldn't persuade them, he tried to intimidate them. ▶ to bully, to frighten, to threaten, to scare, to terrorize

intrepid *adjective*
The snowfalls did not stop the more intrepid skiers. ▶ brave, fearless, daring, bold, courageous, heroic, valiant

intricate *adjective*
The old clock had an intricate mechanism. ▶ complicated, complex, elaborate, involved

intrigue *verb*
We were intrigued by the conversation at the next table. ▶ to fascinate, to interest

introduce *verb*
1 Anil introduced me to a friend of his. ▶ to present, to make known
2 The bus companies want to introduce higher fares. ▶ to bring in, to establish, to propose, to start, to begin, to initiate

intrude *verb*
Ben stood at the door, not wanting to intrude. ▶ to interrupt, to butt in, to break in, to interfere

intruder *noun*
The boys spotted an intruder this morning. ▶ a trespasser, a burglar, a prowler

invade *verb*
The country has been invaded by its neighbours throughout its history. ▶ to occupy, to attack, to overrun

invalid *adjective*
The permit is invalid without an official stamp. ▶ not valid, unusable, unacceptable, worthless, void

invaluable *adjective*
Their help had been invaluable. ▶ indispensable, useful, precious

invent *verb*
They are always inventing excuses. ▶ to make up, to think up, to concoct, to devise, to contrive, to create

investigate *verb*
The police are investigating a number of robberies in the area. ▶ to inquire into, to examine, to explore, to study

investigation *noun*
1 The police investigation will last for weeks. ▶ an inquiry, an examination
2 We are doing an investigation into what kind of transport people use. ▶ a study (of), a survey (of), an analysis (of), a piece of research

invincible *adjective*
The French army proved invincible. ▶ unbeatable, impregnable, unconquerable

invisible *adjective*
The factory was invisible from the road. ▶ hidden, concealed, out of sight, unseen, imperceptible, inconspicuous, obscured (by)

invite *verb*
Perhaps we should invite your friend to join in. ▶ to ask, to encourage, to urge

involve *verb*
1 Our project involves several museum visits. ▶ to include, to require, to entail, to contain
2 The Easter play involved a lot of people. ▶ to affect, to concern, to include, to interest

involved *adjective*
The plot of the play is extremely involved. ▶ complicated, complex, intricate, elaborate, confusing

irate *adjective*
A few very irate people were still waiting at the bus stop. ▶ cross, angry, infuriated, furious, enraged, indignant

irrational *adjective*
Their arguments seem irrational.
▶ illogical, unreasonable, senseless, ridiculous, absurd

irregular *adjective*
1 *In bad weather the buses tend to run at irregular intervals.* ▶ erratic, variable, odd, uncertain, random, unpredictable
2 *Holding a party on a Wednesday was highly irregular.* ▶ unusual, exceptional, peculiar, abnormal

irrelevant *adjective*
Who wrote the letter was quite irrelevant. ▶ immaterial, beside the point, unconnected

irresponsible *adjective*
It was irresponsible to let Julie walk home on her own. ▶ inconsiderate, negligent, reckless, careless, unthinking

irritable *adjective*
The flu was making him irritable.
▶ bad-tempered, grumpy, cross, angry, irascible, morose, sullen, gruff, testy, moody, short-tempered

irritate *verb*
The noise next door began to irritate them. ▶ to annoy, to bother, to make someone cross, to aggravate, to displease, to exasperate, to anger, to upset, to trouble

isolate *verb*
A small group had become isolated by the tide. ▶ to separate, to cut off

issue *verb*
1 *Smoke was issuing from the chimney.*
▶ to emerge, to flow out, to pour out, to gush

2 *The Post Office issued a special set of stamps.* ▶ to bring out, to circulate, to distribute, to give out, to print, to publish, to release, to send out

issue *noun*
1 *The January issue is published after Christmas.* ▶ a number, an edition, a publication
2 *Traffic problems were a major issue in the local elections.* ▶ a matter, a concern, a question, a topic

item *noun*
There were just a few odd items still unsold at the end of the day. ▶ an article, a thing, an object, a piece

J j

jab *verb*
The room was such a squash I kept jabbing people in their backs. ▶ to prod, to dig, to poke

jacket *noun*
The book I want has a bright yellow jacket. ▶ a cover, a wrapper

jagged *adjective*
The broken glass had a jagged edge.
▶ rough, uneven, sharp

jam *verb*
1 *I jammed my things in a suitcase.*
▶ to cram, to crush, to squeeze, to pack
2 *The street was jammed with buses.*
▶ to block, to obstruct, to crowd, to congest
3 *The window has jammed.* ▶ to stick, to become stuck

jam *noun*
They began to realize that they were in a bit of a jam. ▶ a difficulty; (informal) a fix, a tight corner, a spot

jar *noun*
A jar on the table had some dead flowers in it. ▶ a glass, a pot, a vase

jar *verb*
1 I think the impact must have jarred my back. ▶ to jolt, to jerk
2 His voice jarred terribly. ▶ to grate

jaunty *adjective*
Kay felt in a jaunty mood. ▶ lively, cheerful, alert, bright, frisky, perky, sprightly

jealous *adjective*
Jonathan was jealous of the winner, but managed to go up and congratulate him. ▶ envious, resentful, grudging (about)

jeer *verb*
Some unkind people stood by the road jeering the last few runners. ▶ to laugh at, to mock, to make fun of, to taunt, to ridicule

jerk *verb*
Tom jerked the handle hard to get the door open. ▶ to tug, to jolt, to yank, to wrench, to pull

jest *noun*
It was a silly thing to do, but they only did it as a jest. ▶ a joke, a trick, a prank, a hoax

jester *noun*
Edward's uncle was a bit of a jester. ▶ a joker, a clown, a comedian, a comic, a wit

jet *noun*
A jet of water shot right across the garden. ▶ a gush, a stream, a spray, a spurt, a fountain

jetty *noun*
A boat was tied up at the jetty. ▶ a wharf, a quay, a pier, a landing-stage

jewel *noun*
She was wearing a brooch with a bright jewel in the centre. ▶ a gem, a precious stone, a stone

jingle *verb*
Stephen ran for the bus, his money and keys jingling in his pockets. ▶ to clink, to tinkle, to rattle

job *noun*
1 They were all curious about what job this strange person had. ▶ an occupation, a position, a form of employment, a post, a profession, a trade, work
NOTE: You can also say: They were all curious about what this strange person did for a living.
2 Stella had a few jobs to do before she could go out. ▶ a task, a chore, a piece of work, a duty, an errand

jog *verb*
1 Julia jogged my elbow to attract my attention. ▶ to knock, to nudge, to prod, to jolt
2 Shall we jog round the park? ▶ to run, to trot

join *verb*
1 The string wasn't long enough so they had to join several pieces. ▶ to connect, to attach, to put together, to combine, to couple, to link, to fasten together, to fix together
2 The paths join near the river. ▶ to merge, to meet, to converge, to come together
3 Henry's mother had joined a book group and would be out that evening. ▶ to become a member of, to enlist in, to enrol in, to take part in, to sign on for

joint *adjective*
No one had time to do the work by themselves, so it had to be a joint effort.
▶ combined, collective, united, shared, common, communal, general

joke *noun*
1 *The jokes were beginning to get silly.*
▶ a jest, a gag, a trick
2 *They were too old for playing jokes on each other.* ▶ a trick, a prank, a hoax

joke *verb*
We were only joking. ▶ to fool, to be silly, to jest, to tease; (informal) to kid

jolly *adjective*
Terry was a jolly man, always smiling and joking. ▶ happy, cheerful, lively, cheery, jovial, joyful, light-hearted, merry, bright, sunny, friendly, animated

jolt *verb*
1 *An old car was jolting slowly up the road.* ▶ to bump, to shake, to bounce, to jerk, to lurch
2 *Becky jolted him as he was writing.*
▶ to bump, to jog, to knock, to nudge, to shove

jostle *verb*
We were jostled in the crowd. ▶ to hustle, to bump, to push, to shove

jot *verb*
The man jotted down a few details. ▶ to note, to write, to scribble, to take down

journal *noun*
1 *I read about it in a medical journal.*
▶ a magazine, a periodical
2 *My mother kept a journal, which she wrote by hand.* ▶ a diary, a record, a log, an account

journalist *noun*
A group of journalists and photographers were waiting at the gate.
▶ a reporter, a correspondent

journey *noun*
1 *a long journey by land* ▶ a tour, a trek, an expedition
2 *a long journey by ship* ▶ a voyage, a cruise
3 *a journey by air* ▶ a flight
4 *a short journey* ▶ a trip, an outing, an excursion, a drive, a hike, a walk
5 *a special journey* ▶ a safari, a pilgrimage

jovial *adjective*
Fortunately, their grandfather was in a jovial mood that morning. ▶ jolly, happy, cheerful, lively, bright, sunny, friendly, cheery, joyful, light-hearted, merry, animated

joy *noun*
You could see the joy on their faces.
▶ delight, happiness, pleasure, bliss, ecstasy

joyful *adjective*
The couple had a joyful wedding on a Greek island. ▶ cheerful, merry, joyous, happy, festive

judge *verb*
It's hard to judge the distance from here.
▶ to tell, to decide, to estimate, to gauge; (more formal) to assess

judgement *noun*
It was a difficult decision, but they showed good judgement. ▶ discretion, sense, reason, perception

jumble *noun*
His books were in a complete jumble.
▶ muddle, mess, clutter, confusion, disorder, chaos

jumble *verb*
I'm trying not to jumble these piles of papers. ▶ to muddle, to muddle up, to mix up, to confuse

jump *verb*
1 *When the ball came his way, Philip jumped and caught it.* ▶ to leap, to

spring, to bound
2 *The little horse jumped the fence
easily.* ▶ to clear, to go over, to vault
3 *The dogs were jumping about and
barking.* ▶ to bound, to caper, to frisk,
to prance
4 *The noise made us jump.* ▶ to start,
to flinch

jumper *noun*
*Her jumper got stuck on her head as she
tried to pull it on.* ▶ a sweater, a
pullover, a jersey

junction *noun*
*You have to turn right at the next
junction.* ▶ a crossroads, a crossing, an
interchange, an intersection

junior *adjective*
*Sally was only a junior member of the
firm.* ▶ subordinate, minor, young,
less important

junk *noun*
There was a lot of junk to clear away.
▶ rubbish, refuse, litter, mess, clutter,
garbage, trash, odds and ends, waste

just *adjective*
*The judges listened to all the arguments
so they could reach a just decision.*
▶ fair, proper, valid, honest,
appropriate, reasonable, impartial;
(more formal) rightful, right-minded

justice *noun*
*After all the hostile newspaper reports,
it was hard to believe the suspects would
get justice.* ▶ fairness, impartiality

justify *verb*
*Their bad behaviour had been hard to
justify.* ▶ to excuse, to explain, to
defend, to support

jut out *verb*
The rocks jut out above the beach. ▶ to
stick out, to project, to protrude, to
extend

juvenile *adjective*
*For adults, their behaviour seemed
juvenile.* ▶ childish, immature,
infantile

K k

keen *adjective*
1 *They are keen swimmers.* ▶ eager,
enthusiastic, avid, fervent, devoted
2 *James had been keen to sell Michael
his gerbils.* ▶ eager, enthusiastic
(about)
NOTE: If you use **enthusiastic**, you have to
say *James had been enthusiastic about selling
Michael his gerbils.*
3 *Cats have keen eyesight.* ▶ sharp,
strong, acute
4 *A keen wind was blowing.* ▶ severe,
intense, extreme, biting

keep *verb*
1 *I'll keep some money for my holiday.*
▶ to save, to put away, to hang on to;
(more formal) to retain
2 *He has a nephew who keeps chickens.*
▶ to tend, to care for, to breed, to
manage, to look after
3 *Flo kept trying, but it wasn't easy.*
▶ to continue, to carry on, to persevere
in, to persist in
4 *Keeping a family can be expensive.*
▶ to maintain, to feed, to support, to
provide for
5 *We'll try not to keep you.* ▶ to delay,
to detain, to hold up, to hinder
6 *The milk should keep for a few days.*
▶ to last, to stay fresh, to be usable

key *noun*
*The key to good writing is to know what
you want to say.* ▶ an answer, a guide,
a pointer, a clue

kidnap *verb*

Oliver was kidnapped and taken back to Fagin's house. ▶ to abduct, to snatch, to seize, to capture, to carry off

kill *verb*

1 *A man was killed in his house last weekend.* ▶ to murder, to put to death; (informal) to bump off, to do in
NOTE: You use these words about deliberate killing, not about accidents
2 *The soldiers killed an entire village.* ▶ to massacre, to slay, to slaughter, to exterminate, to butcher
3 *The President was killed in broad daylight.* ▶ to murder, to assassinate
NOTE: You use **assassinate** when you are talking about an important leader or politician

kind *noun*

What kind of food do you like? ▶ a type, a sort, a make, a brand, a category, a class, a variety, a form

kind *adjective*

It was kind of them to help us. He's a kind sort of boy, and will do anything for anyone. ▶ friendly, helpful, generous, good-natured, nice, genial, kindly, pleasant, considerate, caring, thoughtful, obliging, agreeable, warm-hearted, understanding, gracious, benevolent, compassionate, tender

kindle *verb*

1 *It was not easy to kindle the fire as the wood was damp.* ▶ to ignite, to light, to set fire to, to burn
2 *Damp wood does not kindle easily.* ▶ to burn, to ignite, to catch fire

kink *noun*

The rope has several kinks in it. ▶ a twist, a loop, a knot

kit *noun*

1 *Have you seen my games kit?* ▶ gear, a strip, an outfit
2 *A bicycle repair kit was spread all over the table.* ▶ a set, equipment

knack *noun*

It takes a special knack to get the lids off these jars. ▶ a skill, a talent, an ability

kneel *verb*

She knelt to pick up a pin. ▶ to stoop, to bend, to get down on your knees, to bow, to crouch

knickers *plural noun*

The drawer was full of knickers and handkerchiefs. ▶ pants, panties, shorts, briefs, underpants
NOTE: All these alternative words are plural as well

knob *noun*

1 *He grabbed the knob and pulled the door closed.* ▶ a handle
2 *The tree trunk was covered in hard knobs.* ▶ a bump, a lump, a swelling, a bulge, a knot

knock *verb*

In her hurry Debbie knocked her elbow against the door and yelled out. ▶ to hit, to bump, to bang; (informal) to bash

knot *verb*

The string was too short so we knotted two pieces together. ▶ to tie, to fasten, to bind, to join

know *verb*

1 *Do you know that man?* ▶ to recognize, to be acquainted with, to be familiar with, to be a friend of
2 *Jenny knows several languages.* ▶ to understand, to comprehend, to speak

knowledge *noun*

1 *She has a good knowledge of French.* ▶ an understanding, a grasp, a comprehension, a skill (in)

2 *Have you any knowledge of where they might be?* ▶ information (about), news (of), facts (about)

knowledgeable *adjective*
He is very knowledgeable about music.
▶ well-informed, educated (in), learned (in)

L l

label *noun*
One of the suitcases had lost its label, and they weren't sure whose it was.
▶ a tag, a sticker, a ticket

laborious *adjective*
Changing the light bulbs on such a high ceiling would be a laborious task.
▶ hard, difficult, strenuous, arduous, exhausting, gruelling, tough

labour *noun*
Sorting out the garden took a great deal of labour. ▶ work, effort, toil, exertion, grind

lack *verb*
The book lacks an index. ▶ to need, to be without, to be deficient in, to be short of, to miss
NOTE: You can also say *The book has no index* or *The book doesn't have an index.*

lack *noun*
In the dry weather there is often a lack of water. ▶ a shortage, a scarcity, an absence, a want, a need

lad *noun*
A lad of twelve or thirteen stood in the doorway. ▶ a boy, a youth, a young man, a youngster

laden *adjective*
An old man trudged up the road, laden with shopping. ▶ burdened, loaded, weighed down

lady *noun*
A lady got off the bus at the next stop.
▶ a woman
NOTE: The normal word is **woman**, but people sometimes use **lady** when they are trying to be polite. A young woman is sometimes called a **girl**.

lag *verb*
It was a long climb, and some of the group began to lag behind. ▶ to fall behind, to fall back, to drop behind, to straggle, to trail
NOTE: You could also say … *some of the group could not keep up.* You can use **linger** or **dawdle** when you are talking about someone who is deliberately going slowly

lair *noun*
They came across what looked like an animal's lair. ▶ a den, a shelter
NOTE: Some animals have lairs with special names. For example, a fox has an **earth** and a badger has a **sett**

lame *adjective*
1 *The man was lame and needed a walking stick.* ▶ disabled, crippled, maimed
2 *We only had a lame excuse for being late.* ▶ feeble, weak, flimsy, poor, tame, unconvincing

lamp *noun*
A lamp was burning in the porch.
▶ a light, a lantern

land *noun*
1 *The travellers reached far-off lands.*
▶ a country, a region, a nation, a state, a territory, a realm, a kingdom
2 *The land in this part of the country is rich and fertile.* ▶ the earth, the soil
3 *The house was built on a large piece of land.* ▶ estate, ground, property

land *verb*
1 *The plane is due to land in an hour's time.* ▶ to touch down, to come down, to arrive

2 *The ship docked at midnight, too late for the passengers to land immediately.*
▶ to disembark, to go ashore

landscape *noun*
The house looked out on a bleak landscape. ▶ a scene, a view, a vista, a panorama, countryside

language
1 *The article was written in clear language.* ▶ words, wording, phrasing, writing
2 *Ken speaks several languages.*
▶ (a poetic word) a tongue
NOTE: A **dialect** is a type of language spoken in part of a country. A **variety** is a form of a language, for example American English and Canadian French

lap *noun*
1 *As soon as she sat down, the cat was on her lap.* ▶ knees, knee
2 *The race takes three laps of the track.*
▶ a circuit

lap *verb*
I spilt some milk and the dog lapped it up. ▶ to drink, to sip, to lick

lapse *noun*
After a lapse of three months work began again. ▶ a break, a gap, a pause, an interval

large *adjective*
1 *a large country large buildings* ▶ big, huge, enormous, sizeable, extensive, vast, grand, massive, colossal, gigantic, immense
2 *a large helping of food* ▶ big, generous, substantial, huge, enormous
3 *a large supply of paper* ▶ big, plentiful, abundant, generous, substantial, ample, considerable
4 *a large person* ▶ big, bulky, huge, enormous, fat, strapping

lass *noun*
She was no more than a lass. ▶ a girl, a young woman, a youngster; (old-fashioned) a maiden

last *adjective*
The last prize is for special effort.
▶ final, concluding

last *verb*
1 *Our supplies won't last much longer.*
▶ to endure, to last out, to survive
2 *The journey lasts for two hours.* ▶ to continue, to go on, to take
NOTE: If you use **take**, you do not use *for* after it: *The journey takes two hours.*
3 *I hope the fine weather will last.* ▶ to continue, to stay, to endure, to hold, to persist

latch *noun*
Tom lifted the latch and opened the door. ▶ a catch, a fastening

late *adjective*
We were late because of a bus strike.
▶ delayed, overdue, unpunctual, tardy

laugh *verb*
Even bad jokes seemed to make him laugh. ▶ to chuckle, to giggle, to snigger, to titter, to guffaw

laugh at *verb*
It was unkind to laugh at them. ▶ to make fun of, to mock, to ridicule, to scoff at

launch *verb*
1 *The rocket was launched this morning.*
▶ to fire, to send off, to set off
2 *The government will launch its new campaign to reduce unemployment.*
▶ to establish, to initiate, to start, to begin, to set up

lavatory *noun*
Jo decided to hide in the lavatory.
▶ a toilet, a WC (= water closet); (informal) a loo

lavish *adjective*
There was a lavish supply of food on the table. ▶ plentiful, sumptuous, generous, copious, extravagant, abundant

law *noun*
A new law will control certain types of guns. ▶ a rule, a regulation, an edict, a decree

lawful *adjective*
1 *Public fishing in the river is not lawful.*
▶ permitted, legal, allowed, authorized, permissible
2 *I am the lawful owner of this car.*
▶ legal, rightful, legitimate

lay *verb*
1 *She laid the rug on the floor.* ▶ to put, to spread, to place, to leave, to set down, to position
2 *The conspirators laid their plans carefully.* ▶ to prepare, to form, to devise, to work out

layer *noun*
The path was covered by a layer of ice.
▶ a film, a coating, a sheet

lazy *adjective*
No one could call Helen lazy again after all she had done. ▶ idle, slack, sluggish, inactive

lead *verb*
1 *The hotel porter led the family to their rooms.* ▶ to escort, to guide, to conduct
2 *She leads a team of research scientists.* ▶ to direct, to head, to be in charge of, to manage, to supervise

leader *noun*
The leaders of several countries were at the meeting. ▶ a head, a ruler, a chief, a president, a prime minister

leaflet *noun*
A clump of leaflets came through the letter box. ▶ a brochure, a pamphlet, a circular

league *noun*
The league has twenty teams playing at weekends. ▶ an association, a group, a federation

leak *verb*
Oil was leaking from one of the pipes.
▶ to escape, to ooze, to drip, to seep, to trickle

lean *verb*
1 *The lorry leaned to one side in the strong wind.* ▶ to tilt, to slant, to incline, to list
NOTE: You use **list** when you are talking about a ship
2 *She leaned her bicycle against the wall.* ▶ to prop, to rest, to put

lean *adjective*
Fashion models tend to have lean figures. ▶ slim, slender, thin, gaunt, lanky, skinny
NOTE: **Lanky** and **skinny** are more unkind than the other words

leap *verb*
1 *The little horse leapt over the fence.*
▶ to jump, to spring, to bound, to vault
2 *The children leapt about in delight.*
▶ to dance, to frisk, to caper, to hop, to prance

learn *verb*
We learned how to tie complicated knots. ▶ to find out, to discover, to be taught, to master

learned *adjective*
The book was written by two learned authors. ▶ knowledgeable, intellectual, scholarly, educated, cultured

learner *noun*
My sister has been playing the violin for years, but I'm just a learner.
▶ a beginner, a novice

leave *verb*
1 *The man had recently left his wife.*
▶ to desert, to abandon
2 *It was soon time to leave.* ▶ to go, to set off, to depart
3 *She left her job in the summer.* ▶ to quit, to retire from, to give up
4 *I left a note on the fridge door.* ▶ to put, to place, to fix
5 *Sandra had left several names off her party list.* ▶ to drop (from), to omit (from), to reject (from)

leave *noun*
How much leave do you get? ▶ time off, holiday

lecture *noun*
The notice was about a lecture on fossils.
▶ a talk, a speech, an address

ledge *noun*
A flowerpot stood on the ledge.
▶ a shelf, a step, a window sill

legal *adjective*
Keeping wild animals is not legal.
▶ permitted, lawful, allowed, authorized, permissible

legendary *adjective*
Dragons are legendary beasts.
▶ mythical, fabulous, fictitious, invented

legible *adjective*
The doctor's writing was hardly legible.
▶ readable, understandable, clear

legitimate *adjective*
We need a legitimate reason for being late. ▶ valid, sound, good, acceptable, plausible, credible

leisure *noun*
We should get a few hours' leisure at the weekend. ▶ free time, rest, recreation, relaxation, ease

leisurely *adjective*
The family went for a leisurely stroll by the beach. ▶ gentle, slow, easy, relaxing

lengthen *verb*
1 *The curtains needed to be lengthened for the new house.* ▶ to extend, to enlarge, to make longer
2 *The days lengthen at this time of year.* ▶ to get longer, to draw out

lenient *adjective*
The judge was lenient and let them off with a warning. ▶ easygoing, forgiving, indulgent, merciful, tolerant; (informal) soft

lessen *verb*
1 *There is a medicine that will lessen the pain.* ▶ to reduce, to relieve
2 *The rain lessened towards evening.*
▶ to decrease, to ease off, to slacken, to subside

let *verb*
Toby's parents let him stay the night at a friend's house. ▶ to allow, to permit; (formal) to authorize

lethal *adjective*
A large dose would be lethal. ▶ deadly, fatal, poisonous

level *adjective*
1 *We have to play the game on a level surface.* ▶ flat, horizontal, even, smooth
2 *At half-time the scores were level.*
▶ even, equal

level *noun*
1 *The new shopping complex has several levels.* ▶ a floor, a storey
2 *James has studied French to a high level.* ▶ a standard, a grade

level *verb*
1 *The grass needs to be levelled.* ▶ to flatten, to smooth, to even out

2 *Part of the city was levelled in an earthquake.* ▶ to destroy, to flatten, to demolish

liable *adjective*
1 *They are liable to forget things.* ▶ apt, prone, inclined, likely
2 *If there is any damage you will be liable.* ▶ responsible, answerable, accountable, to blame

liberal *adjective*
1 *Put a liberal amount of sun cream on your skin.* ▶ generous, plentiful, abundant, lavish, copious
2 *Jed's mother had a more liberal attitude than his father.* ▶ tolerant, broad-minded, easygoing, fair

liberate *verb*
At the end of the war the victors liberated thousands of prisoners. ▶ to free, to release, to set free, to let out, to discharge

liberty *noun*
The country lost its liberty in the war. ▶ freedom, independence

license *verb*
A notice on the shop door read 'Not licensed to sell tobacco or alcohol'. ▶ to authorize, to permit, to allow

lid *noun*
A sell-by date was stamped on the lid. ▶ a top, a cap, a cover, a covering

lie *noun*
It became obvious that the story had been a series of lies. ▶ a falsehood; an untruth; (informal) a fib

lie *verb*
1 *Kenny was sure Stuart had been lying.* ▶ to tell a lie, to tell lies; (informal) to fib, to kid
2 *People were sitting in chairs or lying on the floor.* ▶ to recline, to rest, to sprawl

life *noun*
1 *There is unlikely to be life on Mars.* ▶ human existence, beings, activity
2 *She is full of life.* ▶ energy, vitality, vigour, liveliness, zest

lifeless *adjective*
1 *Under the rubble was the lifeless body of a small child.* ▶ dead, killed; (formal) deceased
2 *After being knocked down he lay lifeless for several minutes.* ▶ unconscious, motionless

lift *verb*
The block was too heavy to lift without a crane. ▶ to raise, to pick up, to hoist, to pull up, to carry; (more formal) to elevate

light *adjective*
1 *The suitcase was light enough for him to carry himself.* ▶ lightweight, portable
2 *We could see her clearly as she was wearing light clothes.* ▶ pale, bright
3 *A light breeze rustled in the trees.* ▶ gentle, faint, slight, moderate

light *noun*
The climbers found their way back by the light of the moon. ▶ the glow, the shining, the shine, the brightness, the gleam

light *verb*
1 *It was time to light the barbecue.* ▶ to kindle, to ignite, to set fire to
2 *The tree lights lit a corner of the garden beautifully.* ▶ to illuminate, to brighten, to lighten

like *verb*
1 *Victoria liked her friend's Mum, but thought her a bit bossy at times.* ▶ to be fond of, to admire, to approve of, to have a liking for
2 *What sort of food does he like?* ▶ to enjoy, to be keen on, to fancy, to prefer, to be partial to

likely *adjective*
It's likely that Sam will be hungry when he gets home. ▶ probable, possible, plausible

likeness *noun*
Diana had a strong likeness to one of Mary's friends. ▶ a resemblance, a similarity

limit *noun*
1 *A high wall marked the limit of the estate.* ▶ the boundary, the edge, the border, the perimeter
2 *They could invite up to a limit of twelve people.* ▶ a maximum

limit *verb*
The cost had to be limited to £100. ▶ to restrict, to keep, to confine, to curb

limp *adjective*
1 *The plants started to go limp in the dry conditions.* ▶ drooping, floppy, flabby, wilting
2 *He offered her a limp handshake.* ▶ weak, feeble, slack

line *noun*
1 *I'll tie the line to a hook on the wall.* ▶ a rope, a cord, a cable, a string, a wire
2 *The wallpaper was green with pale lines.* ▶ a stripe, a streak, a strip, a band
NOTE: You use **band** when the lines go across rather than down
3 *A line of cars headed the parade.* ▶ a row, a procession, a column, a file, a queue, a series
4 *At this point the railway line went through a tunnel.* ▶ a track

linger *verb*
I'd rather not linger out here in the cold. ▶ to dally, to wait about, to hang about, to delay, to loiter

link *noun*
There is a close link between smoking and heart disease. ▶ a connection, an association, a relationship

link *verb*
1 *There is a special fitting to link the trailer to the back of a car.* ▶ to connect, to couple, to attach, to join
2 *The police couldn't find anything to link her with the break-in.* ▶ to connect, to tie, to associate

list *noun*
1 *a list of names* ▶ a register, an inventory
2 *a list of books a list of things a shop sells* ▶ a catalogue
3 *a list of food in a restaurant* ▶ a menu

listen *verb*
It was hard to listen with all the noise going on outside. ▶ to pay attention, to attend, to concentrate, to hear

listless *adjective*
A young woman was clutching a pale, listless child. ▶ tired, weak, weary, sluggish, lethargic, feeble

litter *noun*
After the fair, the park was covered in litter. ▶ refuse, rubbish, waste, garbage, clutter

little *adjective*
1 *She lived in a little house by the river.* ▶ small, tiny, minute, wee; (informal) teeny, titchy
2 *Her son had died when he was still little.* ▶ young, small
3 *It was only a little problem.* ▶ small, minor, trivial, slight, insignificant

live *adjective*
Live lobsters were crawling about in the water. ▶ living, active

live *verb*
1 *The dinosaurs lived millions of years ago.* ▶ to be alive, to exist
2 *We live in a small apartment.* ▶ to occupy; (formal) to reside in

lively *adjective*
1 *Three lively young girls lived in the flat above.* ▶ energetic, active, animated, boisterous, high-spirited, vigorous, vivacious, frisky, playful
2 *The party turned out to be a lively occasion.* ▶ exciting, jolly, cheerful, happy

livid *adjective*
Tom could see that his father was not just annoyed but quite livid. ▶ angry, furious, cross, enraged, infuriated, irritated, incensed, bad-tempered, irate

load *noun*
1 *Donkeys carried heavy loads up the hillside.* ▶ a burden, a weight
2 *A lorry brings a load of supplies each week.* ▶ a consignment, a cargo

load *verb*
Will you help to load the van? ▶ to pack, to fill, to stack

loathe *verb*
The children all loathed Sunday evenings. ▶ to hate, to detest, to dislike

loathsome *adjective*
The people up the road had been insulting and loathsome. ▶ horrible, detestable, obnoxious, odious, revolting

lobby *noun*
There's space for a pram in the lobby. ▶ a hall, an entrance hall, a foyer
NOTE: You normally use **foyer** when you are talking about a large public building such as a cinema

local *adjective*
The local supermarket is a ten-minute walk away. ▶ nearby, neighbouring, neighbourhood
NOTE: You only use **neighbourhood** in this way *before* a noun.

locate *verb*
1 *Andy could not locate his keys anywhere in the house.* ▶ to find, to discover, to track down, to unearth
2 *The industrial park is located on the main road out of town.* ▶ to situate, to place, to position

lock *verb*
Make sure you lock the door. ▶ to fasten, to secure, to bolt

lock up *verb*
The prisoners were locked up for months. ▶ to imprison, to confine, to gaol, to shut in

lodge *verb*
1 *They lodged the visitors in a cottage on the estate.* ▶ to accommodate, to board, to house, to put up
2 *The ball lodged in the branches.* ▶ to stick, to become (or get) stuck, to become (or get) fixed, to become (or get) caught

lofty *adjective*
The family lived at the top of a lofty house. ▶ tall, high, towering

logical *adjective*
It was logical to wait for an answer to their letter before doing anything. ▶ sensible, reasonable, rational, wise

loiter
Ruth loitered in the wood, reluctant to return. ▶ to linger, to dally, to hang about, to dawdle

lonely *adjective*
1 *Douglas felt lonely and went out to look for his friends.* ▶ alone, lonesome, forlorn

2 *After a while they passed a lonely farmhouse.* ▶ isolated, secluded, remote

long *adjective*
After dinner there were some long speeches. ▶ lengthy, prolonged, endless, interminable

long for *verb*
I was longing for something to eat. ▶ to crave, to desire, to fancy, to hanker after, to yearn for, to want

look *noun*
1 *The house had a deserted look.* ▶ an appearance
2 *His look changed when he heard the news.* ▶ an expression, a face, an appearance, a countenance

look *verb*
1 *The others came in to look at what Frank had been doing.* ▶ to see, to take a look at, to observe; (not an everyday word) to behold
2 *Jerry came in, looking pleased.* ▶ to appear, to seem

look after *verb*
Our neighbours will look after the parrot while we're away. ▶ to mind, to take care of, to attend to, to care for

look for *verb*
I'm looking for my glasses. ▶ to search for, to hunt for, to seek

loom *verb*
1 *An iceberg loomed out of the fog.* ▶ to emerge, to appear, to stand out
2 *Tall buildings loomed over them.* ▶ to tower, to soar, to rise, to hang

loop *noun*
The gift was wrapped in pretty paper with a loop of ribbon. ▶ a coil, a twist

loop *verb*
The rope was looped round a post. ▶ to coil, to wind, to twist, to curl, to entwine

loose *adjective*
1 *The door handle had become loose.* ▶ wobbly, insecure, unsteady
2 *The string is too loose.* ▶ slack, unfastened, untied
3 *The dog got loose.* ▶ free
NOTE: You can also say *The dog escaped.*

loosen *verb*
Someone had loosened the ropes. ▶ to slacken, to undo, to ease, to free, to loose, to release

loot *noun*
The soldiers had taken masses of loot. ▶ booty, plunder

loot *verb*
People had no food and had begun to loot damaged buildings. ▶ to plunder, to ransack, to rob, to steal from

lose *verb*
1 *I've lost my pen.* ▶ to mislay
2 *The local team lost on Saturday.* ▶ to be defeated, to be beaten, to fail

lot *noun*
1 *She has a lot of friends.* ▶ many, plenty of
2 *You'll need a lot of money.* ▶ much, plenty of
NOTE: When *a lot of* is followed by a plural noun (*friends*) you use **many**, and when it is followed by a singular noun (*money*) you use **much**

loud *adjective*
There was loud music coming from a parked car. ▶ noisy, deafening, blaring, piercing, shrill, raucous

lounge *verb*
We lounged about, waiting for something to happen. ▶ to loaf, to loiter, to laze, to idle, to slouch

lovable *adjective*
I realized what an attractive, lovable person she was. ▶ lovely, endearing, charming, appealing

love *verb*
1 *If they love each other, why are they always quarrelling?* ▶ to be fond of, to adore, to cherish, to dote on
2 *I love doughnuts.* ▶ to like, to be fond of, to adore, to fancy

love *noun*
She showed a lot of love for her family. ▶ fondness, devotion

lovely *adjective*
1 *When she came in she looked lovely.* ▶ attractive, appealing, charming, pretty
2 *We had a lovely time.* ▶ enjoyable, fine, nice

loving *adjective*
Emma was relieved to be back among her loving family. ▶ affectionate, devoted, adoring, fond, tender

low *adjective*
1 *They are soldiers of a low rank.* ▶ junior, subordinate, inferior
2 *She spoke in a low whisper.* ▶ quiet, soft
3 *The dog let out a low growl.* ▶ deep

lower *verb*
1 *The flag is lowered each evening.* ▶ to let down, to take down, to bring down, to drop
2 *The local shops have lowered some of their prices.* ▶ to reduce, to drop, to cut, to decrease, to lessen

loyal *adjective*
Helen had been a loyal friend for years. ▶ faithful, devoted, true, reliable, constant, staunch

lucid *adjective*
The man gave a lucid description of what had happened. ▶ clear, intelligible, understandable, coherent, comprehensible

luck *noun*
1 *It was just by luck that we happened to meet.* ▶ chance, accident, coincidence
2 *What they needed was a piece of luck.* ▶ good fortune

lucky *adjective*
Keith had got the right answer by a lucky guess. ▶ fortunate, accidental, chance, happy

ludicrous *adjective*
The idea seemed ludicrous. ▶ silly, ridiculous, absurd, crazy, laughable, mad, preposterous, nonsensical

luggage *noun*
The family always took a lot of luggage on their holiday. ▶ baggage, bags, cases, suitcases
NOTE: All these nouns, except for **baggage**, are plurals

lull *verb*
She held the frightened child in her arms and lulled him back to sleep. ▶ to soothe, to calm, to quieten, to pacify

lull *noun*
There was a short lull in the motorway traffic. ▶ a break, a pause, a gap, an interval, a respite, a rest (from)

lumber *verb*
Someone was lumbering about upstairs. ▶ to clump, to shuffle, to plod, to trudge

luminous *adjective*
The clock had a luminous dial. ▶ glowing, phosphorescent, shining

lump *noun*

1 *The builder had dropped lumps of putty on the floor.* ▶ a hunk, a piece, a chunk, a dollop, a knob

2 *He fell and got a lump on his head.* ▶ a swelling, a bump

lurch *verb*

The drunken man lurched clumsily from one lamp-post to the next. ▶ to stagger, to totter, to stumble, to reel, to pitch

lure *verb*

The city wants to lure more visitors next year. ▶ to attract, to draw, to entice, to persuade, to tempt, to coax

lurid *adjective*

1 *The walls were painted in lurid colours.* ▶ gaudy, bright, startling, vivid

2 *The newspaper report included many lurid details.* ▶ sensational, shocking, unpleasant

lurk *verb*

When he went into the shop someone seemed to be lurking behind the counter. ▶ to hide, to crouch, to lie in wait

luscious *adjective*

The peaches were luscious. ▶ delicious, juicy, sweet

lush *adjective*

The room was full of lush furnishings. ▶ luxurious, rich, plush, lavish, sumptuous

lust *noun*

He was kept going by an energetic lust for life. ▶ an appetite, a passion, a longing, a desire, a greed, a hunger

luxurious *adjective*

The royal apartments were grand and luxurious. ▶ lavish, sumptuous, lavish, plush, lush, rich

luxury *noun*

They now had enough money to live in luxury. ▶ comfort, ease, wealth

M m

machine *noun*

A machine could do the job in half the time. ▶ a device, an appliance, an apparatus, a mechanism, a contraption
NOTE: You might use **contraption** if you are talking about a machine that is strange or difficult to use. You use **machinery** to mean 'a collection of machines'

mad *adjective*

1 *They must have been mad to go out in such bad weather.* ▶ crazy, stupid, insane

2 *He seemed pretty mad with them.* ▶ angry, cross, infuriated, enraged

madden *verb*

It maddened her that so much money had been wasted. ▶ to anger, to infuriate, to exasperate, to incense, to enrage, to vex

magazine *noun*

A woman in the corner was reading a magazine. ▶ a periodical, a journal

magic *noun*

1 *She didn't know whether to believe in magic.* ▶ sorcery, witchcraft, wizardry

2 *A conjuror will do some magic at the party.* ▶ tricks, conjuring

magnificent *adjective*

The view from the top of the tower was magnificent. ▶ splendid, glorious, superb, wonderful, spectacular, beautiful, gorgeous, marvellous

magnify *verb*

The picture needs to be magnified to see all the details. ▶ to enlarge, to increase, to blow up

mail *noun*

The mail comes at eight o'clock. ▶ post, letters, parcels

mail *verb*
You can order books by phone and they'll mail them to you. ▶ to post, to dispatch, to send

maim *verb*
Her eldest son had been badly maimed in a fight. ▶ to injure, to disable, to cripple, to mutilate

main *adjective*
The main reason for choosing Greece was the weather. ▶ principal, chief, primary, prime, basic, essential, foremost

mainly *adverb*
The birds mainly ate nuts. ▶ chiefly, mostly, predominantly, primarily, usually, generally

maintain *verb*
1 *The farmer has several tractors to maintain.* ▶ to keep, to preserve, to take care of, to service
2 *I maintain that travelling by train is best.* ▶ to claim, to assert, to declare, to insist

majestic *adjective*
The building was tall and majestic. ▶ grand, imposing, impressive, splendid, noble, magnificent

major *adjective*
The major roads are shown in red on the map. ▶ chief, principal, important

make *noun*
We've never heard of this make of computer. ▶ a brand, a kind, a sort

make *verb*
1 *The factory down the road makes furniture.* ▶ to produce, to manufacture, to create, to build, to construct, to assemble
2 *We don't want to make any difficulties.* ▶ to cause, to bring about, to provoke
3 *Ann and Jemima made the boys tell them the secret.* ▶ to force, to compel, to oblige, to order, to require
NOTE: If you use these words you need to use *to* after them: *Ann and Jemima forced the boys to tell them the secret.*
4 *You can make the sofa into a bed.* ▶ to convert, to turn, to alter, to change, to modify, to transform
5 *She makes money selling jewellery.* ▶ to earn, to get, to gain, to obtain, to receive
6 *Do you think we can make the 7 o'clock train?* ▶ to get to, to reach, to achieve
7 *Five and seven make twelve.* ▶ to add up to, to come to, to amount to, to total
8 *Karen needed to make an appointment to see the dentist.* ▶ to arrange, to fix

make out *verb*
It was hard to make out what they were saying. ▶ to discern, to understand, to hear, to follow, to perceive

make up *verb*
Hamish was not very good at making up excuses. ▶ to invent, to concoct, to think up

make-believe *noun*
The story is only make-believe. ▶ fantasy, imagination, pretence

malevolent *adjective*
She tried to avoid the malevolent gaze of his eyes. ▶ evil, wicked, cruel, spiteful, hostile, baleful

malicious *adjective*
Someone had been spreading malicious gossip. ▶ hurtful, harmful, vicious, nasty, spiteful, vindictive

man *noun*
A man stood by the door.
▶ a gentleman, a fellow, a male; (informal) a chap, a bloke, a guy

manage *verb*
1 *The old man leaves his sons to manage the business now.* ▶ to run, to supervise, to control, to direct, to lead, to look after, to be in charge of, to administer
2 *I think I can manage by myself for a bit.* ▶ to cope, to get along, to succeed
3 *How much work can you manage this week?* ▶ to cope with, to take on, to undertake, to achieve, to complete, to accomplish

manager *noun*
Mr Jarvis was the manager of a local building firm. ▶ the head, the director, the proprietor, the chief; (informal) the boss

mangle *verb*
The police had the unpleasant task of pulling out bodies that had become mangled in the crash. ▶ to crush, to mutilate, to injure

mania *noun*
They have a mania for board games. ▶ a craze, a fad, a passion, an enthusiasm, an obsession (with)

mankind *noun*
Mankind has been on earth for a relatively short time. ▶ human beings, humankind
NOTE: If you use **human beings**, you need to use a plural verb: *Human beings have been on earth for a relatively short time.*

manner *adjective*
1 *He looked at me in a suspicious manner.* ▶ a way, a fashion, a style
2 *He has a very gentle manner.* ▶ a disposition, a demeanour, an attitude, a bearing

manoeuvre *noun*
Getting the lorry through would be a tricky manoeuvre. ▶ a move, an operation, an exercise

manoeuvre *verb*
It would not be easy to manoeuvre the lorry down a side street. ▶ to guide, to negotiate

many *adjective*
Many people will be coming. ▶ a lot of, numerous, countless; (informal) lots of, heaps of

map *noun*
I'll draw you a map so you can find the way. ▶ a diagram, a plan

mar *verb*
The success of the party was marred by some rowdy behaviour. ▶ to spoil, to taint, to blemish, to undermine, to ruin

march *verb*
The soldiers were made to march across the square. ▶ to troop, to parade, to stride

margin *noun*
The grass was turning yellow at the margins. ▶ a border, an edge, a verge

mark *noun*
Daniel had a large greasy mark on the front of his shirt. ▶ a stain, a streak, a smear, a spot, a blot, a smudge, a trace

mark *verb*
1 *He was careful not to mark the table when he put his glass down.* ▶ to scratch, to scar, to stain
2 *Our work is marked at the end of each week.* ▶ to correct, to evaluate, to assess

market *noun*
We bought some old lamps at the local market. ▶ a bazaar, a fair, a sale

maroon *verb*
A group of children are marooned on an alien planet. ▶ to strand, to abandon, to desert, to leave, to forsake

marsh *noun*
Some of the estuary was quite good land, though a lot of it was marsh. ► bog, marshland, swamp, fen, fenland

martial *adjective*
The band played martial music. ► military, warlike

marvel *verb*
We marvelled at the height of the buildings. ► to wonder at, to admire, to be amazed by

marvellous *adjective*
What a marvellous actor he is. ► excellent, very good, outstanding, first-class, superb, fine, great, remarkable, wonderful, admirable, magnificent, exceptional; (informal) fabulous, fantastic, terrific, tremendous

mash *verb*
The dogs had mashed the flowers into the ground. ► to crush, to squash, to grind, to mangle, to pound, to smash

mask *verb*
A row of trees masked the ugly buildings behind. ► to hide, to conceal, to screen, to obscure, to cloak, to disguise, to blot out

mass *noun*
1 She stared down at the mass of papers on the kitchen table. ► a pile, a heap, a mound, a stack, a load, a quantity
2 A mass of melted chocolate had stuck to the spoon. ► a lump, a hunk, a chunk, a dollop
3 A mass of people were waiting outside the gate. ► a crowd, a throng, a mob, a large number, a lot

massacre *noun*
There had been a massacre in the village during the war. ► a slaughter, a mass killing

massive *adjective*
It took a massive effort to move the stone. ► huge, enormous, giant, gigantic, immense, colossal, mighty, vast, big

master *noun*
He was used to being the master in his own house. ► a chief, a boss, a head, a ruler

master *verb*
1 The family enjoyed living abroad, but some of them had trouble mastering the language. ► to learn, to grasp, to understand; (informal) to get the hang of
2 He found it hard to master all his feelings. ► to control, to overcome, to conquer, to suppress, to govern

match *noun*
The hockey match has been postponed to next week. ► a game, a tie, a contest

match *verb*
1 The jacket and trousers don't match. ► to go together, to blend, to harmonize
2 It won't be easy to match their achievement. ► to equal, to measure up to, to live up to, to rival
3 Choose a hat that matches your coat. ► to go with, to suit, to tone with, to blend with

mate *noun*
Keith is my brother's mate. ► a friend, a chum, a companion

material *noun*
The curtains were made of strong material. ► fabric, cloth

matter *noun*
1 We scooped a lot of filthy matter out of the drain. ► material, stuff, substance
2 It was a matter only the manager could deal with. ► an affair, a concern, a business, a subject, a topic, an issue,

a question, a thing
3 *We all wondered what the matter with Kerry was.* ▶ the trouble, the problem, the difficulty

matter *verb*
We may be a bit late but I don't think it will matter. ▶ to be important, to make a difference

mature *adjective*
He is mature for his age. ▶ grown-up, developed, adult

maximum *adjective*
The maximum number allowed in the lift is 6. ▶ largest, greatest, highest

maybe *adverb*
Maybe I'll go for a walk. ▶ perhaps, possibly

meadow *noun*
Sheep were grazing in a meadow. ▶ a field, a pasture

meagre *adjective*
The helpings look rather meagre. ▶ small, scanty, thin, sparse, inadequate, mean; (informal) measly

mean *verb*
1 *What does this sign mean?* ▶ to communicate, to convey, to express, to imply, to indicate, to say, to stand for, to suggest, to symbolize
2 *What do you mean to do? I didn't mean to hurt you.* ▶ to intend, to plan, to propose

mean *adjective*
1 *He's too mean to give a donation.* ▶ stingy, miserly, tight-fisted; (informal) mingy
2 *It was mean to send them away.* ▶ unkind, unfriendly, nasty, sneaky

meaning *noun*
Some words have more than one meaning. ▶ a sense, a significance, an explanation

means *noun*
1 *The princess had no means of escaping from the tower.* ▶ a way, a method
2 *We do not have the means to pay for an air fare.* ▶ money, resources, funds

measure *noun*
The government is taking measures to control pollution. ▶ a step, an action

measurement *noun*
The measurements of the room were written on a piece of paper. ▶ the dimensions, the size, the extent
NOTE: If you use **size** or **extent** you need to use a singular verb: *The size of the room was written on a piece of paper.*

medal *noun*
Her uncle had received a medal for bravery. ▶ an award, a decoration, a prize

meddle *verb*
Kate thought she was helping, but she was accused of meddling. ▶ to interfere, to pry, to snoop, to intrude

medicine *noun*
The doctor told him which medicine to take. ▶ medication, a drug, a prescription

mediocre *adjective*
Their new song is very mediocre. ▶ ordinary, uninteresting, unexciting, second-rate, indifferent, undistinguished

meditate on *verb*
The men spent an hour or so meditating on what had happened. ▶ to contemplate, to reflect on, to consider, to ponder on, to think about, to brood over

medium *adjective*
The suspect was described as being fair and of medium height. ▶ average, middling, middle, normal, moderate, ordinary

meek *adjective*
Patsy just stood there looking meek.
▶ docile, obedient, quiet, unassuming, gentle, modest

meet *verb*
1 *I met my friend in the park.* ▶ to encounter, to come across, to see
2 *There is a statue where the two roads meet.* ▶ to converge, to merge, to join, to come together
3 *The reading group will meet this evening.* ▶ to gather, to come together, to assemble

meeting *noun*
1 *The chairman addressed the meeting.* ▶ an assembly, a gathering, a conference
2 *The friends had another unexpected meeting the next week.* ▶ an encounter, a rendezvous

melancholy *adjective*
She had a melancholy expression on her face. ▶ sad, unhappy, dejected, depressed, despondent, wretched, miserable, gloomy

mellow *adjective*
The room is painted in mellow colours. ▶ soft, rich, ripe, pleasant

melody *noun*
She played a melody on her flute. ▶ a tune, an air, a theme

melt *verb*
1 *The ice was beginning to melt in the sun.* ▶ to thaw, to soften
2 *The crowd slowly melted into the nearby streets.* ▶ to disperse, to melt away, to fade, to dissolve, to disappear, to vanish

memorable *adjective*
The trip proved to be an enjoyable and memorable one. ▶ outstanding, notable, impressive, unforgettable

memorize *verb*
It was going to be hard to memorize the whole poem. ▶ to learn, to remember

memory *noun*
Their conversation brought back some happy memories. ▶ a recollection, a reminder

menace *verb*
The man had been menacing people in the area for some time. ▶ to threaten, to frighten, to intimidate, to scare

mend *verb*
1 *I'm not sure we can mend your bike in time for tomorrow's outing.* ▶ to repair, to fix
2 *My gloves need mending.* ▶ to darn, to patch

mention *verb*
1 *Has anyone mentioned tomorrow's arrangements?* ▶ to refer to, to speak about, to allude to, to comment on
2 *Sarah mentioned that she was meeting them later.* ▶ to remark, to say, to observe

merchant *noun*
Our uncle is a timber merchant. ▶ a dealer, a supplier, a trader

merciful *adjective*
The rebel leader was not often merciful towards his enemies. ▶ kind, lenient, forgiving, compassionate, sympathetic, tolerant

merciless *adjective*
The attack on the town was sudden and merciless. ▶ vicious, pitiless, savage, ruthless, callous, heartless, inhumane

mercy *noun*
The attackers showed no mercy. ▶ compassion, clemency, kindness, pity, sympathy, feeling, forgiveness

merge *verb*
1 *Our school merged with the one down the road.* ▶ to amalgamate, to combine, to come together, to unite
2 *The paths merge by the pond on the common.* ▶ to converge, to meet, to join

merit *noun*
Their work shows real merit. ▶ worth, value, quality, distinction, importance

merit *verb*
Philip thought his letter merited a personal reply. ▶ to deserve, to be entitled to, to earn

merry *adjective*
The music made everyone feel merry. ▶ happy, cheerful, lively, bright, cheery, jovial, joyful, light-hearted, jolly, animated, sunny, friendly

mess *noun*
There is an awful mess in the kitchen. ▶ a muddle, a jumble, a clutter, a confusion, a shambles

mess about *verb*
(informal) *Some people were messing about at the bus stop.* ▶ to play about, to fool around; (informal) to muck about

mess up
(informal) *The builders messed up the job completely.* ▶ to bungle, to botch, to spoil

message *noun*
Kate said she never got my message. ▶ a note, a letter; (more formal) a communication

messy *adjective*
The room looked drab and messy. ▶ dirty, untidy, disorderly, filthy; (informal) mucky

method *noun*
The next time he built a set of shelves he tried a different method. ▶ a means, a manner, a way, a technique, a system

methodical *adjective*
This kind of work needs people who are methodical. ▶ systematic, organized, well organized, meticulous, careful, businesslike, orderly, painstaking

middle *noun*
On the way home the boys got caught in the middle of a crowd. ▶ the centre, the midst, the core, the heart

middle *adjective*
The middle post had been knocked over. ▶ centre, central, inner

might *noun*
It took a lot of might to move away the stone. ▶ force, strength, energy, power, vigour

mighty *adjective*
He gave a mighty blow with his axe. ▶ powerful, forceful, vigorous, enormous, great, hefty, huge

mild *adjective*
1 *The weather should be mild tomorrow.* ▶ warm, calm, pleasant, moderate, balmy
2 *John's father was normally a mild man but now he looked angry.* ▶ gentle, docile, genial, placid, good-tempered, kind

militant *adjective*
The demonstrators were becoming more and more militant. ▶ aggressive, belligerent, hostile

milky *adjective*
Ruth dropped a tablet in the glass and the liquid turned milky. ▶ cloudy, whitish, misty

mimic *verb*
Comedians like to mimic famous people.
▶ to imitate, to impersonate, to copy

mind *noun*
She may be old but her mind is as sharp as ever. ▶ brain, intelligence, intellect, understanding

mind *verb*
1 *Mind you don't trip on the step.* ▶ to take care, to be careful, to watch out
2 *He doesn't usually mind if we're a bit late.* ▶ to bother, to care, to complain, to grumble, to object, to worry
3 *Will you mind my suitcase for a while?* ▶ to take care of, to look after, to keep an eye on, to watch

mingle *verb*
The pop stars mingled with the crowds.
▶ to mix, to circulate

miniature *adjective*
The shelf was covered in miniature ornaments. ▶ tiny, small-scale, minute, diminutive, small, little

minimum *adjective*
The minimum charge is £5. ▶ lowest, smallest, least

minor *adjective*
We were relieved to hear that the accident had only been a minor one.
▶ insignificant, unimportant, small, trivial

minute *adjective*
The cover is fixed on with three minute screws. ▶ tiny, small-scale, miniature, diminutive, small, little

miracle *noun*
It was a miracle they weren't all badly hurt. ▶ a wonder, a marvel

miraculous *adjective*
It was miraculous that she found her earring again after such a long time.
▶ amazing, extraordinary, unbelievable, incredible, marvellous

misbehave *verb*
All three were told off for misbehaving.
▶ to behave badly, to be naughty, to disobey, to play up; (informal) to fool about, to mess about

misbehaviour *noun*
They promised to avoid misbehaviour in future. ▶ misconduct, bad behaviour, naughtiness, disobedience, mischief

miscellaneous *adjective*
The chest was full of miscellaneous bits of old jewellery. ▶ various, varied, assorted, different, diverse, mixed

mischief *noun*
They'd got up to some mischief while their parents were away.
▶ misbehaviour, misconduct, naughtiness

mischievous *adjective*
He had a mischievous look in his eyes.
▶ naughty, playful, impish

miserable *adjective*
She went home feeling tired and miserable. ▶ sad, unhappy, dejected, depressed, despondent, wretched, melancholy, gloomy

misery *noun*
The family suffered much misery during the war. ▶ sorrow, distress, unhappiness, hardship, grief

misfortune *noun*
Our next misfortune was to break down on the bypass. ▶ bad luck, a calamity, a disaster; (more formal) adversity, a mischance, a mishap, an affliction

mishap *noun*
Wednesday turned out to be a day full of mishaps. ▶ a misfortune, an accident, a difficulty, a misadventure

mislead *verb*
They misled us into thinking we were safe. ▶ to deceive, to delude, to fool, to hoodwink, to bluff, to trick; (informal) to kid

miss *verb*
1 *Kate had missed a few things from her list.* ▶ to forget, to overlook, to ignore, to leave out, to disregard, to neglect, to omit
2 *I'll miss my friends when they go home.* ▶ to long for, to pine for, to yearn for, to want

mission *noun*
After that she made her way home, her mission a success. ▶ a task, an assignment, an errand, a purpose, an objective

mist *noun*
The fields were covered in mist. ▶ fog, haze

mistake *noun*
There are several mistakes in this report. ▶ an error, a blunder; (informal) a howler, a slip-up

mistrust *verb*
She had no reason to mistrust us. ▶ to disbelieve, to distrust, to suspect

misty *adjective*
The windows had become misty. ▶ hazy, steamy, blurred, clouded

mix *verb*
You have to mix the eggs and flour in a bowl. ▶ to blend, to combine, to whisk, to integrate

mix up *verb*
I've mixed up these papers. ▶ to jumble, to muddle, to confuse, to shuffle

mixed *adjective*
A mixed collection of paintings and photographs were hung on the walls. ▶ varied, assorted, different, miscellaneous

mixture *noun*
There was a strange mixture of things in the cupboard. ▶ an assortment, a variety, a collection, a jumble

moan *verb*
They are always moaning about the weather. ▶ to complain, to grumble, to grouse; (informal) to whinge

mob *noun*
A mob of people stood outside the gates. ▶ a crowd, a throng, a horde, a swarm, a rabble

mobile *adjective*
She always carries a mobile phone now. ▶ portable, movable

mock *verb*
The other children used to mock him because of the way he spoke. ▶ to make fun of, to laugh at, to ridicule, to sneer at, to scoff at, to jeer at

model *noun*
1 *Our car is an older model than yours.* ▶ a design, a type, a version
2 *Choose a design to use as a model.* ▶ a pattern, an example, a prototype

moderate *adjective*
Jack earned a moderate amount of money. ▶ fair, reasonable, average, middling, ordinary

modern *adjective*
The family live in a modern house on the edge of town. ▶ new, fashionable, contemporary, up-to-date

modernize *verb*
The kitchen needs to be modernized. ▶ to renovate, to improve, to rebuild, to update

modest *adjective*
1 *She was always modest about her achievements.* ▶ unassuming, humble, bashful, coy, shy
2 *The staff will get a modest pay rise next year.* ▶ moderate, small, reasonable, limited

modify *verb*
Some features of the design need to be modified. ▶ to adjust, to alter, to adapt, to change, to revise

moist *adjective*
The ground was moist and spongy.
▶ damp, wet, watery, soft

molest *verb*
A group of youths were molesting an old man. ▶ to harass, to abuse, to assault, to attack, to annoy, to pester, to bother

moment *noun*
1 *I will be with you in a moment.* ▶ an instant, a second
2 *Maybe this was the moment to mention the broken windows.* ▶ an opportunity, a time, an occasion

momentous *adjective*
A year ago today the president made his momentous decision to resign.
▶ important, crucial, significant, grave, serious

monarch *noun*
The monarch lives in a grand palace.
▶ a ruler, a king, a queen, an emperor, an empress

money *noun*
1 *I didn't have any money with me.*
▶ cash, change, notes, coins, silver, funds
2 *The family has a great deal of money.*
▶ capital, resources, income, wealth, assets

monotonous *adjective*
The work was well paid but very monotonous. ▶ dull, boring, dreary, tedious, repetitive

monstrous *adjective*
1 *The barbecue stood beside a monstrous bonfire.* ▶ huge, enormous, colossal, gigantic, immense, mighty
2 *They had committed a monstrous crime.* ▶ wicked, terrible, dreadful, evil, gross, hideous, horrible, outrageous, repulsive, shocking

mood *noun*
The next day everyone felt in a better mood. ▶ a temper, a humour, a disposition, a state of mind

moody *adjective*
The boys had been moody all week.
▶ sulky, sullen, bad-tempered, cross, grumpy, irritable, morose, melancholy

mope *verb*
People tend to mope when they haven't got enough to do. ▶ to sulk, to brood, to be unhappy

moral *adjective*
She is a very moral person. ▶ honest, virtuous, honourable, upright, just, trustworthy

morbid *adjective*
He walked quickly, his head full of morbid thoughts. ▶ gloomy, glum, melancholy, gruesome, unhappy, unhealthy

more *adjective*
Can we have more money? ▶ extra, additional, further

morose *adjective*
He came into the room looking angry and morose. ▶ bad-tempered, gloomy, depressed, moody, sullen, unhappy

morsel *noun*
He hasn't eaten a morsel of food all day.
► a bite, a bit, a mouthful, a scrap

mostly *adverb*
1 *Fortunately the walk was mostly downhill.* ► mainly, chiefly, predominantly, primarily, generally
2 *People mostly like to win money prizes.* ► usually, normally, generally

motive *noun*
Most crimes have a motive. ► a reason, a cause, a purpose

mottled *adjective*
The birds are camouflaged by their mottled brown feathers. ► speckled, spotted, spotty, blotchy

motto *noun*
Our motto has always been 'waste not, want not'. ► a saying, a slogan, a proverb

mould *noun*
The bread has mould on it. ► mildew, fungus

mould *verb*
The figures had been moulded from clay.
► to shape, to sculpt, to form, to cast

mouldy *adjective*
The cheese looked mouldy.
► mildewed, musty, rotten

mound *noun*
1 *There was a mound of potato peel in the sink.* ► a heap, a pile, a mass
2 *They laid out their picnic on a small mound.* ► a hill, a hillock, a knoll, a rise, a hump

mount *verb*
1 *The old man mounted his bicycle and rode away.* ► to climb on, to get on
2 *The excitement was mounting.* ► to grow, to increase
3 *The drawer was full of pictures ready for mounting.* ► to frame

mourn *verb*
The family went on mourning for weeks after he died. ► to grieve, to sorrow, to lament

mouth *noun*
The sea was beginning to fill the mouth of the cave. ► an entrance (to), an opening

move *verb*
1 *If we move the cupboard out we'll have more space.* ► to shift, to carry, to take
2 *When the others wanted to sit down, Tom refused to move.* ► to budge, to shift, to stir, to change position, to leave
3 *The car was moving at high speed.* ► to travel, to race, to shoot, to rush, to speed, to hurtle
4 *People were moving along slowly.* ► to walk, to amble, to stroll
5 *The dancers moved gracefully across the stage.* ► to glide, to sweep, to dance, to flow, to skim, to slide, to slip
6 *The old bus moved clumsily up the road.* ► to lumber, to lurch, to trundle, to sway
7 *The soldiers moved slowly forward.* ► to advance, to proceed, to progress
8 *The music moved them deeply.* ► to affect, to touch, to stir
NOTE: For some of these meanings you can also use **come** or **go**

move *noun*
Whose move is it? ► a turn, a go, a chance, an opportunity

muck *noun*
There was a lot of muck on the floor.
► dirt, filth, rubbish, mess

muddle *verb*
1 *So many different ideas had muddled them.* ► to confuse, to bewilder, to puzzle, to perplex
2 *Someone had muddled the books.*
► to jumble, to mix up

muddle *noun*
The room is in a terrible muddle.
▶ a jumble, a mess, a shambles, a confusion

muffle *verb*
Jenny tried to muffle her cough. ▶ to stifle, to soften, to deaden, to quieten, to suppress

mug *verb*
They were mugged on their way home.
▶ to attack, to assault, to rob, to molest

muggy *adjective*
Next day the weather was warmer and almost muggy. ▶ humid, close, oppressive, sultry

multiply *verb*
The number of houses has multiplied in the past few years. ▶ to increase, to grow

munch *verb*
She stood at the back, munching biscuits. ▶ to crunch, to chew, to chomp, to bite, to eat

murky *adjective*
The pond was cold and murky. ▶ dim, gloomy, cloudy, dark

music *noun*
SOME MUSICAL INSTRUMENTS ARE:
stringed instruments: banjo, cello, double-bass, fiddle (violin), guitar, harp, lute, lyre, mandolin, sitar, ukulele, viola, violin, zither;
woodwind instruments: bagpipes, bassoon, clarinet, flute, harmonica, mouth organ, oboe, piccolo, recorder;
brass instruments: bugle, cornet, horn, saxophone, trombone, trumpet, tuba;
keyboard instruments:accordion, barrel organ, clavichord, grand piano (large and with a long body), harmonium (small organ), harpsichord, organ, piano, spinet (small harpsichord);
percussion instruments: castanets, cymbals, drum, glockenspiel, gong, kettledrum, maracas, side drum, snare drum, tambourine, timpani (kettledrums), tomtom, triangle, tubular bells, xylophone;
electronic instruments: keyboard (with keys like a piano), synthesizer

musty *adjective*
Sarah opened a window to get rid of the musty smell. ▶ mouldy, stale, damp

mute *adjective*
He stood there, mute and terrified.
▶ silent, dumb, speechless

mutilate *verb*
The statue in the park had been mutilated. ▶ to damage, to disfigure, to deface, to vandalize

mutiny *noun*
The crew was on the point of mutiny.
▶ rebellion, revolt, rising

mutual *adjective*
They promised each other mutual help.
▶ joint, shared, common

mysterious *adjective*
The family had disappeared in mysterious circumstances. ▶ strange, puzzling, baffling, inexplicable, unknown

mystery *noun*
The cause of the death remained a mystery. ▶ a puzzle, a problem, an enigma

mystify *verb*
Toby's strange behaviour had mystified his friends. ▶ to puzzle, to perplex, to baffle, to bewilder, to confuse

mythical *adjective*
The picture showed winged dragons and other mythical monsters. ▶ legendary, fabulous, imaginary, fictional

N n

nag *verb*
Susan was determined not to nag the children. ▶ to keep on at, to pester, to bully, to chivvy, to scold

naked *adjective*
Without the towel round her she would be naked. ▶ unclothed, undressed, bare, nude, uncovered

name *noun*
What is the name of the book? ▶ a title

name *verb*
1 *They named their baby Jonathan.*
▶ to call
2 *They named Amanda leader of the group.* ▶ to appoint, to choose (as), to nominate
NOTE: If you use **choose**, you have to say *They chose Amanda as leader of the group* or *They chose Amanda to be leader of the group.*

nap *noun*
The old woman always had a nap after lunch. ▶ a sleep, a snooze, a rest

narrate *verb*
She narrated the story in great detail.
▶ to relate, to recount, to describe, to tell

narrow *adjective*
The window was tall and narrow.
▶ thin, slender, slim, fine

nasty *adjective*
1 *There is a nasty smell in the bathroom.* ▶ bad, unpleasant, horrid, foul, stinking, disagreeable
2 *The mess on the floor looked nasty.*
▶ dirty, filthy, disgusting, revolting
3 *The man had been nasty to them.*
▶ unkind, unpleasant, unfriendly, cruel
4 *They had a nasty experience in London.* ▶ bad, unpleasant, dreadful, awful, terrible, frightening

nation *noun*
Leaders of several nations came to New York. ▶ a country, a land, a state, a people

native *noun*
Jean is a native of France. ▶ a citizen, a national, an inhabitant, a resident

natural *adjective*
1 *Jackie has a natural gift for music.*
▶ instinctive, inherited
2 *Anger was a natural reaction to the news.* ▶ normal, unsurprising, ordinary, regular

nature *noun*
Everyone admired William's loving nature. ▶ a character, a personality, a disposition, a temper, a temperament, a manner

naughty *adjective*
Most of the children were good, but one or two were quite naughty.
▶ disobedient, bad, mischievous, troublesome, impish, unruly
NOTE: You can also say *... one or two of them behaved badly* or *... one or two of them were badly behaved.*

navigate *verb*
It was not easy to navigate the little boat against such a strong current. ▶ to steer, to direct, to guide, to pilot, to sail

near *adjective*
The house is near the station. ▶ close to, beside, adjacent to

nearly *adverb*
It was nearly time to leave. ▶ almost, practically, about

neat *adjective*
1 *The boys' room was small but extremely neat.* ▶ orderly, tidy
2 *Her clothes were neat and bright.*
▶ smart, pretty, elegant, spruce, trim

necessary *adjective*
It had been necessary to move the car out of the way. ► required, essential, important, needed, unavoidable, vital

need *noun*
There was no need for them to stay.
► a necessity, an obligation, a requirement

need *verb*
I needed another £10. ► to want, to be short of, to lack; (more formal) to require

needless *adjective*
All that worry turned out to be needless.
► unnecessary, pointless, unwanted

needy *adjective*
Needy people find it hard to ask for help.
► poor, deprived, destitute, impoverished, penniless

neglect *verb*
We've been neglecting the housework recently. ► to forget, to ignore, to overlook, to disregard, to shirk, to skip

negotiate *verb*
The school council negotiated a new policy on homework. ► to work out, to agree on, to conclude, to arrange

neighbourhood *noun*
We are moving to a quieter neighbourhood. ► a district, an area, a locality, a region, a vicinity

neighbourly *adjective*
Most people in this street are neighbourly types. ► friendly, helpful, obliging

nerve *noun*
1 *It needed some nerve to walk through the wood after dark.* ► courage, pluck, daring, bravery; (informal) guts
2 (informal) *Then she had the nerve to complain about our noise.* ► the cheek, the impudence, the audacity, the effrontery

nervous *adjective*
As the day of the exam grew near, I became more and more nervous.
► anxious, worried, apprehensive, concerned, uneasy, fearful, jittery

nestle *verb*
The young animals had nestled together against the barn wall. ► to snuggle, to cuddle

neutral *adjective*
It was hard to believe that the referee was entirely neutral. ► impartial, detached, disinterested, uninvolved, unbiased, unprejudiced

new *adjective*
1 *Anthony pulled out a new £10 note.*
► unused, brand new, clean, fresh
2 *We are trying to introduce new methods.* ► modern, recent, up-to-date

news *noun*
There may be some news about their friends. ► information, word, a report, an announcement; (old-fashioned) tidings

next *adjective*
1 *Charlie lives in the next street.*
► neighbouring, adjacent, closest, nearest
2 *The next bus may be ours.*
► following, subsequent, succeeding

nibble *verb*
Some sheep were nibbling the grass.
► to chew, to munch, to eat

nice *adjective*
1 *I hope tomorrow is a nice day.*
► pleasant, beautiful, fine, sunny, warm
2 *We all think Kate is a nice person.*
► friendly, likeable, pleasant, good, kind, generous
3 *Paris is a nice place to live in.*
► agreeable, pleasant, attractive, good, enjoyable

nimble *adjective*
She worked at her sewing with nimble fingers. ▶ agile, deft, lively, skilful, quick

nip *verb*
An insect has nipped my arm. ▶ to bite, to sting, to pinch

noble *adjective*
1 *She comes from a noble family.*
▶ aristocratic, high-born, upper-class
2 *The rescue was a noble deed.*
▶ brave, courageous, chivalrous, gallant, heroic, honourable, worthy
3 *The noble building on the corner was a bank.* ▶ stately, imposing, grand, majestic, elegant, impressive

noise *noun*
A loud noise came from the next room.
▶ a din, a row, a racket, a hubbub, a clamour, an uproar, a rumpus, a commotion

noisy *adjective*
The party had been very noisy. ▶ loud, deafening, rowdy, blaring

nominate *verb*
The king's brother was nominated as his successor. ▶ to appoint, to designate, to select, to choose, to name

nonsense *noun*
Everyone thought Tara had spoken a lot of nonsense. ▶ rubbish, balderdash, drivel, gibberish

non-stop *adjective*
Non-stop shouting made it difficult to speak. ▶ ceaseless, constant, continuous, incessant, uninterrupted, persistent

non-stop *adverb*
Sara talks non-stop. ▶ ceaselessly, constantly, continuously, persistently, without stopping

normal *adjective*
This is my normal route to work.
▶ usual, accustomed, regular, habitual, customary, ordinary, typical

nosy *adjective*
I'll try to find out without appearing too nosy. ▶ inquisitive, snooping, meddlesome, curious, prying

notable *adjective*
1 *Their success was a notable achievement.* ▶ remarkable, extraordinary, striking
2 *Her grandfather had been a notable politician.* ▶ famous, well-known, distinguished, eminent, prominent, renowned, celebrated, important

notch *noun*
The stick had a notch cut in one end.
▶ a cut, a nick, a mark

note *noun*
1 *Mark wrote his friends a note to thank them for their help.* ▶ a letter, a message; (more formal) a communication
2 *There was a note of anger in his voice.*
▶ a sound, a tone, a feeling

note *verb*
1 *Note everything they say.* ▶ to notice, to remember, to heed, to mark, to mind
2 *Note this in your book.* ▶ to write, to jot, to record

notice *verb*
I noticed that the car park was empty.
▶ to observe, to see, to note, to find

notice *noun*
1 *A notice had been put on the board.*
▶ an announcement, a message, a note, a poster
2 *It escaped my notice.* ▶ attention
3 *We weren't given any notice that there was going to be a fire practice.*
▶ warning, notification

notify *verb*
This letter is to notify you that you have been successful in applying for the job.
▶ to inform, to tell, to advise, to warn

notion *noun*
The notion that the earth might be flat seemed to amuse him. ▶ an idea, a belief, a concept, a theory, a thought

nourish *verb*
We need the right food to nourish us.
▶ to feed, to sustain, to strengthen

novel *adjective*
It was a novel way of solving the problem. ▶ new, original, different, unusual

novice *noun*
The computer program is for novices and advanced users. ▶ a beginner, a learner

nude *adjective*
A row of nude statues stood in the corridor. ▶ naked, bare, unclothed, undressed, uncovered

nudge *verb*
Kelly nudged him gently and grinned.
▶ to prod, to poke, to touch, to push

nuisance *noun*
The slugs in the garden are a nuisance.
▶ a pest, an annoyance, a bother, a worry, an irritation, a trouble

numb *adjective*
Our fingers were numb with cold.
▶ dead, deadened, insensitive, frozen

number *noun*
1 *It was hard to read the number on the door.* ▶ a figure, a digit, a numeral
2 *A large number of people were still waiting.* ▶ an amount, a quantity, a collection
3 *The buskers were playing old numbers from the sixties.* ▶ a song, an piece, an item

number *verb*
The crowd numbered 10,000. ▶ to add up to, to total, to work out at

numeral *noun*
The book had a date in roman numerals. ▶ a figure, a digit, a number

numerous *adjective*
There are numerous kinds of cat.
▶ many, plenty of, countless, innumerable, several
NOTE: You use **several** when you do not mean very many

nurse *verb*
Jenny went on nursing her sick mother for several months. ▶ to look after, to care for, to tend, to cherish

nutritious *adjective*
The family started the day with a light but nutritious breakfast. ▶ nourishing, wholesome

oath *noun*
Witnesses in law trials have to take an oath. ▶ a vow, a pledge, a promise
NOTE: You use **make** or **give** with these words

obedient *adjective*
Tim's an obedient boy but his brother can be quite difficult. ▶ well-behaved, compliant, dutiful, law-abiding

obey *verb*
There are a lot of rules you have to obey.
▶ to abide by, to keep to, to follow, to conform to, to submit to

object *noun*
1 *We found a strange object on the beach.* ▶ an article, a thing, an item
2 *One object of the meeting was to tell*

people about the summer camps.
▶ a purpose, an aim, a point, an intention, a goal, an objective

object *verb*
The older people objected to the noise.
▶ to complain (about), to protest (about, at), to disapprove (of), to grumble (about)
NOTE: Notice the way you use these words. For example, you would say *The older people complained about the noise* or *The older people disapproved of the noise.*

objection *noun*
We had a strong objection to the idea.
▶ a protest (at), an opposition, disapproval (of)

objectionable *adjective*
They were saying things that we thought objectionable. ▶ nasty, unpleasant, offensive, disagreeable

obligation *noun*
Anyone staying in the house has an obligation to keep it clean.
▶ a responsibility, a duty, a requirement

obligatory *adjective*
Are swimming hats obligatory here?
▶ compulsory, necessary, essential, required, mandatory

oblige *verb*
1 *We were obliged to leave.* ▶ to force, to compel, to require
2 *Will you oblige me by closing the window?* ▶ to please, to help

oblong *noun*
The garden is shaped like an oblong.
▶ a rectangle

obnoxious *adjective*
The smell from the dustbins was obnoxious. ▶ disgusting, unpleasant, foul, nasty, revolting, nauseating

obscene *adjective*
Some of the pictures were obscene.
▶ indecent, offensive, coarse, improper, disgusting

obscure *adjective*
1 *The reasons for his decision are obscure.* ▶ unclear, uncertain, confusing, puzzling, unimportant, unknown
2 *Terry's family was descended from obscure English lords.* ▶ unknown, forgotten, unimportant, minor

observant *adjective*
You have to be observant if you want to be a writer. ▶ alert, attentive, sharp-eyed, vigilant, astute, perceptive

observation *noun*
I had a few observations to make.
▶ a comment, a remark, an opinion

observe *verb*
1 *We observed Susan going into the supermarket.* ▶ to see, to notice, to catch sight of, to watch; (more formal) to perceive, to discern
2 *She observed that it was starting to snow.* ▶ to remark, to comment, to say
3 *We must observe the law.* ▶ to obey, to keep, to follow

obsolete *adjective*
Mechanical calculating machines have become obsolete. ▶ out-of-date, antiquated, old-fashioned, disused

obstacle *noun*
1 *Someone had put obstacles in the road.* ▶ an obstruction, a barrier, a barricade
2 *When you are abroad, not knowing the language can be an obstacle.*
▶ a difficulty, a hindrance

obstinate *adjective*
The man was obstinate and refused to move. ▶ stubborn, defiant, dogged, unyielding

obstruct *verb*
A fallen tree was obstructing the traffic.
▶ to block, to hamper, to hinder, to impede, to interfere with, to slow down

obstruction *noun*
An overturned lorry formed a large obstruction in the road. ▶ an obstacle, a barrier, a barricade, a blockage

obtain *verb*
Where can I obtain tickets for the theatre? ▶ to get, to buy, to acquire, to purchase, to get hold of, to procure

obvious *adjective*
The bank had made a mistake, but fortunately it was obvious. ▶ clear, unmistakable, plain, evident

occasion *noun*
1 *We need the right occasion to tell them.* ▶ an opportunity, a chance, a moment, a time
2 *The coronation was a grand occasion.* ▶ an event, a ceremony, a function

occasionally *adverb*
We all make mistakes occasionally. ▶ sometimes, from time to time, now and then

occupation *noun*
Medicine is a worthwhile occupation. ▶ a profession, an activity, a business, a job, work
NOTE: If you use **work**, you would say *Medicine is worthwhile work.*

occupied *adjective*
Everyone in the office is occupied at the moment. ▶ busy, engaged, active

occupy *verb*
1 *A young family occupies the flat downstairs.* ▶ to live in, to dwell in; (more formal) to reside in
2 *The country had been occupied during the last war.* ▶ to invade, to capture, to overrun, to take over

occur *verb*
Tell us what occurred. ▶ to happen, to take place, to come about; (more formal) to befall someone

occurrence *noun*
Burglary is a rare occurrence in our small village. ▶ an event, a happening, a phenomenon, an incident

odd *adjective*
1 *It was odd that nobody saw us.* ▶ strange, curious, peculiar, weird, funny
2 *They all agreed that Martin was a little odd.* ▶ strange, eccentric, abnormal, unusual, unconventional

odious *adjective*
We agreed that Nero was an odious person. ▶ hateful, horrible, unpleasant, detestable

offence *noun*
1 *It is an offence to use a television without a licence.* ▶ a crime, an illegal act, a misdeed
2 *Steve's remark caused great offence.* ▶ annoyance, hurt, insult

offend *verb*
I didn't mean to offend you. ▶ to hurt, to upset, to insult, to give offence to, to displease, to annoy

offensive *adjective*
Some people found his remarks offensive. ▶ insulting, abusive, unpleasant, objectionable

offer *verb*
1 *Offer them a chocolate.* ▶ to give
2 *I offered to collect her from the station.* ▶ to propose, to volunteer

offer *noun*
The children next door made a kind offer of help. ▶ a proposal, a suggestion
NOTE: You can also say *The children next door kindly offered to help.*

official *adjective*
The case held official documents.
▶ formal, authorized

official *noun*
An official came to meet us at the door.
▶ an officer, an authorized person

officious *adjective*
He heard an officious voice telling him to leave. ▶ self-important, bossy, bumptious, interfering

often *adverb*
We often go to the cinema. ▶ frequently, regularly, constantly, repeatedly

oily *adjective*
The food looked oily. ▶ greasy, fatty

old *adjective*
1 *The centre of the town has many old buildings.* ▶ ancient, early, historic, antiquated, antique
NOTE: You normally use **antique** when you are talking about valuable items that people collect, such as furniture and ornaments
2 *An old woman was waiting for a bus.* ▶ elderly, aged
3 *The book was written in an old style.* ▶ old-fashioned, out-of-date, obsolete
4 *Wear old clothes to do the painting.* ▶ worn, shabby, scruffy
5 *I went back to my old school for a visit.* ▶ former

old-fashioned *adjective*
The house had a big old-fashioned bathroom with noisy pipes. ▶ old, outmoded, dated, unfashionable

ominous *adjective*
Ominous clouds had gathered in the distance. ▶ sinister, threatening, menacing, forbidding, grim

omit *verb*
1 *Several names had been omitted from the list.* ▶ to leave out, to overlook, to forget, to exclude, to drop, to reject, to eliminate

NOTE: If you use **exclude**, **drop**, **reject**, or **eliminate**, you normally mean that something was omitted on purpose, whereas **leave out**, **overlook**, and **forget** mean that something was omitted by mistake
2 *I omitted to lock the door.* ▶ to fail, to neglect, to forget

ooze *verb*
A thick black liquid was oozing out of the crack. ▶ to escape, to leak, to drip, to seep, to trickle

opaque *adjective*
The man was hidden behind opaque windows. ▶ dark, misty, blurred, dingy, grimy, murky, unclear, cloudy

open *adjective*
1 *Someone had left the door open.* ▶ ajar, unfastened, unlocked
2 *There is a lot of open space behind the houses.* ▶ clear, broad, empty, unfenced, unused
3 *They were quite open about what they had done.* ▶ honest, frank, candid, sincere, straightforward

open *verb*
1 *Let's open a window.* ▶ to unfasten, to undo, to unlock
2 *The sale opens at 2 o'clock.* ▶ to begin, to commence, to start

opening *noun*
1 *Some children had made an opening in the fence.* ▶ a gap, a hole, a crack, a breach
2 *A guest speaker was invited for the opening of the conference.* ▶ beginning, start; (more formal) commencement

operate *verb*
1 *No trains operate after midnight.* ▶ to run, to function
2 *I realized I couldn't operate the answering machine.* ▶ to work, to use

operation *noun*
Moving house is a difficult operation.
▶ an activity, an exercise, an affair, a business, a project, a process

opinion *noun*
Della wanted to know other people's opinions. ▶ a view, a point of view, a thought, a judgement, an attitude, a belief, a conclusion

opponent *noun*
Frances turned out to be his next opponent in the chess tournament.
▶ an adversary, an antagonist, a rival, an enemy

opportunity *noun*
This evening we'll have an opportunity to go out. ▶ a chance, an occasion, a time

oppose *verb*
A group of people opposed the plan for a new road. ▶ to resist, to fight, to be against, to attack, to contest, to defy

opposite *adjective*
1 *They have opposite opinions about many things.* ▶ different, opposing, conflicting, contrary, contradictory, clashing
2 *The sisters lived on opposite sides of the road.* ▶ facing

opposition *noun*
There was a lot of opposition to the idea.
▶ hostility, resistance, antagonism, disapproval (of)

oppress *verb*
1 *The military government oppressed its opponents.* ▶ to persecute, to crush, to subdue
2 *Many of the refugees were oppressed by grief over dead relatives.* ▶ to burden, to weigh down, to crush, to deject, to afflict, to trouble

oppressive *adjective*
1 *The country has an oppressive ruler.*
▶ harsh, cruel, severe, tyrannical, unjust
2 *The weather is oppressive today.*
▶ humid, close, muggy, stifling, sultry, hot

opt for *verb*
I opted for the cash prize. ▶ to choose, to pick, to settle for, to select

optimistic *adjective*
We felt optimistic about winning.
▶ confident, hopeful, positive, cheerful, expectant

option *noun*
We did not have much option.
▶ a choice, an alternative

oral *adjective*
Your report can be either written or oral. ▶ spoken, verbal

orbit *noun*
The satellite makes an orbit of the earth every 48 hours. ▶ a circuit, a revolution

ordeal *noun*
Many tourists faced the ordeal of breaking down on foreign motorways.
▶ the distress, the anguish, the suffering, the torment, the trouble

order *noun*
1 *The general gave the order to attack.*
▶ a command, an instruction
2 *After all the fun it was difficult to restore order.* ▶ peace, calm, control, discipline, good behaviour
3 *The car was old but still in good order.*
▶ condition, a state
NOTE: If you use **state**, you say *The car was old but still in a good state.*
4 *I'll put these cards in the right order.*
▶ a sequence, an arrangement

order *verb*
1 *The general ordered the troops to attack.* ▶ to command, to instruct, to

direct
2 *If you want a newspaper you'll have to order it.* ▶ to book, to reserve, to send off for

orderly *adjective*
1 *We need to work in a more orderly fashion.* ▶ tidy, careful, methodical, neat, organized, well-organized, systematic
2 *During a fire drill, everyone needs to be orderly.* ▶ disciplined, restrained, controlled, well behaved, calm

ordinary *adjective*
1 *Instructions should be written in ordinary language.* ▶ normal, usual, everyday, familiar, plain, average, routine
2 *It's just an ordinary sort of house.* ▶ conventional, average, normal, common, nondescript, standard, unexceptional, undistinguished, modest

organization *noun*
She works for an international business organization. ▶ an institution, an establishment, a firm, a company; (informal) an outfit

organize *verb*
1 *Someone needs to organize the books.* ▶ to sort, to sort out, to arrange, to classify, to group, to put in order
2 *It's our job to organize the parade.* ▶ to plan, to set up, to coordinate, to see to

origin *noun*
The idea had its origin in a suggestion of my father's. ▶ a beginning, a start, a source

original *adjective*
1 *The original idea was to go by train.* ▶ first, earliest, initial
2 *The furniture has an original design.* ▶ new, fresh, unique

originate *verb*
Supermarkets originated in America. ▶ to begin, to start, to arise, to emerge

origins *plural noun*
The family has Irish origins. ▶ beginnings, sources, ancestry, descent, roots

ornament *noun*
The fireplace was cluttered with cheap ornaments. ▶ a decoration, an adornment, a trinket

orthodox *adjective*
They have orthodox religious views. ▶ conventional, normal, traditional, accepted

outbreak *noun*
Frank had been in Paris at the outbreak of war. ▶ the beginning, the start

outcome *noun*
All your good work has had a happy outcome. ▶ a result, a consequence, an effect, a conclusion, a sequel

outcry *noun*
There would be an outcry if the local library were closed. ▶ a row, a protest, an uproar, a clamour

outdo *verb*
Liz spent her whole childhood trying to outdo her older sister. ▶ to excel, to surpass, to beat, to exceed, to do better than

outfit *noun*
Jean chose a smart outfit for her interview. ▶ a costume, a set of clothes, a suit, a dress, an ensemble

outing *noun*
An outing to the hills would be fun. ▶ a trip, an excursion, a jaunt, a journey, an expedition

outlaw *noun*
The mountains were once the home of outlaws. ▶ a bandit, a robber, a criminal, a fugitive, a renegade

outlet *noun*
The tank has an outlet at the side. ▶ an opening, a vent, a mouth, a spout, a channel

outline *noun*
1 *The outline of buildings could be seen in the distance.* ▶ a shape, a figure, a form, a silhouette, a profile
2 *Give us an outline of your plans.*
▶ a summary, a sketch, a rough idea

outlook *noun*
1 *The house has a fine outlook towards the sea.* ▶ a view, a prospect
2 *He's very nice but he has a rather gloomy outlook.* ▶ an attitude, a point of view, a frame of mind, a perspective

outrage *noun*
1 *The last bombing outrage was in the city centre.* ▶ an atrocity, a crime, an enormity
2 *A rise in taxes would cause outrage.*
▶ anger, fury, disgust, indignation, horror

outrageous *adjective*
When he's drunk his behaviour is outrageous. ▶ shocking, appalling, disgraceful, disgusting, offensive, scandalous

outside *noun*
The outside of the building was rather drab. ▶ the exterior, the face, the front, the surface; (more formal) the façade

outskirts *noun*
We live on the outskirts of town. ▶ the edge, the fringe, (in) the suburbs

outspoken *adjective*
She tends to be outspoken when she's angry. ▶ blunt, frank, candid, direct, forthright, plain-speaking

outstanding *adjective*
1 *David is an outstanding athlete.*
▶ very good, excellent, first-class, superb, fine, great, remarkable, marvellous, wonderful, admirable, magnificent, exceptional, notable, distinguished; (informal) fabulous, fantastic, terrific, tremendous
2 *There are a lot of outstanding debts to settle.* ▶ unpaid, remaining, overdue

outward *adjective*
There was no outward sign of any trouble. ▶ visible, noticeable, external

outwit *verb*
Tom was too clever to be easily outwitted. ▶ to deceive, to trick, to get the better of, to cheat, to dupe, to fool

overcast *adjective*
The sky was grey and overcast.
▶ cloudy, dull, gloomy

overcome *verb*
I am trying to overcome my fear of heights. ▶ to defeat, to beat, to master, to conquer, to suppress

overflow *verb*
The water has overflowed. ▶ to spill over, to flood, to pour over

overgrown *adjective*
The garden was overgrown and hard to get through. ▶ wild, unkempt, untidy, tangled

overhaul *verb*
Someone needs to overhaul the car.
▶ to service, to check, to repair

overjoyed *adjective*
We were overjoyed to hear that Mary was coming. ▶ delighted, very pleased, very happy, ecstatic, elated, joyful

overlook *verb*
1 *I'll overlook your mistake this time.*
► to disregard, to forget, to ignore
2 *They have completely overlooked the problems caused by the extra traffic.*
► to forget, to miss, to leave out
3 *The house overlooks the sea.* ► to face, to look on to

overpower *verb*
In the end she managed to overpower her attacker. ► to overcome, to beat off, to get the better of

overrun *verb*
The garden was overrun with worms.
► to infest, to inundate

oversight *noun*
The phone bill was still unpaid, not deliberately but by an oversight.
► a mistake, an error, a lapse, a slip-up

overtake *verb*
Someone was trying to overtake us on a dangerous bend. ► to pass, to go past, to pull in front of

overturn *verb*
The car overturned, leaving its driver trapped. ► to turn over, to tip over, to topple over
NOTE: If you are talking about a boat, you can also use **capsize**

overwhelm *verb*
1 *During the gales the sea overwhelmed several coastal villages.* ► to swamp, to submerge, to engulf, to inundate
2 *The country was overwhelmed by invading armies.* ► to crush, to beat, to conquer, to overcome, to overpower
3 *She was overwhelmed with grief.*
► to overcome, to overpower, to shake
NOTE: If you use **overpower**, you have to say *She was overpowered by grief.*

owing to *preposition*
The ship could not leave port owing to bad weather. ► because of, on account of, thanks to
NOTE: You normally use **thanks to** only when you are talking about something good. For example, you might say *The ship was able to leave port thanks to a change in the weather.*

own *verb*
Many young students owned cars. ► to have, to possess

P p

pace *noun*
1 *Harriet took another pace towards the door.* ► a step, a stride
2 *The leaders set a fast pace.* ► a speed, a rate, a time, a tempo

pacify *verb*
Dad told Mum he would replace the broken mirror, and this seemed to pacify her. ► to calm, to quieten, to soothe, to appease

pack *noun*
It was tempting to buy an extra-large pack of cereal. ► a packet, a carton, a box, a package

pack *verb*
1 *We'll have to pack everything into a chest.* ► to put, to load, to store, to stow
2 *The stadium was packed with people.*
► to crowd, to fill, to cram, to stuff, to mob

package *noun*
The postman handed Kate a package.
► a parcel, a packet, a bundle

pact *noun*
The two countries signed a pact to control drug smuggling. ► an agreement, a deal, a treaty, an understanding

pad *noun*
1 *The seats are hard, so you'll need a pad to sit on.* ▶ padding, a cushion
2 *Everyone had a pad to write on.* ▶ a notebook, a jotter

pad *verb*
The gloves are thickly padded with foam. ▶ to fill, to stuff, to pack

page *noun*
1 *The book has pictures on every page.* ▶ a side, a leaf, a sheet
2 *The king called for his page.* ▶ an attendant, a boy, a servant

pageant *noun*
The town holds a pageant in July. ▶ a parade, a procession, a spectacle, a show

pain *noun*
Jack fell over and felt a pain in his leg. ▶ a hurt, a pang, an ache, a twinge

painful *adjective*
He was suffering from a painful wrist injury. ▶ sore, hurting, tender, agonizing
NOTE: Note that **agonizing** is a much stronger word than the others

paint *verb*
Let's paint the walls blue. ▶ to decorate, to colour

pair *noun*
The twins looked a fine pair together. ▶ a couple

pal *noun*
(informal) *Tim was a good pal to me.* ▶ a friend; (informal) a chum, a mate

pale *adjective*
1 *Tessa looked pale and had a headache.* ▶ white, pallid, pasty, colourless, wan
2 *The room was painted in pale colours.* ▶ light, faint

pamper *verb*
The baby is pampered by the older children. ▶ to cosset, to mollycoddle, to fuss over, to indulge, to spoil

pandemonium *noun*
An overturned lorry was causing pandemonium on the motorway. ▶ chaos, confusion, turmoil, bedlam, disorder

panel *noun*
The panel will answer questions about food safety. ▶ a team, a group

panic *noun*
People ran for the doors in panic. ▶ terror, alarm, fear, fright

pant *verb*
It had been a hard climb and we were all panting. ▶ to gasp, to wheeze, to puff

pantry *noun*
There was plenty of food in the pantry. ▶ a larder, a food cupboard

pants *plural noun*
Tod was wearing bright red pants. ▶ underpants, briefs, shorts, trunks, knickers
NOTE: In America, **pants** means 'trousers'

paper *noun*
1 *The box contained important papers.* ▶ documents, records
NOTE: Be careful how you use **records**, which has other meanings as well as 'papers'
2 *Have you got any paper?* ▶ stationery, notepaper, writing paper, drawing paper
3 *Today's paper has an article on the new swimming pool.* ▶ a newspaper

parade *noun*
The parade passes Meg's house. ▶ a procession, a cavalcade

paralyse *verb*
Injuries from a road accident had paralysed her. ▶ to disable, to

immobilize, to incapacitate, to cripple
NOTE: It is a good idea to avoid the word
cripple, which many people dislike

paraphernalia *noun*
*A lot of paraphernalia was cluttering up
the hall.* ► equipment, gear, tackle,
stuff

parcel *noun*
The postman handed Kevin a parcel.
► a package, a packet, a bundle

parched *adjective*
1 *The ground was hard and parched.*
► dry, arid, barren
2 (informal) *Running in hot weather
makes me feel parched.* ► thirsty,
dehydrated

pardon *noun*
*The new president issued a pardon for
all political prisoners.* ► an amnesty, a
reprieve

pardon *verb*
*Her mother found it hard to pardon her
rudeness.* ► to forgive, to excuse, to let
off
NOTE: If you use **let off**, you have to say
*Her mother found it hard to let her off for her
rudeness.*

part *noun*
1 *I've read the first part of the story.*
► a bit, a section, a portion, a piece
2 *His brother worked in another part of
the business.* ► a section, a
department, a branch, a division, a
sector
3 *The repair man is waiting for some
spare parts.* ► a component, a unit
4 *Which part of town do you live in?*
► an area, a district, a region

part *verb*
*My sister and her boyfriend have
decided to part.* ► to split up, to break
up, to separate

part with *verb*
*Lucy didn't want to part with her
melting ice cream.* ► to give up, to let

go of, to relinquish, to abandon, to
surrender

partial *adjective*
1 *We only got a partial answer to our
question.* ► incomplete, limited,
imperfect, unfinished
2 *I am partial to fudge.* ► fond of
NOTE: You could also say *I like fudge* or *I
enjoy fudge.*

participate *verb*
*He didn't want to participate in our
game.* ► to take part, to join, to be
involved

particle *noun*
Particles of dust covered the window sill.
► a piece, a bit, a speck, a grain, a
crumb, a fragment

particular *adjective*
1 *Is there a particular day you'd like me
to come?* ► special, specific, distinct
2 *I'm afraid I'm rather particular about
what I eat.* ► fussy, finicky, choosy,
fastidious

particulars *plural noun*
*Jessica brought home some particulars
about a new house.* ► details,
information

partner *noun*
Rajiv and Henry were business partners.
► an associate, a colleague, a comrade,
an ally

party *noun*
1 *A school party got on the train at
Newcastle.* ► a group; (more formal)
a contingent; (informal) a crowd, a
bunch
2 *We're having a party on Saturday.*
► a gathering, a celebration, a social

pass *noun*
Emma's bus pass was about to run out.
► a permit, a ticket

pass *verb*
1 *The parade took hours to pass.* ► to
go by, to go past

2 *Sharon was trying to pass the car in front.* ▶ to overtake, to get in front of
3 *How can we pass the time?* ▶ to spend, to use, to while away
4 *After a while the feeling of fear began to pass.* ▶ to go away, to disappear, to fade, to subside, to finish
5 *Can I pass you anything?* ▶ to give, to hand, to offer

pass round *verb*
You'd better pass round the cakes. ▶ to offer, to hand round, to distribute, to circulate

passable *adjective*
The hotel was fine but the food was only just passable. ▶ acceptable, adequate, all right, tolerable

passage *noun*
1 *A narrow passage led to the kitchen.* ▶ (indoors) a passageway, a corridor; (outdoors) an alley, a path, a pathway
2 *I'll read you a passage from a poem I like.* ▶ an extract, an excerpt, a piece, a section, a quotation

passion *noun*
My grandfather liked to indulge his passion for cricket. ▶ a love, an enthusiasm, an appetite, an urge, a craving, a desire, an obsession (with)

passionate *adjective*
He had a passionate interest in many sports. ▶ eager, intense, keen, fervent, avid, enthusiastic

paste *noun*
You'll need some paste to make your collage. ▶ adhesive, gum, glue

pastime *noun*
Painting is a popular pastime. ▶ an activity, an interest, a hobby, an amusement, a recreation, a diversion, an entertainment, an occupation

pasture *noun*
Cattle need good-quality pasture.
▶ grassland, grazing land, grass, a field, a meadow, a paddock

pat *verb*
The woman patted the child gently on the head. ▶ to tap, to caress, to dab

patch *verb*
Jean went home to patch the hole in her jumper. ▶ to mend, to darn, to repair, to sew up, to stitch up

path *noun*
The path was covered in weeds.
▶ a footpath, a pathway, an alley, a track

pathetic *adjective*
1 *The programme included pathetic scenes of refugees.* ▶ sad, tragic, moving, piteous, pitiful, touching
2 *He made a pathetic attempt to climb the tree.* ▶ feeble, weak, useless, miserable, wretched

patience *noun*
You need patience when you're looking after small children. ▶ perseverance, restraint, endurance, calmness, self-control

patient *adjective*
He tried to be patient while he waited for the phone to ring. ▶ calm, serene, restrained, forbearing, composed, quiet, tolerant

patrol *verb*
Security guards patrol the buildings at night. ▶ to guard, to keep watch over, to go round, to watch

pattern *noun*
1 *If they were going to make the clothes themselves they'd need a pattern to follow.* ▶ an example, a guide, a specimen, a model
2 *Billy lay in bed staring at the patterns the light made on the ceiling.* ▶ a shape, a design, a form, a figure

pause *noun*
There was a pause as he pulled a T-shirt over his head. ► a break, a delay, a gap, an interruption, an interval, a lull, a rest

pause *verb*
In the hall, Rachel paused at the bottom of the stairs. ► to stop, to wait, to halt, to hang back, to hesitate, to rest

pay *verb*
1 How much did you pay for your house? ► to spend, to give
2 It pays to be honest. ► to be worthwhile, to help, to be advantageous

pay *noun*
My pay has gone up this year.
► income, earnings, salary, wages
NOTE: If you use **earnings** or **wages**, you have to use a plural verb: *My earnings have gone up this year*, not *My earnings has gone up this year*.

peace *noun*
1 Everyone hopes for peace and an end to war. ► agreement, friendliness, harmony, concord
2 After the noise of the city the peace of the countryside is welcome. ► quiet, peacefulness, calmness, tranquillity, serenity, stillness

peaceful *adjective*
It would be nice to have a peaceful afternoon by the river. ► quiet, calm, gentle, restful, tranquil

peak *noun*
1 The peak of the mountain was hidden in the clouds. ► a top, a summit, a tip, a crest, a pinnacle
2 The storm reached a peak during the night. ► a climax, a height, a high point

peculiar *adjective*
1 The jelly had a peculiar taste, although it was supposed to be strawberry. ► odd, unusual, funny, strange, curious, queer, weird
2 You would never mistake Charlie's peculiar way of laughing. ► special, distinctive, individual, characteristic, personal

peel *noun*
A piece of orange peel had fallen on the floor. ► rind, skin

peep *noun*
Kim couldn't resist a quick peep in the cupboard. ► a peek, a look, a glance

peep *verb*
Someone was peeping through the keyhole at them. ► to peek, to peer, to spy, to look

peer *verb*
A man peered round the corner, and then darted back again. ► to glance, to peep, to look

pelt *verb*
On the way home the children picked up chestnuts to pelt each other with. ► to bombard, to attack, to shower, to batter

penalty *noun*
In some countries the penalty for murder is death. ► a punishment

penetrate *verb*
The bullets had penetrated the man's head and chest. ► to pierce, to puncture, to cut through, to enter

penniless *adjective*
Van Gogh died penniless because no one bought his paintings. ► destitute, impoverished, poor, poverty-stricken

pensive *adjective*
Stella looked pensive, and shook her head. ► thoughtful, reflective, serious

people *plural noun*
The room was full of noisy people.
▶ folk, individuals, human beings;
(more formal) persons

people *noun*
*The country is inhabited by a peaceful
people.* ▶ a population, a nation, a
race

perceive *verb*
1 *We perceived a reflection of the trees in
the water.* ▶ to recognize, to notice, to
discern, to detect, to see
2 *Harry perceived that something was
wrong.* ▶ to understand, to realize, to
grasp

perceptive *adjective*
*It was perceptive of her to work out who
was missing.* ▶ clever, astute,
observant, shrewd

perfect *adjective*
1 *The diamond looked almost perfect.*
▶ faultless, flawless, pure,
undamaged, excellent
2 *The painting was a perfect copy of an
old master.* ▶ exact, accurate, precise
3 (informal) *The man was a perfect
stranger.* ▶ complete, total, absolute

perforate *verb*
*The newspaper was perforated by what
looked like teeth marks.* ▶ to puncture,
to pierce, to penetrate, to punch

perform *verb*
1 *The surgeon performed the operation
on Tuesday.* ▶ to carry out, to do, to
complete
2 *They performed a play in the school
hall.* ▶ to present, to produce, to put
on

performer *noun*
*The theatre likes to give opportunities to
local performers.* ▶ an entertainer, a
player, an actor, an artist

perfume *noun*
*A delicious perfume of roses drifted in
from the garden.* ▶ a scent, a
fragrance, an aroma, a smell

perhaps *adverb*
Perhaps you'd like to come with us.
▶ maybe, possibly

peril *noun*
*You are allowed to defend yourself if
your life is in peril.* ▶ danger, (at) risk,
(under) threat
NOTE: Notice that you would say *You are
allowed to defend yourself if your life is at risk*
or *if your life is under threat.*

perimeter *noun*
*There is an electric fence round the
perimeter of the ground.* ▶ the
boundary, the border, the
circumference, the edge

period *noun*
1 *You have to make your complaint
within a certain period.* ▶ a time, a
length of time, an interval
2 *Which period of history are you
studying?* ▶ an age, a time, an era

perish *verb*
1 *Many more birds would have perished
but for our nesting box.* ▶ to die, to be
killed, to expire
2 *The tyres on the old bike had
perished.* ▶ to rot, to decay, to
disintegrate

permanent *adjective*
1 *Noise is a permanent problem in big
cities.* ▶ constant, continuous,
perpetual, persistent, chronic,
incessant, lasting, enduring,
everlasting
2 *James is looking for a more
permanent job.* ▶ long-term, stable,
secure, firm, fixed

permissible *adjective*
It's permissible to be in love with film stars when you are twelve. ▶ allowable, allowed, acceptable, permitted, proper; (informal) OK

permission *noun*
We need permission to take photographs in the museum. ▶ authorization, authority, approval, consent

permit *verb*
The council does not permit parking in the High Street. ▶ to allow, to agree to, to authorize, to consent to, to approve of, to tolerate

permit *noun*
Have you got a fishing permit? ▶ an authorization, a ticket, a pass, a warrant

perpetual *adjective*
Kim seems to be on a perpetual diet of cornflakes. ▶ everlasting, permanent, endless, eternal, ceaseless, unending, never-ending, continuous, enduring, infinite

perplex *verb*
The crime has perplexed the police for months. ▶ to baffle, to mystify, to fox, to puzzle, to frustrate, to bewilder, to confuse, to confound, to stump

persecute *verb*
People are still often persecuted for their beliefs. ▶ to oppress, to terrorize, to mistreat, to molest, to torment, to victimize, to bully, to intimidate

persevere *verb*
It wouldn't be easy and they'd all have to persevere. ▶ to persist, to keep on, to keep trying, to be patient, to be resolute, to continue

persist *verb*
1 *If you persist you may get your way in the end.* ▶ to persevere, to keep on, to keep trying, to be patient, to be resolute, to continue
2 *The rain persisted for hours.* ▶ to keep on, to last, to go on, to continue

persistent *adjective*
1 *There have been persistent rumours about a new manager.* ▶ continual, constant, repeated, endless, unending, incessant, ceaseless
2 *She is very persistent in her efforts to raise money.* ▶ resolute, determined, dogged, persevering, steadfast

person *noun*
He is a most unpleasant person. ▶ an individual, a human being, a character
NOTE: You can of course use other words such as **man** or **woman**: see the entries for those words

personal *adjective*
1 *Judy wanted her personal mug with her name on it.* ▶ private, own, individual, particular, special
2 *We have personal business to discuss.* ▶ private, confidential, intimate, secret

personality *noun*
She has a cheerful personality. ▶ a nature, a character, a temperament, a disposition

perspire *verb*
John was beginning to perspire in the heat. ▶ to sweat

persuade *verb*
1 *I'll try and persuade them to let us go.* ▶ to induce, to urge, to coax
2 *They persuaded us that they were right.* ▶ to convince

persuasive *adjective*
Our arguments didn't seem very persuasive. ▶ convincing, strong, influential

perverse *adjective*
It was perverse of him to leave so early.
▶ obstinate, unreasonable, contrary, wayward

pessimistic *adjective*
We were pessimistic about our chances.
▶ gloomy, despairing, unhappy, negative

pest *noun*
Colin was being a pest. ▶ a nuisance, a bother, an annoyance

pester *verb*
Jane was keeping quiet, trying not to pester her mother. ▶ to disturb, to bother, to trouble, to worry, to annoy

pet *noun*
Everyone could see that Mike was his grandmother's pet. ▶ a favourite, a darling

pet *verb*
Some children were petting a local cat.
▶ to stroke, to caress, to fondle

petrify *verb*
He just stood there, petrified by the noise. ▶ to terrify, to frighten, to scare stiff

petty *adjective*
They were fed up with all the petty rules.
▶ trivial, trifling, minor, insignificant, unimportant, small

phantom *noun*
The story was about scary phantoms.
▶ a ghost, an apparition, a spectre, a spirit; (informal) a spook

phase *noun*
The next phase of the building operation begins in March. ▶ a stage, a period, a step

phenomenal *adjective*
Her success had been phenomenal.
▶ amazing, remarkable, exceptional, extraordinary, astonishing, spectacular

phenomenon *noun*
Earthquakes occur, but they are a rare phenomenon. ▶ an event, an occurrence, a happening

philosophical *adjective*
He tried to be philosophical about his illness. ▶ calm, patient, resigned, reasonable, stoical, sanguine

phone *verb*
Shall I phone your mother now? ▶ to call, to ring, to telephone

phoney *adjective*
(informal) He spoke with a phoney Australian accent. ▶ false, bogus, faked

phrase *noun*
He was trying to think of the right phrase to express his feelings. ▶ an expression, a remark

physical *adjective*
1 Spirits do not have physical forms.
▶ solid, tangible, concrete
2 I need more physical exercise.
▶ bodily

pick *verb*
1 They were each asked to pick a number. ▶ to choose, to select, to decide on
2 Mary was in the garden picking flowers. ▶ to gather, to collect, to cut

picture *noun*
1 There were pictures on all the walls.
▶ a painting, a drawing, a sketch
NOTE: A picture of a person is called a **portrait**, and a picture of a large outdoor scene is called a **landscape**
2 Edward's cousin was taking pictures of the wedding. ▶ a photograph; (less formal) a photo, a snapshot, a snap

3 *I had a picture in my mind of tall forests and bright skies.* ▶ an image, an impression, a scene

picture *verb*
Stuart tried to picture his brother raking through the dustbins. ▶ to imagine, to visualize, to conceive, to think of

picturesque *adjective*
Keith wanted a holiday with more than just picturesque scenery and sandy beaches. ▶ pretty, lovely, attractive, beautiful, charming, colourful

piece *noun*
1 *Would you like a piece of cheese?* ▶ a lump, a chunk, a bit, a portion, a slice, a hunk, a scrap (= small piece), a morsel (= small piece)
2 *She fetched a new piece of soap.* ▶ a bar, a block, a tablet
3 *A piece from his watch had fallen on the floor.* ▶ a component, a part
4 *Jim was writing a piece for the local newspaper.* ▶ an article, a report, a story, an item

pierce *verb*
The splinter had pierced the skin deeply. ▶ to prick, to penetrate, to puncture, to go through, to perforate

piercing *adjective*
1 *We heard a piercing scream.* ▶ sharp, shrill, deafening, loud
2 *The wind was piercing.* ▶ freezing, bitter, biting, intense

pile *noun*
A pile of old newspapers lay on the floor. ▶ a heap, a stack, a mound, a bundle
NOTE: A **bundle** is usually a pile that has been tied up with string or paper

pile *verb*
Cathy's clothes were piled in a corner. ▶ to heap, to stack, to gather, to collect

pilfer *verb*
Sam was wearing the woolly hat he had pilfered from the garage shop. ▶ to steal, to take; (informal) to pinch, to nick

pillar *noun*
The passage had pillars on one side, and the sunlight streamed in. ▶ a column, a post

pimple *noun*
He had a small pimple on his chin. ▶ a spot, a swelling
NOTE: A **swelling** is usually larger than a pimple or a spot

pin *verb*
Someone had pinned a new notice on the board. ▶ to fix, to fasten, to put; (more formal) to attach (to)
NOTE: If you use **attach**, you have to say *Someone had attached a new notice to the board.*

pinch *verb*
1 *James turned round to see who had pinched his arm.* ▶ to nip, to tweak, to squeeze
2 (informal) *Someone has pinched my pen.* ▶ to steal, to take, to pilfer; (informal) to nick

pine *verb*
Frank was away so long the dog began to pine. ▶ to mope, to languish

pine for *verb*
We were all pining for some warmer weather. ▶ to long for, to hanker after, to yearn for, to miss

pinnacle *noun*
She was at the pinnacle of her career. ▶ the peak, the summit, the height, the top

pioneer *noun*
The museum had information about the old pioneers. ▶ an explorer, a discoverer, a settler

pious *adjective*
The priest was both learned and pious.
► devout, religious, holy

pit *noun*
There was a deep pit where the old tree had been. ► a hole, a hollow, a crater, a chasm

pitch *noun*
1 *The pitch was too wet to play on.*
► a ground, a field, a playing-field
2 *The excitement reached a high pitch.*
► a level, a strength, an intensity

pitch *verb*
1 *People had begun to pitch tents in the next field.* ► to put up, to set up, to erect
2 *A small boy was pitching stones into the lake.* ► to throw, to toss, to fling, to hurl, to cast; (informal) to chuck
3 *He tripped over the doorstep and pitched forward.* ► to fall, to tumble, to lurch, to plunge

pitiful *adjective*
1 *After a few days lost on the moors he had become a pitiful sight.* ► wretched, pathetic, piteous, dreadful, sad
2 *It was a pitiful attempt to put things right.* ► feeble, weak, miserable, useless

pitiless *adjective*
He had behaved like a pitiless tyrant.
► cruel, callous, heartless, ruthless, bloodthirsty

pity *noun*
1 *The attackers show no pity for their victims.* ► feeling, sympathy, compassion, mercy
2 *It's a pity they can't come.* ► a shame

pity *verb*
It was hard not to pity them. ► to sympathize with, to feel pity for, to feel sorry for, to feel for

place *noun*
1 *The place was clearly marked on the map.* ► a location, a point, a position, a spot, a locality, a region, an area
2 *Jill lived in a small place in the country.* ► a house, a property, a residence
3 *The table has places for twelve people.*
► a seat, a chair, a setting

place *verb*
Kim placed a hand gently on his arm.
► to put, to lay, to rest, to set

placid *adjective*
Jennifer was normally placid but it did not seem a good idea to provoke her.
► mild, calm, peaceful, quiet, gentle

plague *noun*
1 *A plague broke out in the city.* ► an epidemic, a pestilence
2 *A plague of locusts hit the country.*
► a swarm, a host; (more formal) an infestation

plague *verb*
Sophie was plagued all day by her younger brothers. ► to pester, to disturb, to bother, to annoy, to trouble

plain *adjective*
1 *It was plain that they wanted to come.*
► clear, obvious, apparent, evident, unmistakable
2 *The walls were covered in plain wallpaper.* ► simple, bare, austere, undecorated
3 *This is the plain truth.* ► clear, simple, straightforward, honest, blunt, candid

plaintive *adjective*
The dog gave a plaintive cry. ► sad, sorrowful, doleful, melancholy

plan *noun*
1 *The plan is to meet in town tomorrow afternoon.* ► a scheme, an idea, a

proposal, an intention, an
arrangement
2 *We'll need to get a plan of the city to
find our way around.* ▶ a map, a chart,
a diagram

plan *verb*

1 *The group planned to meet in town the
next day.* ▶ to intend, to propose, to
aim, to plot
2 *We need to plan the journey carefully.*
▶ to organize, to prepare, to arrange,
to work out, to think out

plant *noun*

TYPES OF PLANTS ARE:

plants that produce seeds (with roots,
stems, and leaves, and having either
flowers or cones): some well-known
plants that produce flowers are
acanthus, African violet, alyssum,
anemone, aspidistra, aster, aubrietia
(pronounced or-bree-sha), azalea,
begonia, bluebell, buddleia
(pronounced budd-li-a), busy Lizzie,
buttercup, camellia (pronounced ka-
mee-li-a), carnation, chrysanthemum,
clematis, clover, cowslip, crocus,
cyclamen, daffodil, dahlia, daisy,
dandelion, deadly nightshade,
delphinium, edelweiss, forget-me-not,
forsythia (pronounced with the *y* to
rhyme with eye), foxglove, freesia,
fuchsia (pronounced fyoo-sha),
geranium, gladiolus, harebell, heather,
hibiscus, hollyhock, honeysuckle,
hyacinth, hydrangea (pronounced hie-
drayn-ja), iris, japonica, jasmine,
laburnum, lavender, lilac, lily, lily of
the valley, lobelia, lotus, lupin,
magnolia, marigold, mayflower,
meadowsweet, mimosa, mistletoe,
narcissus, nasturtium, oleander
(pronounced olly-an-der), orchid,
pansy, peony, petunia, phlox, pink,
poinsettia, polyanthus, poppy,
primrose, primula, pyracantha,

rhododendron, rose, sage, shamrock,
snapdragon, snowdrop, sorrel, spider
plant, stock, sunflower, sweet pea,
sweet william, thistle, tulip, verbena,
violet, wallflower, water lily, wisteria,
zinnia

algae (with no roots, stems, or leaves,
and producing tiny cells called spores
instead of seeds): for example various
kinds of seaweed;
mosses and liverworts (with simple
leaves, and producing spores);
ferns (with roots, stems, and leaves,
and producing spores)

plant *verb*

*The children wanted to plant their seeds
in the garden.* ▶ to sow, to put in the
ground

plaster *noun*

Jackie needed a plaster on her cut.
▶ a dressing, a sticking plaster

plate *noun*

1 *The waiter arrived with a load of
plates.* ▶ a dish, a platter
2 *The book has colour plates.* ▶ an
illustration, a picture, a photograph

platform *noun*

*The woman went to the platform and
started to speak.* ▶ a stage, a podium,
a dais

plausible *adjective*

Their excuse was not very plausible.
▶ convincing, likely, believable,
credible, reasonable

play *noun*

There is a short morning break for play.
▶ fun, amusement, recreation

play *verb*

1 *The children were playing happily.*
▶ to have fun, to enjoy yourself, to
amuse yourself
2 *The band played a dance tune.* ▶ to
perform

play up *verb*
Some people began to play up at the back of the room. ▶ to misbehave, to fool about, to be naughty, to make trouble; (informal) to mess about, to muck about

player *noun*
1 The game is for four players. ▶ a competitor, a contestant, a participant
2 There are twenty players in the orchestra. ▶ a performer, a musician, an instrumentalist

playful *adjective*
1 A playful young dog wobbled into the room. ▶ lively, frisky, active, skittish, spirited, vivacious
2 Gary gave me a playful punch on the shoulder. ▶ friendly, teasing, good-natured, light-hearted, jokey

plea *noun*
The villagers made a plea for help after the floods. ▶ an appeal, a request, a petition, an entreaty

plead *verb*
The captives pleaded to be released. ▶ to beg, to appeal, to implore, to entreat, to beseech
NOTE: If you use **implore**, **entreat**, or **beseech**, you have to include a person or people after it, for example The captives implored their jailers to release them.

pleasant *adjective*
1 The hotel was warm and pleasant. We had a pleasant outing to a theme park. ▶ lovely, agreeable, enjoyable, comfortable, delightful, attractive, satisfying
2 Hugh's father was a jolly, pleasant sort of man. ▶ friendly, kind, genial, nice, likeable, amiable, agreeable

please *verb*
Thomas pleased his grandmother by sending her a postcard. ▶ to delight, to gladden, to make happy, to gratify, to content, to satisfy

pleased *adjective*
Carol came in looking pleased. ▶ glad, happy, content, satisfied

pleasure *noun*
1 Carla smiled with pleasure. ▶ happiness, enjoyment, joy, delight, bliss, ecstasy, satisfaction
2 One of her pleasures was playing her flute. ▶ a delight, an amusement, a diversion, an entertainment, a recreation

pledge *noun*
They gave a pledge that they would return. ▶ a promise, an assurance, a guarantee, a vow, an oath, your word
NOTE: If you use **word**, you have to say They gave their word that they would return.

pledge *verb*
They pledged their support for the rebels. ▶ to promise, to vow

plentiful *adjective*
We have a plentiful supply of food. ▶ large, ample, abundant, profuse, liberal, copious, generous, lavish

plenty of *noun*
We have plenty of chairs. ▶ a lot (of), enough

pliable *adjective*
The wire was tough but pliable. ▶ flexible, springy, bendable, supple, easy to bend

plight *noun*
They were stranded for several days before anyone knew of their plight. ▶ a difficulty, a predicament, trouble, straits

plod *verb*
Two of them plodded through the snow to find help. ▶ to trudge, to tramp, to clump

plot *noun*
1 Some soldiers planned a plot against the king. ▶ a conspiracy, an intrigue, a plan, a scheme
2 The plot of the play is quite simple. ▶ a story, a narrative, an outline
3 Sam had a vegetable plot at the end of the garden. ▶ a patch, a bed, an allotment

plot *verb*
A group of army officers plotted to overthrow the government. ▶ to conspire, to scheme, to plan

pluck *noun*
(informal) It took a lot of pluck for her to speak out like that. ▶ courage, determination, daring, audacity, nerve, spirit; (informal) guts, grit

pluck *verb*
1 The young man plucked a rose and handed it to her. ▶ to pick, to take, to pull off
2 Martha plucked her keys from the table and rushed out. ▶ to snatch, to grab, to seize

plug *noun*
The barrel had a large plug at the bottom. ▶ a bung, a stopper, a cork

plug *verb*
1 A piece of putty will plug the hole in the window. ▶ to stop, to stop up, to block up, to close, to fill, to seal
2 (informal) He's only on the show to plug his new film. ´▶ to publicize, to promote, to advertise

plump *adjective*
A jolly man with a plump figure appeared in the door. ▶ stout, podgy, portly, chubby, tubby, dumpy, fat

plunder *verb*
Rioters had plundered most of the grocery stores. ▶ to loot, to raid, to ransack, to ravage, to rob, to steal (from)

plunder *noun*
The soldiers took a lot of plunder back to their camp. ▶ booty, loot, spoils

plunge *verb*
1 Holly ran to the pool and plunged into the deep end. ▶ to dive, to leap
2 You have to plunge the hot metal into water. ▶ to immerse, to submerge, to thrust
3 The killer plunged a knife into the victim's back. ▶ to thrust, to force, to push

podgy *adjective*
The woman was short and podgy.
▶ plump, chubby, dumpy, fat, portly, squat

poem *noun*
I read a poem about a mouse. ▶ a verse, a rhyme, an ode
NOTE: A long poem that tells a story is called a **ballad**. A short poem addressed to someone is called an **ode**. A special kind of romantic poem with fourteen lines is called a **sonnet**.

point *noun*
1 Mark prodded a pea with the point of his knife. ▶ the tip, the end
2 We meet at this point on the map. ▶ a spot, a place, a location, a position
3 They gave up at that point. ▶ a time, a moment, a stage; (more formal) a juncture
4 The point of the game is to finish with no cards. ▶ the aim, the object, the idea, the purpose, the intention

point *verb*
She pointed a gun at us. ▶ to aim, to direct, to level

point out *verb*
Our guide pointed out the spot where the president had been killed. ▶ to indicate, to show, to identify

pointless *adjective*
It would be pointless to argue with them. ▶ futile, useless, fruitless, senseless

poise *noun*
1 *The dancers have great beauty and poise.* ▶ balance, control, grace, calmness, equilibrium, self-confidence, self-control, steadiness
2 *She retained her poise despite the difficulties.* ▶ calm, self-control, composure, dignity, equanimity

poisonous *adjective*
Toadstools are poisonous. ▶ toxic, lethal, deadly, fatal

poke *verb*
1 *Someone poked me in my back.*
▶ to prod, to dig, to jab
2 *Hilary poked a key into the lock.*
▶ to stick, to thrust

pole *noun*
The fence was supported by tall poles.
▶ a post, a column

policy *noun*
The government has a new policy on education. ▶ a plan, a strategy, an approach

polish *noun*
The liquid that Meg spilt on the table had spoilt its polish. ▶ gloss, shine, sheen, brightness, smoothness, glossiness, lustre

polish *verb*
Will you polish the table? ▶ to shine, to buff, to rub

polite *adjective*
1 *He received a polite reply to his letter of complaint.* ▶ courteous,
considerate, civil, thoughtful, respectful
2 *Kevin shocked everyone when he swore, as he was usually so polite.*
▶ civil, well-mannered, courteous, respectful

poll *noun*
The result of the poll will be known by midnight. ▶ an election, a ballot, a vote

pollute *verb*
Oil has polluted a long stretch of the coastline. ▶ to contaminate, to infect, to foul, to poison

pomp *noun*
The royal wedding had all the pomp you would expect. ▶ solemnity, pageantry, splendour, glory, ceremony, magnificence, majesty, show

pompous *adjective*
Adam seemed rather dull and pompous.
▶ self-important, arrogant, haughty; (informal) stuck-up

ponder *verb*
We pondered long and hard about what to do. ▶ to think, to reflect, to consider, to deliberate

pool *noun*
The firm has a pool of cars that people can use. ▶ a supply, a collection, a group

poor *adjective*
1 *There are a lot of poor people in this area.* ▶ needy, badly off, deprived, penniless, destitute, hard up
2 *Their work has been poor.* ▶ inferior, inadequate, unsatisfactory, deficient, faulty, mediocre, shoddy, bad
3 *Poor Jill's got flu.* ▶ unfortunate, wretched, pitiful, unlucky

poorly *adjective*
I felt poorly and stayed at home.
▶ unwell, sick, ill, indisposed

pop *verb*
1 *Guns were popping everywhere.* ▶ to bang, to go off, to explode
2 (informal) *I'd better pop the milk in the fridge.* ▶ to put, to stick, to slip

popular *adjective*
The conjuror is always popular at parties. ▶ well-liked, favourite, in demand

port *noun*
The ship came slowly into the port. ▶ a harbour, a dock

portable *adjective*
The man was carrying a portable computer. ▶ lightweight, compact

portion *noun*
The food was good but the portions were small. ▶ a helping, a share, an amount

portrait *noun*
A portrait of their grandfather hung on the wall. ▶ a likeness, a picture, a painting, a representation

portray *verb*
The article portrayed her as a selfish and uncaring woman. ▶ to depict, to picture, to represent, to describe, to show

pose *verb*
1 *The man was posing as a police officer.* ▶ to impersonate, to pretend to be
2 *I'd like to pose a question.* ▶ to ask, to suggest, to put forward

posh *adjective*
(informal) *Gemma's friend lived in a posh house.* ▶ smart, grand, elegant, rich, fancy

position *noun*
1 *The house is in a convenient position.* ▶ a location, a locality, a situation, a place, a point, a spot
2 *Graham was looking for a position in the local newspaper office.* ▶ a job, a

post, an appointment, employment, work
3 *He was in a sitting position.* ▶ a posture, a pose

positive *adjective*
1 *I am positive I saw them.* ▶ sure, certain, definite, convinced, confident
2 *Do you have positive proof?* ▶ real, definite, absolute

possess *verb*
I have no wish to possess a computer. ▶ to own, to get, to have

possessions *plural noun*
Jack's aunt had a lot of possessions. ▶ belongings, property, goods

possibility *noun*
There's the possibility of snow later. ▶ a chance, a likelihood

possible *adjective*
1 *It is possible that they have left already.* ▶ conceivable, feasible, imaginable
2 *There is no possible way of doing this.* ▶ feasible, practical, workable

possibly *adverb*
They could possibly arrive tomorrow. ▶ perhaps, maybe

post *noun*
1 *The fence is supported by concrete posts.* ▶ a pole, a stake, a column
2 *Graham was looking for a post in the local newspaper office.* ▶ a job, a position, an appointment, employment, work
3 *The post is late today.* ▶ the mail

poster *noun*
The tree had a poster on it about the circus. ▶ a notice, a placard, an advertisement, a sign

postpone *verb*
We have had to postpone our holiday.
▶ to delay, to put off, to adjourn, to defer

potential *adjective*
He's so good he's a potential prizewinner. ▶ likely, possible, probable

potion *noun*
Her mother held her nose with one hand, and poured the potion down her throat with the other. ▶ a medicine, a mixture, a draught

pouch *noun*
He poked his hand in the pouch and pulled out a silver coin. ▶ a bag, a purse

pounce *verb*
Two men pounced on him outside his house on Monday. ▶ to jump, to spring, to leap, to swoop

pound *verb*
You have to pound the garlic into a paste. ▶ to grind, to crush, to beat, to batter, to mash, to smash, to pulp

pour *verb*
After the storm water was pouring from the broken gutters. ▶ to gush, to stream, to flow, to run

poverty *noun*
The family lost everything and lived a life of poverty. ▶ hardship, need, privation, want, beggary

power *noun*
1 No one has the power to see into the future. ▶ the ability, the skill, the competence, the talent
2 As a police officer she has the power to arrest people. ▶ the authority, the right
3 The wind had tremendous power and brought down trees. ▶ force, strength, might, energy, vigour

powerful *adjective*
1 The lion was crunching a bone in its powerful jaws. ▶ strong, mighty
2 The exhibition had powerful images of starving children. ▶ strong, moving, forceful, striking, impressive
3 He had friends who were now powerful people. ▶ important, influential, authoritative

practical *adjective*
1 Any reasonably practical person could make this in a weekend. ▶ capable, competent, efficient, businesslike
2 The boys tried to offer some practical help. ▶ useful, usable, sensible

practically *adverb*
In her job she met famous people practically every day. ▶ almost, nearly

practice *noun*
1 Their normal practice is to go swimming at the weekend. ▶ a custom, a routine, a habit
2 He plays the piano quite well but needs more practice. ▶ preparation, rehearsal
3 It was a good idea but it didn't work out in practice. ▶ reality, fact, action

practise *verb*
Kay was in the gym, practising. ▶ to exercise, to train

praise *verb*
He had done a good job and she praised his efforts. ▶ to applaud, to acclaim, to congratulate, to commend, to pay tribute to

prance *verb*
Some tourists were prancing about taking photographs from every angle. ▶ to jump, to leap, to dance, to skip

prank *noun*
Stella decided to stay out of the way, in case her prank had been discovered. ▶ a trick, a practical joke, an antic, an escapade

precarious *adjective*
Some ornaments stood in a precarious line at the edge of the shelf. ▶ unsafe, insecure, dangerous, perilous, hazardous

precaution *noun*
Use this spray as a precaution against getting bitten. ▶ a safeguard, a defence, a protection

precede *verb*
A police escort preceded the van carrying the prisoners. ▶ to come before, to go before, to go in front of

precious *adjective*
The burglars stole all my precious jewellery. ▶ valuable, invaluable, priceless

precise *adjective*
1 Helen was not sure of the precise time. ▶ exact, correct, right
2 Their work was always neat and precise. ▶ careful, meticulous

predict *verb*
It's hard to predict what might happen. ▶ to forecast, to foretell, to prophesy

prefer *verb*
Would you prefer a seat by the window? ▶ to like better, to rather have, to fancy

prejudice *noun*
They showed a strong prejudice against older people. ▶ a bias, discrimination, intolerance, unfairness

prejudiced *adjective*
They were obviously prejudiced. ▶ biased, intolerant, unfair, one-sided

preliminary *adjective*
Before the concert the guitarist gave a preliminary talk. ▶ introductory, preparatory, opening

premises *plural noun*
The premises were locked up and in darkness. ▶ a property, a building, an establishment

preoccupied *adjective*
Sarah was preoccupied and didn't hear the phone ring. ▶ engrossed, absorbed, busy

prepare *verb*
The museum is preparing a new exhibition. ▶ to organize, to plan, to arrange, to get ready

preposterous *adjective*
The idea was preposterous. ▶ silly, ridiculous, absurd, laughable, ludicrous, crazy, mad, nonsensical

prescribe *verb*
The doctor prescribed some medicine. ▶ to advise, to recommend, to suggest

present *adjective*
1 At least one adult has to be present. ▶ here, there, available, on the scene
2 It is difficult to be sure in the present circumstances. ▶ current, existing

present *noun*
The money was meant to be a present. ▶ a gift, a donation

present *verb*
1 A distinguished guest will present the prizes. ▶ to award, to give, to hand over
2 We will present a play at Easter. ▶ to perform, to put on, to act

presently *adverb*
They will be here presently. ▶ soon, shortly, in a while

preserve *verb*
The council is anxious to preserve the beauty of the town. ▶ to maintain, to protect, to safeguard, to defend, to guard, to keep, to look after, to save; (more formal) to conserve

press *verb*
1 *Press the button and the lift may come.* ▶ to push
2 *Press the soil down firmly round the plant.* ▶ to push, to squash, to squeeze, to smooth, to flatten
3 *I have some clothes to press.* ▶ to iron, to smooth, to flatten

pressure *noun*
They had to apply a lot of pressure to get the door open. ▶ force, power, strength

prestige *noun*
The business was successful and enjoyed a lot of prestige. ▶ fame, reputation, influence, glory, renown, honour

presume *verb*
I presume they are coming. ▶ to suppose, to assume, to imagine, to believe, to guess, to expect, to gather

presumptuous *adjective*
It was a little presumptuous to walk in like that and expect a meal on the table. ▶ arrogant, bold, audacious, insolent, cheeky, forward, impertinent

pretend *verb*
Let's pretend we're on holiday. ▶ to imagine, to make believe, to fancy, to suppose

pretty *adjective*
The flowers looked pretty in the sun. ▶ attractive, lovely, appealing, charming, pleasing, beautiful

pretty *adverb*
It's pretty cold outside. ▶ fairly, rather, quite, moderately, somewhat

prevent *verb*
1 *It was difficult to prevent the men from rushing off.* ▶ to stop, to hinder, to curb, to deter, to discourage, to check
2 *It would be difficult to prevent an accident.* ▶ to avoid, to avert

previous *adjective*
1 *I had seen them the previous week.* ▶ before, earlier
NOTE: If you use these words, you say *I had seen them the week before* or *I had seen them a week earlier.*
2 *I have had no previous experience of rock-climbing.* ▶ past, earlier, former, prior

prey *noun*
The lion had already killed its prey. ▶ a victim, a quarry

prey on *verb*
Some birds prey on mice and other small animals. ▶ to hunt, to kill, to feed on

price *noun*
It sounded a lovely holiday but the price was high. ▶ a cost, a charge, an amount, an expense

priceless *adjective*
Most of the jewels were quite ordinary but one or two were priceless. ▶ valuable, precious, costly

prick *verb*
You have to prick the plastic covering with a fork. ▶ to pierce, to puncture

prickly *adjective*
He fell headlong into a prickly bush. ▶ spiky, thorny

pride *noun*
1 *We can look back with pride on the year's achievements.* ▶ satisfaction, contentment, pleasure
2 *He was puffed up with pride.* ▶ conceit, vanity, arrogance, self-importance, self-satisfaction

prim *adjective*
He tried not to look too prim and serious for his interview. ▶ proper, precise, correct

primarily *adverb*
The hermit lived primarily on wild roots and nuts. ▶ mainly, chiefly, mostly, predominantly

primary *adjective*
His primary concern was always his children. ▶ main, principal, chief, first, prime, major

prime *adjective*
Fog was the prime cause of the accident. ▶ main, principal, chief, major, first, primary

primitive *adjective*
1 *Primitive humans were hunters rather than farmers.* ▶ prehistoric, ancient, early
2 *You can make a primitive sledge from an old tray.* ▶ simple, crude, rough

principal *adjective*
Gardening was his principal source of income for several years. ▶ chief, main, major, first, prime, primary, foremost

principle *noun*
1 *As a general principle it is better not to argue.* ▶ a rule, a theory, a strategy
2 *He is a man of principle.* ▶ honesty, honour, integrity, belief, conscience, scruples

principles *plural noun*
She learned the principles of algebra at an early age. ▶ the rules, the laws, the theory

print *noun*
His thumb left a print on the glass. ▶ a mark, an impression, a stamp

prison *noun*
All three men were sent to prison. ▶ jail

prisoner *noun*
1 *The prisoners were allowed in the yard for an hour each day.* ▶ a convict
2 *The winning army took many prisoners.* ▶ a captive, a hostage

NOTE: A **hostage** is a prisoner who is held captive until someone pays a ransom or agrees to a demand

private *adjective*
1 *These letters are private.* ▶ personal, confidential, intimate
2 *Is there a private place to swim?* ▶ hidden, secluded, quiet

privilege *noun*
The ancient gods had the privilege of being immortal. ▶ an advantage, a benefit, a right

prize *noun*
The prize went to someone they'd never heard of. ▶ an award

prize *verb*
She had prized her jewellery all her life. ▶ to value, to appreciate, to cherish

probable *adjective*
It is probable that they have left by now. ▶ likely, most likely, possible

probe *verb*
Perhaps we should probe a little further to see what happened. ▶ to inquire, to explore, to investigate

problem *noun*
1 *I've got five problems to solve by tomorrow.* ▶ a puzzle, a question, a riddle
2 *The family next door is having a problem with the drains.* ▶ trouble, a difficulty, a complication

procedure *noun*
The leaflet explains the procedure for opening a bank account. ▶ a process, a method, a system

proceed *verb*
Once he had answered all the questions he was allowed to proceed. ▶ to carry on, to continue, to go on

proceeds *plural noun*
The proceeds from the sale amounted to over £500. ► takings, a profit, an income

process *noun*
Robots are now used in the manufacturing process. ► an operation, a procedure, an activity, a system, a method

process *verb*
The information on the form is processed by a computer. ► to deal with, to handle, to convert, to prepare, to treat

procession *noun*
A procession was moving slowly down the road. ► a parade, a cavalcade, a pageant

proclaim *verb*
The king proclaimed a national holiday on his daughter's birthday. ► to declare, to announce, to decree, to pronounce

prod *verb*
Hilary felt someone prod her in the back. ► to dig, to poke, to jab

produce *verb*
1 *The factory produces cars and light vans.* ► to make, to manufacture, to assemble
2 *Martin suddenly produced a letter.* ► to show, to bring out, to reveal, to disclose, to present

profession *noun*
John was thinking about which profession to choose. ► an occupation, a career, a line of work, a calling, a vocation, a job

professional *adjective*
1 *The building work looked professional and solid.* ► competent, expert, skilful, qualified, skilled, trained

2 *The flats were bought by young professional people.* ► qualified, trained, skilled

proficient *adjective*
Harry is a very proficient driver. ► competent, able, capable, qualified, skilled, effective

profit *noun*
The sale made a small profit. ► a gain, a surplus

profound *adjective*
They have a profound knowledge of the subject. ► deep, learned, serious, wise

progress *noun*
Jemima's progress this term has been amazing. ► advance, development, improvement

progress *verb*
Our plans have been progressing. ► to advance, to develop, to move forward

prohibit *verb*
They have prohibited smoking in the shopping centre. ► to forbid, to ban, to bar, to outlaw

project *noun*
1 *In the end the project had to be abandoned for lack of money.* ► a plan, a scheme, a proposal
2 *Our project is on water.* ► an activity, a topic, an assignment, a task

project *verb*
1 *A row of pegs projected from the wall.* ► to stick out, to jut out, to extend, to protrude
2 *The light projected a shadow across the doorway.* ► to cast, to throw

prolong *verb*
Traffic jams prolonged the journey by several hours. ► to lengthen, to increase, to extend, to draw out, to drag out, to make longer, to protract

prominent *adjective*
1 *The house stood in a prominent position.* ▶ conspicuous, noticeable, obvious, pronounced
2 *My grand mother was a prominent member of the local council.*
▶ important, distinguished, eminent, famous, celebrated, well-known

promise *verb*
1 *Bella promised that she would write every day.* ▶ to give your word, to swear, to vow, to guarantee, to agree
2 *Angie promised me that she wouldn't go on the road.* ▶ to assure, to give an undertaking

promise *noun*
I give you my promise. ▶ an assurance, a guarantee, a pledge

promote *verb*
1 *They want to promote the cause of peace.* ▶ to support, to back, to encourage, to help
2 *She is visiting bookshops to promote her latest novel.* ▶ to publicize, to advertise; (informal) to plug

prompt *adjective*
I'd like a prompt answer. ▶ quick, speedy, swift, punctual, immediate

prompt *verb*
Her success in the competition prompted her to take up acting as a career. ▶ to encourage, to inspire, to stimulate, to urge

prone *adjective*
He is prone to lose his temper. ▶ liable, apt, likely, inclined
NOTE: You can also say *He is given to losing his temper.*

pronounce *verb*
1 *You pronounce 'pair' and 'pear' the same way.* ▶ to say, to speak, to utter

2 *After a short rest he pronounced himself fit again.* ▶ to declare, to proclaim, to announce

pronounced *adjective*
The pitch has a pronounced slope.
▶ distinct, definite, noticeable, conspicuous, prominent, obvious

proof *noun*
They knew they had seen the man there, but getting proof would be difficult.
▶ evidence, confirmation

prop *noun*
The stage was strengthened by props underneath it. ▶ a support, a strut, a post

prop *verb*
She had to prop a ladder against the wall. ▶ to lean, to rest, to stand

prop up *verb*
The old building was propped up by scaffolding. ▶ to hold up, to reinforce, to support

propel *verb*
A small petrol engine propels the dinghy through the water. ▶ to drive, to push, to send, to force

proper *adjective*
1 *We tried to behave in a proper fashion.*
▶ decent, respectable, polite, becoming, seemly, tasteful, appropriate, fitting
2 *Show me the proper way to hold a golf club.* ▶ correct, right, suitable

property *noun*
1 *The house was rented and not their own property.* ▶ a possession, an asset
2 *They have property in Italy.*
▶ estates, land, wealth, houses

prophecy *noun*
The prophecy seemed to come true.
▶ a prediction, a forecast

prophesy *verb*
He prophesied that the mist would soon lift. ▶ to predict, to forecast, to warn, to foretell

proportion *noun*
1 *The proportion of women to men is roughly 3 to 1.* ▶ the ratio, the balance
2 *A large proportion of our income is spent on rent and bills.* ▶ a part, a percentage, a fraction, a section, a share

proposal *noun*
A proposal for increased taxes would not be popular. ▶ a scheme, a proposition, a plan, a project, a suggestion

propose *verb*
1 *They have proposed a different idea.* ▶ to suggest, to offer, to plan, to recommend
2 *We propose to leave next week.* ▶ to intend, to aim, to plan, to mean

proprietor *noun*
The proprietor of the shop came over to see us. ▶ a manager, an owner; (informal) a boss

prosecute *verb*
You were lucky not to be prosecuted for shoplifting. ▶ to charge (with)

prospect *noun*
We have good prospects of winning. ▶ a possibility, a hope, a chance, a likelihood

prosper *verb*
The family business started to prosper again after the war. ▶ to flourish, to thrive, to grow, to do well, to succeed, to be successful

prosperous *adjective*
The family had moved to a prosperous London suburb. ▶ rich, successful, affluent, thriving, flourishing, wealthy

protect *verb*
1 *Birds build their nests high up to protect their young.* ▶ to safeguard, to shelter, to look after
2 *High walls protected the house from intruders.* ▶ to defend, to guard, to shield, to keep safe

protest *verb*
Why don't you protest? ▶ to complain, to grouse, to grumble, to object, to moan

protest *noun*
1 *The boy let out a cry of protest.* ▶ complaint, disapproval
2 *Mark decided to organize a protest against the new traffic plans.* ▶ a demonstration, a march, a rally

protrude *verb*
A piece of broken gutter protruded from the side of the house. ▶ to stick out, to jut out, to stand out, to project

proud *adjective*
1 *Fiona was proud of her daughter's singing ability.* ▶ pleased (with), delighted (with)
2 *They were too proud to ask for help.* ▶ dignified, self-respecting
3 *Martin has become very proud and won't mix with us any more.* ▶ arrogant, haughty, conceited, self-important, vain; (informal) stuck-up

prove *verb*
Can you prove that Gary took your ruler? ▶ to establish, to show, to confirm, to demonstrate, to verify

provide *verb*
1 *Can you provide your own sheets and towels?* ▶ to supply, to bring, to furnish, to contribute
2 *The club provides a good opportunity to enjoy yourself and learn something at the same time.* ▶ to offer, to afford, to give

provisions *plural noun*
We have enough provisions to last a week. ▶ food, supplies, rations

provoke *verb*
1 He has a bad temper and it's best not to provoke him. ▶ to annoy, to anger, to upset, to irritate, to enrage, to incense
2 Her remarks provoked a lot of criticism. ▶ to cause, to arouse, to excite, to stir up, to stimulate, to produce

prowl *verb*
Some men were prowling around outside the gates. ▶ to lurk, to creep, to slink

prudent *adjective*
1 It might be more prudent to ring the cinema and book some tickets.
▶ sensible, wise, advisable
2 Tom was being prudent in saving all his money. ▶ careful, sensible, cautious

pry *verb*
We were tempted to stop and pry. ▶ to snoop, to interfere, to meddle, to nose about

public *adjective*
1 They would have to meet in a public place such as the park. ▶ open, communal, common, shared
2 It was public knowledge that George was going to live abroad. ▶ common, general, familiar

public *noun*
The public are allowed to use the gardens. ▶ people, everyone, the community

publish *verb*
1 The newsletter is published every fortnight. ▶ to issue, to bring out, to produce, to print, to release
2 They will publish the results of the competition tomorrow. ▶ to announce, to declare, to disclose, to reveal, to print, to release

puff *noun*
A sudden puff of wind nearly pushed him over. ▶ a gust, a blast

puff *verb*
Running for the bus made her puff.
▶ to pant, to gasp

puff out *verb*
Pigeons seem to puff out their chests.
▶ to swell, to fill, to inflate, to expand

pull *verb*
1 The car was pulling a caravan.
▶ to tow, to drag, to draw, to haul
2 If you pull the rope, a bell rings.
▶ to tug, to jerk, to wrench

pull out *verb*
1 I'm going to have a tooth pulled out.
▶ to extract, to remove
2 Half the competitors pulled out just before the race. ▶ to withdraw, to retire

pull up *verb*
A car pulled up beside them. ▶ to stop, to draw up

pullover *noun*
Colin forced a pullover over his big head.
▶ a sweater, a jumper, a jersey

pulse *noun*
The music had a throbbing pulse.
▶ a beat, a rhythm, a movement

pump *verb*
1 I'd better pump my tyres. ▶ to inflate, to pump up, to blow up
2 The first thing to do was pump out all the water. ▶ to empty, to drain

punch *verb*
Michael had been laughing at her, so she punched him. ▶ to hit; (formal) to strike; (informal) to thump, to clout

punctual *adjective*
It was odd for David to be late when he was usually so punctual. ► on time, prompt

puncture *verb*
A sharp stone had punctured the tyre. ► to pierce, to prick, to penetrate, to make a hole in

punish *verb*
If they did wrong they were usually punished. ► to discipline, to penalize, to correct, to chastise

puny *adjective*
He was never going to force the door open with his puny shoulders. ► weak, feeble, frail; (informal) weedy

pupil *noun*
The photo showed all the pupils with their teacher. ► a schoolchild, a student

purchase *verb*
(not an everyday word) *You can purchase your tickets at the machine.* ► to buy, to get, to obtain, to pay for

pure *adjective*
1 *Use pure olive oil.* ► clean, clear, undiluted
2 *The holiday was pure bliss from beginning to end.* ► sheer, utter, complete, absolute, total, perfect

purify *verb*
A chemical is added to purify the water. ► to clean, to disinfect, to sterilize, to cleanse, to refine

purpose *noun*
1 *I'm not sure what his purpose was in coming this morning.* ► an intention, an aim, a motive, a goal, an objective
2 *The little tool seemed to have no real purpose.* ► a point, a use

purposely *adverb*
He had purposely built the hut with no windows. ► deliberately, intentionally, on purpose

pursue *verb*
1 *He ran down the road, pursued by an angry neighbour.* ► to chase, to follow
2 *She would like to pursue a career as a journalist.* ► to follow, to work at; (more formal) to conduct

pursuit *noun*
1 *The police had to break off their pursuit when the mist came down.* ► a chase, a hunt
2 *It's useful to have an indoor pursuit that doesn't depend on the weather.* ► an interest, an activity, a hobby, a pastime, an occupation

push *verb*
1 *The murderer had pushed the car over the cliff.* ► to force, to shove, to propel
2 *She knelt down and pushed everything back into the box.* ► to force, to pack, to cram, to squeeze, to crush, to press, to thrust
3 *The crowd were pushing forward.* ► to move, to surge, to force a way, to shove
4 *Try pushing the button.* ► to press

put *verb*
1 *Put the shopping down here.* ► to place, to set, to lay, to leave
2 *He tried to put the idea as simply as he could.* ► to express, to explain, to state, to say

put in *verb*
I need to put in new batteries. ► to fit, to insert, to install

put off *verb*
We'll put off the party for a week. ► to postpone, to defer, to delay; (more formal) to adjourn

put out *verb*
We tried to put out the fire. ▶ to extinguish, to quench

put up *verb*
1 Let's put the tent up here. ▶ to erect, to pitch, to set up
2 They are going to put up a new block of flats. ▶ to build, to construct, to erect
3 Let's put up our tent here. ▶ to pitch, to erect, to raise, to set up
4 When we go to London my cousin will put us up. ▶ to accommodate, to house, to lodge, to quarter
5 The landlord had put up the rent again. ▶ to increase, to raise, to step up

put up with *verb*
Jennifer didn't think she could put up with the noise any longer. ▶ to bear, to stand, to tolerate, to endure

puzzle *noun*
1 It was a bit of a puzzle to know who had rung the door bell. ▶ a mystery, a problem, a conundrum, a dilemma
2 Kirstie sat down to do the puzzles in the newspaper. ▶ a question, a riddle, a conundrum; (informal) a brain-teaser

puzzled *adjective*
He was puzzled to find the house empty. ▶ baffled, perplexed, confused, bewildered, stumped, nonplussed

Q q

quaint *adjective*
The choir sang quaint old English folk songs. ▶ charming, old-fashioned, unusual

quake *verb*
Inside himself he was quaking, but he was determined not to show his fear. ▶ to tremble, to shake, to quiver, to shudder

qualified *adjective*
Teresa is a qualified swimming instructor. ▶ trained, certified

quality *noun*
1 The work is of a good quality. ▶ a standard, a class, a grade, a level
2 The paper had a shiny quality. ▶ a look, a condition, a characteristic, a property

quantity *noun*
1 There was a large quantity of garden rubbish waiting to be collected. ▶ an amount, a volume
NOTE: You can also say There was a lot of garden rubbish waiting to be collected.
2 He had gathered a small quantity of pebbles into a pile. ▶ a number
NOTE: You can also say He had gathered a few pebbles into a pile or He had gathered several pebbles into a pile.

quarrel *verb*
They are usually good friends, but they occasionally quarrel. ▶ to argue, to differ, to disagree, to fall out, to fight, to squabble

quarrel *noun*
Kate has had a bad quarrel with her brother. ▶ an argument, a row, a disagreement, a dispute

quarters *plural noun*
The soldiers' quarters were in a nearby town. ▶ lodgings, accommodation, a billet

quaver *verb*
When he's nervous his voice starts to quaver. ▶ to tremble, to waver, to quiver, to quake, to shake

quay *noun*
We went to the quay to look for Sam's boat. ▶ a pier, a jetty, a landing stage, a wharf

queasy *adjective*
So much rich food made me feel queasy. ▶ sick, unwell, queer, bilious

queer *adjective*
The juice had a queer taste. ▶ odd, strange, peculiar, funny, curious, weird, unusual

query *verb*
The bill seemed rather large so Maggie queried it. ▶ to question, to ask about, to dispute

quest *noun*
They went on a quest to find the treasure. ▶ a search, a hunt, an expedition

question *noun*
1 Can you answer this question? ▶ a problem, a query, an enquiry, a puzzle
2 There is some question about whether he is fit. ▶ doubt, uncertainty

question *verb*
1 The police questioned me about the accident. ▶ to ask, to cross-examine, to examine, to interrogate, to interview
2 Nobody questioned my right to speak at the meeting. ▶ to query, to doubt, to dispute, to challenge

queue *noun*
There was a queue of cars at the bridge. ▶ a line, a tailback

queue *verb*
We were told to queue at the door. ▶ to line up, to form a line, to stand in line

quick *adjective*
1 We had a quick trip back because there wasn't much traffic. ▶ fast, rapid, swift, speedy
2 The goats climbed up the rocks with quick movements. ▶ agile, nimble, brisk, deft, lively
3 I expect you would like a quick answer. ▶ prompt, early, immediate, instant
4 Jean is a quick pupil. ▶ bright, clever, sharp, intelligent

quicken *verb*
As he got nearer the door his pace quickened. ▶ to speed up, to grow quicker, to accelerate, to hasten, to get faster

quiet *adjective*
1 Maria was usually quiet and rather shy. ▶ placid, reserved
2 Shaun spoke in a quiet voice that you could hardly hear. ▶ soft, low
3 All they asked for was a quiet life. ▶ calm, tranquil, untroubled, peaceful

quieten *verb*
1 I'll just go and quieten the dogs. ▶ to calm, to hush, to pacify, to silence; (informal) to shut up
2 The noise quietened after a while. ▶ to lessen, to soften, to die down

quit *verb*
1 (informal) He wants to quit smoking. ▶ to stop, to give up; (more formal) to cease
2 Dad had a row with his boss and quit his job. ▶ to give up, to leave, to resign from

quite *adverb*
1 I haven't quite finished. ▶ completely, entirely, absolutely, altogether, totally, utterly, wholly
2 When she came in and saw us, she looked quite horrified. ▶ utterly, totally, completely
3 The news was quite bad, though not as bad as we feared. ▶ fairly, pretty, rather, moderately

quiver *verb*
Steve was quivering with excitement. ▶ to tremble, to shake, to shudder

quiz *noun*
Jamie went in for a general knowledge quiz. ▶ a competition, a test

quota *noun*
By lunch time he had already eaten his quota of calories. ▶ an allowance, a share, a ration, a portion

quotation *noun*
I was trying to remember a quotation from Shakespeare. ▶ an excerpt, an extract, a passage; (informal) a quote

quote *verb*
He quoted a few words from a famous song. ▶ to repeat, to cite, to mention, to refer to

R r

race *noun*
Let's have a race to the windmill and back. ▶ a dash, a chase
NOTE: There are no good alternative words for **race** when it means 'a large group of people who have the same ancestors and the same physical features'. Words such as **people**, **nation**, and **ethnic group** do not mean the same as **race**, but refer to the human beings of a country or place.

race *verb*
Judy raced home to see if there was any post for her. ▶ to dash, to hurry, to run, to tear, to sprint, to fly

rack *noun*
There is a rack for plates over the sink. ▶ a stand, a support, a frame

racket *noun*
1 *The people in the hall were startled by a sudden racket outside.* ▶ a noise, a din, a commotion, a row, an uproar, a hubbub, pandemonium, a rumpus

2 (informal) *The men were arrested when their business was found to be a racket.* ▶ a fraud, a swindle

radiant *adjective*
The wedding couple looked radiant with happiness. ▶ bright, brilliant, splendid, gleaming, shining

radiate *verb*
A light bulb radiates more heat than light. ▶ to give out, to emit, to send out, to transmit

radical *adjective*
The new manager has made radical changes. ▶ drastic, thorough, fundamental, far-reaching, sweeping

rage *noun*
Edward found it hard to hide his rage. ▶ fury, anger, temper; (not an everyday word) wrath

ragged *adjective*
ragged clothes ▶ frayed, torn, tattered, shabby, worn out

raid *noun*
The city had suffered many bombing raids during the war. ▶ an attack, an assault, a blitz, a strike

raid *verb*
Pirates raided the towns along the coast. ▶ to attack, to assault, to plunder, to pillage, to loot, to ravage

rain *noun*
The rain went on all evening. ▶ (heavy rain) a downpour, a deluge; (light rain) drizzle, a shower

rain *verb*
1 *It was still raining when they went out.* ▶ (to rain heavily) to pour, to teem; (to rain gently) to drizzle
2 *Fragments of glass rained on them from above.* ▶ to fall, to drop, to pour, to shower

raise *verb*

1 *They were going to need a crane to raise such a large block.* ▶ to lift, to pick up, to hoist

2 *Several people raised their hands to ask questions.* ▶ to hold up, to put up, to lift

3 *We are trying to raise £5,000 for charity.* ▶ to make, to collect, to get

4 *At the meeting the rabbi raised another topic.* ▶ to mention, to introduce, to put forward

5 *It was difficult to raise children on such a small income.* ▶ to bring up, to rear, to care for, to look after, to educate

6 *The neighbouring farmer raises cattle and sheep.* ▶ to breed, to rear

7 *The local farm raises cereal crops.* ▶ to grow, to produce, to cultivate

rally *noun*

A rally will be held in town next Saturday. ▶ a demonstration, a protest, a public meeting

ram *verb*

1 *The angry man rammed a fist in my face.* ▶ to thrust, to push, to force, to jam

2 *A large lorry had rammed the gate.* ▶ to crash into, to collide with, to bump, to strike, to hit

ramble *verb*

We like to ramble in the country. ▶ to roam, to wander, to rove, to stroll, to walk

rampage *verb*

A gang had rampaged through the park destroying young trees. ▶ to go wild, to go berserk

ramshackle *adjective*

The family was still living in a ramshackle little house off the High Street. ▶ dilapidated, rickety, tumbledown, decrepit

random *adjective*

The police were making random checks on passing cars. ▶ haphazard, chance, irregular, indiscriminate, arbitrary, unplanned

range *noun*

1 *A mountain range lay to the north.* ▶ a chain, a line

2 *The newsagent sells a wide range of magazines.* ▶ a selection, a choice, a variety

range *verb*

1 *Ages ranged from 5 to 25.* ▶ to extend, to stretch, to vary, to reach

2 *Sheep and goats range over the hills.* ▶ to wander, to roam, to rove, to stray

rank *noun*

1 *The people were arranged in several ranks.* ▶ a row, a line, a column, a file

2 *He had the rank of captain.* ▶ a position, a status, a title, a grade, a level

ransack *verb*

1 *We had to ransack the cupboard to find our clothes.* ▶ to search, to rake through, to rummage through, to scour, to turn inside out

2 *When they got home the room had been ransacked.* ▶ to wreck, to ravage, to plunder, to loot

rap *verb*

Someone was rapping on the window. ▶ to knock, to tap, to strike

rapid *adjective*

She has made a rapid recovery from her illness. ▶ quick, fast, swift, speedy

rare *adjective*

1 *Peter had a rare coin in his pocket.* ▶ unusual, uncommon, scarce, exceptional

2 *Opportunities to meet famous people are rare.* ▶ infrequent, occasional, exceptional

rarely *adverb*
The old man rarely went out.
▶ seldom, infrequently, occasionally, hardly ever, scarcely ever

rascal *noun*
She called him a rascal and said he would be in real trouble one day.
▶ a rogue, a knave, a scoundrel, a scamp

rash *adjective*
It had been rather rash of her to offer to pay for the meal. ▶ hasty, impulsive, impetuous, reckless

rate *noun*
1 *Everyone was working at a furious rate.* ▶ a pace, a speed, a tempo
2 *What is the rate for a letter to Europe?* ▶ a charge, a cost, a price

rate *verb*
She is rated very highly as an actor.
▶ to value, to regard, to prize

rather *adverb*
1 *It was rather late.* ▶ fairly, quite, somewhat, moderately; (informal) pretty
2 *We would rather stay here.* ▶ sooner, preferably
NOTE: You can also say *We would prefer to stay here.*

ration *noun*
Henry was generous enough to let Tom have some of his food ration. ▶ an allowance, a share, a portion, a quota

ration *verb*
When the water ran short the leaders had to ration it. ▶ to limit, to restrict, to control, to share out

rational *adjective*
It was not easy to find a rational explanation for what happened.
▶ reasonable, sensible, logical, sound, cogent

rations *plural noun*
Our rations will last a week at the most.
▶ supplies, provisions, food, stores

rattle *verb*
The window was rattling in the wind.
▶ to clatter, to vibrate, to clank, to bang
NOTE: You can also use **chatter** when you are talking about teeth

rave *verb*
1 *The man started to rave and threaten us.* ▶ to rage, to rant, to roar, to fume, to be angry
2 *Steve came back raving about a new act he'd just seen.* ▶ to enthuse, to be excited; (informal) to be wild

ravenous *adjective*
We reached home tired and ravenous.
▶ famished, starved, starving, hungry

raw *adjective*
1 *Jerry said he preferred his vegetables raw.* ▶ uncooked, unprepared
2 *What raw materials do you need?*
▶ natural, crude, basic
3 *There was a raw wind blowing.*
▶ cold, bitter, chilly
4 *Jane's shoe had rubbed a raw patch on her heel.* ▶ sore, grazed, inflamed, red

ray *noun*
A ray of strong light came through the window. ▶ a beam, a shaft, a streak, a gleam

reach *verb*
1 *Diane reached for the milk.* ▶ to stretch, to grab (at), to clutch (at)
2 *I can't reach the top shelf.* ▶ to grasp, to get hold of, to touch
3 *After a while we reached the end of the motorway.* ▶ to get to, to come to, to arrive at

reach *noun*
The house is within easy reach of the station. ▶ distance, range

react *verb*
When Kate heard what had happened, she reacted angrily. ► to respond, to answer, to reply

read *verb*
1 *There was one other person on the train, reading a newspaper.* ► to look at, to study, to peruse, to browse through, to scan
2 *The writing was difficult to read.* ► to understand, to make out, to decipher, to interpret
3 *The thermometer reads 20°.* ► to show, to indicate, to record, to register

ready *adjective*
1 *I'm ready to help you.* ► prepared, willing, eager, keen, glad
2 *Is dinner ready?* ► prepared, available

real *adjective*
1 *Are those pearls real?* ► genuine, authentic
2 *The story is based on real events.* ► factual, actual, true, historical

realistic *adjective*
1 *The characters in the film were very realistic.* ► authentic, genuine, lifelike, natural
2 *The plan should be realistic and not too ambitious.* ► practical, workable, feasible, viable, possible

realize *verb*
After a few minutes I realized that the machine was faulty. ► to understand, to grasp, to become aware, to appreciate, to comprehend, to recognize, to perceive, to see

really *adverb*
1 *I think he is really sorry.* ► truly, indeed, certainly, actually, genuinely, honestly
2 *I thought the party was really good.* ► very, extremely

realm *noun*
The king increased taxes throughout his realm. ► a kingdom, an empire

reap *verb*
The corn is reaped in August. ► to cut, to gather in, to harvest

rear *noun*
The man left by the kitchen door at the rear of the house. ► the back, the end

rear *adjective*
A child was looking out of the rear window. ► back, end

rear *verb*
1 *By the time she was twenty she was rearing three children.* ► to bring up, to raise, to care for, to look after
2 *The neighbouring farmer rears cattle and sheep.* ► to breed, to raise

reason *noun*
1 *There had to be a reason for their change of mind.* ► an explanation, a cause, grounds, a pretext, a justification, a motive, a purpose
2 *Please listen to reason.* ► sense, logic

reason *verb*
1 *The doctor reasoned that the fresh air would do him some good.* ► to consider, to reckon, to think, to conclude, to judge
2 *It's hard to reason with such stubborn people.* ► to argue, to use reason, to discuss things

reasonable *adjective*
1 *He is a reasonable person and won't be angry.* ► sensible, fair, rational, logical, intelligent
2 *She earns a reasonable income now.* ► fair, respectable, adequate, moderate, proper

reassure *verb*
Juliet saw that he was upset and tried to reassure him. ► to comfort, to encourage, to support

rebel *verb*
Unless their demands were met, they would rebel. ▶ to revolt, to rise up, to mutiny (on a ship)

rebellion *noun*
The army was brought in to end the rebellion. ▶ a revolt, a revolution, a rising, a mutiny (on a ship)

rebellious *adjective*
Isabel wasn't rebellious, but she wasn't afraid to stand up to people. ▶ unruly, disobedient, insubordinate, defiant, quarrelsome

rebound *verb*
The ball rebounded off the post. ▶ to bounce back, to ricochet

rebuild *verb*
Part of the house had been rebuilt after a fire. ▶ to repair, to restore, to reconstruct, to renovate

rebuke *verb*
His parents rebuked him for being lazy. ▶ to scold, to reprimand, to reproach, to blame, to censure, to criticize, to find fault with; (informal) to tell off, to tick off

recall *verb*
I remember the incident but I can't recall all the details. ▶ to recollect, to remember

recede *verb*
The floods have receded. ▶ to go back, to ebb, to retreat

receive *verb*
1 *Anne received lots of cards when she was ill.* ▶ to get, to be given, to acquire
2 *Tim received a reward for rescuing the neighbours' cat.* ▶ to earn, to get, to obtain
3 (not an everyday use) *I'll receive my guests in the living room.* ▶ to greet, to meet, to welcome, to entertain

recent *adjective*
Recent discoveries have given us new information about the Romans in Britain. ▶ new, fresh, modern, up-to-date, contemporary

receptacle *noun*
(not an everyday word) *I need some sort of receptacle for all these carrier bags.* ▶ a container, a holder

reception *noun*
They were given a friendly reception. ▶ a welcome, a greeting

recite *verb*
Everyone had to recite a poem of their choice. ▶ to deliver, to perform, to say out loud, to speak, to repeat

reckless *adjective*
The witnesses all said his driving had been reckless. ▶ dangerous, irresponsible, careless, rash

reckon *verb*
1 *We reckon the cost at over a million pounds.* ▶ to calculate, to estimate, to assess, to work out, to compute, to total
2 *I reckon it might snow.* ▶ to think, to believe, to guess, to consider

recline *verb*
Another traveller was reclining on one side of the compartment. ▶ to lie, to lean back, to stretch out, to rest

recognize *verb*
1 *I'm not sure I'd recognize her if I saw her again.* ▶ to remember, to know again, to identify, to recall, to recollect
2 *We recognize that we may have acted unfairly.* ▶ to admit, to accept, to acknowledge, to be aware, to understand

recoil *verb*
He recoiled in fear. ▶ to jump, to jump back, to flinch, to shrink back, to spring back, to cower

recollect *verb*
I recollect that we had a long wait for the train. ▶ to recall, to remember

recommend *verb*
I recommend that you wear your boots. ▶ to suggest, to urge, to advise (to)
NOTE: If you use **advise**, you have to say *I advise you to wear your boots.*

record *verb*
The detective recorded every word the man said. ▶ to write down, to note, to make a note of

record *noun*
The children kept a detailed record of their visit. ▶ an account, a description, a report, a log, a journal, a diary

recover *verb*
1 *Rose had measles and took a long time to recover.* ▶ to get better, to get well, to recuperate, to pull through
2 *I lost a lot of valuables in the burglary and only recovered a few of them.* ▶ to get back, to retrieve, to reclaim

recreation *noun*
The quiz was meant for recreation, not to be educational. ▶ amusement, fun, enjoyment, entertainment, play, leisure

rectify *verb*
The mechanic was unable to rectify the fault. ▶ to put right, to correct, to cure, to remedy, to repair

recuperate *verb*
Kim's mother was recuperating after an operation. ▶ to recover, to get better, to get well, to convalesce

recur *verb*
All his old doubts and worries began to recur. ▶ to come back, to return, to reappear

reduce *verb*
Katie tried to reduce the amount she spent on magazines. ▶ to lessen, to lower, to cut, to decrease, to diminish

reel *noun*
I need to buy a reel of cotton. ▶ a spool

reel *verb*
1 *She reeled back and lost her balance.* ▶ to stagger, to totter, to stumble, to lurch
2 *Too much whisky was making his head reel.* ▶ to swim, to spin, to swirl

refer to *verb*
1 *I won't refer to the matter again.* ▶ to mention, to allude to, to comment on
2 *You'll need to refer to an encyclopedia for the answer.* ▶ to consult, to turn to

refined *adjective*
They spoke and behaved in a very refined way. ▶ well-mannered, polite, cultured, cultivated

reflect on *verb*
They reflected on what had happened that morning. ▶ to think about, to ponder on, to consider, to contemplate, to meditate on

reform *verb*
They are planning to reform the voting system. Prison didn't seem to have reformed her. ▶ to improve, to change

refrain from *verb*
Please refrain from eating in the library. ▶ to stop, to abstain from

refresh *verb*
A rest and a cool drink would refresh us. ▶ to revive, to freshen, to invigorate, to fortify

refuge *noun*
A group of travellers trudged up the road looking for a refuge from the storm. ▶ a shelter, a haven, a cover, a retreat

refund *verb*
If you pay a deposit the shop will not always refund it. ▶ to pay back, to repay

refuse *verb*
1 *They refuse to help.* ▶ to be unwilling, to decline
2 *It was a generous offer, but they still refused it.* ▶ to turn down, to reject, to decline, to say no to, to spurn

regard *verb*
1 *The policeman regarded us closely.*
▶ to contemplate, to eye, to gaze at, to look at, to stare at, to view, to watch
2 *I regard her as a friend.* ▶ to consider, to think of, to look on, to see
NOTE: If you use **consider** you do not use *as*: *I consider her a friend.*

regarding *preposition*
The notice has rules regarding use of the library. ▶ concerning, about, connected with

region *noun*
Many plants only grow in warm regions.
▶ an area, a zone, a part of the world, a locality

register *noun*
Our names are listed on a register.
▶ a list, an index, a roll

register *verb*
The thermometer registered 25°. ▶ to show, to indicate, to read, to record, to say, to point to

regret *verb*
Claudia already regretted her refusal to help. ▶ to be sorry for, to be ashamed of, to be sad about, to repent

regrettable *adjective*
It is regrettable that so few people came to the meeting. ▶ unfortunate, a pity, a shame, disappointing, deplorable
NOTE: **Deplorable** is a much stronger word than **regrettable**

regular *adjective*
1 *The patient's breathing was now more regular.* ▶ even, steady, rhythmic, constant
2 *The bus followed its regular route.*
▶ normal, usual, correct, habitual, customary

regulate *verb*
1 *A system of one-way streets helps to regulate the traffic.* ▶ to control, to manage, to organize
2 *You can regulate the radio's volume with a remote control.* ▶ to adjust, to alter, to change, to vary

regulation *noun*
A list of safety regulations is on the notice board. ▶ a rule, a law, a requirement

rehearse *verb*
Chris went to a practice room to rehearse his music. ▶ to practise, to prepare, to run through, to go over

reign *verb*
The king died without an heir, and his brother reigned after him. ▶ to rule, to be king (or queen), to govern

reinforce *verb*
Steel girders reinforce the roof. ▶ to strengthen, to support, to prop up

reject *verb*
They rejected our offer of help. ▶ to refuse, to decline, to turn down, to say no to, to dismiss

rejoice *verb*
We rejoiced at the good news. ▶ to be happy, to be delighted, to celebrate

relate *verb*
Kim sat down and related what had happened. ▶ to describe, to recount, to narrate, to report, to tell

related to
Road accidents are often related to excessive speed. ▶ connected with, associated with, attributed to, caused by

relationship *noun*
There is a close relationship between age and health. Our village has a special relationship with one in France. ▶ an association, a connection, a link

relative *noun*
A whole lot of our relatives are coming at Christmas. ▶ a relation

relax *verb*
1 It's good to relax in the evenings. ▶ to rest, to be comfortable, to unwind; (informal) to take it easy
2 Try to relax your arm. ▶ to loosen, to slacken

release *verb*
Some of the prisoners were released after a few days. ▶ to free, to set free, to let go, to allow out, to liberate

relent *verb*
She was angry, but when she heard the full story she relented. ▶ to yield, to soften, to be merciful

relentless *adjective*
They faced relentless criticism.
▶ persistent, continual, constant, ceaseless

relevant *adjective*
Your remarks don't seem very relevant.
▶ appropriate, suitable, apt, fitting

reliable *adjective*
Katie is a reliable friend.
▶ trustworthy, dependable, faithful, loyal, steady, responsible

relief *noun*
1 It was a relief to reach home.
▶ a comfort, a help
2 We will give money to famine relief.
▶ support, aid, assistance

relieve *verb*
The doctor gave me some medicine to relieve the pain. ▶ to ease, to reduce, to lessen, to soothe, to calm

religion *noun*
We are studying the religions of the world. ▶ a belief, a faith
SOME IMPORTANT RELIGIONS ARE:
Baha'ism, Buddhism, Christianity, Hinduism, Islam, Jainism (Indian), Judaism, Shinto (Japanese), Sikhism, Taoism (Chinese)

religious *adjective*
1 The marriages took place at a huge religious ceremony. ▶ sacred, divine, holy
2 She is a very religious person.
▶ devout, pious

relish *verb*
I always relish a good argument. ▶ to enjoy, to appreciate, to delight in, to like, to love

reluctant *adjective*
Our friends seemed reluctant to help.
▶ unwilling, disinclined, loath

rely on *verb*
We know we can always rely on you.
▶ to depend on, to count on, to trust; (informal) to bank on

remain *verb*
1 A lot of food remained after the party.
▶ to be left, to be left over, to be still there
2 Your mother will have to remain in hospital a few more days. ▶ to stay, to continue, to wait

remainder *noun*
The first chapter of the book is exciting, but the remainder isn't as good. ▶ the rest

remains *plural noun*
I'll clear away the remains of our meal. ▶ remnants, leftovers, leavings

remark *verb*
She remarked that the rain had stopped. ▶ to comment, to mention, to observe, to state, to say

remark *noun*
I didn't hear your remark. ▶ a comment, an observation, an opinion, a statement, a view, a criticism

remarkable *adjective*
It was a remarkable story. ▶ extraordinary, unusual, amazing, astonishing, astounding, staggering, surprising, incredible

remedy *noun*
Some kinds of leaves are a good remedy for bee stings. ▶ a cure, a medicine, a treatment

remember *verb*
1 *Can you remember what she said?* ▶ to recall, to recollect
2 *There are so many special numbers to remember.* ▶ to learn, to memorize

remind *verb*
I'll remind her to phone you. ▶ to prompt

remnants *plural noun*
The remnants of our meal were still on the table three hours later. ▶ the remains, the leftovers, the leavings

remorse *noun*
Her eyes filled with tears of remorse. ▶ regret, shame, guilt

remorseful *adjective*
Kevin felt deeply remorseful about what he'd done. ▶ ashamed (of), sorry (for), regretful, repentant

remote *adjective*
They were living in a remote village by the sea. ▶ far-away, lonely, desolate, distant, outlying, solitary, inaccessible

remove *verb*
1 *I'd better remove my things from the chair so you can sit down.* ▶ to take away, to clear away, to move, to shift, to transfer
2 *I had removed some of the names from the computer screen by mistake.* ▶ to erase, to get rid of, to delete, to eliminate, to wipe out
3 *Please remove your shoes before going in.* ▶ to take off
4 *People who are a nuisance will be removed.* ▶ to expel, to throw out, to turn out, to eject, to evict, to get rid of

render *verb*
The illness rendered him unfit for work. ▶ to make, to leave

renew *verb*
I must renew my passport before next summer. ▶ to change, to replace, to extend

renovate *verb*
The new owners of the big house are planning to renovate it. ▶ to restore, to improve, to modernize; (informal) to do up

renowned *adjective*
Jane's father was Mr Hunt, the renowned surgeon. ▶ famous, well-known, distinguished, eminent, noted

rent *verb*
It would be nice to rent a house by the sea. ▶ to lease, to hire

repair *verb*
1 *Shaun was repairing a fence in one of the fields.* ► to mend, to fix, to restore
2 *Her trousers need repairing.* ► to mend, to patch, to darn

repay *verb*
We will repay you the cost of your journey. ► to pay back, to refund, to recompense
NOTE: If you use **recompense** you have to say *We will recompense you for the cost of your journey.*

repeat *verb*
1 *Would you repeat what you said?* ► to say again, to restate, to reiterate
2 *You have to repeat the exercise several times.* ► to do again, to redo

repeatedly *adverb*
They had told him repeatedly to wait behind. ► constantly, frequently, often, again and again, over and over, persistently

repel *verb*
1 *The country prepared to repel the invaders.* ► to drive off, to drive out, to repulse, to resist, to fight off
2 *We were repelled by the smell.* ► to disgust, to revolt

repentant *adjective*
He wanted to show how deeply repentant he was. ► ashamed, sorry, remorseful, penitent, regretful

replace *verb*
1 *Please replace the books on the right shelf.* ► to put back, to return
2 *I need to replace some light bulbs.* ► to change, to renew
3 *We are not sure who will replace her when she retires.* ► to succeed, to follow, to come after, to take over from

replica *noun*
The statue was only a plaster replica. ► a copy, a duplicate, a reproduction, an imitation, a likeness

reply *verb*
I replied that I did not know. ► to answer, to respond, to retort
NOTE: You use **retort** when you mean 'to reply angrily'

reply *noun*
The bank's reply came this morning. ► an answer, a response, a retort
NOTE: You use **retort** when you mean 'an angry reply'

report *verb*
1 *It was her duty to report what she had seen.* ► to describe, to declare, to state, to communicate, to announce, to reveal
2 *When you arrive, report to the reception desk.* ► to present yourself, to introduce yourself, to make yourself known
3 *If he discovered that she was lying, he would report her.* ► to complain about, to denounce, to inform against

report *noun*
There is a report of the incident in the local newspaper. ► an account, a description, an article (about), a story (about)

reporter *noun*
A newspaper reporter came to interview the boys. ► a correspondent, a journalist

represent *verb*
The dotted lines represent state boundaries. ► to stand for, to symbolize, to show, to indicate

reprieve *verb*
The prisoner was reprieved with six months of his sentence still to serve. ► to pardon, to let off, to release, to set free

reprimand *verb*
They were reprimanded for their bad behaviour. ▶ to scold, to tell off, to admonish, to rebuke, to reproach

reproduce *verb*
1 *The new photocopier will reproduce documents in colour.* ▶ to copy, to duplicate, to print, to photocopy
2 *Some animals reproduce very quickly.* ▶ to breed, to have young, to multiply, to increase

reproduction *noun*
The painting looks good but it's only a reproduction. ▶ a copy, a duplicate

repulsive *adjective*
The cockroaches in the bathroom were a repulsive sight. ▶ disgusting, revolting, hideous, repellent, nauseating

reputation *noun*
The local garage has a reputation for reliability. ▶ a name

request *verb*
Our neighbours have requested a grant to repair their roof. ▶ to appeal for, to apply for, to ask for, to claim

request *noun*
We've made several requests for help. ▶ an appeal, a plea, an entreaty

require *verb*
1 *We require peace and quiet to do our work.* ▶ to need, to want, to demand, to insist on
2 *The driver was required to show his licence.* ▶ to order, to instruct, to direct

rescue *verb*
1 *The hostages were rescued at midnight.* ▶ to release, to free, to set free, to liberate, to save
2 *They managed to rescue the rest of the barbecue before the rain started.* ▶ to save, to recover, to retrieve, to salvage

resemblance *noun*
There is a strong resemblance between Kirsty and her sister. ▶ a likeness, a similarity

resemble *verb*
Kirsty and her sister resemble each other. ▶ to look like, to be similar to

resent *verb*
I rather resent her having so much money. ▶ to begrudge, to envy, to be jealous of, to be angry about

resentful *adjective*
It's hard not to feel resentful about all the money she has. ▶ envious, jealous, aggrieved, grudging

reserve *verb*
You'd better reserve some seats on the train to London. ▶ to book, to order

reserve *noun*
Each side is allowed three reserves. ▶ a substitute, a replacement

reserved *adjective*
Linda seemed more than usually reserved about what she was doing. ▶ shy, reticent, bashful, withdrawn, aloof, secretive

reside in *verb*
(not an everyday word) *The family resided in a large house by the lake.* ▶ to live in, to dwell in, to inhabit, to occupy

resign *verb*
Molly's mother had an argument at work and threatened to resign. ▶ to leave, to quit, to give up

resign yourself *verb*
In the end we resigned ourselves to staying at home. ▶ to put up with, to agree to, to accept

resist *verb*
1 *The silly cat resisted all attempts to rescue her.* ▶ to fight, to defy, to oppose, to withstand
2 *I can't resist telling her what happened.* ▶ to help

resolute *adjective*
They decided that resolute action was called for. ▶ determined, firm, resolved, adamant, decided

resolve *verb*
1 *We resolved to do better next time.* ▶ to decide, to determine, to undertake
2 *The problem was not an easy one to resolve.* ▶ to solve, to overcome, to sort out

resort to *verb*
Aaron was afraid they might resort to cheating. ▶ to make use of, to rely on, to turn to, to fall back on

resound *verb*
Every sound resounded in the large cathedral. ▶ to echo, to reverberate

resources *plural noun*
1 *Our joint resources only came to a few pounds.* ▶ funds, assets, money, wealth
2 *The land is rich in natural resources.* ▶ materials, raw materials

respect *noun*
1 *Have respect for people's feelings.* ▶ regard, consideration, concern, sympathy
2 *They treated us with great respect.* ▶ honour, courtesy, regard
3 *In some respects, he is like his sister.* ▶ a way, an aspect, a detail, a feature, a point

respect *verb*
1 *I respect her for her honesty.* ▶ to admire, to think well of, to honour
2 *They will try to respect our wishes.* ▶ to consider, to heed

respectable *adjective*
1 *They are very respectable people.* ▶ decent, honest, worthy, honourable
2 *Neil got respectable marks in the exam.* ▶ reasonable, satisfactory, adequate, decent, good

respond *verb*
We asked her but she did not respond. ▶ to answer, to reply, to react

response *noun*
When we wrote we got no response. ▶ an answer, a reply

responsible *adjective*
1 *She is responsible for locking up at night.* ▶ in charge (of)
2 *Who could be responsible for causing such a mess?* ▶ to blame, guilty (of)
3 *We need a responsible babysitter.* ▶ dependable, reliable, trustworthy, dutiful, honest

rest *verb*
1 *The walkers rested for a few minutes before their climb.* ▶ to relax, to take a rest, to sit down
2 *Jason's mother was resting.* ▶ to sleep, to have a nap, to doze, to snooze
3 *Rest the ladder on the roof.* ▶ to lean, to stand, to prop, to put, to place, to support

rest *noun*
1 *We are going to need a short rest before our climb.* ▶ a break, a pause, a respite
2 *You need to get some rest.* ▶ relaxation, comfort, ease
3 *I'll keep the rest for later.* ▶ the remainder, the surplus

restless *adjective*
Tim was tired and feeling restless. ▶ fidgety, unsettled, jumpy, jittery, agitated, nervous

restore *verb*
1 *The police arrested the thief and restored our property to us.* ▶ to give back, to return, to bring back
2 *The old house will be restored and opened to visitors.* ▶ to renovate, to repair, to refurbish; (informal) to do up

restrain *verb*
The crowd was noisy and had to be restrained. ▶ to control, to check, to hold back, to curb

restrict *verb*
After the accident his life became restricted to sitting in a wheelchair. ▶ to confine, to limit

result *noun*
The man died as a result of his injuries. ▶ a consequence, an effect, an outcome

result *verb*
1 *Several ideas resulted from our discussions.* ▶ to arise, to emerge, to develop, to come about, to follow
2 *Food shortages resulted in riots in the streets.* ▶ to cause, to bring about, to lead to, to provoke

resume *verb*
Fighting resumed on the following day. ▶ to begin again, to continue, to restart, to carry on; (more formal) to recommence

retain *verb*
Retain your tickets for inspection. ▶ to keep, to hang on to, to hold on to

retire *verb*
1 *Frank is 64 and will retire next year.* ▶ to stop work, to give up work
2 *I'll retire to my room now.* ▶ to withdraw, to retreat

retreat *verb*
He retreated towards the door in alarm. ▶ to move back, to go back, to back away, to fall back, to retire, to withdraw

retrieve *verb*
Before he could leave James had to retrieve his coat. ▶ to get back, to recover, to trace, to rescue

return *verb*
1 *The geese return every summer.* ▶ to come back, to reappear
2 *I will return home tomorrow.* ▶ to go back
3 *I forgot to return Janet's pen.* ▶ to give back, to send back, to take back
NOTE: If you are talking about money, you can also use **repay** or **refund**

reveal *verb*
1 *The door opened to reveal a room full of people.* ▶ to display, to expose, to show, to uncover
2 *In the end we had to reveal our secret.* ▶ to declare, to disclose, to divulge, to make known, to announce, to communicate

revenge *noun*
The killing was an act of revenge. ▶ vengeance, retaliation, reprisal, retribution

revere *verb*
Everyone who knew Donald revered him. ▶ to admire, to respect, to adore, to honour, to idolize

reverse *noun*
They seem to do the reverse of what I say. ▶ the opposite, the contrary

reverse *verb*
1 *Let's try reversing the two wires.* ▶ to change round, to swap, to invert
2 *Jan reversed the car into the garage.* ▶ to back

review *noun*
1 *The council will hold a review of the library services.* ▶ an inspection, a survey, an examination, a study, an appraisal
2 *There is a review of the book in today's paper.* ▶ a report, a criticism, an appraisal
NOTE: If you use **criticism** this can also mean 'a bad comment or report'

review *verb*
We need to review the situation and decide what to do. ▶ to study, to look at, to survey, to assess, to consider, to examine, to inspect, to discuss

revise *verb*
The essay needed revising and shortening. ▶ to correct, to alter, to amend, to adapt, to rewrite

revive *verb*
1 *It was three days before she revived from the coma.* ▶ to recover, to come round, to regain consciousness
2 *The village wants to revive its traditional pancake race.* ▶ to bring back, to start up again, to restore, to resurrect, to reintroduce
3 *A hot meal will soon revive us.* ▶ to restore, to refresh, to invigorate

revolt *verb*
1 *People in the cities began to revolt against the government.* ▶ to rebel, to rise up
2 *All the bloodshed revolted them.* ▶ to disgust, to horrify, to repel, to sicken, to nauseate

revolting *adjective*
The stench from the dustbins was revolting. ▶ disgusting, horrid, horrible, dreadful

revolution *noun*
1 *After the revolution many people had to leave the country.* ▶ a rebellion, a revolt, an uprising

2 *The wheel made three complete revolutions and slowly came to rest.* ▶ a turn, a circuit
NOTE: A revolution by a planet round the sun or satellite round a planet is called an **orbit**

revolve *verb*
The wheels slowly started to revolve. ▶ to turn, to go round, to rotate

reward *noun*
When Sam handed in the money he was given a reward. ▶ an award, a payment

reward *verb*
You will be rewarded for your efforts. ▶ to recompense, to pay, to compensate

rewarding *adjective*
Reading is a rewarding activity. ▶ satisfying, worthwhile, valuable, profitable, beneficial

rhyme *noun*
There was a rhyme she knew off by heart. ▶ a verse, a poem

rhythm *noun*
The music had a strong rhythm. ▶ a beat, a pulse

rich *adjective*
1 *The large house is owned by a rich family.* ▶ wealthy, well-to-do, well-off, prosperous
2 *The house has rich furnishings.* ▶ splendid, sumptuous, luxurious, costly

riches *plural noun*
They dreamt of riches and foreign travel. ▶ wealth, prosperity

rickety *adjective*
The building looks old and rickety. ▶ dilapidated, decrepit, unsteady, ramshackle, tumbledown

rid *verb*
We have to rid the house of mice. ▶ to clear, to free, to purge

get rid of *verb*
We have to get rid of the mice. ▶ to remove, to dispose of, to do away with

riddle *noun*
I'm trying to solve a riddle. ▶ a puzzle, a mystery, a problem, a conundrum

ridicule *verb*
When ideas are new, people often ignore them or ridicule them. ▶ to make fun of, to deride, to laugh at, to mock, to scoff at

ridiculous *adjective*
It was ridiculous to feel angry about something so unimportant. ▶ silly, absurd, laughable, ludicrous, crazy, mad, preposterous, nonsensical

right *adjective*
1 Is the answer right? ▶ correct, accurate, true
2 It's not right to cheat. ▶ honest, fair, good, proper, just, lawful, moral
3 I'm not sure I have the right books. ▶ suitable, proper, appropriate, correct

right *noun*
You have the right to vote when you are 18. ▶ the power, the authority, the entitlement

rightful *adjective*
Give the money back to its rightful owner. ▶ proper, legitimate

rigid *adjective*
1 The ceiling is supported by rigid beams. ▶ firm, stiff, hard, solid, inflexible, unbending
2 The rules seem very rigid. ▶ strict, harsh, stern, unyielding

rim *noun*
There was a crack in the rim of the glass. ▶ the brim, the edge

ring *noun*
1 Someone had drawn a ring round the spelling mistake. ▶ a circle, a loop
2 The clock had a round glass case with a gold ring at the bottom. ▶ a band

ring *verb*
1 A line of trees ringed the field. ▶ to circle, to surround, to encircle, to enclose
2 The church bells began to ring. ▶ to peal, to chime, to toll, to sound, to ring out
3 Someone had rung Mary and left a message. ▶ to phone, to call, to telephone

rinse *verb*
The campers rinsed their socks in the stream. ▶ to wash, to wash out

riot *noun*
The food shortages led to a riot. ▶ a revolt, a disturbance, a commotion, a rumpus, an uproar

riot *verb*
Soon the people were rioting. ▶ to go on the rampage, to rampage, to rebel, to revolt

riotous *adjective*
The behaviour of the crowd was becoming riotous. ▶ rowdy, disorderly, unruly, wild

rip *verb*
I ripped my shirt climbing over the fence. ▶ to tear, to split

ripe *adjective*
The fruit is not yet ripe. ▶ mature, ready

ripen *verb*
Leave the pears by the window to ripen. ▶ to mature, to develop, to grow ripe, to get ripe

rise *verb*

1 *The men all rose as she came into the room.* ▶ to get up, to stand up, to get to your feet

2 *Prices have risen again this year.* ▶ to increase, to go up

3 *The balloon got smaller and smaller as it rose into the sky.* ▶ to climb, to go up, to ascend

4 *The mountains rose behind the house.* ▶ to loom, to tower, to stand out

rise *noun*

The rise in prices was caused by a bad harvest. ▶ an increase

risk *noun*

There is a slight risk of snow. ▶ a danger, a chance, a possibility

risky *adjective*

They were on the wrong road, but it was too risky to stop and turn round. ▶ dangerous, hazardous, unsafe, chancy

ritual *noun*

Molly completed the tea-making ritual. ▶ a ceremony, a rite

rival *noun*

The local radio station now has a rival. ▶ a competitor, an opponent

rival *verb*

In a good summer the weather here rivals the south of France. ▶ to compare with, to compete with

rivalry *noun*

The brothers enjoyed a friendly rivalry. ▶ competition, competitiveness

river *noun*

We are going to have a picnic by the river. ▶ (a small river) a stream, a brook

road *noun*

1 *We live in a long road off the High Street.* ▶ a street, an avenue

2 *There is a little road leading down to the harbour.* ▶ a lane, a path, a track

3 *Take the road to York and turn off at Leeds.* ▶ a route; (a main road) a highway, a motorway

roam *verb*

Some sheep had got out and were roaming through the village. ▶ to wander, to stray, to ramble

roar *verb*

Everyone roared with laughter. ▶ to shout, to yell, to bellow, to howl, to shriek

rob *verb*

They are going to rob the local shop. ▶ to steal from, to burgle, to loot, to pilfer, to plunder

robber *noun*

The robbers escaped in a fast car. ▶ a thief, a burglar, a crook

robust *adjective*

My shoes are not robust enough for climbing. ▶ strong, sturdy, tough

rock *noun*

I fell on a rock and hurt myself. ▶ a boulder, a stone

rock *verb*

The little boat rocked in the wind. ▶ to sway, to roll

rod *noun*

1 *The fence is made of iron rods.* ▶ a bar, a rail, a pole

2 *The magician used a long rod.* ▶ a wand, a stick

rogue *noun*

People thought him a rogue although he was in fact honest. ▶ a rascal, a scoundrel, a villain; (not an everyday word) a knave

role *noun*
1 *Kim plays the role of a crook in the film.* ▶ a part, a character
2 *Computers have a role in language learning.* ▶ a part, a function, a contribution to make

roll *verb*
1 *She released the brake and the wheels started to roll.* ▶ to turn, to turn round, to spin, to revolve, to rotate
2 *Someone had been rolling pastry on the kitchen table.* ▶ to smooth, to flatten, to level out
3 *The ship was rolling in the rough sea.* ▶ to pitch, to rock, to sway, to lurch

romantic *adjective*
Jean's boyfriend was a warm romantic sort of person. ▶ amorous, passionate, loving, emotional

room *noun*
1 *The Queen retired to her private room.* ▶ (not everyday words) a chamber, an apartment
2 *Is there room for me?* ▶ space

roomy *adjective*
The house was bright and roomy. ▶ spacious, large; (not an everyday word) capacious

root *noun*
Lack of money is the root of our problem. ▶ the cause, the origin, the source, the basis

rope *noun*
The boat was attached to the jetty with a rope. ▶ a cable, a cord, a line, a hawser
NOTE: A **hawser** is a special type of thick rope used to secure a large ship

rosy *adjective*
1 *Her cheeks looked rosy.* ▶ pink, red, glowing
2 *The future looks rosy.* ▶ hopeful, bright, promising, encouraging

rot *verb*
The fruit was beginning to rot. ▶ to go bad, to decay, to perish

rotten *adjective*
1 *The posts were rotten where they went into the ground.* ▶ decayed, soft, rotted, perished, disintegrating
2 *I'll throw away that rotten tomato.* ▶ mouldy, bad, decayed, decomposed

rough *adjective*
1 *There is a rough path across the hills.* ▶ rugged, bumpy, uneven
2 *The crowd was becoming rough.* ▶ rowdy, disorderly
3 *The wind was rough.* ▶ strong, wild, stormy, turbulent, violent
4 *His skin was rough and covered in bristles.* ▶ coarse, scratchy, hairy, harsh
5 *I can make a rough guess.* ▶ approximate, vague, inexact, imprecise
6 *The climbers made a rough shelter to protect themselves from the wind.* ▶ crude, simple, rough-and-ready, basic

roughly *adverb*
There was a girl of roughly his age staying at the farm. ▶ about, approximately, around, close to

round *adjective*
The window on the top floor was small and round. ▶ circular, rounded

round *noun*
The winners go on to the next round. ▶ a stage, a level

round *verb*
A huge lorry rounded the corner. ▶ to go round, to come round, to turn

round off *verb*
We rounded off the day with a cream tea. ▶ to finish, to end, to conclude, to complete

round up *verb*
Go and round up the children. ▶ to gather, to bring together, to assemble, to muster

roundabout *adjective*
We went by a roundabout route.
▶ indirect, meandering, rambling, circuitous, long

rouse *verb*
1 It's not easy to rouse them in the mornings. ▶ to wake up, to arouse, to awaken, to get up
2 The newspaper article roused my curiosity. ▶ to excite, to stimulate, to stir up, to awaken

rout *verb*
The attackers were routed in a battle to the south of the town. ▶ to crush, to conquer, to overwhelm, to defeat

route *noun*
We went home by a different route.
▶ a road, a way

routine *noun*
1 He soon settled into the routine of his new job. ▶ a custom, a habit, a pattern, a way, an order
2 I showed Bridget the routine for getting her dinner tickets. ▶ a system, a procedure, a method

rove *verb*
The sheep rove freely over the hills. ▶ to wander, to roam, to range

row *noun*
A row of books stood on the shelf.
▶ a line, a string, a sequence, a series

row *noun*
1 Julie had a row with her brother.
▶ a quarrel, an argument, a fight, a squabble, a disagreement
2 There was a dreadful row coming from the next room. ▶ a noise, a din, a racket, a disturbance, a rumpus, an uproar

rowdy *adjective*
A rowdy party was going on across the road. ▶ noisy, loud, disorderly, unruly, rough

royal *adjective*
The king was wearing his royal robes.
▶ regal

rub *verb*
1 He rubbed his hands together. ▶ to stroke
2 The cleaner was rubbing the table.
▶ to polish, to clean

rub out *verb*
I've got a few mistakes to rub out. ▶ to erase, to remove, to get rid of

rubbish *noun*
1 Put the rubbish in the bin outside.
▶ refuse, garbage, waste, trash
2 James did talk a lot of rubbish at times.
▶ nonsense; (informal) gibberish

rubble *noun*
A lot of buildings were reduced to rubble in the earthquake. ▶ ruins, debris, wreckage

ruddy *adjective*
Michael has red hair and a ruddy complexion. ▶ red, rosy, glowing, fresh

rude *adjective*
1 She's very nice but sometimes she can be extremely rude. ▶ impolite, discourteous, ill-mannered, badly behaved, insolent, impertinent, offensive, insulting
2 Mark was telling us a rude joke.
▶ dirty, indecent, coarse, crude

ruffian *noun*
Two of the ruffians seized me and forced me against the fence. ▶ a hooligan, a lout, a thug

ruffle *verb*
1 The wind had ruffled my hair. ▶ to mess up, to tousle, to dishevel, to

tangle, to disarrange
2 *The bad news had ruffled him.* ▶ to disturb, to agitate, to bother, to upset

rugged *adjective*
The track became more rugged in the hills. ▶ rough, uneven, bumpy

ruin *verb*
1 *A stomach upset nearly ruined her holiday.* ▶ to spoil, to wreck, to mess up
2 *The crops were ruined in the storms.*
▶ to destroy, to wreck, to devastate, to demolish, to flatten

ruin *noun*
They were facing financial ruin.
▶ disaster, catastrophe, bankruptcy, failure

ruins *plural noun*
They walked through the ruins of the bombed city. ▶ remains, remnants, debris, wreckage, rubble

rule *noun*
1 *A list of club rules is on the notice board.* ▶ a regulation, a law
2 *The country used to be under Spanish rule.* ▶ government, authority, control, jurisdiction
3 *Our normal rule is to have a big meal on Sunday.* ▶ a custom, a practice, a routine

rule *verb*
1 *The king ruled the country with a council of ministers.* ▶ to govern, to run, to control, to administer
2 *The judge ruled that the evidence was unreliable.* ▶ to decide, to decree, to adjudicate, to judge

ruler *noun*
The country has a new ruler.
▶ a monarch, a sovereign, a king, a queen, a governor, a leader

rumble *verb*
The traffic rumbled across the bridge.
▶ to thunder, to roar

rummage *verb*
Someone had been rummaging through her things. ▶ to search, to comb, to scour

rumple *verb*
The curtains had been rumpled. ▶ to crease, to crumple, to ruffle

rumpus *noun*
We could hear a rumpus from the next room. ▶ a disturbance, a noise, a din, a commotion, a hubbub

run *verb*
1 *We had to run to catch the bus.* ▶ to dash, to race, to hurry, to rush
2 *Trains run every hour.* ▶ to go, to travel, to operate
3 *The engine was running smoothly.*
▶ to work, to function, to perform
4 *Water was running from the tap.*
▶ to dribble, to flow, to gush, to pour, to stream, to trickle
5 *She runs a corner shop.* ▶ to manage, to look after, to maintain, to supervise

run away *verb*
The dog must have run away. ▶ to escape, to flee, to get away, to make off

run over *verb*
We ran over a rabbit in the car. ▶ to hit, to run down, to knock over

runny *adjective*
The mixture for the pudding looked too runny. ▶ watery, sloppy, liquid, thin

rural *adjective*
The house was in a rural setting.
▶ country, rustic, pastoral

ruse *noun*
Sam had thought of a ruse to get his sister out of the house. ▶ a scheme, a trick, a ploy, a stratagem

rush *verb*
When the doorbell rang I rushed to see
who it was. ▶ to dash, to race, to
hurry, to run, to hasten

rush *noun*
1 *A rush of cool air came in from the
open window.* ▶ a stream, a flow, a
flood
2 *There was a rush to get tickets for the
concert.* ▶ a dash, a stampede, a
scramble
3 *I'm in rather a rush.* ▶ a hurry

rust *verb*
The car had begun to rust under the
wheel arches. ▶ to go rusty, to corrode

rustic *adjective*
They enjoy the peace of their rustic
surroundings. ▶ country, rural,
pastoral

rustle *verb*
The papers on the table rustled in the
breeze. ▶ to swish

rusty *adjective*
The gate was old and rusty. ▶ rusted,
corroded

rut *noun*
It was difficult to avoid all the ruts in
the soft ground. ▶ a furrow, a groove

ruthless *adjective*
The king was ruthless in hunting down
his enemies. ▶ cruel, callous, heartless,
pitiless, bloodthirsty

S s

sack *noun*
There was a sack of old clothes on the
floor. ▶ a bag, a pouch, a pack

sack *verb*
Ken's brother had been sacked from his
job. ▶ to dismiss, to fire

sacred *adjective*
The Koran is a sacred book. ▶ holy,
religious, divine

sacrifice *verb*
Several people sacrificed their holidays
to help with the rescue. ▶ to give up, to
forgo, to surrender

sad *adjective*
1 *We were sad about having to leave.*
▶ unhappy, despondent, down-
hearted, sorrowful, dejected,
downcast, miserable, glum, gloomy,
melancholy; (informal) low, down
2 *There is a sad story in the newspaper
about an abandoned baby.*
▶ distressing, touching, pathetic,
pitiful
3 *Some of the songs in the show were
quite sad.* ▶ melancholy, touching,
poignant

sadden *verb*
The bad news saddened everyone. ▶ to
upset, to dishearten, to deject, to
dismay, to depress

safe *adjective*
1 *I needed to find somewhere safe to
leave my bags.* ▶ secure, protected,
defended
2 *Jenny had had quite an adventure but
got home safe.* ▶ unharmed,
unscathed
3 *It is important to drive at a safe
speed.* ▶ sensible, prudent
4 *The medicine is quite safe for children.*
▶ harmless, innocuous

safeguard *verb*
The law has to safeguard innocent
people. ▶ to protect, to defend, to look
after

safety *noun*
The precautions were meant for our safety. ▶ protection, security

sag *verb*
Some heavy books made the shelf sag in the middle. ▶ to bend, to bow, to dip, to slump, to hang down

sail *verb*
We sail from Venice tomorrow. ▶ to set sail, to go by ship

sailor *noun*
The boy was the grandson of an old sailor. ▶ a seaman, a seafarer, a mariner

sake *noun*
She went to a lot of trouble for my sake. ▶ benefit, advantage, good, welfare

salary *noun*
She earns a salary of £40,000 a year. ▶ an income
NOTE: You can also say *She receives earnings of £40,000 a year* or *She earns £40,000 a year.*

salvage *verb*
The ship sank and was salvaged many years later. ▶ to recover, to rescue, to retrieve, to reclaim

same *adjective*
1 *He's the same person we saw yesterday.* ▶ identical
NOTE: You can also say *He's the very person we saw yesterday.*
2 *The two houses look the same.* ▶ similar, identical

sample *noun*
We borrowed some carpet samples from the shop. ▶ a specimen, an example, an illustration

sample *verb*
Would you like to sample my cake? ▶ to try, to have some of, to taste

sane *adjective*
It was an odd thing for a sane person to do. ▶ normal, rational, reasonable

sap *verb*
The heat had sapped our energy. ▶ to exhaust, to drain, to reduce, to use up

sarcastic *adjective*
Jack could be very sarcastic and hurtful. ▶ mocking, scornful, derisive

satisfactory *adjective*
We never got a satisfactory explanation of what happened. ▶ acceptable, adequate, reasonable, sufficient, tolerable, fair

satisfied *adjective*
1 *We are satisfied that they are telling the truth.* ▶ convinced, persuaded, content, happy, assured
2 *He had a satisfied look on his face.* ▶ contented, happy, smug

satisfy *verb*
1 *I don't think a sandwich will satisfy me.* ▶ to content, to make happy, to be enough for
2 *There is not enough food to satisfy all our needs.* ▶ to fulfil, to meet

saturate *verb*
My clothes are saturated with rain. ▶ to soak, to drench

saucy *adjective*
She spoke to her mother in a saucy way. ▶ cheeky, pert, rude, disrespectful, impudent, insolent

saunter *verb*
It would be nice to saunter through the gardens. ▶ to stroll, to amble, to wander, to roam

savage *adjective*
They were the victims of a savage attack. ▶ cruel, violent, barbaric, vicious, bloodthirsty, murderous, brutal, ferocious, ruthless

save *verb*
1 *A special force was sent in to save the hostages.* ▶ to free, to liberate, to rescue, to release, to set free
2 *We'd better save some of the food for later.* ▶ to keep, to preserve, to put by, to hold on to
3 *I'm trying to save some money for my holiday.* ▶ to keep, to set aside, to put by, to save up
4 *It is important to save the children from any danger.* ▶ to protect, to safeguard, to keep

say *verb*
1 *Colin tried to say what he really thought.* ▶ to state, to express, to convey, to explain
2 *I said that it was getting late.* ▶ to mention, to remark, to comment
3 *She was too angry to say his name.* ▶ to speak, to utter

saying *noun*
There is a saying that an apple a day keeps the doctor away. ▶ a proverb, an adage, a maxim, a motto, a slogan

scale *verb*
The climbers began to scale the rock face. ▶ to climb, to ascend, to mount

scales *plural noun*
The cat was too heavy to weigh in the scales. ▶ a balance

scamper *verb*
You could hear the mice scampering back into their holes. ▶ to scurry, to scuttle, to dash, to hurry, to run

scan *verb*
1 *We scanned the landscape for signs of a road.* ▶ to study, to survey, to view, to gaze at, to scrutinize, to examine
2 *She scanned the book for a picture of the village.* ▶ to look through, to glance through, to skim, to read quickly

scandal *noun*
1 *Their behaviour caused quite a scandal.* ▶ a sensation, an outrage, an embarrassment
2 *The newspaper article was full of scandal.* ▶ gossip, rumour

scandalous *adjective*
Their behaviour had not just been embarrassing but downright scandalous. ▶ disgraceful, outrageous, shameful, shocking

scanty *adjective*
The furniture in the house was old and scanty. ▶ sparse, meagre, inadequate

scar *noun*
The man had a scar on his left cheek. ▶ a mark, a blemish

scar *verb*
His face had been scarred in an accident. ▶ to mark, to disfigure, to damage

scarce *adjective*
Fresh fruit was scarce because of the war. ▶ short, in short supply, lacking, sparse, meagre, limited, scanty

scarcely *adverb*
Donna had scarcely finished eating when the phone rang. ▶ barely, hardly, only just

scare *verb*
The noise was scaring the animals. ▶ to frighten, to alarm, to startle, to terrify

scare *noun*
You gave me quite a scare. ▶ a fright, a shock

scary *adjective*
(informal) *It was scary in the dark.* ▶ creepy, eerie, frightening, ghostly, spooky, uncanny, weird

scatter *verb*
1 *Roof tiles were scattered on the ground after the gales.* ▶ to throw, to strew, to

spread, to disperse
2 *The crowd scattered when the police arrived.* ▶ to disperse, to run off, to break up

scene *noun*
1 *This is the scene of the incident.*
▶ a location, a setting, a site, a place
2 *They made a scene when they were kept waiting.* ▶ an argument, a fuss, a commotion
3 *The house looked out on a rural scene.* ▶ a view, a landscape, a panorama, a prospect, a vista

scenic *adjective*
The holiday company organized coach trips to scenic areas. ▶ beautiful, pretty, picturesque, attractive, lovely

scent *noun*
The scent of roses was coming into the room. ▶ a fragrance, a perfume, an aroma, a smell, a whiff

sceptical *adjective*
I was sceptical about getting to the station in time. ▶ doubtful, disbelieving, dubious, incredulous, pessimistic, unconvinced

schedule *noun*
The schedule requires him to walk 15 miles every day. ▶ a timetable, a programme, a plan

scheme *noun*
The government will give details of a scheme to help students. ▶ a plan, a project, a proposal, a procedure, a system

scheme *verb*
Some people were scheming to overthrow the government. ▶ to plot, to conspire, to intrigue, to plan

scholar *noun*
He is the son of a distinguished scholar.
▶ an academic, an intellectual

scoff at *verb*
It was hard not to scoff at such nonsense. ▶ to make fun of, to sneer at, to laugh at, to scorn, to ridicule

scold *verb*
Tim's mother scolded him for upsetting his sister. ▶ to reprimand, to rebuke, to tell off, to censure, to criticize; (informal) to tick off

scoop *verb*
The dog had scooped out some earth to bury its bone. ▶ to dig, to hollow, to gouge, to shovel

scope *noun*
1 *That question doesn't come within the scope of this book.* ▶ the range, the extent, the limits
2 *We like to give you plenty of scope for trying out your own ideas.* ▶ room, opportunity

scorch *verb*
The iron had slightly scorched his white shirt. ▶ to singe, to burn

score *noun*
At the end of the game we'll add up the score. ▶ the total, the marks, the points

score *verb*
1 *We have scored ten points.* ▶ to gain, to win, to make, to get, to be awarded
2 *Your hard shoes have scored the wooden floor.* ▶ to scratch, to mark

scorn *noun*
She didn't think she deserved such scorn from us. ▶ contempt, derision, disdain, disgust, mockery

scorn *verb*
He wanted to be artistic and scorned the use of a ruler. ▶ to scoff at, to despise, to deride, to spurn, to reject

scoundrel *noun*
The letter sounded old-fashioned and accused him of being a scoundrel.
▶ a rogue, a villain, a rascal, a knave

scour *verb*
1 *The saucepan needs scouring.* ▶ to scrub, to clean, to polish
2 *We scoured the garden but the tortoise had vanished.* ▶ to search, to comb, to ransack, to rummage through

scowl *verb*
She folded her arms and scowled at us.
▶ to frown, to glare, to glower

scramble *verb*
1 *We scrambled up the steep slope.*
▶ to clamber, to climb, to crawl
2 *Everyone scrambled for the ball.* ▶ to struggle, to fight, to scuffle, to tussle

scrap *noun*
1 *The yard was full of old scrap.* ▶ junk, rubbish, waste
2 *There were still scraps of food on the table.* ▶ a bit, a crumb, a speck, a particle, a morsel, a piece, a fragment
3 *Some dogs were having a scrap in the road.* ▶ a fight

scrap *verb*
In the end we had to scrap the idea.
▶ to give up, to abandon, to discard, to drop, to throw away

scrape *noun*
They were in a bit of a scrape.
▶ trouble, a difficulty, a jam

scrape *verb*
1 *I managed to scrape my hand against the wall.* ▶ to scratch, to graze
2 *It took a long time to scrape off all the old paint.* ▶ to scrub, to rub, to scour

scrape together *verb*
They scraped together enough money for a holiday. ▶ to collect, to save

scratch *verb*
1 *Someone has scratched the paint on the door.* ▶ to mark, to scrape, to damage, to score
2 *If your skin itches you have to scratch it.* ▶ to rub

scream *verb*
He screamed and jumped back in fear.
▶ to screech, to shriek, to yell, to cry out

scream *noun*
We heard a scream in the next room.
▶ a screech, a shriek, a yell, a cry

screen *noun*
There was a screen round his bed.
▶ a partition, a panel, a blind, a curtain

screen *verb*
A tall fence screened the tennis courts from the park. ▶ to conceal, to shield, to hide, to shade, to protect

scribble *verb*
Before rushing off, Sonia had scribbled a note and left it on the table. ▶ to scrawl, to dash off, to jot down, to write

scrub *verb*
First, he scrubbed the boy from head to toe with a piece of hard soap. ▶ to scour, to rub, to brush, to clean, to wash

scruffy *adjective*
I had nothing to wear that day except a scruffy old pair of jeans. ▶ shabby, untidy, dishevelled, dirty, scrappy, tatty

scrutinize *verb*
He picked up the book and scrutinized it carefully. ▶ to examine, to inspect, to study

scuffle *noun*
The argument ended in an ugly scuffle.
▶ a fight, a brawl, a tussle, a struggle

seal *noun*
The document bore an official seal.
▶ a stamp, a crest, an emblem

seal *verb*
1 *Seal the jar before you store it.* ▶ to
fasten, to secure, to stop up
2 *I've sealed the envelope.* ▶ to stick
down, to close

search *verb*
1 *The whole family began searching for
the lost tortoise.* ▶ to hunt, to explore,
to look
2 *The staff searched the supermarket
for the lost child.* ▶ to scour, to comb,
to explore, to look through

search *noun*
The child was found after a long search.
▶ a hunt, a check; (not an everyday
word) a quest

seat *noun*
The room has seats for fifty people.
▶ a chair, a bench, seating

secluded *adjective*
*They found a secluded beach for their
picnic.* ▶ remote, quiet, isolated,
inaccessible, lonely, private, solitary

second *noun*
The buzzing noise lasted a few seconds.
▶ a moment

secret *adjective*
1 *What I told you is secret.*
▶ confidential, private, personal
2 *The house had a secret passage.*
▶ hidden, concealed

secretive *adjective*
*John was quiet and secretive, and told
us very little.* ▶ furtive, reticent,
reserved, uncommunicative

section *noun*
*A section of the train had come off the
rails.* ▶ a part, a portion, a bit

sector *noun*
*The army defended the southern sector
of the town.* ▶ an area, a district, a
section, a part, a zone

secure *adjective*
1 *Check that all the doors and windows
are secure.* ▶ fastened, locked
2 *The castle was secure against attack.*
▶ safe, protected, defended
3 *The shelves are not very secure.*
▶ firm, fixed, steady, solid

sedate *adjective*
*We drove through what looked like a
quiet and sedate town.* ▶ calm,
dignified, tranquil, peaceful, sober

see *verb*
1 *What did you see from the window?*
▶ to observe, to notice, to catch sight
of, to spot, to discern, to distinguish, to
look at, to make out, to perceive, to
recognize; (not an everyday word) to
behold
2 *She saw what I meant.* ▶ to
understand, to comprehend, to grasp,
to follow, to realize, to appreciate, to
know
3 *See that the door is locked when you
leave.* ▶ to ensure, to make sure, to
make certain
4 *I went to see my Mum in her office.*
▶ to visit, to call on, to meet
5 *I'll see you to the gate.* ▶ to escort, to
accompany, to take, to conduct
6 *Can you see yourself as a singer?* ▶ to
imagine, to picture, to visualize, to
conceive of

seek *verb*
1 *You need to seek medical advice.* ▶ to
look for, to try to get
2 *All we seek is a little peace.* ▶ to
want, to need, to wish for, to desire

seem *verb*
They seem happy in their new house.
▶ to appear, to look, to sound

seep *verb*
Water was seeping into the basement.
► to trickle, to ooze, to dribble, to drip, to flow, to leak

seize *verb*
1 *One of the children seized a pillow.*
► to grab, to grasp, to snatch, to clutch
2 *The suspects were seized at the airport.* ► to arrest, to capture, to detain, to catch

seldom *adverb*
It seldom rains here. ► rarely, not often, infrequently, hardly ever
NOTE: If you use **infrequently**, you have to say *It rains here infrequently*, and if you use **not often** you have to say *It doesn't rain here often*.

select *verb*
He selected a cigar and sat back. ► to choose, to take, to pick, to decide on, to settle on

self-centred *adjective*
They thought he was self-centred and idle. ► selfish, egocentric

self-confident *adjective*
Jane is self-confident enough to try anything. ► assertive, assured, sure of yourself, bold, positive

self-conscious *adjective*
I felt rather self-conscious in my floppy hat. ► bashful, shy, embarrassed, reserved

selfish *adjective*
It was selfish of them to leave without offering you a lift. ► self-centred, thoughtless

sell *verb*
The local shop sells a wide range of cheeses. ► to market, to retail, to deal in, to trade in, to stock, to handle

send *verb*
When did they send the parcel? ► to dispatch, to post, to transmit

send away *verb*
When I had finished with them I sent them away. ► to dismiss, to get rid of

send for *verb*
We'd better send for the doctor. ► to fetch, to call for, to call, to summon

sensation *noun*
1 *There's an itching sensation in my leg.*
► a feeling
2 *The news caused quite a sensation.*
► an excitement, a commotion, a thrill, a scandal

sensational *adjective*
1 *The front page of the newspaper was full of sensational stories.* ► lurid, shocking, startling
2 *She looked sensational in her new dress.* ► marvellous, wonderful, dazzling, spectacular, fabulous, fantastic

sense *noun*
1 *A good sense of rhythm will improve your writing.* ► a feeling, an awareness
2 *Fortunately she had the sense to keep quiet.* ► the intelligence, the wisdom, the brains, the gumption, the wit

sense *verb*
1 *She sensed that I had not told her everything.* ► to perceive, to realize, to detect, to discern, to become aware, to feel
2 *The device senses radioactivity.* ► to detect, to record, to pick up

senseless *adjective*
1 *The war was a senseless conflict that could have been avoided.* ► stupid, foolish, pointless, absurd
2 *The wounded man lay senseless on the ground.* ► unconscious

sensible *adjective*
1 *I need someone sensible to look after the children one day a week.* ▶ wise, prudent, intelligent, shrewd, reasonable, thoughtful, practical
2 *It would have been sensible to let us know.* ▶ prudent, wise, advisable

sensitive *adjective*
1 *You should use sun cream if you have sensitive skin.* ▶ delicate, tender, soft
2 *He's quite sensitive about being criticized.* ▶ touchy, difficult

sentimental *adjective*
The film is a sentimental love story.
▶ emotional, romantic, tender, soppy

separate *adjective*
1 *We need to keep these two piles of coins separate.* ▶ apart, separated
2 *I work in a separate part of the building.* ▶ different, distinct, detached

separate *verb*
1 *I'll try to separate the best ones from the others.* ▶ to detach, to divide, to remove, to set apart, to cut off, to break off
2 *The road separates into two at the bottom of the hill.* ▶ to divide, to diverge, to fork
3 *His parents separated when he was quite small.* ▶ to divorce, to split up

sequence *noun*
1 *Put the cards in the right sequence.*
▶ an order, an arrangement
2 *The sequence of events began with a murder.* ▶ a series, a chain, a course, a succession

serene *adjective*
Her face looked serene and beautiful.
▶ calm, peaceful, tranquil, placid

series *noun*
A series of disasters followed.
▶ a sequence, a succession, a chain, a string, a row

serious *adjective*
1 *We have to discuss some serious business.* ▶ important, significant, weighty
2 *He's had a serious car accident.*
▶ bad, severe, nasty, dreadful, terrible
3 *When she heard the news her expression became serious.*
▶ thoughtful, solemn, earnest, grave
4 *They are serious about wanting to come.* ▶ sincere, earnest, genuine, firm

serve *verb*
When I went into the shop a young girl came up to serve me. ▶ to help, to assist, to attend, to look after

service *noun*
1 *He retired after forty years' service.*
▶ work, employment, duty
2 *Doing the shopping for us was a great service.* ▶ a help, a favour, an assistance

service *verb*
My car needs to be serviced. ▶ to maintain, to overhaul, to check

session *noun*
The talk was followed by a session of questions and answers. ▶ a period, a spell, an interval

set *noun*
1 *She didn't want to go with the swimming set.* ▶ a group, a bunch
2 *I'll buy you a new set of tools if you like.* ▶ a collection, a lot

set *verb*
1 *He set the basket down on the low table.* ▶ to put, to place, to stand, to leave, to rest, to lay, to position, to deposit
2 *By the time we returned the cement had set and was hard enough to walk on.* ▶ to harden, to solidify
3 *They were the sort of people who*

always set the table for next morning's breakfast. ▶ to lay, to arrange, to prepare

set off verb
1 We'll have to set off early. ▶ to leave, to depart; (informal) to get going
2 Some people were setting off fireworks. ▶ to detonate, to explode, to let off

set up verb
The bank has set up a new branch in Edinburgh. ▶ to open, to establish

setback noun
We finished on time, despite setbacks. ▶ a difficulty, a snag, a complication, a problem

settle verb
1 Rose settled in a chair and closed her eyes. ▶ to relax, to sit back, to rest
2 The family wants to settle in Australia. ▶ to emigrate (to), to go to live, to move (to)
3 We still have to settle where we are going for our holiday. ▶ to decide, to agree, to fix, to choose, to establish
4 It took years to settle all our debts. ▶ to pay, to repay

sever verb
His hand was severed by a mighty blow with the sword. ▶ to cut off, to chop off, to separate

severe adjective
1 Parents were much more severe in those days. ▶ strict, harsh, stern, hard
2 He was suffering from a severe headache. ▶ bad, acute, strong, intense

sew verb
It's better to sew the pieces by hand. ▶ to stitch

sew up verb
I'll try to sew up the hole in your jacket. ▶ to stitch, to darn, to mend, to repair

shabby adjective
The young woman was wearing a shabby straw hat. ▶ ragged, scruffy, tattered, worn, threadbare

shack noun
The old man lived in a shack in the mountains. ▶ a hut, a hovel

shade noun
1 We ate our food under the shade of an oak tree. ▶ the shadow, the shelter
2 The sea looked a dark shade of green. ▶ a tinge, a hue, a tint, a tone

shade verb
I had to shade my eyes from the strong light. ▶ to shield, to mask, to protect, to screen

shadow noun
The boy stood in the shadow of a tall building. ▶ the shade

shadow verb
Chris was sent to shadow her and report back on her movements. ▶ to follow, to stalk, to pursue, to tail

shady adjective
1 The hotel is located in a shady avenue near the beach. ▶ shaded, shadowy, sheltered, cool
2 He's always making shady deals on his mobile phone. ▶ dishonest, crooked, suspicious, disreputable, dubious; (informal) dodgy

shaft noun
1 He pulled the arrow out by its shaft. ▶ a stem, a rod
2 A shaft of light fell through the window. ▶ a beam, a ray, a gleam

shaggy adjective
The big shaggy head turned to look at me. ▶ hairy, bushy, woolly

shake verb
1 Her grandmother's hand was shaking a little. ▶ to tremble, to quiver, to

shiver, to shudder
2 *'Go away!' he yelled, shaking his fist at them.* ▶ to wave, to raise, to swing, to brandish
3 *Claire picked up the rug and shook it out of the window.* ▶ to wave, to waggle, to wag, to twirl
4 *I think the news shook him pretty badly.* ▶ to shock, to alarm, to distress, to startle, to perturb, to frighten

shaky *adjective*
The table was too shaky to put anything down on it. ▶ unsteady, wobbly, flimsy, rickety, rocky, insecure, precarious

shallow *adjective*
The water was shallow as far as we could see. ▶ not deep

sham *noun*
The excuse had been a sham all along.
▶ a pretence, a deception

shambles *noun*
Our first rehearsal turned into a complete shambles. ▶ a muddle, a mess, chaos

shame *noun*
1 *His face was red with shame.*
▶ disgrace, guilt, humiliation, remorse, dishonour, embarrassment
2 *It was a shame you couldn't come with us.* ▶ a pity, bad luck

shameful *adjective*
What had been an exciting adventure now seemed a shameful thing to have done. ▶ disgraceful, deplorable, shocking, bad

shape *noun*
You can tell what kind of tree it is by its shape. ▶ a form, an outline, a figure, a profile
SOME COMMON SHAPES ARE:
plane shapes (flat shapes that can be cut from paper): polygon (3 or more sides), triangle (3 sides), quadrilateral

(4 sides), rectangle (4 sides and 4 right angles), square (4 sides of the same length and 4 right angles), pentagon (5 sides), hexagon (6 sides), heptagon (7 sides), octagon (8 sides); circle, oval, ellipse;
solid shapes (having three dimensions): polyhedron (a solid shape with straight edges), tetrahedron (4 sides that are triangles), cube (6 sides that are squares), octahedron (8 sides that are triangles); sphere (like a ball), cylinder (with ends that are circles and a circular cross-section), cone (with a circular base and coming to a point)

shape *verb*
She shaped and softened the clay with her long thin fingers. ▶ to mould, to form, to fashion

share *noun*
A lot of people will get a share of the reward. ▶ a part, a portion, an allowance, a quota

share *verb*
1 *The boys stopped to buy a can of drink each and share a bar of chocolate.* ▶ to divide, to split, to halve
2 *They wanted us to share in the good luck.* ▶ to be involved, to take part, to join, to participate

share out *verb*
Let's share out what we have left. ▶ to distribute, to hand out

sharp *adjective*
1 *The rocks on the beach were sharp and hurt her feet.* ▶ pointed, jagged, spiky, razor-sharp
2 *Young Gary possessed a sharp and inquisitive mind.* ▶ clever, bright, quick, acute, astute, smart, shrewd
3 *The apple she chose was not sweet, but had a sharp taste.* ▶ sour, acid, tangy, tart

4 *To the left of the road there is a sharp drop down the side of the hill. There has been a sharp rise in house prices.*
▶ sudden, steep, abrupt, precipitous
5 *I suddenly felt a sharp pain in my back.* ▶ severe, acute, extreme, intense, serious, violent
6 *There is a sharp distinction between borrowing and stealing.* ▶ clear, clear-cut, distinct, definite, marked

shatter *verb*
He closed the dishwasher with a crash that shattered a wine glass. The crash made a wine glass shatter. ▶ to smash, to splinter, to fracture, to break

shed *noun*
The gardener put his tools back in the shed. ▶ a hut, an outhouse, a shack

shed *verb*
1 *He was so badly hurt he was shedding blood.* ▶ to spill, to drip, to drop
2 *The road was blocked by a lorry that had shed its load.* ▶ to spill, to scatter, to drop

sheen *noun*
The table had been polished to a fine sheen. ▶ a shine, a gloss, a lustre

sheepish *adjective*
He greeted his mother with a sheepish grin. ▶ bashful, coy, self-conscious, shy, timid, embarrassed

sheer *adjective*
1 *It was sheer chance that Martha had been there at the same time.*
▶ complete, pure, absolute, total, utter
2 *A few yards away was the top of a sheer cliff.* ▶ abrupt, precipitous, vertical

sheet *noun*
1 *Write the answer on a sheet of paper.*
▶ a leaf, a page
2 *The builder brought in a sheet of glass.* ▶ a pane, a plate
3 *The pond was covered by a sheet of ice.* ▶ a layer, a film

shell *noun*
The nut has a hard shell. ▶ a case, a covering

shelter *noun*
1 *The travellers looked for shelter for the night.* ▶ refuge, safety, protection
2 *A row of trees offered a shelter from the rain.* ▶ a refuge, a cover, a haven

shelter *verb*
A hill shelters the house from the wind.
▶ to protect, to shield, to defend, to guard

shield *noun*
The fence acts as a shield against the wind. ▶ a protection, a defence, a guard, a safeguard

shield *verb*
A plastic roof shielded us from the rain.
▶ to protect, to shelter

shift *verb*
1 *It will take a long time to shift all the furniture.* ▶ to move, to carry
2 *The man looked angry and refused to shift.* ▶ to move, to budge, to change position

shine *verb*
A light was shining in the distance. ▶ to glow, to gleam, to glimmer

shiny *adjective*
He was very proud of his shiny new shoes. ▶ polished, gleaming, glossy, bright, shining

shiver *verb*
Donna shivered and decided to get back in the car. ▶ to tremble, to quiver, to shudder, to quaver, to shake

shock *noun*
1 *It was a shock to discover that he had failed the exam.* ▶ a surprise, a blow; (informal) a bombshell
2 *The shock of the explosion was felt several miles away.* ▶ the impact, the blast (from), the jolt

shock *verb*
The villagers were shocked to see houses collapsing around them. ▶ to appal, to horrify, to alarm, to startle, to dismay, to stun, to daze, to stupefy

shocking *adjective*
Conditions in the prison were shocking. ▶ appalling, dreadful, awful, frightful, terrible, scandalous

shoddy *adjective*
We are not paying good money for shoddy goods. ▶ inferior, poor-quality, cheap, nasty

shoot *verb*
1 *Shoot the rifle to hit the target.* ▶ to fire, to aim, to discharge
2 *The sentry on duty shot at the intruders.* ▶ to fire, to open fire (on), to aim
3 *A sports car shot past.* ▶ to streak, to flash, to fly, to speed

short *adjective*
1 *The book is quite short and won't take long to read.* ▶ brief, concise, compact
2 *The man was short and aged about fifty.* ▶ small, squat, dumpy
3 *They are here on a short visit.* ▶ brief, quick, cursory, passing
4 *In a dry summer, water can be short.* ▶ scarce, in short supply, sparse, lacking, limited, scanty
5 *He was rather short with me.* ▶ curt, abrupt, sharp, irritable, bad-tempered, snappy, testy, cross, grumpy

shortage *noun*
There seems to be a shortage of paper. ▶ a lack, a deficiency, a scarcity, a want

shortcoming *noun*
The plan was generally good but had a few shortcomings. ▶ a fault, a failing, a defect, an imperfection, a weakness, a vice
NOTE: A **vice** is a bad habit that a person has

shorten *verb*
The story is too long and needs to be shortened. ▶ to cut, to abridge, to compress, to condense, to reduce

shortly *adverb*
The plumber is arriving shortly to fix the bath tap. ▶ soon, presently, in a short while, in a little while, directly

shot *noun*
1 *We heard a shot from the trees.* ▶ a bang, a blast, a crack, a report
2 *I'm going to have a shot at the competition.* ▶ a try, an attempt

shout *verb*
They soon became angry and started shouting. ▶ to call out, to yell, to cry out, to bawl, to shriek

shout *noun*
The conversation was interrupted by shouts from the garden. ▶ a yell, a cry, a call

shove *verb*
Some lads pushed past and shoved us out of the way. ▶ to push, to jostle, to hustle

show *noun*
We went to see a fashion show. ▶ an exhibition, a display

show *verb*
1 *The cinema shows four or five films each fortnight.* ▶ to present, to put on
2 *Emma showed me how to mend a*

puncture. ▶ to explain, to tell, to teach, to demonstrate (to)

3 *It's only a scratch and it won't show.* ▶ to be seen, to be visible, to stand out

4 *I'll show them round the house.* ▶ to direct, to guide

5 *One of the photographs showed the old fire station.* ▶ to depict, to illustrate, to picture, to portray

6 *Research shows that fire alarms can cause panic.* ▶ to demonstrate, to prove

show off *verb*
Some people can't help showing off.
▶ to boast, to brag, to swank

shower *verb*
She showered them with kisses. ▶ to overwhelm, to inundate

showy *adjective*
The house was decorated in showy colours. ▶ brash, bright, flashy, gaudy, lurid, conspicuous, striking

shred *noun*
Shreds of paper lay on the floor.
▶ a strip, a piece, a scrap

shrewd *adjective*
Rashid was a shrewd man, and good with numbers. ▶ clever, astute, ingenious, crafty, sharp, smart, intelligent, knowing, wise

shriek *verb*
Steve leapt to his feet, shrieking, and knocked his chair over. ▶ to scream, to yell, to shout, to screech

shriek *noun*
Someone pinched him, and he let out a shriek. ▶ a screech, a scream, a yell, a shout

shrill *adjective*
The shrill ringing of the telephone woke her up. ▶ harsh, piercing, high-pitched, sharp

shrink *verb*
1 *The woodwork started to shrink, leaving gaps and causing draughts.*
▶ to contract, to shrivel

2 *After a few years the costs begin to shrink.* ▶ to lessen, to reduce, to decrease, to contract, to diminish, to dwindle

shrink back *verb*
Isabel shrank back in fright, stumbling over a bench. ▶ to recoil, to jump back, to flinch, to spring back, to cringe

shrivel *verb*
All they could find to eat was a piece of cold meat that had started to shrivel.
▶ to shrink, to dry up, to wither, to wilt

shroud *verb*
The countryside was shrouded in mist.
▶ to cover, to envelop, to hide, to veil, to blanket, to wrap

shudder *verb*
The thought of all the things he had to do made him shudder. ▶ to shake, to quiver, to tremble, to shiver

shuffle *verb*
1 *The old man shuffled down the road.*
▶ to hobble, to shamble

2 *Have you shuffled the cards?* ▶ to mix, to jumble

shut *verb*
1 *Elaine came in and shut the door. The door shut suddenly.* ▶ to close
NOTE: To shut something very hard is to **slam** it

2 *Make sure you shut the windows at night.* ▶ to close, to fasten, to secure, to lock

shut in *verb*
The dogs are all shut in for the night.
▶ to confine, to enclose, to keep in, to coop up

shut up *verb*
Tell them to shut up. ▶ to be quiet, to keep quiet, to be silent

shy *adjective*
I was too shy to say anything.
▶ nervous, timid, bashful, coy, modest, self-conscious, inhibited

sick *adjective*
1 *The next day he felt sick and had to stay away.* ▶ ill, unwell, poorly, queer; (more formal) indisposed
2 *Laura was sick of hearing about Ted's problems.* ▶ tired, fed up (with), bored (with)

sicken *verb*
It sickened them to see so much poverty.
▶ to disgust, to revolt, to repel, to nauseate

sickly *adjective*
Emma had been a sickly child.
▶ unhealthy, weak, frail, delicate

side *noun*
1 *There are six sides to a cube. There are no windows on this side of the house.* ▶ a face, a surface
2 *A triangle has three sides.* ▶ an edge
3 *There is a path down one side of the garden.* ▶ an edge, a verge, a border, a fringe, a margin
4 *The two sides came on the pitch together.* ▶ a team

siege *noun*
The siege of the city lasted for several months. ▶ a blockade

sift *verb*
Sift the flour to take out all the lumps.
▶ to strain, to sieve

sight *noun*
1 *Karen has good sight and had no trouble spotting the boys in the distance.*
▶ eyesight, vision
2 *After a few miles we turned a corner*

and had a sight of the village. ▶ a view
3 *The garden is a lovely sight in spring.*
▶ a scene, a spectacle, a vision

sight *verb*
The boy was sighted at a bus stop. ▶ to spot, to observe, to recognize, to see, to notice

sign *noun*
1 *She gave them a sign to be quiet.*
▶ a signal, a gesture, an indication
2 *There were no signs of life at the cottage.* ▶ a clue, an indication, a symptom
3 *A no-entry sign had been put across the road.* ▶ a signpost, a notice
4 *= is the sign for 'equals'.* ▶ a symbol, a mark

sign *verb*
1 *You have to sign your name on the form.* ▶ to write
2 *We have signed three new players.*
▶ to recruit, to take on, to enrol, to contract

signal *noun*
The police officer raised a hand as a signal to stop. ▶ a sign, a gesture, an indication

signal *verb*
The speaker signalled that he was ready to start. ▶ to gesture, to indicate

significance *noun*
Jerry suggested 16 April, but the significance of the date was not clear at the time. ▶ the importance, the meaning, the relevance, the implication

significant *adjective*
1 *The new manager made some significant changes.* ▶ important, considerable
2 *She lost a significant amount of money.* ▶ considerable, large, sizeable

signify *verb*
A cross on the map signifies a church.
▶ to indicate, to mean, to stand for, to represent

silence *noun*
The room fell into silence. ▶ quiet, hush, tranquillity

silence *verb*
The anger in his voice silenced her for a moment. ▶ to quieten

silent *adjective*
1 *The room was as silent as a graveyard.*
▶ quiet, still, soundless, noiseless
2 *While Harry was speaking, the others remained silent.* ▶ quiet, unspeaking, dumb, mute

silly *adjective*
Natalie was sensible and didn't usually do silly things. ▶ foolish, unwise, stupid, senseless, ridiculous, crazy, mad, foolhardy; (informal) daft

similar *adjective*
The houses are all similar in appearance. ▶ alike, identical, the same, much the same, comparable

similarity *noun*
There is a strong similarity between them. ▶ a resemblance, a likeness, a closeness

simple *adjective*
1 *She was wearing light shoes and a simple dress.* ▶ plain, undecorated
2 *We have a few simple questions to answer.* ▶ easy, elementary, uncomplicated
3 *The explanation was simple.* ▶ clear, straightforward, obvious

simply *adverb*
It's simply a question of time. ▶ only, purely, merely, solely

sin *noun*
He was afraid he might have committed a sin. ▶ a wrong, a misdeed, an evil, a wrongdoing

sincere *adjective*
I gave them my sincere good wishes.
▶ honest, genuine, earnest, real, candid

sincerity *noun*
Jack nodded his head, but the gesture had little sincerity. ▶ genuineness, honesty, seriousness

sinful *adjective*
Avoid behaviour that people might think is sinful. ▶ wrong, wicked, bad, evil

sing *verb*
The sun shone and the birds were singing. ▶ to tweet, to chirp
NOTE: There are various words for people singing, such as **croon**, **chant**, and **trill**, but they all have special meanings

singe *verb*
I singed my shirt with the iron. ▶ to scorch, to char, to burn

single *adjective*
1 *A single red rose stood in a vase.*
▶ solitary, sole, isolated
2 *All her cousins were married, except one who was single.* ▶ unmarried

single out *verb*
Jane and Francis were singled out for special praise. ▶ to choose, to pick, to pick out, to select

single-handed *adjective*
Meg managed to finish the job single-handed. ▶ unaided, unassisted, on your own, without help

singular *adjective*
It was a singular piece of luck that she was at home at the time.
▶ extraordinary, remarkable, peculiar

sinister *adjective*
The men lurked in a corner, looking sinister. ▶ menacing, threatening, frightening, ominous

sink *verb*
1 *The ship sank in a storm.* ▶ to go under, to go down, to founder, to submerge
2 *The sun sank behind the trees.* ▶ to go down, to descend
3 *He sank to his knees.* ▶ to fall, to drop, to go down (on)

sit *verb*
Tania was sitting on the bed reading a magazine. ▶ to be seated, to be settled, to perch, to squat, to rest

site *noun*
The site for the new building was close to the river. ▶ a location, a position, a place, a situation, a spot

situation *noun*
1 *Their house is in a pleasant situation near the shops.* ▶ a location, a position, a spot, a place, a site
2 *We saw a programme about the situation in Bosnia.* ▶ conditions, state of affairs, circumstances, affairs

size *noun*
Despite the size of the factory there was only one set of toilets. ▶ the dimensions, the proportions, the magnitude, the area, the extent

sizeable *adjective*
A sizeable crowd had collected outside the gates. ▶ largish, fairly large, considerable, biggish

sketch *noun*
The architect brought some sketches of the house. ▶ a drawing, an outline

sketch *verb*
Joanna sat down to sketch the scene. ▶ to draw, to outline

skilful *adjective*
Gina is a skilful dancer. ▶ able, skilled, capable, accomplished, competent, gifted, proficient, talented

skill *noun*
1 *He grasped her hand and led her with great skill over the rocks.* ▶ ability, competence, expertise, dexterity
2 *Everyone admired Fiona's skill in languages.* ▶ an ability, a talent (for)

skim *verb*
1 *Small birds skimmed the surface of the pond.* ▶ to glide over, to brush
2 *I skimmed across the hard ice.* ▶ to glide, to slide

skin *noun*
1 *The cocoa was getting cold by now and it had a skin on top.* ▶ a film, a covering, a crust, a layer
2 *The fruit has a hard skin.* ▶ a peel, a rind

skinny *adjective*
The old woman lifted her skinny hand. ▶ thin, bony, scraggy, emaciated

skip *verb*
1 *Children were skipping about on the green.* ▶ to jump, to spring, to leap, to frisk, to prance, to bound, to hop, to dance
2 *You'll have to skip a few pages to finish the book in time.* ▶ to miss out, to leave out, to ignore, to pass over

slab *noun*
A slab of stone was leaning against the fence. ▶ a block, a chunk, a hunk, a piece

slack *adjective*
1 *The rope was slack.* ▶ loose, limp
2 *Business is often slack on Mondays.* ▶ light, slow, quiet, sluggish
3 *They have been rather slack about their work.* ▶ lazy, idle, neglectful, careless

slacken *verb*
1 *He slackened his arm as the screw began to turn more easily.* ▶ to relax
2 *The pace slackened towards the end of the race.* ▶ to ease, to reduce, to decrease, to lessen

slam *verb*
The gate kept slamming in the wind. She went over to the window and slammed it shut. ▶ to bang

slant *verb*
The post slanted slightly to the right. ▶ to slope, to lean, to tilt, to incline

slap *verb*
She went over and slapped his face. ▶ to smack, to hit

slapdash *adjective*
Their work had been slapdash. ▶ careless, slovenly, shoddy, untidy, messy

slash *verb*
Someone had slashed the picture with a knife. ▶ to gash, to rip, to hack, to cut

slaughter *verb*
The army slaughtered everyone in the village. ▶ to kill, to massacre, to slay

slaughter *noun*
A scene of slaughter followed. ▶ carnage, bloodshed, killing, massacre, murder

slave *verb*
Everyone slaved for hours to get the job finished. ▶ to toil, to labour, to work

slay *verb*
The king decided to slay all his enemies. ▶ to kill, to slaughter, to massacre, to put to death, to murder

sleek *adjective*
The cat has lovely sleek fur. ▶ smooth, soft, glossy, silky

sleep *verb*
I tried to sleep for a while. ▶ to doze, to snooze, to slumber, to nod off, to take a nap
NOTE: All these words mean 'to sleep for a short time'

sleepy *adjective*
By ten o'clock I was feeling sleepy. ▶ drowsy, tired, weary

slender *adjective*
She had long arms and a slender figure. ▶ slim, thin, fine, slight

slice *verb*
I'll slice some more bread. ▶ to cut, to cut into slices
NOTE: If you are talking about meat you can also use **carve**

slice *noun*
Would you like a slice of bread? ▶ a piece

slick *adjective*
The salesman was very slick and we didn't trust him. ▶ quick, cunning, artful, smart, wily

slide *verb*
He slid down the slope on a toboggan. ▶ to glide, to skate, to skim, to slip

slight *adjective*
Her health has shown a slight improvement. ▶ small, little, modest

slim *adjective*
Eve wore a summer dress with a belt round her slim waist. ▶ slender, thin, narrow, fine

sling *verb*
They were slinging stones into the lake. ▶ to throw, to hurl, to fling, to toss, to lob, to cast; (informal) to chuck

slink *verb*
The burglar slunk past the window. ▶ to sneak, to creep, to steal, to slip, to edge

slip *verb*
1 *Karen wore new shoes, which kept slipping on the polished floor.* ▶ to slide, to skid, to slither
2 *I slipped and nearly fell.* ▶ to stumble, to lose your balance
3 *We slipped out of the house.* ▶ to sneak, to creep, to steal, to slink
4 *Slip this in your pocket.* ▶ to put, to drop, to tuck

slippery *adjective*
The floor had been washed and was still slippery. ▶ slithery; (informal) slippy

slit *noun*
1 *I peeped through a slit in the tent.* ▶ an opening, a chink, a crack
2 *He made a slit in his jeans.* ▶ a gash, a tear, a cut, a split

slit *verb*
I rushed in to slit open the envelope. ▶ to tear, to cut

slither *verb*
Kate fell and slithered across the floor. ▶ to slip, to skid, to slide

slope *noun*
The ball rolled down to the bottom of the slope. ▶ an incline, a ramp, a hill, a gradient

slope *verb*
1 *The grass slopes gently towards the river.* ▶ to fall, to descend, to shelve
2 *The floor sloped at one end.* ▶ to tilt, to lean, to slant, to tip

sloppy *adjective*
1 *The paint was sloppy and dripped down the walls.* ▶ runny, watery, liquid, wet
2 (informal) *Their work is sloppy.* ▶ slovenly, careless, shoddy, slapdash, slipshod
3 *The story was long and rather sloppy.* ▶ sentimental, soppy

slot *noun*
You put the cassette into a slot at the front. ▶ a slit, an opening

slouch *verb*
Nicky slouched back in his chair. ▶ to slump, to droop, to lounge

slovenly *adjective*
Jill's writing had become slovenly. ▶ sloppy, careless, shoddy, slapdash, slipshod

slow *adjective*
1 *They were making slow progress.* ▶ gradual, steady, moderate
2 *They had been slow to finish their work.* ▶ sluggish
3 *He was slow to admit he had been wrong.* ▶ reluctant, hesitant, unwilling

slow down *verb*
You'll have to slow down at the traffic lights. ▶ to brake, to go slower

sly *adjective*
He turned and gave her a sly grin. ▶ cunning, mischievous, wily, artful, crafty, furtive, sneaky

smack *verb*
She didn't want to lose her temper with Jake and smack him. ▶ to slap, to hit, to strike, to spank

small *adjective*
1 *I'd like some coffee, but only a small cup.* ▶ little
2 *The insect was so small you could hardly see it.* ▶ tiny, minute
3 *The food is good but the helpings are rather small.* ▶ meagre, scanty, mean, stingy, ungenerous
4 *If your problem is just a small one you can get help by phone.* ▶ trivial, minor, insignificant, slight, trifling

smart *adjective*
1 *She always looked smart.* ▶ well-dressed, stylish, elegant, fashionable, neat, trim, chic

2 *It was smart of Henry to work out where we'd been.* ► clever, intelligent, bright, astute, shrewd
3 *You can get to the station in ten minutes at a smart pace.* ► brisk, fast, quick

smart *verb*
My eyes were smarting from the cigarette smoke. ► to sting, to hurt, to be sore

smash *verb*
1 *Dan dropped his glass and smashed it.* ► to break, to shatter
2 *The lorry left the road and smashed into a wall.* ► to crash, to bang, to run, to collide (with), to hit
NOTE: If you use **hit** you do not use *into*

smear *verb*
The little boy had smeared jam all over his face. ► to wipe, to rub, to spread, to dab

smell *noun*
1 *There was a strong smell of burning.* ► an odour, a stink, a stench, a reek
2 *What a lovely smell of roses.* ► an aroma, a fragrance, a scent, a perfume, a whiff

smile *verb*
She saw us and smiled. ► to beam, to grin
NOTE: To smile in a silly or unpleasant way is to **smirk**

smooth *adjective*
1 *The top of the table was smooth and polished.* ► level, even
2 *We had a smooth ride.* ► gentle, calm, comfortable
3 *The sea was smooth for most of the crossing.* ► calm, still, flat
4 *Our dog has a lovely smooth coat.* ► sleek, silky, soft, velvety

smooth *verb*
Louise smoothed the newspaper and looked for her article. ► to press, to flatten, to even out

smother *verb*
1 *Be careful not to smother the baby with too many bedclothes.* ► to stifle, to suffocate
2 *They both enjoyed hunks of bread smothered in peanut butter.* ► to cover

smudge *noun*
Someone's fingers had left smudges on the wallpaper. ► a mark, a stain, a spot, a streak, a smear, a blot, a trace

smudge *verb*
I was in too much of a hurry and smudged the page. ► to blot, to smear, to stain, to mark

smug *adjective*
They both sat back with smug smiles on their faces. ► self-satisfied, superior, conceited

snag *noun*
Unless there's a snag we should finish the job today. ► a complication, a setback, a problem, a difficulty, an obstacle

snap *verb*
I pressed too hard and snapped the pencil. I pressed too hard and the pencil snapped. ► to crack, to break

snatch *verb*
She snatched the bag and ran out of the house. ► to seize, to grab, to grasp, to clutch

sneak *verb*
When they aren't looking we can sneak out of the house. ► to slink, to creep, to steal, to slip, to edge

sneaky *adjective*
(informal) *It was a sneaky trick to play on Liz.* ▶ mean, deceitful, devious, sly, underhand

sneer *verb*
He'll sneer if I come back without you. ▶ to scoff, to jeer, to smirk, to make fun of someone

snippet *noun*
There were a few snippets of information in the newspapers. ▶ a scrap, a piece, a fragment, a morsel

snivel *verb*
The children were upset and some of them started to snivel. ▶ to grizzle, to whimper, to blubber, to sob, to cry

snobbish *adjective*
Kim seemed snobbish and didn't want to talk to us. ▶ snooty, snobby, arrogant, superior, haughty, disdainful; (informal) stuck-up

snoop *verb*
He made sure he'd put everything back so no one would suspect he'd been snooping. ▶ to pry, to meddle, to interfere, to intrude, to nose about

snooze *verb*
A cat was snoozing in the corner of a chair. ▶ to doze, to drowse, to sleep, to slumber

snub *verb*
I tried to help, but Ginny snubbed me and walked away. ▶ to be rude to, to scorn, to disdain

snug *adjective*
It was a snug little room with a log fire. ▶ comfortable, cosy, warm

snuggle *verb*
The child snuggled against his mother and went to sleep. ▶ to curl up, to cuddle, to huddle, to nestle

soak *verb*
The driving rain had soaked us. ▶ to drench, to saturate, to wet thoroughly

soak up *verb*
A cloth will soak up the mess. ▶ to absorb, to take up

soar *verb*
The bird gently soared and then dived. ▶ to climb, to rise, to glide, to fly upwards

sob *verb*
She sobbed loudly, and Richard put a hand on her shoulder. ▶ to cry, to weep

sober *adjective*
Myra had a sober expression on her face. ▶ solemn, serious, dignified, grave, sombre

sociable *adjective*
Peter had become more sociable as he grew older. ▶ friendly, genial, affable, outgoing, gregarious

society *noun*
Harry was a member of a local poetry society. ▶ an organization, a club, a group

soft *adjective*
1 *He sank back into the soft leather seat.*
▶ supple, flexible, pliable, springy
2 *The bed was warm and soft.*
▶ comfortable, cosy
3 *The blouse is made of a soft material.*
▶ silky, velvety, smooth, sleek
4 *We heard a soft voice in the next room.* ▶ quiet, gentle, mild, tender
5 *The umpire was accused of being too soft.* ▶ lenient, easygoing, kind

soggy *adjective*
Kate had dropped her towel and it was now soggy. ▶ sodden, sopping, drenched, saturated, soaked, wet through

sole *adjective*
A young child was the sole survivor of the attack. ► single, only, solitary, one

solemn *adjective*
1 The people moved forward in a solemn procession. ► dignified, grave, formal, serious
2 The man looked solemn but said nothing. ► serious, grave, thoughtful

solid *adjective*
1 The house was well built with solid walls. ► firm, sturdy, strong, dense, rigid
2 They gave solid support. ► strong, substantial, reliable, dependable

solitary *adjective*
1 He lived a solitary life. ► lonely, friendless, secluded, unsocial
2 The house was situated in a solitary spot. ► remote, isolated, desolate
3 There was a solitary van in the car park. ► single

solution *noun*
There may be no solution to the problem. ► an answer, an explanation, a key

solve *verb*
The riddle proved difficult to solve. ► to work out, to explain, to answer

sombre *adjective*
1 The room was painted in sombre colours. ► sober, dark, dull, drab, cheerless
2 His grandfather was a sombre and lonely man. ► gloomy, serious, sober, sad, grave

somewhat *adverb*
It was somewhat late. ► rather, fairly, pretty

soon *adverb*
It will be time to go soon. ► shortly, presently, in a while

soothe *verb*
Molly took the baby into another room to try to soothe him. ► to calm, to comfort, to quieten, to pacify, to mollify

soothing *adjective*
The warm water was soft and soothing. ► pleasant, relaxing, gentle, mild, healing

sore *adjective*
He had a sore leg for weeks after his fall. ► painful, hurting, aching, raw, tender, smarting

sorrow *noun*
It was a time of great sorrow for everyone. ► sadness, regret, grief, remorse, anguish

sorrowful *adjective*
They both looked sorrowful as they said goodbye to each other. ► sad, dejected, unhappy, wretched, disconsolate

sorry *adjective*
1 Susan was sorry she hadn't told them. ► regretful, apologetic, remorseful, repentant
2 I was sorry about what had happened. ► sad, unhappy, distressed

sort *noun*
Meg had bought a new sort of car. ► a kind, a make, a brand, a type

sort *verb*
There was a pile of papers waiting to be sorted. ► to arrange, to put in order, to tidy, to organize, to classify

sort out *verb*
I'll have to sort out this problem later. ► to deal with, to attend to, to cope with, to tackle, to handle, to manage

sound *noun*
There was a sound of arguing in the street. ► a noise

sound *adjective*
1 *We all got home safe and sound.*
▶ healthy, well, fit
2 *They wanted to choose a sound investment for their money.* ▶ safe, dependable, reliable, solid
3 *He says odd things but his ideas are sound.* ▶ reasonable, logical, sensible, valid, coherent, right

sour *adjective*
1 *The fruit wasn't yet ripe and tasted sour.* ▶ sharp, acid, tart
2 *His brother had become quite sour, even towards him.* ▶ peevish, grumpy, morose, irritable, disagreeable, testy, bad-tempered, unpleasant

source *noun*
We're not sure what the source of the rumour is. ▶ an origin, a beginning, a cause, a starting point

sow *verb*
The farmer was sowing seed. ▶ to plant, to scatter

space *noun*
1 *There is plenty of space for a car.* ▶ room, capacity
2 *There is a large space between the two houses.* ▶ a gap, an opening, a break
3 *They moved house twice in the space of a year.* ▶ a period

spacious *adjective*
The house was comfortable and spacious. ▶ roomy, large, sizeable; (not an everyday word) commodious

span *noun*
The bridge has a span of half a mile. ▶ a distance, an extent, a length, a width

span *verb*
Several bridges span the river. ▶ to cross, to stretch over, to reach over, to pass over

spare *verb*
1 *Sally needed some money, but her mother could only spare two pounds.* ▶ to afford, to manage, to provide, to give
2 *The king was willing to spare his enemies.* ▶ to pardon, to be merciful to, to forgive, to let off, to reprieve

spare *adjective*
I don't have any spare money. ▶ extra, odd, unused, additional

spark *noun*
The machine ground to a halt as sparks flew out. ▶ a flash, a sparkle

sparkle *verb*
Her huge brown eyes sparkled as she turned her head. ▶ to glint, to gleam, to glitter, to twinkle, to glow

sparse *adjective*
The old man had missing teeth, and his hair was sparse. ▶ thin, scanty, meagre, scarce

spatter *verb*
The lorry spattered mud over the pavement. ▶ to splash, to spray, to shower, to sprinkle

speak *verb*
1 *She was too upset to speak.* ▶ to talk, to say something, to express yourself
2 *Do you speak Spanish?* ▶ to talk, to know

special *adjective*
1 *It had been a special day that everyone enjoyed.* ▶ unusual, notable, important
2 *I like the special smell of fresh bread.* ▶ distinctive, characteristic, unique
3 *Jenny had her special chair.* ▶ personal, individual
4 *There's a special tool for taking out broken screws.* ▶ specific

specialist *noun*
His grandfather had been a specialist in Chinese languages. ▶ an expert, an authority

specific *adjective*
We have to know the specific day it happened. ▶ definite, precise, exact, particular

specimen *noun*
There are some fine specimens of birds on the island. ▶ an example, a sample, an instance, a type

speck *noun*
There was a speck of soot on Angela's cheek. ▶ a spot, a mark, a piece, a bit, a dot, a particle, a grain

speckled *adjective*
Some of the eggs were speckled, and others were pure white. ▶ spotted, flecked, mottled, freckled

spectacle *noun*
The game was exciting and proved a marvellous spectacle. ▶ a display, a show, a sight, an exhibition

spectacular *adjective*
George made a spectacular dive at the other end of the pool. ▶ magnificent, splendid, superb, wonderful, marvellous

spectators *plural noun*
The spectators cheered. ▶ the audience, the crowd, the onlookers

speech *noun*
She gave a short speech after handing out the prizes. ▶ a talk, an address

speed *noun*
They worked with amazing speed. ▶ quickness, swiftness, rapidity

speed *verb*
The car sped up the road. ▶ to race, to shoot, to streak, to zoom, to flash, to tear, to hurtle, to hurry, to rush

speedy *adjective*
We need a speedy reply. ▶ prompt, immediate, instant

spell *noun*
We are going to spend a short spell in the country. ▶ a period, a time, an interval

spend *verb*
1 *He spent a year in Singapore.* ▶ to pass, to live
2 *We had to go home because we had spent all our money.* ▶ to pay, to use up

sphere *noun*
The lamp was made of a large glowing sphere on a tall stand. ▶ a globe, a ball

spike *noun*
The gate post had a dangerous spike at the top. ▶ a point, a prong

spill *verb*
1 *Water was spilling over the edge of the basin.* ▶ to pour, to run, to overflow, to flow, to slop
2 *A lorry had spilled its load on the motorway.* ▶ to shed, to drop, to scatter

spin *verb*
The wheel was spinning in the thick mud. ▶ to turn, to whirl, to revolve, to rotate

spine *noun*
June injured her spine in an accident. ▶ backbone

spirit *noun*
1 *The house was said to be haunted by spirits.* ▶ a ghost, a phantom, a spectre, an apparition; (informal) a spook
2 *She is a person of great spirit.*

► courage, bravery, fortitude, daring, pluck, determination, enthusiasm, resolution

spiteful *adjective*
His behaviour had been cruel and spiteful. ► vindictive, malicious, vicious, revengeful, hateful, malevolent

splash *verb*
Ben stood there with the brush in his hand, splashing us with paint. ► to spatter, to splatter, to shower

splendid *adjective*
The city at night is a splendid sight. ► magnificent, glorious, superb, wonderful, spectacular, sumptuous, beautiful, gorgeous, marvellous, dazzling

splendour *noun*
The splendour of the room never failed to impress him. ► magnificence, grandeur, brilliance, sumptuousness

splinter *noun*
There were splinters of wood in her fingers. ► a fragment, a chip, a flake

split *verb*
1 *All they had was some chocolate, which they split four ways.* ► to divide, to separate, to share
2 *Ted split the log with an axe.* ► to cut open, to cleave, to divide
3 *The child's dress had split at the back.* ► to tear, to rip

split *noun*
The curtain has a split in it. ► a tear, a rip

spoil *verb*
1 *Karen didn't want to spoil the story by giving away the ending.* ► to ruin, to wreck, to mess up
2 *He had had a lifetime of being spoiled by women.* ► to indulge, to pamper

spooky *adjective*
(informal) *James thought the lane looked dark and spooky.* ► eerie, ghostly, creepy, scary

sport *noun*
Tim was beginning to enjoy sport a lot more now. ► exercise, recreation, games

spot *noun*
1 *There were spots of ink on the wallpaper.* ► a mark, a stain, a blot, a blotch, a speck
2 *They could see spots of rain on the windscreen.* ► a drop, a bead
3 *Let's find a shady spot by the trees.* ► a place, a position, a location, a site
NOTE: A **site** is usually a larger area for a building or for caravans

spot *verb*
It took a while before we spotted our friends. ► to see, to catch sight of, to observe, to spy, to make out

spotless *adjective*
He cleaned the floor until it was spotless. ► clean, immaculate

spout *verb*
She turned on the tap and steaming water spouted out. ► to pour, to gush, to spurt, to squirt, to stream, to flow

sprawl *verb*
The children were sprawling on the sofas. ► to lounge, to spread out, to recline, to lean back, to lie, to relax, to stretch out

spray *noun*
A spray of water shot into the air. ► a fountain, a shower

spray *verb*
Maggie shook the pen fiercely, spraying ink everywhere. ► to sprinkle, to scatter, to shower, to splash, to spatter

spread *verb*
1 *I spread the newspaper on the table.*
▶ to unfold, to open out, to lay out
2 *Someone has been spreading rumours.*
▶ to circulate, to pass on, to put out
3 *The rain will spread to all parts of the country this afternoon.* ▶ to extend, to increase

sprightly *adjective*
The nurse was a sprightly middle-aged woman. ▶ lively, energetic, active, animated

spring *verb*
1 *She sprang to her feet.* ▶ to jump, to leap, to bound, to bounce
2 *The trouble has sprung from carelessness.* ▶ to develop, to arise, to originate

sprinkle *verb*
A hose was sprinkling water on the grass. ▶ to spray, to scatter, to splash

sprout *verb*
The seeds had begun to sprout. ▶ to develop, to germinate, to spring up, to shoot up, to grow

spruce *adjective*
Helen was looking spruce in her new dress. ▶ neat, smart, trim, well-dressed

spur *verb*
Promise of a reward spurred us to action. ▶ to stimulate, to urge, to encourage, to prompt

spurt *verb*
1 *Water spurted from the tap.* ▶ to pour, to gush, to spout, to squirt, to stream, to flow
2 *The car spurted past us.* ▶ to speed, to shoot, to dash, to accelerate, to surge

spy *noun*
1 *Jill wished her father was something more interesting: a spy for example, or a gangster.* ▶ a secret agent

spy *verb*
We spied the car again later, parked in a side street. ▶ to spot, to notice, to catch sight of, to observe, to see

squabble *verb*
Kim and Peter were squabbling in the garden. ▶ to quarrel, to argue, to fight

squalid *adjective*
The old houses were cramped and squalid. ▶ dirty, foul, sordid, unpleasant

squander *verb*
They squandered money on things they didn't need. ▶ to waste, to fritter

square *verb*
His story doesn't square with yours.
▶ to agree, to fit, to accord

squash *verb*
Sharon squashed her clothes into a suitcase. ▶ to crush, to compress, to press, to squeeze, to flatten

squat *adjective*
A squat little old man was staring at her.
▶ stocky, podgy, dumpy

squat *verb*
He bent his legs and squatted on the floor. ▶ to crouch, to sit

squeeze *verb*
1 *He looked at her and squeezed her arm.* ▶ to grip, to clasp
2 *I squeezed my clothes into the drawer.*
▶ to squash, to push, to shove, to crush, to compress

squirt *verb*
1 *The man was angry because Keith squirted water at him.* ▶ to spray, to shower, to splash
2 *She stuck a thumb in the orange and juice squirted out.* ▶ to spurt, to gush, to spray, to spout

stab *verb*
He stabbed the food with his fork. ▶ to jab, to pierce

stab *noun*
I felt a stab of pain as the needle went into my leg. ▶ a pang, a twinge, a shock

stable *adjective*
1 Make sure the ladder is quite stable before you go up. ▶ steady, secure, firm
2 It was good to have found a stable job at last. ▶ secure, lasting, permanent, continuing

stack *noun*
When he got back home there was a stack of videos to watch. ▶ a heap, a pile, a collection

stack *verb*
Chloe had stacked the newspapers neatly on a shelf. ▶ to pile, to heap

staff *noun*
When the staff arrived for work next morning, the doors were still locked. ▶ the employees, the workforce, the workers, the personnel
NOTE: If you are talking about a school you can also say **teachers**

stage *noun*
1 She stood on the stage and looked at the audience. ▶ a platform
2 You need to plan every stage of the project very carefully. ▶ a phase, a step, a point

stagger *verb*
1 She staggered a little and put her hand on his arm. ▶ to falter, to stumble, to totter
2 Then he staggered us all by walking out. ▶ to astonish, to astound, to amaze, to shock, to surprise, to dismay, to startle, to stun

stain *noun*
The book had a large stain on its cover. ▶ a mark, a smudge, a spot, a blot, a blotch, a smear, a blemish

stain *verb*
Handling the fruit had stained his hands. ▶ to mark, to soil, to make dirty, to discolour

stake *noun*
The fence was held up by a row of stakes. ▶ a post, a pole, a spike

stale *adjective*
The bread was stale by now. ▶ dry, old, not fresh, mouldy

stalk *verb*
A group of hunters were stalking deer. ▶ to hunt, to track, to trail, pursue, to follow

stall *verb*
They tried to stall until Roger returned. ▶ to delay, to hang back, to hesitate, to play for time

stammer *verb*
The boy stammered nervously. ▶ to stutter

stamp *verb*
The official stamped a date in my passport. ▶ to print, to mark

stamp on *verb*
Jamila stamped on a wasp. ▶ to tread on, to trample on, to step on, to squash, to crush

stand *noun*
The statue had fallen off its stand. ▶ a support, a base, a pedestal

stand *verb*
1 Gemma stood to greet us. ▶ to rise, to get up, to get on your feet
2 Michael stood the plant on the table. ▶ to put, to set, to place, to position, to deposit

3 *The offer will stand for three weeks.*
▶ to remain, to continue, to stay, to be available, to be valid
4 *She couldn't stand the thought of leaving without us.* ▶ to bear, to abide, to endure
5 *I really won't stand any arguments.*
▶ to tolerate, to put up with
6 *'MP' stands for 'Member of Parliament'.*
▶ to mean, to represent, to indicate

stand up for *verb*
When Nick was in trouble his sister always stood up for him. ▶ to support, to defend, to help, to stick up for, to speak up for

stand up to *verb*
After months of bullying, she decided it was time to stand up to him. ▶ to resist, to defy, to confront, to face up to, to withstand

standard *adjective*
The book describes the standard methods of measuring speed. ▶ normal, usual, regular, orthodox, accepted, routine, typical, common, conventional, customary

standard *noun*
The work has been done to a high standard. ▶ a level, a quality, a grade

staple *adjective*
Rice is a staple food. ▶ principal, main, basic, primary, important

star *noun*
Dozens of film stars were there.
▶ a celebrity, an idol

stare at *verb*
Samantha stood staring at my new clothes. ▶ to gaze at, to look at, to peer at, to contemplate, to examine, to gape at, to study

start *verb*
1 *Kate's Mum had started her new job the day before.* ▶ to begin, to embark

on; (not an everyday word) to commence
2 *Frank's grandfather had started a bakery business.* ▶ to found, to set up, to establish, to create, to open
3 *We all started when the train rushed past.* ▶ to flinch, to jerk, to jump, to twitch, to wince

start *noun*
1 *Saturday is the start of the new season.* ▶ the beginning; (not an everyday word) the commencement
2 *We gave the young ones a 10 minutes' start.* ▶ an advantage, a lead, a head start

startle *verb*
He jerked his head up, startled by her voice. ▶ to alarm, to surprise, to disturb, to frighten, to jolt, to shake

starving *adjective*
The refugees were cold and starving.
▶ starved, famished, hungry

state *noun*
1 *The room was in an untidy state.*
▶ a condition, a shape
2 *The country had been threatened by a neighbouring state.* ▶ a nation, a country

state *verb*
The new law stated that all citizens had the right to vote. ▶ to say, to declare, to proclaim, to announce, to assert

stately *adjective*
A long drive led to a stately mansion.
▶ grand, noble, imposing, majestic

statement *noun*
1 *The government issued an official statement.* ▶ an announcement, a communication, a communiqué, a notice
2 *The report begins with a statement of the facts.* ▶ an account, a declaration, an assertion

static *adjective*
The models were lifelike but static.
▶ motionless, stationary

station *verb*
A man was stationed at the door to take the tickets. ▶ to place, to post, to position, to locate

stationary *adjective*
A row of stationary cars stood at the side of the road. ▶ static, still, immobile, motionless, unmoving

statue *noun*
A statue of the king stood in the town square. ▶ a figure, a sculpture, a carving, an image

status *noun*
She is a woman of high status.
▶ position, rank

staunch *adjective*
Rose was one of the Minister's most staunch supporters. ▶ loyal, faithful, firm, constant, devoted

stay *verb*
1 *I'll stay here while you look for a garage.* ▶ to remain, to wait
2 *We went to stay with our friends in Ireland.* ▶ to visit

steady *adjective*
1 *Make sure the ladder's steady.*
▶ secure, stable, fast, firm
2 *The runners kept up a steady pace.*
▶ constant, regular, even

steal *verb*
1 *It seems Joel had stolen some money from us.* ▶ to take; (informal) to pinch
NOTE: You can also use **rob**; then you have to say *It seems Joel had robbed us of some money.*
2 *When it was dark he stole out of the house.* ▶ to slip, to creep, to slink

stealthy *adjective*
There was a lot of stealthy coming and going of people during the morning.
▶ furtive, sneaky, sly, shifty, secretive, secret, quiet

steamy *adjective*
1 *Two children were peering through the steamy windows.* ▶ misty, hazy, cloudy
2 *The bathroom was hot and steamy.*
▶ humid, damp, muggy, close, moist

steep *adjective*
I had to be helped up the steep wooden steps. ▶ sheer, precipitous, abrupt, vertical

steer *verb*
She steered the car slowly into the tiny garage. ▶ to drive, to guide

stem *noun*
1 *The roses grew wild, their stems trailing over the bank of herbs.*
▶ a stalk, a shoot
2 *Wild flowers grew round the stem of the tree.* ▶ a trunk

stem *verb*
1 *Their interest in the area stems from yearly holidays spent there.* ▶ to arise, to originate (in), to be based (on)
2 *I managed to stem the rush of water with a piece of rag.* ▶ to stop, to check, to contain, to hold back

stench *noun*
There was a stench coming from behind the fridge. ▶ a stink, an odour, a reek, a smell

step *noun*
1 *I was across the stream in three large steps.* ▶ a stride, a pace
2 *Violet put her foot gently on the first step.* ▶ a stair, a rung
NOTE: You use **stair** if you are talking about stairs in a house, and **rung** if you are talking

about a ladder

3 *The first step is to make a plan.* ▶ an action, a stage, a phase

step *verb*

We had to be careful where we stepped.
▶ to tread, to put your feet, to walk

step up *verb*

The police decided to step up the search for the missing child. ▶ to increase, to intensify

sterile *adjective*

1 *The woman was sterile.* ▶ infertile, barren

2 *The land is sterile.* ▶ arid, barren, dry, infertile, lifeless

3 *The bandages are sterile.*
▶ sterilized, germ-free, disinfected, antiseptic

stern *adjective*

Debbie went on chattering, but a stern look silenced her. ▶ strict, severe, harsh, forbidding

stick *noun*

1 *We put some more sticks on the fire.*
▶ a branch, a stalk, a twig

2 *The old man was walking with a stick.*
▶ a walking stick, a cane

stick *verb*

1 *The woman stuck her head round the door. Philip stuck his hand in the air. I'll stick these things in the bin.* ▶ to put, to poke, to thrust

2 *He stuck a pin in the balloon.* ▶ to jab, to thrust, to prick, to pierce, to puncture, to stab

NOTE: If you use **prick**, **pierce**, **puncture**, or **stab**, you have to say, for example, *He pricked the balloon with a pin.*

3 *James was sticking pictures into his scrapbook.* ▶ to fix, to paste, to glue, to fasten

4 *The door keeps sticking.* ▶ to jam, to become wedged

stick out *verb*

He fell asleep with his legs sticking out.
▶ to project, to protrude, to poke out, to jut out

stick up *verb*

One or two trees stuck up above the others. ▶ to rise, to tower, to stand up

stick up for *verb*

Lizzie always stuck up for her little brother. ▶ to support, to defend, to help, to stand up for, to speak up for

sticky *adjective*

1 *I'll put a sticky label on the jar.*
▶ adhesive, gummed, tacky

2 *We felt hot and sticky after our long journey.* ▶ sweaty, clammy, damp

stiff *adjective*

1 *Mix the ingredients into a stiff paste.*
▶ solid, thick, firm

2 *Sam made a model out of stiff cardboard.* ▶ rigid, hard, inflexible

3 *We came back from our walk with stiff muscles.* ▶ tense, taut

4 *If you pay late you may get a stiff penalty.* ▶ severe, harsh, hard, heavy

5 *Keeping everyone happy is a stiff task.*
▶ difficult, hard, severe, tough, uphill

6 *The opposition put up a stiff resistance.* ▶ strong, vigorous, powerful, dogged

stifle *verb*

1 *The heat and the fumes were beginning to stifle them.* ▶ to choke, to suffocate

2 *Kay shook her head, stifling a yawn.*
▶ to suppress, to deaden, to muffle

still *adjective*

1 *The guns stopped, and all was still.*
▶ quiet, silent, calm, peaceful, tranquil

2 *They all stood still and waited.*
▶ stationary, immobile, motionless, unmoving, static

stimulate *verb*
1 *The exhibition stimulated a lot of interest.* ► to excite, to interest, to arouse, to rouse, to prompt, to provoke, to stir up
2 *The television programme stimulated her to go and visit Italy herself.* ► to encourage, to spur, to prompt, to urge

stimulus *noun*
The children used the story as a stimulus to make up their own play. ► an incentive, an encouragement, an inspiration

sting *verb*
The wound was beginning to sting. ► to smart, to hurt, to tingle

stingy *adjective*
Joe's uncle had plenty of money, but was too stingy to help him. ► mean, miserly; (informal) mingy

stink *noun*
A nasty stink was coming from the sink. ► an odour, a reek, a stench, a smell

stink *verb*
The compost heap was beginning to stink. ► to reek, to smell

stir *noun*
The news caused quite a stir. ► a fuss, a commotion, a disturbance

stir *verb*
Stir the mixture until it is creamy. ► to mix, to blend, to beat, to whisk

stir up *verb*
They always seem to stir up trouble. ► to cause, to provoke, to start

stirring *adjective*
We were watching a stirring adventure serial. ► rousing, exciting, thrilling

stitch *verb*
Someone had stitched the hole by hand. ► to sew, to mend, to repair

stock *noun*
There is still a large stock of firewood. ► a store, a supply, a reserve, a hoard

stock *verb*
The supermarket stocks children's clothes. ► to sell, to keep, to handle, to supply

stocky *adjective*
He was a stocky young man with a beard. ► sturdy, solid, thickset, dumpy

stodgy *adjective*
At this time of year we tend to have rich stodgy puddings. ► starchy, heavy, solid

stomach *noun*
The boy seemed to have a pain in his stomach. ► belly, abdomen; (informal) tummy

stone *noun*
1 *Some children were throwing stones in the water.* ► a pebble, a rock
2 *A large stone blocked the road.* ► a boulder, a rock

stony *adjective*
They walked further on to where the beach was stony. ► pebbly, rocky, shingly

stoop *verb*
He stooped to pick up a plate. ► to crouch, to bend, to lean down, to bow down

stop *verb*
1 *The noise suddenly stopped.* ► to end, to finish, to break off, to come to an end, to cease, to discontinue
2 *They were determined to stop the killing.* ► to put an end to, to halt
3 *It was time to stop working.* ► to finish, to break off, to quit, to conclude, to cease
4 *There's not much they can do to stop*

us. ▶ to prevent, to hinder, to impede
5 *The buses stop round the corner.* ▶ to
draw up, to halt, to pull up

stop *noun*
Gradually the train came to a stop.
▶ a halt, a standstill

store *noun*
1 *You will need a good store of sugar.*
▶ a stock, a supply, a reserve, a hoard
2 *You can buy them at the local store.*
▶ a shop, a supermarket

store *verb*
1 *We store the paper in a large
cupboard.* ▶ to keep, to stow, to stock
2 *Some animals store food for the
winter.* ▶ to hoard, to put away, to
save

storey *noun*
*The building had a restaurant on the
top storey.* ▶ a floor, a level

storm *noun*
*Many houses had been damaged in a
storm.* ▶ (a storm with wind) a gale,
a hurricane, a whirlwind, a tornado, a
typhoon; (a storm with rain or snow)
a rainstorm, a deluge, a blizzard; (a
storm with thunder and lightning)
a thunderstorm; (old-fashioned word)
a tempest

storm *verb*
The king's army stormed the castle.
▶ to attack, to assault

story *noun*
*The story was so exciting that I couldn't
wait to hear more.* ▶ a tale, an
account, a narrative, a yarn

stout *adjective*
1 *He set off walking, with a stout stick in
his hand.* ▶ strong, solid, sturdy, thick
2 *The brothers were both rather stout.*
▶ stocky, chubby, portly, tubby, plump,
dumpy, fat

3 *The defenders put up a stout
resistance.* ▶ spirited, courageous,
bold, brave, gallant, heroic, valiant,
strong

stove *noun*
*A saucepan was bubbling away on an
old stove.* ▶ a cooker

stow *verb*
*There is space under the stairs for
stowing coats and shoes.* ▶ to store, to
put away, to keep

straggle *verb*
1 *Some of the younger runners were
straggling a bit.* ▶ to lag, to linger, to
fall behind
2 *Black hair straggled down over her
shoulders.* ▶ to trail, to spread, to
dangle

straight *adjective*
1 *The road seemed to go on for ever in a
straight line.* ▶ direct, continuous,
unswerving
2 *We need to get the house straight for
our visitors.* ▶ tidy, neat, orderly
3 *She said she wanted a straight answer
to her question.* ▶ honest, frank,
truthful, straightforward, direct

straightforward *adjective*
It's a straightforward question.
▶ simple, easy, uncomplicated

strain *verb*
1 *Colin was straining to keep his head
above the water.* ▶ to struggle, to make
an effort, to exert yourself, to strive
2 *Be careful not to strain yourself.* ▶ to
exhaust, to tire out, to weary, to wear
out
3 *The doctor said I had strained a
muscle in my back.* ▶ to damage, to
hurt, to injure
4 *I'll strain the orange juice to get the
bits out.* ▶ to filter, to sieve

strain *noun*
By Wednesday, John was beginning to feel the strain of a hard week. ▶ stress, tension, pressure, anxiety

strand *noun*
The cable was made of hundreds of thin strands. ▶ a thread, a fibre, a wire

stranded *adjective*
She was afraid of being stranded in some unknown place. ▶ lost, deserted, abandoned, left helpless, stuck

strange *adjective*
1 It had been a strange day, but at least she had made a new friend. ▶ odd, unusual, extraordinary, peculiar, curious, funny, weird
2 No one could explain Dan's strange behaviour. ▶ odd, eccentric, peculiar, cranky, unconventional
3 He did not like the idea of being stuck in a strange place with no money.
▶ unfamiliar, unknown, alien, foreign

stranger *noun*
Kate didn't want to say too much in front of the stranger. ▶ a visitor, a newcomer, an outsider, a foreigner

strangle *verb*
The report said the victim had been strangled. ▶ to throttle, to suffocate

strap *noun*
The case was held shut by a leather strap. ▶ a belt, a cord, a thong

stray *verb*
The place was so unusual he felt as if he had strayed into a foreign country. ▶ to wander, to roam, to drift

streak *noun*
A streak of sunlight caught the corner of the flower bed. ▶ a line, a band, a stripe

streak *verb*
1 When he returned, his face was streaked with soot. ▶ to smear, to smudge, to mark
2 A ginger cat streaked past them up the stairs. ▶ to race, to shoot, to speed, to flash, to tear, to rush; (informal) to zoom

stream *noun*
1 She must have dropped her keys in the stream. ▶ a brook, a burn, a creek
2 The machine dropped a stream of sticky soap into his hands. ▶ a flow, a jet, a cascade, a rush
3 He had to cross the main road with its usual stream of vehicles heading for the coast. ▶ a flow, a string, a series, a succession, a line

stream *verb*
Blood was streaming from the wound in his head. ▶ to flow, to pour, to gush, to spurt, to squirt, to spout

street *noun*
The street was lively and brightly lit.
▶ a road, an avenue

strength *noun*
It took all his strength to get the door open. ▶ force, might, energy, power

strengthen *verb*
1 The wind began to strengthen. ▶ to grow stronger, to intensify
2 She took up swimming to strengthen her back. ▶ to build up, to toughen, to make stronger, to fortify

strenuous *adjective*
1 The most strenuous part of the climb was right at the top. ▶ difficult, laborious, tough, demanding, arduous, exhausting, gruelling
2 People made strenuous efforts to observe the eclipse. ▶ vigorous, determined, energetic, resolute, active, firm

stress *noun*
After only three days in the job he began to show signs of stress. ▶ strain, tension, anxiety, worry, pressure

stress *verb*
All of them stressed that a holiday would do Val the world of good. ▶ to emphasize, to insist, to underline, to assert

stretch *verb*
1 Knead the dough by stretching it away from you. ▶ to draw, to draw out, to pull, to pull out, to extend, to spread, to lengthen, to elongate
2 For this exercise you stretch your hands above your head. ▶ to reach, to extend, to spread
3 The road stretched ahead for miles. ▶ to extend, to reach, to continue, to go on

stretch *noun*
1 Her mother had spent a long stretch in hospital. ▶ a period, a spell, a time
2 Rex reached a stretch of dual carriageway and put his foot down. ▶ a length, a section, a piece, a distance

strict *adjective*
1 Her parents have always been strict. ▶ harsh, severe, firm, stern
2 I'm telling you this in strict confidence. ▶ complete, total, absolute, utter

stride *noun*
He took two strides forward. ▶ a step, a pace

strife *noun*
On the day of the wedding, just for a while, the family put aside its usual strife. ▶ conflict, fighting, hostility, quarrelling

strike *verb*
He struck his head as he fell. ▶ to hit, to bang, to knock

striking *adjective*
Nicky had striking blonde hair.
▶ impressive, prominent, conspicuous, remarkable, distinctive, stunning, beautiful

string *noun*
1 The radio was held together with string and sticky tape. ▶ cord, twine, rope
2 Dave discovered that she had had a string of boyfriends before him.
▶ a series, a sequence, a chain, a row, a succession, a stream

strip *verb*
1 We'll have to strip the old wallpaper first. ▶ to peel off, to remove
2 He stripped and climbed into the shower. ▶ to undress, to undress yourself, to take your clothes off

strip *noun*
The house has a small strip of garden at the front. ▶ a band, a ribbon, a line, a piece

stripe *noun*
She wore a dress with blue and brown stripes. ▶ a band, a line

strive *verb*
He strove to understand nature, and went for long walks in the woods. ▶ to try hard, to endeavour, to strain, to struggle, to attempt, to exert yourself

stroke *noun*
He knocked the man down with one stroke. ▶ a blow, a hit

stroke *verb*
She sat gently singing, stroking the baby's head. ▶ to caress, to rub, to pat, to pet, to smooth

stroll *verb*
We strolled round the park. ▶ to amble, to saunter, to wander, to take a walk

strong *adjective*
1 *The little boy wasn't strong enough to lift the box.* ▶ tough, hardy, fit
2 *He put a strong arm round her and led her back to the house.* ▶ sturdy, muscular, powerful, brawny, athletic
3 *There was a strong wind blowing.* ▶ powerful, fierce, severe, vigorous, blustery
4 *You'll need strong shoes in this weather.* ▶ robust, durable, sound, well-made
5 *They made a strong case for extending the library hours.* ▶ forceful, powerful, persuasive, clear, substantial, solid
6 *He came back with a strong cardboard box.* ▶ stout, sturdy
7 *A strong smell of coffee came up from the kitchen.* ▶ pronounced, definite, marked, prominent, obvious, unmistakable
8 *He has a strong interest in archaeology.* ▶ eager, keen, enthusiastic, fervent, earnest

structure *noun*
1 *The house was a very solid stone structure.* ▶ a building, a construction; (not an everyday word) an edifice
2 *The diagram shows the structure of the human eye.* ▶ the construction, the form, the composition, the make-up

struggle *verb*
1 *The family is struggling to earn enough money.* ▶ to strive, to endeavour, to work hard, to make an effort, to strain, to try
2 *The prisoners struggled to get free.* ▶ to fight, to wrestle, to wriggle, to writhe

struggle *noun*
There was a struggle and Mr Collins was hit over the back of the head. ▶ a fight, a scuffle, a tussle, a brawl

strut *verb*
He strutted out of the room like an angry peacock. ▶ to prance, to flounce

stubborn *adjective*
Last week I found out just how stubborn he could be. ▶ obstinate, determined, wilful, defiant, dogged

stuck-up *adjective*
The new people who have moved in seem a bit stuck-up. ▶ proud, conceited, arrogant, cocky, self-important

student *noun*
A group of students got on the bus at the next stop. ▶ a pupil, a schoolchild, a scholar, an undergraduate
NOTE: A student at a school is called a **pupil**, **schoolchild**, **schoolboy**, or **schoolgirl**. A student at a college or university is called an **undergraduate**.

studious *adjective*
Karen seemed quiet and studious, but she liked dancing. ▶ academic, intellectual, bookish, scholarly

study *verb*
1 *She lowered her head to study the menu.* ▶ to examine, to scrutinize, to investigate, to consider, to think about
2 *Her brother is studying medicine.* ▶ to learn, to read

stuff *noun*
1 *The toy broke open on the floor and some green stuff came out.* ▶ substance, material, matter
2 *We have to go and collect our stuff from the house.* ▶ belongings, possessions, things, articles

stuff *verb*
She stuffed everything back in her bags, and made for the door. ▶ to pack, to cram, to squeeze, to shove

stuffy *adjective*
The attic bedroom was small and stuffy. ▶ close, airless, humid, muggy

stumble *verb*
He stumbled over the rough ground until he reached the gate. ▶ to stagger, to falter, to tumble, to totter, to trip

stump *verb*
The last question stumped everyone. ▶ to baffle, to puzzle, to mystify, to perplex

stun *verb*
1 *We think he was stunned by a blow on the head.* ▶ to knock out, to daze, to make unconscious
2 *I was stunned when I arrived for work to find fire engines outside the office.* ▶ to stagger, to astonish, to shock, to astound, to amaze, to dumbfound

stunt *noun*
The stunts became more daring as the evening went on. ▶ a trick, a feat, an exploit

stupendous *adjective*
There are stupendous views from the top of the hill. ▶ magnificent, spectacular, glorious, wonderful, marvellous, fantastic

stupid *adjective*
1 *It would be stupid to give up now, after coming so far.* ▶ silly, foolish, crazy, absurd, daft, ridiculous, idiotic, irrational
2 *They all agreed that they had been stupid to try.* ▶ foolish, silly, unwise, unintelligent

sturdy *adjective*
1 *The man was sturdy with square shoulders.* ▶ stocky, hefty, burly, tough-looking
2 *The farmhouse was squat and sturdy.* ▶ strong, solid, durable, well-built
NOTE: With some other words, such as shoes, you say **well-made** instead of **well-built**

stutter *verb*
The girl began to stutter nervously. ▶ to stammer

style *noun*
1 *She always dresses in the latest style.* ▶ a fashion, a trend, a mode
2 *They lived in a tall house built in the Dutch style.* ▶ a manner, a design, a pattern, a fashion, a model
3 *They like to do things with style.* ▶ taste, elegance, flair, finesse, panache

stylish *adjective*
They went to eat in a stylish restaurant. ▶ fashionable, smart, elegant; (informal) posh, trendy

subdue *verb*
1 *The new king quickly subdued his opponents.* ▶ to overcome, to beat, to conquer, to defeat, to crush
2 *The girl managed to subdue her weeping.* ▶ to control, to restrain, to overcome, to check, to curb, to suppress

subdued *adjective*
Jenny had been in a subdued mood all day, but now she livened up. ▶ quiet, downcast, dejected, depressed, sombre

subject *noun*
Kelly handed round a list of subjects for people to write about. ▶ a topic, a theme, an affair, an issue, a matter

subject *verb*
The audience subjected the speaker to a flood of questions. ▶ to expose, to submit

submerge *verb*
1 *His whole body slowly submerged, and he stayed under for quite a while.* ▶ to go under, to sink, to dip, to dive, to subside
2 *She submerged herself in the soft soapy water.* ▶ to immerse, to engulf,

to plunge, to cover
3 *The river burst its banks and submerged a large part of the town.* ► to flood, to engulf, to inundate, to overwhelm, to deluge

submit *verb*
1 *They said they would never submit to the rule of the English.* ► to surrender, to yield, to capitulate, to give in
2 *Both players submitted to the umpire's ruling.* ► to abide by, to conform to, to obey
3 *Please submit your name to Beryl if you want to attend the course.* ► to give in, to hand in, to present

subordinate *noun*
His subordinates were not happy about the way he treated them. ► an inferior, a junior, an assistant, an underling

subscription *noun*
I must pay my subscription by Friday. ► a contribution, a payment
NOTE: If you use **payment**, you say *I must make my payment by Friday* or *I must send my payment by Friday.*

subsequent *adjective*
Subsequent events proved that she was right. ► later, following, next, succeeding

subside *verb*
1 *After a few days the flood water began to subside.* ► to go down, to recede, to diminish, to lessen
2 *The pain in her head began to subside.* ► to ease, to wear off, to abate, to let up, to lessen, to diminish

substance *noun*
The rocks were covered in a slimy substance. ► a material, a stuff

substantial *adjective*
1 *The garden has a substantial wall round it.* ► strong, solid, sturdy, well-built

2 *A substantial part of the cost goes on food.* ► large, significant, sizeable, considerable, major, big

substitute *noun*
If they don't have the one you want, you'll have to choose a substitute. ► an alternative, a replacement

substitute *verb*
After six months you should substitute a new battery for the old one. ► to exchange, to change, to swap, to replace
NOTE: If you use **replace**, you have to say: *After six months you should replace the old battery with a new one.*

subtle *adjective*
1 *It was a subtle plan to get more money.* ► clever, ingenious, sophisticated
2 *There was a subtle perfume in the room.* ► delicate, gentle, mild, faint

subtract *verb*
The shop subtracted £5 from the bill because one of the books was damaged. ► to deduct, to take away

suburb *noun*
The house is in a suburb of Manchester. ► the outskirts

succeed *verb*
1 *She has a lot of ambition and wants to succeed.* ► to be successful, to do well, to prosper
2 *I'm not sure the idea is going to succeed.* ► to work, to be effective
3 *James I succeeded Elizabeth to the throne of England.* ► to follow, to come after

success *noun*
1 *The party achieved success in the local elections.* ► a victory, a win
2 *The trip was a great success.* ► a triumph, an achievement

successful *adjective*
1 *Her aunt ran a successful business in Brighton.* ▶ flourishing, thriving, booming, prosperous, fruitful
2 *Ingrid was successful in the dancing competition.* ▶ victorious

succession *noun*
We heard a succession of explosions. ▶ a series, a string, a sequence, a run

suck up *verb*
A machine trundled along the road sucking up the snow and hurling it out again. ▶ to draw up, to absorb

sudden *adjective*
1 *Then there was a sudden clap of thunder.* ▶ unexpected, abrupt, sharp
2 *She made a sudden dash for the door.* ▶ quick, swift, hasty, abrupt

suffer *verb*
1 *He suffered head and chest injuries in the accident.* ▶ to experience, to endure, to sustain, to undergo
2 *We had to suffer a lot of criticism.* ▶ to endure, to tolerate, to bear, to put up with

suffering *noun*
He came home after years of suffering in a foreign prison. ▶ hardship, misery, pain

sufficient *adjective*
I'm not sure we have sufficient time. ▶ enough, adequate

suffocate *verb*
The crush of the crowd almost suffocated him. ▶ to smother, to choke, to stifle, to throttle

suggest *verb*
1 *Karen suggested that we go back to the hotel.* ▶ to propose, to advise, to recommend
2 *His tone of voice suggested he was angry.* ▶ to imply, to indicate, to mean, to hint

suggestion *noun*
Here is our suggestion for raising some money. ▶ a proposal, a plan, a recommendation

suit *verb*
The red hat suits you. ▶ to be suitable for, to look right on, to fit

suitable *adjective*
Make sure you bring suitable clothes for the trip. ▶ appropriate, fitting, apt, proper, satisfactory

sulk *verb*
When George didn't get his way he spent the day sulking. ▶ to brood, to mope, to be sulky

sulky *adjective*
I'm afraid my sulky look gave away my feelings. ▶ bad-tempered, sullen, moody, cross, disgruntled

sullen *adjective*
The girl glanced back at him with a sullen look. ▶ sulky, moody, bad-tempered

sultry *adjective*
The day turned out hot and sultry. ▶ humid, close, muggy, oppressive

sum *noun*
1 *We will need a large sum of money.* ▶ an amount, a quantity, a number, a total
2 *What is the sum of all these numbers?* ▶ the total

summary *noun*
There is a one-page summary of the story at the beginning of the book. ▶ an outline, a synopsis

summit *noun*
The climbers reached the summit of the mountain at dawn. ▶ the peak, the top

summon *verb*
The king summoned his doctors. ▶ to call, to send for

sunny *adjective*
The next day was warm and sunny.
▶ fine, bright, clear

sunrise *noun*
We woke up at sunrise. ▶ dawn, daybreak

sunset *noun*
Sunset is early in winter. ▶ dusk, twilight, evening

super *adjective*
We had a super time last week.
▶ marvellous, excellent, splendid, wonderful

superb *adjective*
The food was superb. ▶ excellent, marvellous, splendid, wonderful

superficial *adjective*
1 *It's only a superficial cut.* ▶ slight, shallow, trivial, unimportant
2 *I have a superficial interest in politics.*
▶ slight, casual, trivial

superfluous *adjective*
We began to think a car might be superfluous in the big city.
▶ unnecessary, redundant, unwanted, excessive

superior *adjective*
1 *Now we can move to superior accommodation.* ▶ better-quality, better, grander, good-quality, exclusive, high-class
2 *Henry was superior to me in rank.*
▶ senior, higher (than)
3 *He walked over with a superior look on his face.* ▶ proud, conceited, haughty, arrogant, self-important

supervise *verb*
He now had two assistants to supervise.
▶ to control, to direct, to manage, to look after, to watch over

supple *adjective*
I do yoga to make my body more supple.
▶ flexible, pliable, soft, graceful

supplies *plural noun*
The aircraft carried food and medical supplies. ▶ equipment, provisions, stores

supply *verb*
The village shop supplied us with all we needed for the weekend. ▶ to provide, to equip, to furnish

supply *noun*
Ted kept a large supply of whisky.
▶ a stock, a store, a reserve

support *verb*
1 *A pair of thick beams helped to support the roof.* ▶ to hold up, to carry, to bear, to prop up
2 *If Robin is in trouble his family is sure to support him.* ▶ to defend, to protect, to back, to speak up for, to stand up for, to stick up for
3 *The men all sent back to money to support their families.* ▶ to maintain, to keep, to help, to provide for, to feed

support *noun*
1 *They were very glad of our support.*
▶ help, aid, assistance, backing, encouragement
2 *The platform was held up by a row of supports.* ▶ a prop, a pillar, a post

suppose *verb*
1 *I suppose you must be right.* ▶ to assume, to presume, to expect, to believe, to reckon, to guess, to imagine
2 *Just suppose they give us what we want.* ▶ to imagine, to fancy

suppress *verb*
The rebellion was brutally suppressed.
▶ to crush, to quell, to overcome, to put down, to subdue

supreme *adjective*
The victims of the earthquake showed supreme courage. ▶ extreme, the utmost, outstanding, the greatest, the highest

sure *adjective*
1 *I'm sure I shut the door.* ▶ positive, convinced, confident, certain
2 *They are sure to come.* ▶ bound, certain

surface *noun*
1 *The table has a washable plastic surface.* ▶ a covering, a top, a coat, an exterior
2 *A dice has six surfaces.* ▶ a side, a face

surge *verb*
The crowd began to surge forward. ▶ to rush, to push, to move

surly *adjective*
He tended to be rather surly at breakfast time. ▶ bad-tempered, grumpy, sullen, irascible, peevish, sulky, unfriendly

surpass *verb*
Her world record of ten years ago has never been surpassed. ▶ to beat, to exceed, to better, to improve on, to excel, to outdo, to top

surplus *noun*
When the farm produces too much fruit it often gives the surplus away. ▶ the excess, the extra, the remainder

surprise *verb*
1 *The success of the day surprised us both.* ▶ to astonish, to amaze, to astound, to stagger, to take aback, to dumbfound
NOTE: If you are talking about something unwelcome or unpleasant, you can also use **dismay**

2 *We surprised a man trying to break into our car.* ▶ to discover, to catch, to take unawares

surprise *noun*
1 *She knew she had won, but the amount was a complete surprise.* ▶ a shock, a bombshell
2 *When he saw us, he got up in surprise.* ▶ amazement, astonishment, incredulity

surprising *adjective*
We've had a surprising amount of good luck recently. ▶ astonishing, amazing, unexpected, unforeseen

surrender *verb*
The city surrendered after a short siege. ▶ to capitulate, to submit, to yield, to give in

surround *verb*
The country is small and is surrounded by enemies. ▶ to encircle, to enclose, to fence in, to ring

surroundings *plural noun*
The house had lovely surroundings. ▶ an environment, a setting

survey *noun*
The paper will publish a survey of local library facilities. ▶ a study, an assessment, an investigation

survey *verb*
They stopped and surveyed the wreckage. ▶ to inspect, to examine, to view, to look over, to investigate, to review, to assess

survive *verb*
Some of the crash victims survived for several days in the mountains. ▶ to endure, to live, to stay alive, to last, to keep going

suspect *verb*
1 *When the calculator went missing they all suspected me.* ▶ to distrust, to

doubt, to mistrust
2 *When no one turned up they began to suspect it had been a trick.* ▶ to suppose, to imagine, to presume, to think

suspend *verb*
1 *You can suspend a row of lights from a branch of a tree.* ▶ to hang, to dangle, to swing
2 *The meeting was suspended for an hour.* ▶ to adjourn, to interrupt, to break off, to defer, to delay, to postpone

suspense *noun*
There was a strong feeling of suspense as everyone waited for the results.
▶ excitement, tension, drama, uncertainty

suspicion *noun*
He tried to hide his suspicion, but it showed. ▶ distrust, doubt, misgivings, uncertainty

suspicious *adjective*
1 *I'm suspicious about what happened.*
▶ disbelieving, incredulous, sceptical, distrustful, unconvinced, wary
2 *There are suspicious footprints along the path.* ▶ dubious, questionable, peculiar, odd

sustain *verb*
It's difficult to sustain such an effort.
▶ to maintain, to keep up

swagger *verb*
She saw him swaggering along the road.
▶ to prance, to strut

swallow up *verb*
A whole lot of unexpected bills swallowed up the extra money.
▶ to absorb, to take up, to use up

swamp *noun*
For the rest of the day we skirted a large swamp. ▶ a bog, a marsh, a quagmire, a fen, a mire

swamp *verb*
A huge wave swamped the boat. ▶ to engulf, to overwhelm, to submerge, to flood, to inundate

swap *verb*
Points can be swapped for cash prizes.
▶ to change, to exchange, to switch

swarm *verb*
The town is swarming with tourists in summer. ▶ to be overrun, to be teeming, to be infested

sway *verb*
The long branch began to sway in the breeze. ▶ to swing, to bend, to rock, to wave

swear *verb*
He swore he would return. ▶ to promise, to give your word, to pledge, to vow

sweat *verb*
We began to sweat in the heat. ▶ to perspire

sweater *noun*
The girls were wearing old sweaters and jeans. ▶ a jersey, a pullover, a jumper

sweep *verb*
It's time I swept the floor. ▶ to brush, to clean

sweet *adjective*
1 *The pudding tasted very sweet.*
▶ sugary
2 *The perfume has a sweet smell.*
▶ fragrant, fresh

swell *verb*
The ship's sails began to swell in the wind. ▶ to blow out, to billow, to bulge, to enlarge, to grow, to puff up; (more formal) to distend

swerve *verb*
The car swerved to avoid a cyclist. ▶ to turn, to veer, to dodge, to swing out

swift *adjective*
We got a swift reply to our letter.
▶ quick, prompt, fast, rapid, speedy

swim *verb*
The weather was warm enough to swim in the lake. ▶ to bathe, to go swimming

swindle *verb*
The man had tried to swindle us. ▶ to cheat, to defraud; (informal) to con

swing *verb*
1 *A bare light bulb was swinging on the end of a wire.* ▶ to sway, to dangle, to hang, to flap, to rock
2 *The back of the vehicle swung round and nearly hit the hedge.* ▶ to turn, to swerve

swirl *verb*
Leaves were swirling about on the path. ▶ to whirl, to twirl, to spin

switch *verb*
We've switched from gas to electricity. ▶ to change, to swap

swivel *verb*
The telescope swivelled automatically. ▶ to rotate, to revolve, to turn, to swing

swoop *verb*
1 *The hawk swooped on its prey.* ▶ to dive, to plunge, to drop, to pounce
2 *Police swooped on the house in a dawn raid.* ▶ to descend, to pounce

symbol *noun*
The crescent is a symbol of Islam. ▶ an emblem, a sign

sympathetic *adjective*
When Pippa hurt herself her mother was sympathetic. ▶ understanding, caring, comforting, supportive, compassionate

sympathize *verb*
He was upset, and I sympathized with him. ▶ to be sorry for, to pity, to feel for

sympathy *noun*
It was hard to have much sympathy for them. ▶ compassion, consideration, understanding, feeling, pity

synthetic *adjective*
The curtains were made of a synthetic fabric. ▶ artificial, man-made, manufactured

system *noun*
1 *The office had installed a new computer system.* ▶ a network, a set-up, an organization
2 *We have devised a new system for recording telephone messages.* ▶ a method, a procedure, a process, a plan, a routine, a technique

systematic *adjective*
You need to work through the book in a systematic manner. ▶ organized, planned, orderly, methodical

T t

table *noun*
The book has a table of countries at the back. ▶ a list, an index

tablet *noun*
1 *There is a new tablet of soap in the bathroom.* ▶ a bar, a block, a piece, a cake
2 *Take a tablet with some water and you will feel better.* ▶ a pill, a capsule

tack *verb*
1 *I'll tack down the carpet.* ▶ to pin, to nail, to fasten
2 *You need to tack the hem of your skirt.* ▶ to sew, to stitch

tackle *verb*
It's time I tackled the weeds in the garden. ▶ to attend to, to deal with, to sort out, to grapple with, to manage, to undertake

tackle *noun*
Don't forget to bring your fishing tackle. ▶ equipment, gear, kit, stuff

tact *noun*
You need tact to deal with awkward people like that. ▶ understanding, diplomacy, discretion, sensitivity

tactful *adjective*
She tried to be tactful but they were easily offended. ▶ diplomatic, discreet, considerate, polite

tactics *plural noun*
They used clever tactics to win the deal. ▶ a method, a procedure, a strategy, a policy, a plan, a scheme, a manoeuvre

tactless *adjective*
Gareth thought it might be tactless to leave so early. ▶ indiscreet, insensitive, impolite, undiplomatic, inconsiderate

tag *noun*
His coat still had the price tag on it. ▶ a label, a sticker, a ticket

tag *verb*
The cows are all tagged with a metal clip in their ears. ▶ to label, to mark

tail *noun*
No one was sitting in the tail of the aircraft. ▶ the back, the rear

tail *verb*
Sam had an idea someone was tailing him. ▶ to follow, to stalk, to pursue, to shadow

tail off *verb*
Their energy started to tail off in the afternoon. ▶ to decline, to lessen, to slacken, to subside, to reduce

take *verb*
1 *The boy took his mother's hand.* ▶ to grasp, to hold, to clutch, to grab, to seize
2 *She took a cake from the plate.* ▶ to grab, to seize, to snatch, to help yourself to
3 *The army took several prisoners.* ▶ to capture, to seize, to arrest, to detain
4 *Who do you think took the money?* ▶ to pick up, to remove, to steal; (informal) to pinch, to nick, to swipe
5 *I'll take you to the station. Take this parcel to the post office.* ▶ to convey, to carry, to transport, to bring
6 *Ginny wanted me to take her to the cinema.* ▶ to accompany, to escort
7 *Has she taken her medicine?* ▶ to have, to swallow
8 *The local shop doesn't take credit cards.* ▶ to accept, to receive
9 *It took a lot of time to finish the job.* ▶ to need, to require, to use up
10 *Take two from ten and you get eight.* ▶ to subtract, to deduct

take in *verb*
We weren't taken in by their offer. ▶ to deceive, to fool

take place *verb*
The sale will take place on Saturday. ▶ to happen, to occur, to be held, to come about

tale noun
The tale is a long and complicated one.
▶ a story, an account, a narrative, a yarn

talent noun
She shows a great talent for acting.
▶ an ability, a gift, an aptitude, an accomplishment, a skill (in)

talented adjective
He is a talented musician. ▶ able, accomplished, skilled, skilful, expert, gifted

talk verb
1 *A group of people were talking in the corner.* ▶ to speak, to chat, to chatter, to natter, to communicate
2 *Owen was talking a lot of nonsense.* ▶ to say, to speak, to utter

talk noun
1 *I wanted a quick talk with Don.* ▶ a conversation, a chat, a discussion
2 *Did you hear the talk about spiders?* ▶ a lecture, an address

talkative adjective
Fran's mother was in a talkative mood. ▶ chatty, communicative

tall adjective
1 *The church has a tall steeple.* ▶ high, lofty
2 *Molly is tall for her age.* ▶ big, lanky

tame adjective
1 *The animals are all tame.* ▶ docile, gentle, domesticated, safe
2 *The ride turned out to be a bit tame.* ▶ dull, feeble, uninteresting, boring

tamper verb
The television isn't working because someone tampered with it. ▶ to interfere, to tinker, to fiddle, to meddle, to play about, to mess about

tang noun
The drink has a slight tang of orange. ▶ a taste, a flavour, a hint

tangle verb
Try not to tangle the puppet's strings. ▶ to twist, to entangle, to muddle, to knot

tangled adjective
My hair has become tangled. ▶ matted, knotted, entangled, dishevelled

tantalize verb
1 *The cat was tantalizing its prey.* ▶ to tease, to torment
2 *It tantalized us to have so little information.* ▶ to torment, to frustrate

tap verb
A boy tapped the window pane and peered in. ▶ to hit gently, to knock, to rap

tape noun
1 *The package was held together with tape.* ▶ sticky tape, ribbon, braid
2 *Do you want to play a tape?* ▶ a cassette

target noun
We reached our target of £100 by lunchtime. ▶ a goal, an objective, an aim

tarnish verb
The metal has become tarnished. ▶ to corrode, to discolour

tart adjective
The apples are tart. ▶ sharp, sour, tangy, acid

task noun
They faced a difficult task in clearing up all the leaves. ▶ a job, a chore, an activity, an assignment, an undertaking

taste *noun*
1 *The fruit had a strange taste.*
▶ a flavour, a quality, a character
2 *Their choice of clothes shows good taste.* ▶ judgement, discernment

taste *verb*
Richard tasted the chocolate. ▶ to try, to sample

tasteful *adjective*
The room was decorated in tasteful colours. ▶ smart, stylish, attractive, elegant, pleasant, pleasing, fashionable

tasteless *adjective*
1 *His sense of humour is often tasteless.* ▶ crude, vulgar, improper
2 *The mushroom soup was rather tasteless.* ▶ bland, flavourless, weak, insipid, thin, boring

tasty *adjective*
The sandwiches were fresh and tasty. ▶ delicious, appetizing

tattered *adjective*
His clothes were worn and tattered. ▶ ragged, torn, frayed, in shreds

tatty *adjective*
The car was smart but rather tatty inside. ▶ shabby, worn, scruffy

taunt *verb*
It seems she had only come back to taunt them. ▶ to mock, to jeer at, to scoff at, to sneer at, to ridicule, to insult

taut *adjective*
As they pulled, the rope became more taut. ▶ tight, stretched, tense

teach *verb*
She had taught them at the local school when they were much younger. ▶ to instruct, to educate, to coach, to train

tear *verb*
1 *Be careful not to tear your clothes on the fence.* ▶ to rip, to split, to slit
2 *He tore the picture off the wall.* ▶ to pull, to rip, to grab
3 *Children were tearing home down the street.* ▶ to rush, to race, to run

tear *noun*
There's a tear in the curtain. ▶ a split, a slit, a gash, a hole

tease *verb*
Stella never liked being teased. ▶ to make fun of, to laugh at, to annoy, to irritate, to pester, to tantalize

tedious *adjective*
The film was tedious and much too long. ▶ boring, dull, uninteresting, dreary, monotonous, tiresome

teem *verb*
1 *The river was teeming with fish.* ▶ to be full of, to be swarming with
2 *By now the rain was teeming down.* ▶ to pour

tell *verb*
1 *The boy told what had happened.* ▶ to describe, to explain, to reveal, to make known, to relate, to disclose, to divulge
2 *Tell me when you have decided.* ▶ to let someone know, to inform, to advise
3 *Margaret told the children a story.* ▶ to relate, to narrate, to recount
4 *The man at the garage told us it wouldn't take long.* ▶ to inform, to advise, to assure, to promise
5 *I'll tell those people to go away.* ▶ to instruct, to order, to command, to direct
6 *Can you tell whose this is?* ▶ to recognize, to identify, to make out, to distinguish, to discover

tell off *verb*
They were told off for being rude. ▶ to rebuke, to scold, to reprimand, to censure; (informal) to tick off

temper *noun*

1 *Is John in a good temper?* ▶ a mood, a humour

2 *The bus driver was in a temper.* ▶ a fury, a rage, a bad mood

NOTE: You can also say *The bus driver was angry* or *The bus driver was furious.*

temporary *adjective*

The delay was only temporary. ▶ brief, passing, momentary, short, transient

tempt *verb*

The good weather might tempt us to go out after all. ▶ to persuade, to coax, to entice

tend *verb*

1 *The gardener was tending his plants in the greenhouse.* ▶ to look after, to mind, to attend to, to take care of

2 *The older boys tend to go out on Friday evenings.* ▶ to be inclined to, to be liable to

NOTE: You can also say *The older boys usually go out on Friday evenings.*

tender *adjective*

1 *Some of the more tender plants need special treatment.* ▶ delicate, fragile, sensitive

2 *The meat is nice and tender.* ▶ soft, juicy

3 *The sick children need tender care.* ▶ fond, kind, loving, affectionate

4 *Her face opened into a tender smile.* ▶ gentle, loving, soft

5 *His wound was still tender.* ▶ sore, painful, sensitive

tense *adjective*

1 *Most of the runners felt tense before the race.* ▶ nervous, anxious, edgy, excited, jittery, jumpy

2 *He felt stiff and his muscles were tense.* ▶ stretched, tight, taut

tension *noun*

There was a lot of tension among the musicians before the big concert.
▶ anxiety, nervousness, suspense

term *noun*

1 *The judge sentenced him to a long term in prison.* ▶ a period, a spell, a stretch

2 *The book uses a lot of technical terms.* ▶ an expression, a word, a phrase

terminate *verb*

(not an everyday word) 1 *The meeting was terminated at three o'clock.* ▶ to close, to conclude, to end

2 *The train terminates at Birmingham.* ▶ to stop, to finish

NOTE: If you use **stop**, this can mean 'stop for a while and then carry on', but **terminate** means 'stop completely'

terrible *adjective*

We had a terrible time getting to London. ▶ dreadful, awful, ghastly, horrible, unpleasant

terrific *adjective*

(informal) 1 *The cars were moving at a terrific speed.* ▶ great, immense, tremendous

2 *That sounds a terrific idea.* ▶ very good, great, wonderful, marvellous, splendid

terrify *verb*

The noise of fireworks terrified them. ▶ to frighten, to scare, to petrify

territory *noun*

They were moving into unexplored territory. ▶ land, an area, a district, a region

terror *noun*

Isabel was shaking with terror. ▶ horror, fright, fear, alarm, panic

test *noun*

1 *Greg went to have an eye test.* ▶ an examination, a check-up

2 *They will do a test to find out the car's performance.* ▶ a trial, an investigation, a check

test *verb*
The garage will have to test the brakes. ▶ to check, to try out, to inspect, to examine

thankful *adjective*
We were thankful that a taxi came quickly. ▶ grateful, appreciative, pleased

thanks *plural noun*
Jan bought us flowers to express her thanks. ▶ gratitude, appreciation

thaw *verb*
The snow began to thaw. ▶ to melt, to unfreeze, to soften, to defrost

theft *noun*
All four of them were accused of theft. ▶ stealing, burglary, robbery
NOTE: **Burglary** is stealing things from a building. Theft from a shop is called **shoplifting**. Theft of small cheap things is called **pilfering**.

theme *noun*
1 *Everyone has to choose a theme to talk about.* ▶ a topic, a subject, an issue, a matter
2 *The song has a well-known theme.* ▶ a tune, a melody

theory *noun*
1 *One theory is that the baby fell out of its pushchair.* ▶ an idea, a belief, a notion, a view, an argument, an explanation; (not an everyday word) a hypothesis
2 *Do you understand the theory of how computers work?* ▶ laws, principles, rules, science

therefore *adverb*
The house was in darkness and therefore we assumed no one was in.
▶ consequently, so, accordingly, thus

thick *adjective*
1 *The castle's outer walls were thick and strong.* ▶ broad, solid, substantial
2 *It would take a long time to read such a thick book.* ▶ fat, big
3 *The boat was held by a thick rope.* ▶ stout, sturdy, strong
4 *The path was blocked by thick foliage.* ▶ dense, impenetrable, solid
5 *The wheels sank in to the thick mud.* ▶ heavy, stiff

thief *noun*
The thief got away through an open window. ▶ a robber, a burglar, a mugger, a pickpocket, a shoplifter
NOTE: A **burglar** is someone who steals things from a building. A **shoplifter** steals things from a shop, a **mugger** takes money from people in the street by threatening them, and a **pickpocket** steals things from people's pockets and bags without them realizing it.

thin *adjective*
1 *A thin young woman walked into the room.* ▶ slim, slender, lean, slight
NOTE: Other less kind words are **lanky** (meaning thin and tall) and **skinny**
2 *He drew a thin line on the board.* ▶ narrow, fine
3 *The audience was fairly thin.* ▶ sparse, small, scanty, meagre

thing *noun*
1 *I've got room for one more thing in my case.* ▶ an item, an article, an object
2 *A strange thing happened yesterday.* ▶ an event, an incident, a happening, an occurrence
3 *There are one or two things they want to talk about.* ▶ a topic, a subject, an idea

think *verb*
1 *We were thinking about going to the zoo.* ▶ to consider, to contemplate, to ponder, to meditate
NOTE: If you use **consider**, **contemplate**, or **ponder**, you do not use *about*: *We were*

contemplating going to the zoo.
2 *I think that's a good idea.* ▶ to
believe, to admit, to consider, to
accept, to conclude, to judge
3 *Think hard about what you are doing.*
▶ to concentrate (on), to attend (to)

think up *verb*
The boys thought up a plan. ▶ to
devise, to conceive, to concoct, to
make up

thorn *noun*
Greta pricked herself on a thorn.
▶ a prickle, a spike, a spine

thorough *adjective*
1 *The windows needed a thorough clean
inside and out.* ▶ careful, exhaustive,
complete, comprehensive, systematic
2 *She is very thorough in all she does.*
▶ careful, meticulous, painstaking,
methodical

thought *noun*
1 *Jennifer seemed lost in thought.*
▶ thinking, deliberation, meditation,
contemplation, reflection
2 *I gave the matter some thought.*
▶ attention, consideration
3 *A thought has come into my head.*
▶ an idea, a notion

thoughtful *adjective*
1 *Danny looked thoughtful.* ▶ pensive,
reflective, serious, absorbed
2 *Mark was a good son, always
courteous and thoughtful.*
▶ considerate, kind, caring, helpful,
obliging, attentive

thoughtless *adjective*
*Kate had been thoughtless in leaving the
children by themselves.* ▶ selfish,
uncaring, irresponsible, negligent,
careless, inattentive, reckless

thrash *verb*
1 *He took the villains out and thrashed
them.* ▶ to flog, to beat, to whip

2 *They thrashed their opponents in the
next game.* ▶ to trounce, to crush, to
beat, to overwhelm
3 *She was thrashing her arms and legs
about in the water.* ▶ to fling, to wave,
to toss, to flail

threadbare *adjective*
*By now his clothes were old and
threadbare.* ▶ worn, frayed, ragged,
shabby, tattered

threat *noun*
1 *She knew he would carry out his
threat and have her sacked.*
▶ a warning
2 *There is a real threat of
thunderstorms.* ▶ a danger, a risk

threaten *verb*
*They claimed they had been threatened
by a group of men in the park.* ▶ to
intimidate, to menace, to bully, to
frighten

thrill *verb*
I was thrilled to be back in America.
▶ to delight, to excite

thrilling *adjective*
The journey across China was thrilling.
▶ exciting, stirring, gripping

thrive *verb*
Fish thrive on a varied diet. ▶ to do
well, to flourish, to prosper, to
succeed, to grow

throb *noun*
*The throb of music came up from the
disco.* ▶ a beat, a rhythm, a pulse

throb *verb*
The music throbbed in their ears. ▶ to
pound, to beat

throng *noun*
*A throng of people waited outside the
door.* ▶ a crowd, a mass, a mob, a
horde, a swarm

throttle *verb*
The murderer killed his victims by throttling them. ▶ to choke, to suffocate, to strangle, to stifle

throw *verb*
1 *She threw the ball against a tree.* ▶ to fling, to hurl, to bowl, to lob, to pitch, to toss, to cast; (informal) to chuck
2 *He came in and threw his coat on the chair.* ▶ to fling, to hurl, to toss; (informal) to chuck

throw away *verb*
When you've finished with the newspaper you can throw it away. ▶ to discard, to dispose of, to get rid of

thrust *verb*
1 *Cathy thrust a book into my hand.* ▶ to push, to shove, to force
2 *He thrust at the enemy with his sword.* ▶ to jab, to lunge, to stab

thug *noun*
A postman was attacked by thugs yesterday. ▶ a ruffian, a hooligan

thump *verb*
He yelped as someone thumped him in the back. ▶ to hit, to strike, to punch, to knock, to slap, to clout

tick *verb*
We have to tick the correct answer. ▶ to mark, to put a tick against, to indicate

tick off *verb*
(informal) *They were ticked off for being rude.* ▶ to rebuke, to scold, to reprimand, to censure, to tell off

ticket *noun*
You can get a ticket from the machine. ▶ a voucher, a coupon, a permit

tickle *verb*
1 *It tickled her to think of all those people waiting to see her.* ▶ to amuse, to cheer, to delight
2 *My throat was starting to tickle.* ▶ to irritate, to tingle, to itch

tidy *adjective*
1 *Maggie tried to make the children look tidy.* ▶ neat, smart, spruce, presentable
2 *I'm afraid the house isn't very tidy.* ▶ orderly, shipshape, in good order, neat
3 *There was a tidy sum of money in the drawer.* ▶ considerable, sizeable

tie *verb*
1 *George couldn't tie his laces.* ▶ to fasten, to do up, to bind
2 *He tied some string round the parcel.* ▶ to knot, to loop, to bind
3 *The two teams still tied after extra time.* ▶ to draw, to be level, to be equal

tie up *verb*
The goat had to be tied up at night. ▶ to tether, to secure

tight *adjective*
1 *Close the window and make sure it is tight.* ▶ secure, firm, fixed
2 *The lid is too tight to open.* ▶ stiff, rigid
3 *Make the rope tight.* ▶ stretched, taut, tense
4 *Space was tight in the little kitchen.* ▶ cramped, close, crowded
5 *He was wearing tight jeans and a jumper.* ▶ close-fitting, narrow

tilt *verb*
1 *The train tilted on each curve.* ▶ to lean, to slant, to incline, to tip, to slope
2 *He tilted his chair as he got up.* ▶ to tip

time *noun*
1 *The best time to call is in the evening.* ▶ a moment, an occasion, an opportunity
2 *I've been to Paris several times.* ▶ an occasion
NOTE: If you use **occasion** in this meaning,

you have to say *I've been to Paris on several occasions.*
3 *She spent a long time in the library.*
▶ a spell, a period, a while, a session
4 *They were studying life in the time of the Vikings.* ▶ the age, the period, the era

timid *adjective*
She handed him her keys with a timid smile. ▶ nervous, bashful, shy, coy, apprehensive, sheepish

tingle *verb*
Her left arm had gone to sleep and was still tingling. ▶ to sting, to tickle

tinker *verb*
Someone had been tinkering with the bicycles. ▶ to interfere, to tamper, to fiddle, to meddle, to play about, to mess about

tinkle *verb*
A bell tinkled in the distance. ▶ to jingle

tint *noun*
The paint has a slight tint of yellow.
▶ a shade, a hue, a tinge, a tone

tiny *adjective*
The baby reached out a tiny hand.
▶ minute, little, wee, small

tip *noun*
1 *I managed to get the pin out with the tip of a pencil.* ▶ the point, the end
2 *You could just see the tip of the mountain poking through the clouds.*
▶ a peak, a top
3 *The book gives you some useful cooking tips.* ▶ a hint, a suggestion, advice
4 *On the way they left some rubbish at the tip.* ▶ the dump
5 *We'd better give the waiter a tip.*
▶ a gratuity

tip *verb*
The old tree was starting to tip. ▶ to lean, to tilt, to slant

tip over *verb*
On the bridge the wind nearly tipped us over. ▶ to knock over, to topple, to overturn

tip up *verb*
If you lean back your chair will tip up.
▶ to topple over, to fall over, to overturn

tire *verb*
The long day had tired the younger ones. ▶ to exhaust, to wear out, to weary

tired *adjective*
We all felt tired after the steep climb.
▶ weary, worn out, exhausted

tiresome *adjective*
Weeding is such a tiresome job.
▶ laborious, boring, tedious, uninteresting, dull

title *noun*
1 *The book had a long title she could never remember.* ▶ a heading, a name
2 *The duke inherited his title from his uncle.* ▶ a status, a rank, a position

toil *noun*
It took years of toil to build the wooden bridge. ▶ work, labour, effort, exertion, drudgery

toil *verb*
The old man toiled up the hill. ▶ to struggle, to labour, to slog

toilet *noun*
There is another toilet downstairs.
▶ a lavatory, a WC (= water closet); (informal) a loo

token *noun*
1 *A white flag is a token of surrender.*
▶ a sign, a mark, an indication
2 *Collect five tokens and you get a free burger.* ▶ a voucher, a coupon

tolerable *adjective*
The food is tolerable but we've had better. ▶ bearable, acceptable, adequate, satisfactory, all right, passable

tolerant *adjective*
His parents seemed extremely tolerant. ▶ easygoing, liberal, forgiving, lenient, sympathetic

tolerate *verb*
1 *The pain is hard to tolerate.* ▶ to endure, to bear, to put up with, to stand, to abide
2 *They don't tolerate smoking in the office.* ▶ to permit, to accept, to allow, to approve of
NOTE: You can also say *They don't let people smoke in the office.*

toll *noun*
There is a toll to use the road bridge. ▶ a charge, a fee

tone *noun*
1 *I didn't like the tone of his voice.* ▶ the expression, the note, the sound
2 *The tone of the meeting was friendly.* ▶ the mood, the atmosphere, the feeling
3 *The room is painted in a gentle tone.* ▶ a shade, a tint, a hue

tone down *verb*
She tried to tone down her anger. ▶ to lessen, to soften, to reduce, to subdue

tool *noun*
The carpenter went back to fetch some more tools. ▶ an instrument, a device, a gadget, an implement, a utensil

top *noun*
1 *The top of the hill was visible through the mist.* ▶ the tip, the peak, the summit, the crown
2 *Can you get the top off this jar?* ▶ a lid, a cap, a cover

top *verb*
The charity collection this year topped £100. ▶ to exceed, to go beyond

topic *noun*
Everyone chooses a topic for discussion. ▶ a subject, a theme, an issue, a matter

topical *adjective*
The programme has a strong topical theme. ▶ contemporary, current

topple over *verb*
Several lamp-posts toppled over in the gales. ▶ to fall over, to fall, to tumble, to tip over, to crash down

topsy-turvy *adjective*
Everything seemed topsy-turvy during the war. ▶ confused, chaotic, muddled, jumbled, disorderly, haphazard, higgledy-piggledy, mixed up, upside-down

torment *verb*
The picnickers were tormented by flies. ▶ to trouble, to afflict, to annoy, to pester, to plague, to persecute

torment *noun*
He was so badly sunburned that the slightest movement was torment. ▶ agony, torture, suffering

torrent *noun*
A torrent of icy water soaked Mrs Harding from head to toe. ▶ a flood, a deluge, a stream, a downpour

torture *verb*
The prisoners were tortured almost every day. ▶ to persecute, to torment, to abuse, to maltreat

torture *noun*
When she woke up she had a headache that was torture. ▶ agony, suffering, torment

toss *verb*

1 *The man tossed the bag over the wall and then climbed up himself.* ► to throw, to fling, to hurl, to heave, to sling, to lob; (informal) to chuck

2 *Some lads were tossing balls at a wall.* ► to throw, to bowl, to hurl

3 *The storm was tossing the little boats about.* ► to rock, to shake, to roll, to pitch, to heave, to move

4 *We tossed a coin to see who would start.* ► to flip

total *noun*

Add up the figures and tell me the total. ► an amount, an answer, a sum

total *adjective*

1 *The total length of the walk was about seven miles.* ► full, whole, entire, complete

2 *What happened next was a total mystery.* ► utter, complete, absolute, perfect

total *verb*

Next day we received a repair bill totalling more than £500. ► to amount to, to add up to, to come to

totter *verb*

The old man grabbed his coat and tottered away. ► to stagger, to stumble, to reel

touch *verb*

1 *She touched him gently on the arm.* ► to pat, to tap, to stroke, to press, to feel

2 *She had been deeply touched by their friendship.* ► to move, to affect

3 *His temperature touched 104 degrees.* ► to reach, to rise to

touchy *adjective*

Ken's job in the library leaves him tired and touchy at the end of the day. ► irritable, testy, grumpy, peevish, snappy, jumpy, sensitive

tough *adjective*

1 *Picnic equipment needs to be made of tough materials.* ► durable, robust, strong, sturdy, unbreakable, hard-wearing, indestructible

2 *He was a tough individual who played rugby for a local team.* ► strong, sturdy, brawny, burly, hardy

3 *The vegetables are fine but the meat is a bit tough.* ► hard, chewy, gristly, leathery, rubbery

4 *Farming can be tough work.* ► hard, difficult, gruelling, arduous, strenuous

tour *noun*

The rest of the day was spent on a tour round the local countryside. ► an excursion, an outing, a trip, a journey

tourist *noun*

In summer the town is full of tourists. ► a visitor, a sightseer, a holiday-maker, a tripper, a traveller

tournament *noun*

I'm taking part in a chess tournament. ► a competition, a contest, a championship, a match

tow *verb*

The car moved slowly up the hill, towing a caravan. ► to pull, to haul, to drag, to draw

tower *noun*

The church has two tall towers. ► a steeple, a spire, a turret

tower *verb*

The skyscrapers towered above the city. ► to soar, to rise, to stand out, to stick up

trace *noun*

They found a trace of blood on the carpet. ► a sign, a mark, evidence

trace *verb*
Andrew still couldn't trace the missing money. ▶ to find, to discover, to recover, to retrieve, to track down, to get back

track *noun*
1 *We walked along a track by the river.* ▶ a path
2 *The dog left a clear track in the soft ground.* ▶ a trail, a trace, marks, footprints
3 *Be careful crossing the railway track.* ▶ the line, the rails

track *verb*
The hunters were tracking animals in the woods. ▶ to trail, to follow, to pursue, to stalk, to hunt

track down *verb*
I'm trying to track down my lost suitcase. ▶ to find, to discover, to recover, to retrieve, to trace, to get back

trade *noun*
1 *The company carries on trade with the Far East.* ▶ business, buying and selling, commerce
2 *His uncle works in the cloth trade.* ▶ a business, an industry
3 *Some school-leavers want to learn a trade.* ▶ an occupation, a business, a job

trade *verb*
1 *Some shops trade on Sundays.* ▶ to do business
2 *The business trades with the Far East.* ▶ to deal, to do business, to buy and sell

trade in *verb*
He traded in his motorcycle for a car. ▶ to exchange, to swap

trader *noun*
Local traders are worried about the new bypass. ▶ a shopkeeper, a dealer, a retailer

tradition *noun*
Street parties are an old local tradition. ▶ a custom, a convention, a practice, an institution

traditional *adjective*
They went to see the traditional May Day celebrations. ▶ customary, conventional, established, regular, usual

traffic *noun*
1 *Most local businesses use road traffic.* ▶ transport, vehicles
2 *They were involved in the traffic in drugs.* ▶ trade, business
NOTE: You usually use **traffic** when you are talking about an illegal trade

tragedy *noun*
It would be a tragedy if another firm got the contract. ▶ a catastrophe, a disaster, a calamity, a misfortune

tragic *adjective*
It had all been a tragic mistake. ▶ dreadful, awful, sad, distressing, disastrous, terrible, unfortunate, unlucky

trail *noun*
The animals left a clear trail to follow. ▶ a track, a trace, marks, footprints

trail *verb*
1 *He trailed an old cart behind him.* ▶ to drag, to draw, to haul, to pull, to tow
2 *The police trailed the stolen car for several miles.* ▶ to follow, to pursue, to track, to stalk

train *verb*
1 *Margaret is training me in judo.* ▶ to coach, to instruct, to teach
NOTE: If you use **teach**, you do not use *in*: *Margaret is teaching me judo.*
2 *I need to train every week.* ▶ to practise, to exercise

tramp *noun*
A tramp was lying on the park bench.
▶ a vagrant, a destitute person, a homeless person

tramp *verb*
We tramped round the town looking for her. ▶ to plod, to trudge, to trek, to march, to stride

trample on *verb*
Someone had trampled on the flowers.
▶ to tread on, to crush, to flatten, to stamp on, to walk over

tranquil *adjective*
The house overlooked a tranquil lake. I didn't want to disturb the tranquil scene. ▶ quiet, calm, peaceful, placid, serene, restful, still

transfer *verb*
The patient was transferred to another hospital. ▶ to move, to carry, to convey, to take, to transport

transform *verb*
A new coat of paint would transform the bathroom. ▶ to alter, to change
NOTE: If you use **alter** or **change** you also need to use an adverb such as *completely*: *A new coat of paint has completely changed the bathroom.*

translate *verb*
Can you translate these French words?
▶ to interpret

transmit *verb*
1 *The news programme is transmitted throughout Europe.* ▶ to broadcast, to send out
2 *We don't know how the disease is transmitted.* ▶ to pass, to pass on, to carry, to convey

transparent *adjective*
The box has a lid made of transparent plastic. ▶ clear, see-through

transport *verb*
The army agreed to transport the villagers to the nearest town. ▶ to take, to drive, to carry, to convey, to move, to transfer

trap *noun*
The poor dog had got caught in a trap.
▶ a snare

trap *verb*
The enemy soldiers were trapped in a bombed house. ▶ to corner, to catch, to hold, to ensnare

trash *noun*
1 *I'll put the trash in the bin.*
▶ rubbish, refuse, garbage, junk, litter, waste
2 *What they said sounded like trash to me.* ▶ nonsense, rubbish, drivel

travel *verb*
We like to travel by train. ▶ to journey, to go, to make your way

treacherous *adjective*
1 *As he grew older he became more sly and treacherous.* ▶ disloyal, unfaithful, untrustworthy, false
2 *It's been snowing and the roads are treacherous.* ▶ dangerous, hazardous, unsafe, perilous

treachery *noun*
She does not deserve such treachery from her friends. ▶ betrayal, disloyalty

tread *verb*
Be careful where you tread. ▶ to step, to walk

tread on *verb*
Someone had trodden on the plants.
▶ to step on, to crush, to trample

treasure *noun*
The explorers stumbled across hidden treasure. ▶ riches, wealth, a hoard, a fortune

treasure *verb*
The old woman treasured her memories.
▶ to cherish, to value, to prize, to appreciate

treat *verb*
1 *His stepmother always treats him very kindly.* ▶ to behave towards, to deal with
2 *The nurse treated his wound.* ▶ to tend, to dress

treatment *noun*
1 *The army was criticized for its rough treatment of the prisoners.* ▶ handling
2 *She needs treatment for her skin rashes.* ▶ care, medication

treaty *noun*
The two countries signed a peace treaty.
▶ an agreement, an alliance, a pact
NOTE: A treaty to end a war is also called an **armistice**

tree *noun*
SOME WELL-KNOWN TREES ARE:
coniferous (bearing cones): cedar, cypress, fir, larch, pine, redwood, spruce;
deciduous (shedding leaves in the autumn): almond, apple, ash, beech, birch, cherry, chestnut, elder, elm, hawthorn, hazel, larch, lime, maple, oak, peach, pear, plane, plum, poplar, sycamore, walnut, willow;
evergreen (having leaves all the year): cedar, cypress, eucalyptus, fir, holly, lemon, lime, olive, orange, palm, pine, spruce, yew

tremble *verb*
1 *Some of the children were trembling with cold.* ▶ to shake, to shiver, to quiver
2 *The ground began to tremble under their feet.* ▶ to shake, to vibrate, to shudder

tremendous *adjective*
1 *Then they heard a tremendous explosion.* ▶ loud, deafening, huge, resounding
2 *We had a tremendous time.*
▶ excellent, wonderful, marvellous, exceptional, great, remarkable; (informal) fabulous, fantastic, terrific

tremor *noun*
We could feel a tremor just before the earthquake. ▶ a trembling, a shaking, a vibration

trend *noun*
1 *There is a trend towards people retiring early.* ▶ a tendency, a shift, an inclination, a movement
2 *The magazine shows you the latest trends.* ▶ a fashion, a style

trendy *adjective*
(informal) *He was dressed from head to toe in trendy clothes.* ▶ fashionable, stylish, modern, up-to-date, contemporary

trial *noun*
The new cars are having a series of trials. ▶ a test, an experiment, a try-out

tribe *noun*
The population is made up of three main tribes. ▶ a people, a community

tribute *noun*
People wrote emotional tributes to the dead man. ▶ an appreciation (of), a eulogy (of), a compliment, praise (for)

trick *noun*
Chloe found it hard to be friendly to him after all the tricks he had played on her.
▶ a prank, a deception, a stunt, a cheat, a hoax, a ruse

trick *verb*
He tricked my mother into signing the agreement. ▶ to deceive, to cheat, to fool, to hoodwink, to dupe, to mislead

trickle *verb*
Water began to trickle from under the car. ▶ to drip, to dribble, to flow, to leak, to seep, to ooze

tricky *adjective*
The next question was much more tricky. ▶ difficult, awkward, complicated

trim *adjective*
They walked out into a trim little garden. ▶ neat, tidy, orderly

trim *verb*
She went out to trim the hedge. ▶ to clip, to cut

trip *verb*
He tripped on the kerb and fell in the road. ▶ to stumble, to lose your balance, to catch your foot

trip *noun*
The trip will last three days. ▶ an excursion, an outing, a journey

triumph *noun*
The climbers returned to the scene of their greatest triumph. ▶ a success, an achievement, a conquest, a victory

trivial *adjective*
He had done wrong, but it was only a trivial offence. ▶ small, minor, insignificant, negligible, petty, trifling, unimportant

troop *noun*
A troop of soldiers landed on the island. ▶ a force, a company, a squad

troop *verb*
The audience trooped out at the end of the show. ▶ to flock, to stream, to surge, to march

trophy *noun*
A ten-year-old won the chess trophy this year. ▶ an award, a prize, a cup

trouble *noun*
1 We've been having trouble with our car. ▶ difficulty, bother
2 There had been some trouble in the crowd. ▶ disturbance, disorder, commotion, violence
3 A ship was in trouble off the North Sea coast. ▶ difficulty, distress
4 We don't want to cause you any trouble. ▶ worry, unhappiness, difficulty, burden
NOTE: If you use **burden** you have to say We don't want to be a burden to you.
5 Our neighbours took a lot of trouble to help us. ▶ care, an effort
NOTE: It you use **effort** you have to say Our neighbours made a lot of effort to help us.

trouble *verb*
1 Something was troubling Gopal's mother. ▶ to worry, to bother, to upset, to disturb, to afflict, to torment
2 I am sorry to trouble you. ▶ to annoy, to bother, to disturb
3 Nobody troubled to ask us what we wanted. ▶ to bother, to take the trouble, to make the effort

troublesome *adjective*
Henry went to the doctor with a troublesome knee problem.
▶ annoying, irritating, worrying, distressing, tiresome, trying, inconvenient

truce *noun*
Both sides agreed to a truce.
▶ a ceasefire, a peace, an armistice

trudge *verb*
We trudged slowly home. ▶ to plod, to tramp

true *adjective*
1 This is a true story. ▶ real, factual, genuine, authentic, actual
2 He is the true heir to the estate.
▶ legal, legitimate, rightful

3 *You are a true friend.* ▶ real, good, loyal, steady, trusty, constant, dependable, faithful

trunk *noun*
1 *The tree had a slender trunk.* ▶ a stem
2 *Put your clothes in the trunk.*
▶ a chest, a box, a case

trust *verb*
I trust you to do your work while I am out. ▶ to rely on, to depend on, to count on, to have faith in

trust *noun*
He placed his trust in her and signed the form. ▶ faith, confidence

trustworthy *adjective*
Helen wanted to prove to them that she was trustworthy. ▶ reliable, dependable, responsible, honest

truth *noun*
Please tell me the truth. ▶ the facts

truthful *adjective*
1 *They gave a truthful account of what happened.* ▶ accurate, honest, frank, correct, straight
2 *They are truthful people.* ▶ honest, sincere, frank

try *verb*
1 *Try to finish by tomorrow.* ▶ to attempt, to aim, to endeavour, to make an effort, to strive
2 *Dad tried a new car.* ▶ to experiment with, to test, to try out

try *noun*
He said he would have a try. ▶ an attempt, a go, (to make) an effort
NOTE: If you use **effort**, you have to say *He said he would make an effort.*

trying *adjective*
We had a trying time getting the broken window mended. ▶ annoying, irritating, troublesome, tiresome

tub *noun*
1 *She poured hot water into the tub.*
▶ a basin, a bowl, a bath
2 *I went and looked for a tub of ice cream.* ▶ a pot

tuck *verb*
She tucked the flap in the envelope and put it in the postbox. ▶ to push, to fold, to insert, to stuff

tug *verb*
1 *It took two of them to tug the huge sofa across the room.* ▶ to drag, to pull, to haul, to draw, to lug
2 *Celia felt a hand tugging at her arm.*
▶ to pull, to jerk, to yank

tumble *verb*
I slipped and tumbled down the stairs.
▶ to topple, to fall, to stumble, to collapse, to go head over heels, to drop

tumult *noun*
It was hard to hear anyone speak in the tumult. ▶ the uproar, the din, the commotion, the turmoil, the racket, the disturbance, the pandemonium

tune *noun*
The girl was humming a tune.
▶ a melody, an air, a theme

tunnel *noun*
The engineers dug a tunnel under the road. ▶ a passage, a shaft, an underpass

turn *noun*
1 *There is a turn in the road a bit further on.* ▶ a bend, a curve, a turning, a junction
2 *It was Harry's turn to buy the drinks at last.* ▶ a go, a duty, a chance, an opportunity
3 *Seeing her like that after all this time gave me a bit of a turn.* ▶ a shock, a fright, a surprise, a scare, a funny feeling

turn *verb*

1 *The wheels began to turn and the car moved off.* ► to revolve, to rotate, to spin, to twirl, to whirl

NOTE: You use **spin**, **twirl**, and **whirl** about things that turn quickly

2 *The bus slowly turned the corner.*
► to go round

3 *When he heard the news he turned pale.* ► to become, to go, to look

turn down *verb*

Ken was offered a job but he turned it down. ► to refuse, to decline, to reject

turn into *verb*

The frog turned into a prince. ► to become, to change into

turn out *verb*

1 *The weather turned out fine after all.*
► to end up, to become

2 *She turned out her pockets.* ► to empty, to clear out, to clean out

turn up *verb*

Dan turned up after lunch. ► to arrive, to appear, to come, to drop in, to drop by

tussle *noun*

It looked like the row might have led to some kind of tussle. ► a struggle, a fight, a scuffle, a scrap

twinge *noun*

As she bent down she felt a twinge in her back. ► a pain, a pang

twinkle *verb*

Polly's eyes twinkled as she threw back her head. ► to glimmer, to glint, to sparkle, to glitter

twirl *verb*

She leaned back in her chair, slowly twirling her glass. ► to turn, to rotate, to spin, to twist, to whirl

twist *verb*

1 *She stood up and twisted her hair round her head, making a long plait.*
► to coil, to wind, to curl, to turn, to loop

2 *The show went well until the puppet's strings got twisted.* ► to tangle, to entangle, to entwine

3 *The road twisted through the hills.*
► to curve, to bend, to meander, to zigzag

twitch *verb*

He tried to smile but his mouth merely twitched. ► to jerk, to quiver, to tremble

type *noun*

What type of computer have you got?
► a kind, a sort, a make, a category

typical *adjective*

1 *Her typical day would begin with a good breakfast.* ► normal, average, ordinary, usual

2 *The soldiers fought with typical courage.* ► characteristic, usual

NOTE: If you use **usual**, you have to say *The soldiers fought with their usual courage.*

tyrant *noun*

The country seemed to be ruled by one tyrant after another. ► a despot, a dictator, an autocrat

U u

ugly *adjective*

1 *What an ugly house it was.*
► hideous, unattractive, unsightly, frightful, horrid

2 *He was usually kind but he had an ugly temper.* ► nasty, unpleasant, dangerous, threatening

ultimate *adjective*

His ultimate goal was to get a job in television. ► final, last, principal

un-

NOTE: There are hundreds of words beginning with **un-**. Those listed here are the ones that have good alternative words. With many words you can use *not* instead of *un-*, for example *not able* instead of **unable**, *not finished* instead of **unfinished**, and *not suitable* instead of **unsuitable**. But you cannot always do this; for example, not with **uneasy**.

unable *adjective*

She was unable to walk after her accident. ▶ incapable (of)
NOTE: If you use **incapable**, you have to say *She was incapable of walking after her accident.*

unaided *adjective*

Chris managed to finish the job unaided. ▶ single-handed, without help

unavoidable *adjective*

A long delay looks unavoidable. ▶ certain, inevitable, inescapable

unbearable *adjective*

The heat was unbearable. ▶ intolerable

unbelievable *adjective*

We had a piece of unbelievable good luck. ▶ incredible, extraordinary, remarkable

uncertain *adjective*

1 Jill and Judy are uncertain whether they can come. ▶ unsure, doubtful, undecided
2 The weather is rather uncertain at the moment. ▶ changeable, variable, unreliable, erratic

uncomfortable *adjective*

1 Her new shoes began to feel uncomfortable. ▶ awkward, ill-fitting
2 I felt uncomfortable about speaking in public. ▶ embarrassed, awkward, self-conscious

uncommon *adjective*

Some serious diseases are uncommon today. ▶ rare, scarce, infrequent

unconscious *adjective*

1 The poor man lay unconscious on the pavement. ▶ senseless, knocked out
2 We were entirely unconscious of the time. ▶ unaware, ignorant
3 He gave an unconscious gesture of annoyance. ▶ automatic, involuntary, spontaneous, unthinking

uncover *verb*

1 When at last he uncovered his head, we saw that he was totally bald. ▶ to bare, to expose
2 The police have uncovered a huge fraud. ▶ to discover, to come across, to reveal, to unearth

undergo *verb*

His uncle had to undergo a serious operation the next day. ▶ to endure, to go through, to have, to experience

underhand *adjective*

He was accused of some underhand business dealings. ▶ deceitful, dishonest, devious, secretive, sly, sneaky

understand *verb*

1 We didn't understand what she was telling us. ▶ to grasp, to comprehend, to appreciate, to follow, to see
2 I understand Liam has measles. ▶ to believe, to hear

understanding *noun*

1 Chloe has a good understanding of French. ▶ an ability (in), an awareness, a grasp, a knowledge
2 In the end the two brothers came to an understanding. ▶ an agreement, an accord, an arrangement
3 You need a lot of understanding to look after young children. ▶ sympathy, tolerance, compassion, consideration, sensitivity, feeling

undertake *verb*

1 Our neighbours undertook to look after our cat while we were away. ▶ to

agree, to promise, to consent
2 *She can't undertake any more work at the moment.* ▶ to handle, to take on, to deal with, to attend to, to tackle, to cope with

undo *verb*
1 *There seemed to be endless buttons and laces to undo.* ▶ to unfasten, to untie
2 *He didn't want the huge dog to undo all his good work in the garden.* ▶ to spoil, to wreck, to destroy, to wipe out

uneasy *adjective*
He felt uneasy when he thought he could hear voices. ▶ anxious, worried, apprehensive, concerned, nervous, jittery

unemployed *adjective*
He had been unemployed for six months. ▶ out of work

uneven *adjective*
1 *The pavement was very uneven and she nearly tripped over.* ▶ rough, bumpy, irregular
2 *The contest seemed to be uneven.* ▶ unfair, one-sided, unequal

unexpected *adjective*
Next day we had an unexpected piece of luck. ▶ sudden, surprising, unforeseen

unfair *adjective*
They all agreed the decision had been unfair. His mother tried not to be unfair with him. ▶ unjust, unreasonable, biased, one-sided, prejudiced

unfaithful *adjective*
Her friends had been unfaithful. ▶ disloyal, false, treacherous

unfamiliar *adjective*
They found themselves in an unfamiliar part of the town. ▶ strange, unknown

unfortunate *adjective*
1 *They had been unfortunate in missing the train.* ▶ unlucky
2 *It was an unfortunate thing to say and he was sorry for it.* ▶ regrettable, unsuitable, inapt, unhappy, ill-advised

unfriendly *adjective*
1 *They got an unfriendly welcome when they returned.* ▶ cool, hostile, unenthusiastic
2 *We were surprised at how unfriendly they could be.* ▶ disagreeable, unpleasant, unkind, hostile, cool, cold, nasty

unhappy *adjective*
Talk to your Mum if you are unhappy. ▶ sad, distressed, dejected, miserable, troubled, downhearted, upset

unhealthy *adjective*
1 *The conditions in the old building were becoming unhealthy.* ▶ insanitary, dirty
2 *A boy came in, an unhealthy-looking lad.* ▶ poorly, sick, unwell

unimportant *adjective*
Some of the things he had worried about now seemed unimportant.
▶ insignificant, trivial, inconsequential, trifling, petty

uninteresting *adjective*
The talk was long and uninteresting.
▶ dull, boring, tedious

unique *adjective*
1 *We were given a unique opportunity to visit the museum before it opened.*
▶ special, incomparable, singular, unprecedented
2 *The new car has some unique features.* ▶ distinctive, exclusive

unjust *adjective*
They all agreed the decision had been unjust. His mother admitted that she

might have been unjust. ► unfair, unreasonable, biased, one-sided, prejudiced

unkind *adjective*
He was upset because his sister had been unkind to him. ► unfriendly, unpleasant, hard-hearted, nasty, mean, beastly

unlikely *adjective*
Their story seemed very unlikely.
► improbable, far-fetched, incredible, unbelievable, unconvincing

unlucky *adjective*
They had been unlucky enough to lose all their money. ► unfortunate

unmistakable *adjective*
There were unmistakable signs that a dog had been in the garden. ► clear, distinct, obvious

unnecessary *adjective*
She told him that excuses were unnecessary. ► superfluous, redundant, unwanted, uncalled-for

unpleasant *adjective*
1 *The boys' aunt could be quite unpleasant at times.* ► cross, bad-tempered, angry, harsh, hateful, odious, unfriendly, rude, disagreeable
2 *Chris had an unpleasant time on a ferry in a storm.* ► disagreeable, horrible, horrid, uncomfortable, dreadful, ghastly, awful, terrible
3 *An unpleasant smell of burnt vegetables came up the stairs.* ► nasty, disagreeable, disgusting, revolting, obnoxious

unreasonable *adjective*
1 *They had come a long way and it would be unreasonable not to help them.*
► unfair, unjust, unacceptable
2 *We thought their demands were unreasonable.* ► excessive, absurd, unacceptable

unreliable *adjective*
Some of the people on the trip proved to be unreliable. ► untrustworthy, irresponsible, erratic

untidy *adjective*
1 *He didn't want to hand in untidy work.* ► careless, slapdash, slovenly, messy, disorganized; (informal) sloppy
2 *She went into the bathroom to sort out her untidy hair.* ► dishevelled, unkempt, tangled, uncombed, bedraggled
3 *There was a small untidy room at the top of the house.* ► messy, confused, jumbled, muddled, disorderly, scruffy, chaotic, topsy-turvy

untie *verb*
It took a long time to untie all the knots.
► to undo, to unravel, to release

untrue *adjective*
Their excuse was not only feeble but also untrue. ► false, fictional, fabricated

unusual *adjective*
1 *His behaviour had been most unusual.*
► strange, odd, peculiar, exceptional
2 *Jeroboam is an unusual name.*
► rare, uncommon

unwell *adjective*
She had been unwell for several days.
► ill, sick

unwilling *adjective*
James was unwilling to go without his sister. ► reluctant, disinclined, loath

unwise *adjective*
It was probably unwise to be so rude.
► foolish, stupid, silly, crazy

update *verb*
The records are updated every five years. ► to revise, to bring up to date, to modernize

upheaval *adjective*
The building works caused a great deal of upheaval. ▶ disruption, disturbance, turmoil, commotion

upkeep *noun*
The upkeep of the large house was very expensive. ▶ maintenance, running

upright *adjective*
1 *He was barely able to stand upright.*
▶ straight, erect, vertical
2 *She seemed a good and upright member of the community.* ▶ honest, just, fair, honourable, trustworthy

uproar *noun*
The meeting ended in uproar. ▶ chaos, pandemonium, confusion, turmoil, a rumpus, a hubbub, a riot, bedlam, a commotion

upset *verb*
1 *Someone upset the cat's milk bowl.*
▶ to tip over, to knock over, to spill, to overturn
2 *The storm was upsetting the younger children.* ▶ to alarm, to disturb, to trouble, to distress, to agitate, to scare, to frighten, to worry, to terrify

upside down *adjective*
1 *The box was standing upside down in the road.* ▶ upturned, the wrong way up, inverted
2 *Everything in the room was upside down.* ▶ chaotic, disorganized, untidy, topsy-turvy, in a mess

up to date *adjective*
1 *The encyclopedia was not very up to date.* ▶ modern, new, recent
2 *She likes to wear up-to-date clothes.*
▶ modern, fashionable, stylish; (informal) trendy
NOTE: Notice that you spell it **up-to-date** (with hyphens) when you use it in front of a noun

urge *verb*
1 *The man was urging his old donkey on.* ▶ to drive, to spur, to push
2 *His parents were always urging him to save his money.* ▶ to encourage, to entreat, to advise, to press, to appeal to

urge *noun*
We all felt an urge to laugh. ▶ a desire, a wish, a need, a longing

urgent *adjective*
1 *Doctors said that the operation was urgent.* ▶ critical, crucial, vital, essential, important, pressing
2 *The town has an urgent need for a bypass.* ▶ pressing, immediate

use *verb*
1 *His grandfather had to use a hearing aid.* ▶ to employ, to utilize, to make use of
2 *I am not sure how to use this machine.*
▶ to work, to operate, to manage

use *noun*
I'm sure I can find a use for this jar.
▶ a purpose, an application

useful *adjective*
1 *She gave us some useful advice.*
▶ helpful, beneficial, practical, constructive, valuable, worthwhile
2 *This looks like a useful gadget.*
▶ handy, practical, effective, convenient

useless *adjective*
1 *The knife was blunt and almost useless.* ▶ ineffective, unusable, worthless
2 *It would be useless to complain.*
▶ pointless, fruitless, futile

usual *adjective*
1 *We met at our usual spot.* ▶ normal, habitual, customary, familiar, accustomed, regular
2 *The usual answer is no.* ▶ expected, typical, normal, standard

utensil *noun*
The local shop now stocks kitchen utensils. ▶ a tool, a device, a gadget, an implement, an instrument, an appliance

utter *adjective*
People rushed along in utter panic.
▶ complete, total, absolute, sheer
NOTE: When you are talking about something good, you can also use **perfect**: *The holiday had been perfect bliss.*

utter *verb*
Before he had time to utter a word, the door burst open. ▶ to say, to speak

utterly *adverb*
His parents had been utterly thrilled by the news. ▶ completely, absolutely, totally, positively

V v

vacant *adjective*
1 *The house had been vacant for several months.* ▶ empty, uninhabited, unoccupied, deserted
2 *He gave a vacant stare.* ▶ blank, expressionless

vacation *noun*
The summer vacation begins next week.
▶ a holiday
NOTE: In Britain, **vacation** normally means a break between terms in a university or college. In North America, **vacation** also means an ordinary holiday.

vague *adjective*
1 *She could only give a vague description of the man.* ▶ inexact, imprecise, general, broad, indefinite, uncertain, hazy, unclear
2 *He is rather vague, always forgetting something.* ▶ absent-minded, forgetful, scatter-brained, inattentive, thoughtless

vain *adjective*
1 *She thought he was a rather vain young man.* ▶ conceited, proud, self-important, arrogant, boastful
2 *They made vain attempts to save him.*
▶ unsuccessful, fruitless, futile, ineffective

valiant *adjective*
The city put up a valiant resistance to the invading army. ▶ brave, courageous, bold, daring, heroic, gallant, spirited, intrepid

valid *adjective*
I'm afraid this passport is not valid.
▶ legal, authorized, genuine, legitimate

valour *noun*
The soldiers showed great valour.
▶ courage, daring, bravery, audacity, spirit, heroism; (informal) pluck, guts, grit

valuable *adjective*
1 *The trunk contained some valuable pieces of jewellery.* ▶ precious, priceless
2 *She made some valuable suggestions for improving my model.* ▶ helpful, positive, useful, worthwhile, constructive, beneficial, advantageous

value *noun*
1 *The value of the houses in this area has gone up a lot.* ▶ the worth, the price
2 *We understand the value of getting plenty of exercise.* ▶ the benefit, the advantage, the importance, the merit

value *verb*
1 *Film stars value their privacy.* ▶ to appreciate, to cherish, to prize, to treasure, to esteem
2 *The estate agent is coming to value the house.* ▶ to assess, to price, to evaluate, to put a value on

vanish *verb*
By the next morning the fog had vanished. ▶ to disappear, to clear, to evaporate, to fade

vanity *noun*
You could see the prince's vanity in the clothes he wore. ▶ pride, conceit, self-importance

vanquish *verb*
The country rapidly vanquished its weaker neighbours. ▶ to defeat, to conquer, to subdue, to overcome, to overpower

variable *adjective*
The weather is variable at this time of year. ▶ changeable, erratic, unpredictable, unreliable, temperamental

variation *noun*
There is a lot of variation in the level of noise. ▶ difference, change, alteration

variety *noun*
1 We have a life full of variety.
▶ change, diversity, variation
2 There was a large variety of magazines to choose from. ▶ an assortment, an array, a choice
3 There are many rare varieties of butterfly. ▶ a kind, a sort, a type, a species, a form

various *adjective*
The loudspeakers are sold in various sizes. ▶ different, diverse, miscellaneous, varied

vary *verb*
1 She varies her walk to the office from day to day. ▶ to change, to alter, to adjust
2 The temperature in the house varies quite a bit. ▶ to change, to differ, to fluctuate

vast *adjective*
Asia is a vast continent. ▶ huge, immense, enormous, extensive, massive

vault *noun*
The wine was stored in an enormous vault. ▶ a basement, a cellar

vault over *verb*
He vaulted over the gate and landed in a field. ▶ to jump over, to leap over, to spring over, to clear

veer *verb*
The car veered into the path of a lorry coming the other way. ▶ to swerve, to turn, to change direction

velocity *noun*
The aircraft reached a high velocity.
▶ speed

vengeance *noun*
The victims' families demanded vengeance. ▶ revenge, retribution, reprisal, retaliation

venomous *adjective*
Not all snakes are venomous.
▶ poisonous

vent *noun*
Fumes from the boiler escape through a vent. ▶ an opening, a hole, an outlet, a slit

venture *noun*
His father had got involved in a new business venture. ▶ a project, an enterprise, an undertaking, a deal

verdict *noun*
The jury did not need long to reach a verdict. ▶ a decision, a judgement, a conclusion

verge *noun*
1 *A dead cat lay on the verge of a road.*
▶ the edge, the side, the border
2 *She was on the verge of leaving.*
▶ the point, the brink

verify *verb*
I could not verify that the amount was correct. ▶ to check, to show, to confirm, to establish, to prove

versatile *adjective*
Larger cars are more versatile and can be used in rough country. ▶ adaptable, flexible

version *noun*
1 *Mandy's version of the incident was a lot different from Emma's.* ▶ an account, a report, a description
2 *We looked at an English version of the Koran.* ▶ a translation, an adaptation
3 *I bought the wide-screen version of the video.* ▶ a form, a variety, a type, a design

vertical *adjective*
He put the ladder into an almost vertical position. ▶ upright, erect

very *adverb*
It was a very warm afternoon.
▶ extremely, exceedingly, exceptionally, truly

very *adjective*
Those were her very words. ▶ actual, exact, precise

vessel *noun*
1 *The harbour was crammed with fishing vessels.* ▶ a boat, a ship, a craft
2 *Pour the liquid into a clean vessel.*
▶ a container, a receptacle

veto *verb*
A committee has vetoed the minister's decision. ▶ to forbid, to prohibit, to ban, to bar

veto *noun*
There is a veto on end-of-term parties.
▶ a ban, a prohibition, an embargo

vex *verb*
The boys' mother was vexed by all the large bills she was getting. ▶ to bother, to trouble, to upset, to worry, to disturb, to annoy, to irritate, to harass, to exasperate

vibrate *verb*
When the fridge came on it started to vibrate. ▶ to shake, to shudder, to rattle, to throb, to tremble, to quake, to quiver, to shiver

vice *noun*
1 *There is a lot of vice in the big city.*
▶ evil, wickedness, sin, wrongdoing, immorality
2 *He has few vices, apart from an angry temper.* ▶ a fault, a failing, a weakness, a defect

vicinity *noun*
There are few shops in this vicinity.
▶ a neighbourhood, an area, a district, a locality, a region

vicious *adjective*
1 *He suffered a vicious attack from muggers in the park. The man was known to be a vicious character.*
▶ violent, brutal, savage, fierce, ferocious, callous, ruthless
2 *The dog looked extremely vicious.*
▶ ferocious, fierce, dangerous, wild

victim *noun*
1 *The newspaper had pictures of the hurricane victims.* ▶ a casualty, a fatality, an injured person
2 *Ellie was the victim of a flu bug.*
▶ a sufferer
3 *The lioness chose her victim and pounced.* ▶ a prey, a quarry

victimize *verb*
Some bullies were victimizing one of the younger children. ▶ to intimidate, to bully, to oppress, to pick on, to persecute, to torment, to treat unfairly

victor *noun*
The victors got a marvellous reception back home. ▶ a winner, a champion

victorious *adjective*
The victorious team returned in triumph. ▶ winning, conquering, successful, triumphant

victory *noun*
Rebecca was celebrating her victory in the chess tournament. ▶ a success, a win, a triumph, a conquest

view *noun*
1 *There's a fine view from the top of the hill.* ▶ an outlook, a prospect, a vista, a panorama
2 *She has strong views about smoking.* ▶ an opinion, a thought, an idea, a conviction, an attitude, a belief

view *verb*
1 *Some officials came to view the damage.* ▶ to inspect, to survey, to examine, to assess, to observe, to look at
2 *They seemed to view us with suspicion.* ▶ to regard, to consider, to contemplate

vigilant *adjective*
The police officer told us all to be vigilant. ▶ alert, observant, watchful, attentive, wary, careful

vigorous *adjective*
1 *He is a vigorous man.* ▶ strong, energetic, active, dynamic, powerful
2 *We need some vigorous exercise.* ▶ strenuous, energetic

vigour *noun*
She always does everything with great vigour. ▶ energy, vitality, enthusiasm, keenness, zeal, zest, force, liveliness

vile *adjective*
1 *What a vile smell.* ▶ revolting, disgusting, unpleasant, foul, filthy, foul, horrible
2 *The murder had been a particularly vile one.* ▶ loathsome, nasty, contemptible, wretched, obnoxious

villain *noun*
The story was about a villain who tried to steal money from old people. ▶ a rogue, a scoundrel, a crook, a wretch

violate *verb*
They have violated all the rules. ▶ to break, to disobey, to disregard, to ignore; (not an everyday word) to infringe

violent *adjective*
1 *They suffered a violent attack from thugs in the street.* ▶ savage, vicious, fierce, brutal
2 *A violent storm hit the town.* ▶ severe, powerful, strong, tempestuous

virtue *noun*
They all admired her virtue. ▶ goodness, decency, honesty, honour, integrity, righteousness, sincerity, morality

virtuous *adjective*
Their behaviour had always been virtuous. ▶ right, honourable, good, honest, just, worthy, moral, pure, upright

visible *adjective*
The house was visible through the trees. ▶ perceptible, discernible, noticeable, apparent

vision *noun*
1 *My eye test showed I had good vision.* ▶ sight, eyesight

2 *He thought he had seen a vision of his dead grandfather.* ▶ an apparition, a hallucination, a ghost, a phantom, a spirit

visit *verb*
I went to visit my friend up the road.
▶ to call on, to see; (informal) to drop in on, to stay with
NOTE: You can use **stay with** if you are talking about a longer visit

visit *noun*
Some friends have come for a visit.
▶ a stay, a call
NOTE: A **stay** is a longer visit and a **call** is a short one

visitor *noun*
1 *Our visitors are leaving tomorrow.*
▶ a guest, a caller
2 *The town has a lot of visitors in the summer.* ▶ a tourist, a sightseer, a holidaymaker

visualize *verb*
It is hard to visualize Penny with short hair. ▶ to imagine, to picture, to conceive

vital *adjective*
It is vital that we catch the last bus.
▶ essential, crucial, important, necessary, imperative

vitality *noun*
The old woman still had plenty of vitality. ▶ energy, vigour, liveliness, life, zest, vim, stamina

vivid *adjective*
1 *The room was painted in vivd colours.*
▶ bright, brilliant, intense, colourful
2 *She gave a vivid description of the storm.* ▶ clear, graphic, powerful, colourful, lively, lifelike

vogue *noun*
There is a vogue for yo-yos at the moment. ▶ a craze, a fashion, a trend

volume *noun*
1 *The volume of traffic has increased.*
▶ the amount, the quantity
2 *The library contains many old volumes.* ▶ a book; (more formal) a tome
3 *The man went to turn down the volume of the television.* ▶ the loudness

voluntary *adjective*
The weekend camp is voluntary.
▶ optional

vomit *verb*
The sight of the dead cat made me want to vomit. ▶ to be sick; (informal) to throw up

vote *noun*
There will be a vote for a new leader next month. ▶ an election, a ballot, a poll

vote for *verb*
They voted for an outing to London.
▶ to choose, to opt for, to pick, to settle on

voucher *noun*
If you collect three vouchers you get the next packet at half price. ▶ a token, a coupon, a ticket

vow *verb*
He vowed he would return one day.
▶ to promise, to pledge, to swear, to give your word, to take an oath

vow *noun*
He made a vow that he would return.
▶ a pledge, a promise, an oath

voyage *noun*
They were going on a long voyage.
▶ a journey, a trip

vulgar *adjective*
1 *He was behaving in a rather vulgar way.* ▶ coarse, crude, impolite, uncouth, offensive

2 *They were telling each other vulgar jokes.* ▶ indecent, improper, dirty, lewd

vulnerable *adjective*
The city had no walls and was always vulnerable. ▶ unprotected, exposed, defenceless, weak

wad *noun*
The teacher brought in a wad of drawing paper. ▶ a bundle, a pad

wag *verb*
She wagged her finger at him as a warning. ▶ to wave, to shake, to waggle, to wiggle

wage *noun*
Pauline's wages had gone up quite a lot in the last year. ▶ pay, earnings, income
NOTE: Another word is **salary**: this means money that you get every month. Wages are paid every day or every week.

wage *verb*
The country waged a long war against its neighbours. ▶ to pursue, to carry on, to conduct

wager *noun*
I made a wager that I'd arrive first. ▶ a bet

wail *verb*
A young child was wailing because it had lost its mother. ▶ to howl, to bawl, to cry, to shriek

wait *verb*
The children waited outside while their mother went into the shop. ▶ to remain, to stay, to stop

wait *noun*
We had a long wait till the bus came. ▶ a delay, a hold-up

wake *verb*
A noise in the street woke her early in the morning. ▶ to arouse, to awaken, to rouse

wake up *verb*
I usually wake up about 7 o'clock. ▶ to awaken, to stir, to rise, to get up

walk *verb*
Ruth walked to the window. ▶ to step, to move; (to walk slowly) to amble, to saunter, to stroll; (to walk fast) to stride, to march, to pace, to trot

walk *noun*
Tomorrow we'll go for a walk in the country. ▶ a stroll, a ramble, a hike

wallow *verb*
The pigs were wallowing in thick mud. ▶ to roll, to roll about, to lie, to flounder

wan *adjective*
The illness made Molly look wan. ▶ pale, poorly, sickly, pasty, ashen

wand *noun*
The magician had left his wand behind. ▶ a stick, a rod, a baton

wander *verb*
1 *Sheep and goats were wandering over the hillside.* ▶ to ramble, to range, to roam, to drift, to rove, to stray
2 *The boys must have wandered off the path and got lost.* ▶ to stray, to turn, to deviate (from)

wane *verb*
Towards evening the light began to wane. ▶ to fade, to fail, to dim, to weaken, to dwindle, to decline, to diminish

want *verb*
1 *What she wanted at that moment was a plate of hot food.* ▶ to wish for, to long for, to desire, to fancy, to crave, to hanker after, to yearn for
2 *Your hair wants cutting.* ▶ to need, to require

want *noun*
The plants began to droop from a want of water. ▶ a lack, a need, a shortage; (not an everyday word) a dearth

war *noun*
War broke out between the two countries. ▶ fighting, hostilities

ward off *verb*
She warded off the dog with a large umbrella. ▶ to fend off, to push away, to repel, to drive back, to parry

warder *noun*
A prison warder took her back to her cell. ▶ a guard, an officer, a keeper

warehouse *noun*
The goods were stored in a warehouse by the docks. ▶ a store, a depot

wares *plural noun*
The woman had set out her wares on a table in the market. ▶ goods, merchandise, produce, stock

warlike *adjective*
The people in the hills had a reputation for being warlike. ▶ belligerent, aggressive, hostile, militant, pugnacious

warm *adjective*
1 *The water was warm.* ▶ tepid, lukewarm, quite hot, heated
2 *It's usually warm in August.* ▶ sunny, hot, pleasant
3 *You're getting warm now.* ▶ close, near
4 *They gave us a warm welcome.* ▶ friendly, cordial, eager, hearty, affectionate, genial, enthusiastic

warn *verb*
She warned us not to go out after dark. ▶ to caution, to remind, to advise

warning *noun*
There was no warning of the sharp bend ahead. ▶ a notice, an indication, a signal, a sign

warp *verb*
The rails had warped in the strong heat. ▶ to bend, to buckle, to twist, to become deformed, to distort

wary *adjective*
Our dog is always wary of visitors. ▶ suspicious, careful, apprehensive, heedful, cautious, chary, distrustful

wash *verb*
1 *Terry promised to wash the car.* ▶ to clean, to sponge down
2 *I must go and wash my hair.* ▶ to shampoo, to rinse
3 *It's a long time since anyone washed the kitchen floor.* ▶ to mop, to sponge, to scrub, to wipe
4 *Have the children washed yet?* ▶ to have a wash, to bath
5 *Waves were washing over the rocks.* ▶ to splash, to dash, to break (against)
6 *The boxes were washed overboard.* ▶ to sweep

waste *noun*
The council now recycles a lot of household waste. ▶ rubbish, refuse, garbage

waste *adjective*
1 *What shall we do with all this waste paper?* ▶ scrap, used, discarded
2 *Waste land stretched for miles.* ▶ empty, barren

waste *verb*
We have wasted a good opportunity. ▶ to squander, to misuse

waste away *verb*
The dog became ill and began to waste away. ► to pine, to weaken, to become thin, to become emaciated

wasteful *adjective*
They are very wasteful with their money. ► extravagant; (not an everyday word) prodigal

watch *verb*
1 *We went into the garden and watched the eclipse.* ► to look at, to contemplate, to gaze at, to stare at
2 *Watch what happens when I pull this lever.* ► to observe, to note, to heed, to mark, to take notice of, to concentrate on
3 *Katie said she'd watch the children while we went out.* ► to look after, to keep an eye on, to mind, to care for, to guard, to supervise

watchful *adjective*
You need to be watchful out alone at night. ► alert, vigilant, attentive, wary; (not an everyday word) circumspect

water *verb*
Have you watered the garden? ► to irrigate, to sprinkle, to spray

waterlogged *adjective*
After the storm the ground was waterlogged. ► soaked, saturated

watery *adjective*
1 *The paint is too watery.* ► thin, runny, liquid
2 *Nathan's eyes looked watery.* ► damp, moist, wet

wave *verb*
1 *We saw Kerrie on the other side of the road and waved to her.* ► to signal, to gesture
2 *He called a taxi by waving his stick.* ► to swing, to brandish, to flourish, to twirl

3 *The corn in the fields was waving in the wind.* ► to sway, to ripple, to flutter, to stir, to move to and fro
4 *Flags were waving from tall posts.* ► to flap, to flutter

wave *noun*
Waves were rolling on the shore. ► a breaker

waver *verb*
1 *Lights wavered on the horizon.* ► to flicker, to quiver, to tremble
2 *She wavered when she realized how much it would cost to go abroad.* ► to hesitate, to pause, to falter, to dither

way *noun*
1 *Do you know the way to London?* ► a route, a road, a direction
2 *I know a good way of making paper aeroplanes.* ► a method, a technique; (not an everyday word) a procedure (for)

NOTE: If you use **procedure** you say *Shall I show you a better procedure for doing that?* or *She showed them the correct procedure for making paper aeroplanes.*

3 *He has a very odd way of thanking people.* ► a manner, a style, a fashion
4 *Things were in a bad way.* ► a state, a condition

weak *adjective*
1 *The illness left him feeling very weak.* ► sickly, poorly, feeble, delicate, frail, infirm
2 *The house had weak foundations and might collapse.* ► defective, faulty, unsafe, insecure, flimsy, fragile, unsteady, shaky
3 *The army had camped in a weak position.* ► vulnerable, exposed, defenceless
4 *He offered a weak excuse and left.* ► unconvincing, feeble, lame, unsatisfactory
5 *She seemed to enjoy her weak tea and stale biscuits.* ► watery, tasteless

weaken *verb*
Tammy's interest began to weaken as she grew tired. ▶ to fade, to flag, to dwindle, to decline, to decrease, to diminish, to lessen, to reduce, to wane

weakness *noun*
There was one major weakness in their plan. ▶ a defect, a flaw, a failing, a fault, an imperfection

wealth *noun*
1 *The family's three large cars were a sign of their wealth.* ▶ money, a fortune, riches, means, affluence
2 *The picture has a wealth of detail.* ▶ a mass, an abundance; (not an everyday word) a profusion

wealthy *adjective*
Their neighbour was a wealthy businessman. ▶ rich, prosperous, well-off, well-to-do, affluent

wear *verb*
1 *I think I'll wear my green sweatshirt.* ▶ to put on, to dress in
2 *The carpet has worn in several places.* ▶ to become thin, to go thin

wear off *verb*
The pain began to wear off. ▶ to fade, to ease, to lessen, to subside

wear out *verb*
The long journey wore us out. ▶ to exhaust, to tire, to weary, to fatigue, to drain

weary *adjective*
She felt weary, and longed for a warm bath. ▶ tired, exhausted, worn out

weather *noun*
The weather is unreliable at this time of year. ▶ the climate
WORDS TO DO WITH THE WEATHER INCLUDE:
hot weather: fine weather, sun, sunshine, heatwave, warm front,
anticyclone;
cold weather: chill, frost, ice, freeze, cold front;
storms: thunderstorm, thunder and lightning, tempest, tornado, typhoon, whirlwind, blizzard, monsoon, cyclone;
wet weather: rain, hail, sleet, slush, snow, snowstorm;
heavy rain: downpour, deluge;
light rain: shower, drizzle;
no rain for a long time: drought;
strong wind: gale, squall, hurricane;
light wind: breeze;
weather in the sky and the air: cloud, fog, mist, smog, haze

weave *verb*
He weaved his way skilfully through the traffic. ▶ to wind, to make your way, to zigzag

wedding *noun*
Their wedding was on a Thursday. ▶ a marriage

weep *verb*
I was so upset I felt like weeping. ▶ to cry, to shed tears, to sob

weight *noun*
1 *The machine measures the weight of large vehicles.* ▶ the heaviness
2 *My brother was only small but was a dreadful weight to carry.* ▶ a load, a burden

weird *adjective*
1 *It gave us a weird feeling being out in the moonlight.* ▶ strange, unnatural, eerie, creepy; (informal) scary, spooky
2 *It was a weird thing to say.* ▶ odd, strange, peculiar, curious

welcome *noun*
We got a friendly welcome when we were home. ▶ a reception, a greeting

welcome *adjective*
The money was a welcome surprise.
▶ pleasant, pleasing, agreeable, acceptable

welcome *verb*
The old woman welcomed us and showed us into the house. ▶ to greet, to receive

welfare *noun*
Her main concern was the welfare of her children. ▶ well-being, happiness, health

well *adjective*
1 *They returned looking well.*
▶ healthy, fit, in good health, strong
2 *I hope everything is well.*
▶ satisfactory, all right

well known *adjective*
Her uncle was a well-known television presenter. ▶ famous, celebrated, distinguished
NOTE: When you use **well known** before a noun (as in the example given here), it has a hyphen (*well-known*).

well off *adjective*
The family had succeeded and was now well off. ▶ prosperous, wealthy, rich
NOTE: When you use **well off** before a noun, it has a hyphen (as in *a well-off family*).

wet *adjective*
1 *The ground was too wet for cutting the grass.* ▶ soaked, damp, saturated, soggy, waterlogged, sodden
2 *Our clothes were wet from being out in the rain.* ▶ drenched, soaked, dripping, sopping
3 *The weather has turned wet.* ▶ rainy, showery, drizzly

wheel *verb*
The soldiers wheeled to the right. ▶ to turn, to veer, to swing, to change direction

whiff *adjective*
There was a strong whiff of onions in the kitchen. ▶ a smell, an aroma, a fragrance
NOTE: For unpleasant smells you can also use **odour**, **stink**, and **stench**, and for sweet smells you can use **perfume** and **scent**

whirl *verb*
She whirled round to see who was following. ▶ to spin, to twirl, to turn

whisk *verb*
You have to whisk three eggs with some flour. ▶ to beat, to whip, to mix

whisper *verb*
She whispered something in his ear.
▶ to murmur

whole *adjective*
He ate a whole packet of biscuits. That is the whole truth. ▶ complete, entire, total, full

wholesome *adjective*
You need wholesome food.
▶ nutritious, healthy

wholly *adverb*
She said she was wholly to blame for the situation. ▶ completely, entirely

wicked *adjective*
It was a wicked thing to do. They are wicked people. ▶ evil, bad, sinful, wrong, shameful

wide *adjective*
1 *The room was wide and had a high ceiling.* ▶ broad, expansive, extensive, spacious
2 *There is a wide choice.* ▶ large, extensive, generous, ample

widespread *adjective*
The news caused widespread anger.
▶ general, universal, extensive

wield *verb*
The knight wielded a sword. ▶ to brandish, to flourish, to handle, to hold, to use

wild *adjective*
1 *The zoo has many wild animals.*
▶ untamed, undomesticated
2 *They drove across some wild country.*
▶ desolate, uninhabited, rough,
rugged, barren, uncultivated
3 *It was a wild night, with heavy rain
and strong winds.* ▶ rough, stormy,
violent, blustery, tempestuous
4 *You do have some wild ideas.*
▶ foolish, strange, unreasonable

wilful *adjective*
1 *George is a wilful child.* ▶ obstinate,
stubborn
2 *She was accused of wilful
disobedience.* ▶ deliberate, calculated,
conscious, persistent

will *noun*
1 *She has a strong will to succeed in life.*
▶ a desire, a wish, a determination, a
resolution
2 *He did it against his mother's will.*
▶ a wish, wishes, an intention

willing *adjective*
1 *We are willing to come with you.*
▶ ready, prepared, inclined, disposed
2 *Her brother is always a willing helper.*
▶ eager, helpful, obliging, cooperative

wilt *verb*
*Some plants in the window were
beginning to wilt.* ▶ to shrivel, to
droop, to wither, to flag, to flop, to
fade

wily *adjective*
*The wily old king knew there was a plot
to get rid of him.* ▶ cunning, crafty, sly,
clever, astute, shrewd, foxy, knowing

win *verb*
1 *I must find out which team won.* ▶ to
be victorious, to come first, to succeed
2 *She has won a prize.* ▶ to gain, to
get, to receive, to obtain, to earn

wind *noun*
The next day there was a stronger wind.
▶ a breeze, a gust
NOTE: A **breeze** is a light wind, and a **gust** or
a **squall** is a short spell of strong wind

wind *verb*
1 *The road winds gently through the
hills.* ▶ to curve, to twist, to bend, to
loop, to zigzag
2 *I wound the wool into a ball.* ▶ to
roll, to coil, to wrap, to twine, to loop

windy *adjective*
It was windy up on the cliffs. ▶ gusty,
breezy, blustery, blowy, squally

wink *verb*
*The lights in the shop window winked on
and off.* ▶ to flicker, to twinkle, to
blink, to flash

winner *noun*
The winner came up to receive a prize.
▶ a victor, a champion

wipe *verb*
I'll wipe the table before we eat. ▶ to
rub, to clean, to dust

wipe out *verb*
*The town was wiped out by bombing
during the war.* ▶ to destroy, to
obliterate, to annihilate, to
exterminate

wire *noun*
Electric wires trailed across the floor.
▶ a cable, a lead, a flex

wisdom *noun*
*She had gained her wisdom from years
of experience.* ▶ good sense,
knowledge, judgement, prudence

wise *adjective*
1 *He is a wise old man and he gave us
good advice.* ▶ intelligent, astute,
shrewd, knowledgeable, knowing,

prudent, perceptive
2 *We think she made a wise decision.*
▶ sensible, sound, shrewd, prudent

wish *noun*
Matthew's strongest wish was to go to the fair. ▶ a longing, a desire, an ambition, a goal, an aim

wish for *verb*
The children all wished for snow at Christmas. ▶ to want, to long for, to hanker after; (not an everyday word) to desire

wistful *adjective*
She gave a wistful smile as she thought about the holiday she would miss.
▶ sad, forlorn

wit *noun*
You'll need to use all your wit to solve the problem. ▶ brains, intelligence, reason

withdraw *verb*
1 *She withdrew some money from her account.* ▶ to take out
2 *Several people have withdrawn from the trip.* ▶ to pull out, to drop out, to back out
3 *The troops have withdrawn from the frontier.* ▶ to fall back, to move back, to retire, to retreat

wither *verb*
Some of the plants were already withering in the heat. ▶ to shrivel, to wilt, to dry up, to droop

withhold *verb*
It is important not to withhold any information. ▶ to keep back, to conceal, to refuse

withstand *verb*
Few animals and plants can withstand such high temperatures. ▶ to endure, to tolerate, to stand up to, to cope with, to resist

witness *noun*
The police took statements from all the witnesses. ▶ an observer, a bystander, an eyewitness, an onlooker

witness *verb*
A young girl had witnessed the whole incident. ▶ to observe, to see, to view

witty *adjective*
It was a good poem with a witty ending.
▶ amusing, clever, funny, humorous

wobble *verb*
The table began to wobble with so much on it. ▶ to shake, to tremble, to quiver, to be unsteady

wobbly *adjective*
The chair had a broken leg and was very wobbly. ▶ unsteady, shaky, rocky, insecure

woe *noun*
She woke them all up with her cries of woe. ▶ sorrow, misfortune, misery, unhappiness, distress, grief

woman *noun*
A woman opened the door and came in.
▶ a lady
NOTE: You can also use **girl** for a young woman

wonder *noun*
The sight of a mighty waterfall fills you with wonder. ▶ awe, admiration, amazement, reverence

wonder *verb*
I wondered what to do next. ▶ to ponder, to consider, to think about

wonder at *verb*
The audience wondered at the acrobats' daring. ▶ to marvel at, to be amazed by, to admire

wonderful *adjective*
We had a wonderful time. ▶ excellent, very good, marvellous, outstanding,

superb, fine, great, remarkable;
(informal) fabulous, fantastic, terrific,
tremendous

wood *noun*
1 *The little house was made of wood.*
▶ timber, planks, logs
2 *We went for a walk in the wood.*
▶ woods, a forest, woodland
NOTE: You can also use **coppice** and **copse**
if you are talking about a small groups of
trees. A **forest** is a large wood

woolly *adjective*
1 *She wore a thick scarf and a woolly
red hat.* ▶ woollen, fluffy, fleecy,
furry, fuzzy
2 *He has a few ideas but they are rather
woolly.* ▶ vague, unclear, indefinite,
confused, uncertain

word *noun*
1 *I'm looking for another word meaning
'smell'.* ▶ a term, an expression
2 *He gave me his word.* ▶ a promise, a
pledge, a guarantee
3 *Start when I give the word.* ▶ the
order, the instruction, the command,
the signal
4 *We sent word that we had arrived
safely.* ▶ information, a message

work *noun*
1 *You deserve a rest after all that work.*
▶ labour, toil, drudgery, exertion
2 *What work do you do?* ▶ a job,
business
3 *I have to hand in my work on Monday.*
▶ homework, an assignment, a project

work *verb*
1 *I've been working on my nature
project.* ▶ to be busy, to labour, to toil
2 *She works in a bank.* ▶ to have a job,
to be employed
3 *Is the lift working?* ▶ to function, to
operate, to run
4 *She didn't think my idea would work.*
▶ to succeed, to be effective

work out *verb*
1 *Things have worked out well for them.*
▶ to develop, to turn out, to evolve
2 *I'm trying to work out how much I
owe you.* ▶ to calculate, to find out, to
figure out, to determine

world *noun*
*By the time she was 40 she had travelled
all over the world.* ▶ the earth, the
globe, the planet

worn *adjective*
The carpet was worn at the edges.
▶ ragged, frayed, tattered, threadbare,
shabby

worried *adjective*
She had a worried look on her face.
▶ anxious, concerned, troubled,
disturbed, apprehensive, agitated,
distressed, bothered

worry *verb*
1 *I told him his work was good and he
need not worry.* ▶ to be anxious, to be
concerned, to fret, to feel uneasy
2 *Don't worry Dad while he's working.*
▶ to disturb, to pester, to trouble, to
bother, to annoy

worry *noun*
*Keeping the younger children happy was
a real worry.* ▶ a care, a concern, an
anxiety, a problem, a trouble

worsen *verb*
1 *In the afternoon the weather
worsened.* ▶ to get worse, to
deteriorate
2 *Getting angry would only worsen the
situation.* ▶ to make worse, to
aggravate

worship *verb*
1 *He had been married to Angela for
many years, and he worshipped her.*
▶ to adore, to idolize, to be devoted to,
to love, to dote on, to revere
2 *People have worshipped gods for*

thousands of years. ► to praise, to glorify, to honour, to show reverence to

worth *noun*
He has some beautiful stamps but they are of little worth. ► value

worthless *adjective*
They paid a lot for the painting but it turned out to be worthless. ► valueless, useless

worthwhile *adjective*
We'll need to save enough money to make the trip worthwhile.
► rewarding, useful, beneficial, profitable

worthy *adjective*
The teams raise money for worthy causes. ► honourable, respectable, deserving, praiseworthy, worthwhile, admirable, commendable, creditable

wound *verb*
Several people were wounded in the shooting. ► to injure, to hurt

wound *noun*
He was suffering from a painful wound.
► an injury

wrap *verb*
1 *I'll wrap the presents in pretty paper.*
► to bind, to cover, to do up
2 *Meg wrapped the old woman in a warm blanket.* ► to cover, to enclose, to muffle, to shroud, to swaddle, to bundle up

wrath *noun*
There was a danger that his wrath would become violent. ► rage, fury, anger, temper

wreck *verb*
The building was wrecked in the explosion. ► to destroy, to demolish, to ruin, to break up

wreckage *noun*
Wreckage from the ship had been washed up on the beach. ► debris, remains, remnants

wrench *verb*
He fetched a screwdriver and wrenched the lid off. ► to force, to prise, to lever, to twist

wrestle *verb*
The two men wrestled on the floor. ► to grapple, to struggle

wretched *adjective*
She felt wretched at having to leave us behind. ► miserable, sad, unhappy, dejected, despondent, melancholy

wriggle *verb*
Cathy wriggled when we tickled her.
► to squirm, to writhe, to twist

wring *verb*
He went into the kitchen to wring his wet clothes. She smiled and wrung my hand. ► to squeeze, to press

wrinkle *verb*
She wrinkled her nose and put her head on one side. ► to crinkle, to crease

wrinkle *noun*
The curtains were full of wrinkles.
► a crease, a crinkle, a fold, a furrow

write *verb*
I sat down to write a shopping list. ► to compose, to compile, to draw up
NOTE: You can also use **scribble**, **scrawl**, or **dash off** if you are talking about writing something quickly or carelessly. A more formal word for writing something serious is **pen**: *She penned a few words to her parents.*

writer *noun*
Her grandfather had been a famous writer. ► an author, (a writer of novels) a novelist, (a writer of plays) a playwright, a dramatist, (a writer of

poems) a poet, (a writer for newspapers) a journalist, a reporter, a correspondent

writhe *verb*
He writhed on the floor in pain. ▶ to squirm, to wriggle, to twist

writing *noun*
The writing is hard to read. ▶ the handwriting, the script

wrong *adjective*
1 *The answer was wrong.* ▶ incorrect, mistaken, false, inaccurate
2 *They all laughed when Lisa said something wrong.* ▶ inappropriate, funny, unsuitable, improper, unacceptable, incongruous
3 *It is wrong to cheat.* ▶ bad, sinful, evil, wicked, dishonest, naughty, unfair, unjust, unethical
4 *There's something wrong with the engine.* ▶ amiss, faulty, out of order

wry *adjective*
He has a wry sense of humour.
▶ mocking, sarcastic

X x

X-ray *noun*
The nurse made an X-ray of his broken leg. ▶ a radiograph

Y y

yard *noun*
There was a yard to play in at the back of the house. ▶ a courtyard, an enclosure

yarn *noun*
1 *She used a fine yarn to make her clothes.* ▶ a thread
2 *The old man told us a yarn about the sea.* ▶ a story, a tale, a narrative

yearly *adjective*
The family always went for their yearly holiday in July. ▶ annual

yearn for *verb*
We yearned for the beach and the sun.
▶ to long for, to wish for, to crave, to hanker after, to want; (informal) to be dying for, to fancy

yell *verb*
The man yelled at us to stop. ▶ to shout, to call (to), to cry out (to), to roar

yield *verb*
1 *In the end they yielded to persuasion.* ▶ to give in, to give way, to submit
2 *These trees yield good apples.* ▶ to produce, to grow, to bear, to give

young *adjective*
1 *She was young and pretty.* ▶ youthful
2 *He is rather young for his age.*
▶ immature, childish

Z z

zany *adjective*
She has a zany sense of humour.
▶ strange, odd, eccentric, weird, absurd, crazy, mad

zealous *adjective*
They are both very zealous about doing their homework when they get home.
▶ conscientious, diligent, enthusiastic, keen, eager

zero *noun*
She pressed zero instead of 8 and got the wrong number. ▶ nought

zest *noun*
Their performance was full of zest.
▶ energy, enthusiasm, enjoyment, eagerness, liveliness

zone *noun*
The pedestrian zone begins here. ▶ an area, a sector, a district, a locality

zoom *verb*
(informal) *The car zoomed up the road.*
▶ to speed, to race, to shoot, to streak, to flash, to tear, to hurtle